always up to date

The law changes, but Nolo is always on top of it! We offer several ways to make sure you and your Nolo products are always up to date:

1 **Nolo's Legal Updater**
We'll send you an email whenever a new edition of your book is published! Sign up at **www.nolo.com/legalupdater**.

2 **Updates @ Nolo.com**
Check **www.nolo.com/update** to find recent changes in the law that affect the current edition of your book.

3 **Nolo Customer Service**
To make sure that this edition of the book is the most recent one, call us at **800-728-3555** and ask one of our friendly customer service representatives. Or find out at **www.nolo.com**.

please note

We believe accurate and current legal information should help you solve many of your own legal problems on a cost-efficient basis. But this text is not a substitute for personalized advice from a knowledgeable lawyer. If you want the help of a trained professional, consult an attorney licensed to practice in your state.

5th edition

The
Small Business
Start-Up Kit
for California

by Peri H. Pakroo

Fifth Edition	APRIL 2004
Editor	BARBARA KATE REPA
Cover Design	SUSAN PUTNEY
Book Design	TERRI HEARSH
Illustration	ALEXIS MOLLOMO
Production	SARAH HINMAN
Index	JANET PERLMAN
CD-ROM Preparation	JENYA CHERNOFF & ANDRÉ ZIVKOVICH
Proofreading	SUSAN CARLSON GREENE
Printing	CONSOLIDATED PRINTERS, INC.

Pakroo, Peri.
    The small business start-up kit for California / by Peri H. Pakroo.--5th ed.
       p. cm.
    ISBN 1-4133-0037-5 (alk. paper)
     1. Small business--Law and legislation--California--Popular works. 2. New business enterprises--Law and legislation--California--Popular works. I. Title.

    KFC84.B87P35 2004
    346.794'0652--dc22

                        2004043468

For information on bulk purchases or corporate premium sales, please contact the Special Sales Department. For academic sales or textbook adoptions, ask for Academic Sales. Call 800-955-4775 or write to Nolo at 950 Parker Street, Berkeley, CA 94710.

Acknowledgments for the First Edition

All authors should be so lucky to have such a swell team of people helping them through the process of writing a book. Thanks to Jake Warner for giving me the inspiration and encouragement to start this book, and to finish it when my mind and fingertips were weary. Major thanks to Beth Laurence for tightening up the information and streamlining it into a finished product. And thanks to the whole editorial staff at Nolo for convincing me I would eventually reach the light at the end of the tunnel with my brain intact.

Thanks to Terri Hearsh for her layout and design of the book. And also to Ely Newman for patiently walking me through the technicalities of putting forms on disk. Sincere thanks to David Rothenberg for lending a CFO's eye to my discussion of small business finances.

Thanks to all my family and friends for their patience and sensitivity in not asking too often "Is your book done yet?"

Most of all, love and thanks to Turtle for keeping my soul happy and free when my mind was not.

PHP 1998

Dedication

I dedicate this book to my mom and dad, Kay and Reza Pakroo, who for better or worse somehow convinced me I could do anything—even write a book.

About the Author

Peri Pakroo is a media developer and consultant, specializing in legal and start-up issues for businesses and nonprofits. She owns and runs p-brain media (www.pbrainmedia.com), a media and communications firm that develops informational content for print, Web, video, and other media. She received her law degree from the University of New Mexico School of Law in 1995, and a year later began editing and writing for Nolo, specializing in small business and intellectual property issues. She has edited such titles as Nolo's *Starting & Running a Successful Newsletter or Magazine*; *Getting Permission: How to License & Clear Copyrighted Materials Online & Off*; *Music Law*; and *How to Write a Business Plan*. Besides working with legal and business issues, Peri has also headed the editorial departments of two arts and entertainment weeklies and a monthly food and lifestyle magazine. She lives with Juno, Kitty B, and Turtle in New Mexico.

Table of Contents

5 Drafting an Effective Business Plan

6 Pricing, Bidding, and Billing Projects

7 Federal, State, and Local Start-Up Requirements

8 Risk Management and Insurance

Appendixes

A Resources and Contact Information

B How to Use the Forms CD-ROM

C Tear-Out Forms

Partnership Agreement

LLC Articles of Organization

Sample Articles of Incorporation

Certificate of Limited Partnership

Limited Liability Partnership Registration

Application for Employer Identification Number (Form SS-4)

California Fictitious Business Name Statement

California Seller's Permit Application and Instructions
(Individuals and Partnerships)

California Seller's Permit Application and Instructions
(Corporations, LLCs, and Organizations)

California Resale Certificate

Swap Meets, Flea Markets, or Special Events Certification

California Board of Equalization Publications Order Form

IRS Form 1040-ES: Estimated Tax Form and Instructions

California Estimated Tax Form and Instructions

Limited Liability Company Tax Voucher

Entity Classification Election (Form 8832)

Election To Have a Tax Year Other Than a Required Tax Year (Form 8716)

Determination of Employee Work Status for Purposes of Federal Employment
Taxes and Income Tax Withholding (Form SS-8)

Icons Used Throughout This Book

Throughout the text, we have included the following icons to help you find the information you need.

   Tip. A commonsense tip to help you understand or comply with legal requirements.

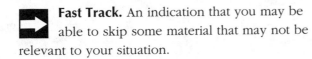 **Warning.** A caution to slow down and
consider potential problems.

See an Expert. A suggestion to seek the
advice of an attorney or tax expert.

 Fast Track. An indication that you may be
able to skip some material that may not be
relevant to your situation.

Other Resources. A suggestion to consult
another Nolo book or another legal or tax resource.

Checklist. A quick summary of the start-up
steps included in each chapter.

■

Working for Yourself Is Easier Than You Think

You don't have an MBA. Hell, you've never taken a business class. You spent your college years studying literature and art history, and periodically dropping out to travel the world. And now you find yourself thinking about going into business for yourself—maybe restoring antiques, illustrating books, running a café, or selling software. "Me, a businessperson?" you skeptically ask. You keep trudging to work each morning, but as the hours tick by you find yourself fantasizing more and more about kissing your 9-to-5 job goodbye. You jot down some notes, work out some kinks in your plan, and continue to wonder whether it just might fly….

Unfortunately, most people who have toyed with business ideas this way never get to find out whether they would have worked or not. For a variety of practical, financial, and psychological reasons, most folks just don't take the leap from idea to reality. This is really a shame, since there's nothing that complex or difficult about turning a business idea into an actual working business. Most prospective entrepreneurs would be surprised—and encouraged—to know that they can get most of the way across the line between "I'm thinking about starting my own business" and "I own and run my own business" simply by completing a short list of bureaucratic tasks. This book will explain what those tasks are and how to complete them.

Stephen Parr, owner and director of Oddball Film and Video, a stock film and video footage company in San Francisco:

I started making video art in the 1970s. After a while I started collecting all these weird bits of film because it was cheaper than shooting it myself. I gathered all kinds of old, found footage like military training films, educational films, home movies, and all kinds of other images and put them together into montages, which I screened in nightclubs as background visuals. I was showing them all over—nightclubs in New York, Chicago, San Francisco—and I made some money by selling the tapes to the clubs.

Then I started getting calls from these companies in Silicon Valley that produce industrial videos, like training films and promotional programs for corporate trade shows. Video game companies were calling, too. Companies like Sega, Sun Microsystems, and Silicon Graphics wanted to pay me for my footage. The guy I lived with at the time thought I should go into business selling the stock footage I had collected, but at the time, I didn't know if I could make a living doing it. I didn't know anything about the stock footage business. There were a few companies doing it, but they were in New York or L.A., and they seemed really huge.

But since I liked working with images and since the business had already started to take off on its own, I finally decided to formalize it. I started by picking a company name. I wanted something interesting that conveyed what I did. We came up with Oddball. It's a word that people don't really use anymore, more of a '40s or '50s expression—an oddball is someone kind of weird, unbalanced, or unusual, you know? Well, from there, I just kept compiling more footage, and over the years I started logging it, and buying more.

At the most basic level, my business involves finding, organizing, and preserving historical footage. And then distributing it. Our clients include ad agencies, news organizations, documentary and feature filmmakers, industrial, corporate, and music video producers, educational filmmakers, and anyone who needs offbeat and unusual images. In one way we're like a library. We archive and license historical visual information.

These days, I spend most of my time trying to organize and publicize my business. We just launched our website, and that takes time to maintain. And I spend a lot more time trying to obtain films than actually looking at them. Still, what I do at Oddball is an extension of the work I've been doing since the 1970s. I guess it became a business the day I decided I wasn't going to do anything else.

A. Get Started—And Get On With Your Business

You undoubtedly already know that getting a business off the ground isn't easy. You've got a million different details to work out—how you'll produce your product or service, how much you'll charge, what marketing strategies to use, how to manage your cash flow—and you need to nail all of this down before you stand to make a dime. You'll likely find that very few, if any, other businesspeople have done exactly what you're setting out to do, so you'll have to answer a lot of questions on your own (or with your partners). It can be scary and lonely—and while exhilarating, it's almost always stressful.

But compared to working out the details of how your business will run and become successful, clearing the bureaucratic hurdles isn't a big deal at all. Dealing with governmental start-up requirements has been done millions of times before by all types of different businesses. While the bureaucracy governing small business often seems like a convoluted maze, you can take comfort in the fact that the procedures are standard; they apply more or less the same to everybody and the answers *are* out there. Unlike your unique business strategy that you'll need your best creative wits to devise, conquering the bureaucracy is essentially a nobrainer. Yes, it requires some patience and fortitude, but by no means do you need any special skill, education, or experience. As long as you do a bit of homework and arm yourself with an overview of the process (as you're doing by reading this book), you'll be able to meet all the small business registration requirements without breaking a sweat.

You can usually start a sole proprietorship (the legal term for a one-owner business) or a partnership (a business with more than owner) by registering with just one government office. And for business owners who want protection from personal liability for business debts—often referred to by the legal jargon "limited liability"—the simplest corporations or limited liability companies (LLCs) require only a couple more registration tasks. In other words, once you've got your business idea developed to a certain degree, all you need to do is visit a few government offices, fill out some forms, and pay some fees—and suddenly your idea will have become an actual, legitimate business.

Keep in mind that there's certainly a lot more to starting a successful small business than dealing with bureaucratic requirements. For starters, you'll need to have a sound business idea, and you'll need to be able to develop good management skills to guide it to success. This book, however, largely leaves these issues for other resources to cover. Unlike many other small business guides, this one will not take up your precious time quizzing you on whether you have the right personality to be your own boss, evaluating your business idea, or helping you to identify the personal goals that you hope to achieve by starting a business. If you need more help deciding whether or not you want to start a business or what kind of business you should start, you should probably buy a different book. If, on the other hand, you want a book that cuts to the chase and explains systematically what you need to do to launch a business in California, this book is for you.

Free online resources. If you need more guidance on other aspects of starting a small business, consult the Small Business section of Nolo's Legal Encyclopedia at www.nolo.com. You'll find several articles on business start-up issues, such as starting the right kind of business and raising start-up money.

But this book is also for those of you who are somewhere in between: fairly certain you want to give your idea a try but not quite ready to march down to city hall to register your business. In addition to explaining the start-up requirements in California, this book also outlines the preliminary work you should do before heading out to file all your official forms. In Chapters 2 through 6, we discuss fundamental tasks such as choosing the right legal structure for your business (sole proprietorship, partnership, LLC, or corporation), coming up with a catchy and legally sound business name, and finding a location that's good for business. We also explain how to draft a business plan that will help you define your business, plan for profitability, and attract lenders and investors. If you've already taken care of some or all these tasks, you can either skip these chapters or use them as a guide to evaluate what you've already done.

Finally, to help you through your start-up days, later chapters introduce you to a number of basic issues that every ongoing business needs to master. These include insurance, taxes, contracts and agreements, and bookkeeping and accounting. Though they're not exactly start-up requirements, you should devote some time to them in the dawning days of your business so that you'll be up to speed when business is fast and furious.

Finally, keep in mind that businesses with employees have significant additional responsibilities. In Chapter 12, we offer a general overview of the laws and regulations that govern businesses with employees. If you're thinking about hiring employees, that chapter will help you figure out if you're ready to tackle the many requirements that come with your first hire. Chapter 12 also explains the difference between employees and independent contractors—an important distinction, because using independent contractors does not subject you to most of the laws that apply when you hire employees.

Help with employment matters. If you do decide that you need to hire any employees, you'll probably need to do further reading. An excellent and exhaustive resource is Nolo's *The Employer's Legal Handbook,* by Fred S. Steingold.

B. Making the Decision to Go Official

Some of you may be facing a different question. Instead of wondering whether or not to start a business, you may be trying to decide whether or not to formalize your business—to go the official route and register your business with the appropriate agencies. For instance, maybe you've been doing freelance graphics work on the side for a number of years, but now you're thinking of quitting your 9-to-5 job to take on graphics work full-time. If you're not sure whether you want to register your business and open it up to the world of government regulations, the information about registration requirements in this book will put you in a better position to make a decision. Chapter 7 walks you through the many governmental requirements that apply to all new businesses, and explains how to go about finding and satisfying any additional requirements that may apply to your specific business.

Stephen Parr, owner and director of Oddball Film and Video, a stock footage company in San Francisco:

What a business really is, is you deciding you have a business. It's really nothing more than that.

Generally speaking, anyone with a good-sized or otherwise visible business should bite the bullet and complete all of the necessary registration tasks to become official. Operating under the table can all too easily be exposed, and the government can come after you for fines and penalties—and might even shut your business down—simply for operating without the necessary paperwork. And if you're making a profit, ignoring the IRS is definitely a bad idea. In addition to fines and back taxes, you could even face criminal charges and jail time.

On the other hand, tiny, home-based, hobby-type businesses can often operate for quite some time without meeting registration requirements. If you're braiding hair or holding an occasional junk sale out of your garage, for instance, you can probably get by without formal business registration—at least for a while. Keep in mind, however, that just because it may be possible doesn't mean it's the best option. Often, formally registering your business can benefit you as well, since you can then write off business expenses and reduce your personal taxes. In Chapter 9, Section A3, we discuss hobby businesses in more depth, including how tax laws deal with businesses that continually lose money.

C. Get Ready for the Ride

One of the main ideas we want you to take away from this book is that there's nothing mysterious or even terribly complex about the process of starting your own business. Whether you've drafted a highly specific business plan with the help of accountants and consultants or you've scratched it out on a cocktail napkin, the process of turning your idea into a legitimate business is the same. That process is covered in this book.

How you build and run your business, on the other hand, is where the real challenge comes in.

You'll need confidence to get your business rolling—and you'll need guts, too. You may well find that some of the questions burning in your mind have no defined answer, because no one has asked that question or tried that idea before. You probably wanted to start a business in the first place so that you could make your own decisions—but this can often be quite a heavy burden. You may not believe it now, but some days you'll probably find yourself wishing you had a boss.

You'll need to learn to trust yourself, both when you feel optimistic and when you suspect that one of your ideas is less than brilliant. You'll also have to develop a sense for when you need help, and to be judicious in taking the advice of people around you. Part of the art of controlling your own destiny is accepting the wisdom of others, while maintaining your own focus and direction. It's not always an easy balance to maintain, but you'll undoubtedly get better at it as you gain experience in running your own show. The bottom line: Think hard, keep your mind open—and fight like hell to make your ideas a reality.

Take the leap.

More Small Business Products From Nolo

BUSINESS PLANS

Business Plan Pro 2004

by Palo Alto Software (available through Nolo)
A fast, easy way to generate the plan you need to launch or expand your business.

How to Write a Business Plan

by Mike McKeever
Explains how to write a business plan, whether for your own purposes or to attract money from lenders or investors—including how to evaluate the profitability of your business idea; estimate operating expenses; determine assets, liabilities, and net worth; and find potential sources of financing.

BUSINESS OPERATIONS

Drive a Modest Car & 16 Other Keys to Small Business Success

by Ralph Warner
Ideas, strategies, and lessons for successful entrepreneurs.

Leasing Space for Your Small Business

by Janet Portman and Fred S. Steingold
A guide to the ins and outs of finding a space for your business, negotiating a lease, and solving problems that arise from it.

Legal Forms for Starting & Running a Small Business

by Fred S. Steingold
Dozens of legal forms and documents crucial for the success of a small business.

Legal Guide for Starting & Running a Small Business

by Fred S. Steingold
All the legal info you need to get your business off the ground and running—including how to raise start-up money, attract the best help, buy or sell a business or franchise, negotiate a favorable lease, insure your business, and resolve legal disputes.

Quicken Legal Business Pro 2004

A software package containing more than 140 legal forms and the complete text of six of Nolo's bestselling business titles—including *Legal Guide for Starting & Running a Small Business, Tax Savvy for Small Business, Everyday Employment Law: The Basics, Everybody's Guide to Small Claims Court, Marketing Without Advertising,* and *Leasing Space for Your Small Business.*

FORMS OF OWNERSHIP

Buy-Sell Agreement Handbook: Plan Ahead for Changes in the Ownership of Your Business

by Anthony Mancuso and Bethany K. Laurence
Explains how to protect your business interests by drawing up a "premarital" agreement between you and your business owners that sets out a plan for what happens if you or a co-owner leaves the company. A must for any new business with more than one owner.

Form Your Own Limited Liability Company

by Anthony Mancuso
Offers instructions and forms to create an LLC in your state, as well as a full explanation of LLCs and how they work.

LLC Maker

by Anthony Mancuso
Windows software that assembles LLC articles of organization according to state legal requirements, plus an operating agreement and other LLC formation paperwork.

Nolo's Quick LLC: All You Need to Know About Limited Liability Companies

by Anthony Mancuso
Explains the basics of limited liability companies, and helps you figure out whether structuring your business as an LLC is the right way to go.

More Small Business Products From Nolo

The Partnership Book: How to Write a Partnership Agreement
by Denis Clifford and Ralph Warner

Describes the legal and practical issues of creating a partnership—including financial and tax liabilities, contributions and distributions, and changes in ownership.

MARKETING

How to Get Your Business on the Web
by Fred S. Steingold

The legal forms you need to get your business on the Internet—and make it a success.

Marketing Without Advertising: Inspire Customers to Rave About Your Business & Create Lasting Success
by Michael Phillips and Salli Rasberry

Explains the secret of attracting customers without pricey ads—including how to build trust with potential customers, encourage customer recommendations, improve customer service, list products and services widely and inexpensively, and use the Internet to market services and products.

PROTECTING BUSINESS ASSETS

Domain Names: How to Choose & Protect a Great Name for Your Website
by Stephen R. Elias and Patricia Gima

Teaches you how to select, register, and protect a great domain name.

Nondisclosure Agreements: Protect Your Trade Secrets & More
by Richard Stim and Stephen Fishman

This book, with forms on CD-ROM, explains how to protect your trade secrets with a non-disclosure agreement (or "confidentiality agreement") before sharing them with potential partners and employees, and includes 19 different legal forms.

TAX

Tax Savvy for Small Business
by Frederick W. Daily

Offers plain-English tax laws and rules on business deductions, plus tax info on LLCs, partnerships, corporations, and more.

WORKPLACE LAWS

The Employer's Legal Handbook
by Fred S. Steingold

All the basics of employment law in one place. It covers safe hiring and firing practices, wages, hours, employee benefits, taxes and liability, discrimination, and sexual harassment.

Hiring Independent Contractors: The Employer's Legal Guide
by Stephen Fishman

This book explains all the tricky IRS rules and provides forms and instructions for hiring ICs.

☑ **Chapter 1 Checklist**

☐ Decide whether to formalize your business.

☐ Research business start-up steps.

☐ Brace yourself for start-up mayhem.

■

Choosing a Legal Structure

You probably already have a rough idea of the type of legal structure your business will take, whether you know it or not. That's because in large part, the ownership structure that's right for your business—a sole proprietorship, partnership, LLC, or corporation—depends on how many people will own the business and what type of services or products it will provide, things you've undoubtedly thought about quite a bit.

For instance, if you know that you will be the only owner, then a partnership is obviously not your thing. (A partnership by definition has more than one owner.) And if your business will engage in risky activities (for example, trading stocks or repairing roofs), you'll want not only to buy insurance, but also to consider forming an entity that provides personal liability protection (a corporation or a limited liability company), which can shield your personal assets from business debts and claims. If you plan to raise capital by selling stock to the public, or want to give your employees stock options, then you should form a corporation.

If you've considered these issues, then you'll be ahead of the game in choosing a legal structure that's right for your business. Still, you'll need to consider the benefits and drawbacks of each type of business structure before you make your final decision.

In California, the basic types of business structures are:

- sole proprietorships
- partnerships
- limited liability companies (LLCs), and
- corporations.

To help you pick the best structure for your business, this chapter explains the basic attributes of each type. And we will help you answer the most common question new entrepreneurs ask about choosing a business form: Should I choose a business structure that offers protection from personal liability (a corporation or an LLC)? Here's a hint as to what our advice will be: If you focus your energy and money on getting your business off the ground as a sole proprietorship or a partnership, you can always incorporate or form an LLC later.

Limited Liability

One basic distinction that you'll probably hear mentioned lots of times is the difference between businesses that provide their owners with "limited liability" and those that don't. Corporations and LLCs both provide owners with limited personal liability. Sole proprietorships and general partnerships do not.

Limited liability basically means that the creditors of the business cannot normally go after the owners' personal assets to pay for business debts and claims arising from lawsuits. (We discuss liability for business debts in detail later in this chapter.)

As you read about specific business types in this chapter, you'll see how a decision to form a limited liability entity (a corporation or an LLC, mainly) can dramatically affect how you run your business. On the other hand, while sole proprietorships and partnerships are somewhat simpler to run than corporations and LLCs, they may leave an owner personally vulnerable to business lawsuits and debts.

A. Sole Proprietorships

Sole proprietorships are one-owner businesses. Any business with two or more owners cannot, by definition, be a sole proprietorship. If you know that there will be two or more owners of your business, you can skip ahead to Section B, below.

Technically, a sole proprietorship is simply a business that is owned by one person and that hasn't filed papers to become a corporation or an LLC. Sole proprietorships are easy to set up and to maintain—so easy that many people own sole proprietorships and don't even know it. For instance, if you are a freelance photographer or writer, a craftsperson who takes jobs on a contract basis, a salesperson who receives only commissions, or an independent contractor who isn't on an employer's regular payroll, you are automatically a sole proprietor. This is true whether or not you've registered your business with your city or obtained any licenses or permits. And it makes no difference whether you also have a regular day job. As long as you do for-profit work on your own (or sometimes with your spouse—see below) and have not filed papers to become a corporation or a limited liability company, you are a sole proprietor.

Kimberly Torgerson, owner of Your Word's Worth, a freelance editing and writing service in Northern California:

I like the variety and flexibility of freelancing. Until a short while ago, I tended to take on projects that would enable me to work intensely, then take lots of time off to write, travel, or just putter. Recently, though, I bought property— which means I'm not taking much time off these days. I just say YES to new projects. The challenge is setting my course as people's deadlines shift. So far, so good.

⚠ Don't ignore local registration requirements.
If you've started a business without quite realizing it—for example, you do a little freelance computer programming, which classifies you as a sole proprietor by default—don't let the fact that you're technically already a sole proprietor fool you into thinking that you've satisfied the governmental requirements for starting a business. Most cities and counties require businesses—even tiny home-based sole proprietorships—to register with them and pay at least a minimum tax. And if you do business under a name different from your own, such as Custom Coding, you must register that name—known as a fictitious business name—with your county. In practice, lots of businesses are small enough to get away with ignoring these requirements. But if you are caught, you may be subject to back taxes and other penalties. We explain how to make the necessary filings with the appropriate government offices in Chapter 7.

Running a Business With Your Spouse

If you plan to start a sole proprietorship and expect that your spouse may occasionally help out with business tasks, you should be aware of a fuzzy area in federal tax law that you can use to your advantage. The IRS typically allows a spouse to pitch in without pay without risking being classified as an owner or as an employee of the other spouse's business. This situation is sometimes erroneously called a "husband-wife sole proprietorship."

The normal rule is that someone who does work for a business must be one of three things from a legal standpoint: a co-owner, an employee, or an independent contractor. But when that someone is your spouse, this rule is softened somewhat. Your spouse can volunteer—that is, work without pay—for your sole proprietorship without being classified as an employee, freeing the business from paying payroll tax.

That saves you money—and, if you have no other employees, also allows you to avoid the time-consuming record keeping involved in being an employer. Similarly, a spouse who is not classified as a partner or an independent contractor won't have to pay self-employment taxes and your business won't have to file a partnership tax return.

Also consider that under marital property laws that vary from state to state, if a business is started or significantly changed when a couple is married, both spouses may have an ownership interest in the business regardless of whose name is on the ownership document.

If you are concerned about the possible consequences of divorce, read Chapter 12, "Planning for Changes in Ownership." It discusses how divorce and other life events such as retirement and death can affect ownership of a business, and explains how to plan in advance to accommodate the possibilities. You may also want to check with a lawyer who is experienced in handling marital property issues to see how your business could be affected in the event of a divorce in your particular state.

Finally, if you and your spouse both want to be active partners in a co-owned business—each with an official say in management—you should create a partnership or an LLC or corporation, even though this will mean filing somewhat more complicated tax returns and other business paperwork. If your spouse tries to squeak by as a volunteer in a so-called husband-wife sole proprietorship when you're really working together as a partnership, you run the risk of being audited, having the IRS declare you're a partnership—and socking your spouse with back self-employment taxes.

1. Pass-Through Taxation

In the eyes of the law, a sole proprietorship is not legally separate from the person who owns it. This is one of the fundamental differences between a sole proprietorship and a corporation or an LLC. And it has two major effects: one related to taxation (explained in this section), and the other to personal liability (explained in the next).

At income tax time, a sole proprietor simply reports all business income or losses on his or her individual income tax return. The business itself is not taxed. The IRS calls this "pass-through" taxation, because business profits pass through the business to be taxed on the business owner's tax return. You report income from a business just like wages from a job except that, along with Form 1040, you'll also need to include Schedule C, on which you'll provide your business's profit and loss information. One helpful aspect of this arrangement is that if your business loses money—and, of course, many start-ups do in the first year or two—you can use the business losses to offset any taxable income you have earned from other sources.

EXAMPLE: Rob has a day job at a coffee shop, where he earns a modest salary. His hobby is collecting obscure records at thrift stores and rummage sales. Contemplating the sad fact that he has no extra money to spend at the flea market on Saturday morning, he decides to start selling some of the vinyl gems he's found. Still working his day job, he starts a small business that he calls Rob's Revolving Records.

During his first full year in business, he sees that a key to consistently selling his records is developing connections and trust among record collectors. Unfortunately, while he is concentrating on getting to know potential buyers and others in the business, sales are slow. At year-end he closes out his books and sees that his website, marketing items such as business cards, and other incidental supplies cost him nearly $9,000, while he made only $3,000 in sales. But there is some good news: Rob's loss of $6,000 can be counted against his income from his day job, which will reduce his taxes and translate into a nice refund check, which he'll put right back into his record business.

Your business can't lose money forever. See our discussion of tax rules for money-losing businesses in Chapter 9, Section A3.

Be ready for the day you'll owe taxes. Once your business is under way and turning a profit, you'll have to start paying taxes. We provide an overview of the taxes small businesses face in Chapter 9. Taxes can get fairly complicated, however, and you may need more in-depth guidance. For detailed information on taxes for the various types of small businesses, see *Tax Savvy for Small Business*, by Frederick W. Daily (Nolo). This book gives exhaustive information on deductions, recordkeeping, and audits—all of which will help you minimize your tax bill and stay out of trouble with the IRS.

2. Personal Liability for Business Debts

Another crucial thing to know about operating your business as a sole proprietor is that you, as the owner of the business, can be held personally liable for business-related obligations. This means that if your business doesn't pay a supplier, defaults on a debt, loses a lawsuit, or otherwise finds itself in financial hot water, you, personally, can be forced to pay up. This can be a sobering possibility, especially if you own (or soon hope to own) a cool house, car, or other treasures. Personal liability for business obligations stems from the fundamental legal attribute of being a sole proprietor: you and your business are legally one and the same.

As explained in more detail in Sections C and D of this chapter, owners of corporations and LLCs enjoy what the law calls "limited personal liability" for business obligations. This means that, unlike sole proprietors and general partners, owners of corporations and LLCs can normally keep their houses, investments, and other personal property, even if the business fails. In short, if you are engaged in a risky business, you may want to consider forming a corporation or an LLC—although a thorough insurance policy can often protect you from lawsuits and claims against the business.

Commercial insurance doesn't cover business debts. While commercial insurance can protect a business and its owners from some types of liability (for instance, slip-and-fall lawsuits), insurance never covers business debts. The only way to limit your personal liability for business debts is to use a limited liability business structure such as an LLC or a corporation (or a limited partnership or limited liability partnership).

3. Creating a Sole Proprietorship

Setting up a sole proprietorship is incredibly easy. Unlike an LLC or a corporation, you generally don't have to file any special forms or pay any special fees to start working as a sole proprietor. You simply declare your business to be a sole proprietorship when completing the general registration requirements that apply to all new businesses, such as getting a business license from your county or city, or a seller's permit from the California Board of Equalization.

For example, when filing for a business tax registration certificate with your city, you'll often be asked to declare what kind of business you're starting. Some cities require only that you check a "sole proprietorship" box on a form, while others have separate tax registration forms for sole proprietorships. Similarly, other forms you'll file, such as those to register a fictitious business name and to obtain a seller's permit, will also ask for this information. (These and other start-up requirements are discussed in detail in Chapter 7.)

B. Partnerships

Bring two or more entrepreneurs together into a business venture, stir gently and—poof!—you've got a partnership. By definition, a partnership is a business that has more than one owner and that has not filed papers with the state to become a corporation or an LLC (or a limited partnership or limited liability partnership).

⚠ Beware of local registration requirements. If you're going into business with others, don't let the fact that you're automatically a partnership fool you into thinking that you've satisfied the governmental requirements for starting a business. Most cities and counties in California require all businesses to register with them and pay at least a minimum tax. And if you do business under a name other than the partners' names, you must register that name—known as a fictitious business name—with your county. We explain how to make the necessary filings with the appropriate government offices in Chapter 7.

1. General vs. Limited Partnerships

Usually, when you hear the term "partnership," it means a general partnership. As we discuss in more detail below, general partners are personally liable for all business debts, including court judgments. In addition, each individual partner can be sued for the full amount of any business debt (though that partner can turn around and sue the other partners for their shares of the debt).

Another very important aspect of general partnerships is that any individual partner can bind the whole business to a contract or business deal—in other words, each partner has "agency authority" for the partnership. And remember, each of the partners is fully personally liable for a business deal gone sour, no matter which partner signed the contract. So choose your partners carefully.

There are also a couple of special kinds of partnerships, called limited partnerships and limited liability partnerships. They operate under very different rules and are relatively uncommon, so we'll touch on them only briefly.

A limited partnership requires at least one general partner and at least one limited partner. The general partner has the same role as in a general partnership: he or she controls the company's day-to-day operations and is personally liable for business debts. The limited partner contributes financially to the business (for example, invests $100,000 in a real estate partnership) but has minimal control over business decisions or operations, and normally cannot bind the partnership to business deals. In return for giving up management power, a limited partner gets the benefit of protection from personal liability. This means that a limited partner can't be forced to pay off business debts or claims with personal assets, but can lose the entire investment in the business. But beware: A limited partner who tires of being passive and starts tinkering under the hood of the business should understand that personal liability can quickly become unlimited that way. If a creditor can prove that the limited partner acted in a way that led the creditor to believe that he or she was a general partner, that limited partner can be held fully and personally liable for the creditor's claims.

Another kind of partnership in California, called a limited liability partnership (LLP), provides all of its owners with limited personal liability. These partnerships are only available to professionals—licensed lawyers, accountants, and architects—and are particularly well suited to them. Most professionals aren't keen on general partnerships because they don't want to be personally liable for another partner's problems—particularly those involving malpractice claims. Forming a corporation to protect personal assets may be too much trouble, and California won't allow these professionals to form an LLC. The solution is often a limited liability partnership. This business structure protects each partner from debts against the partnership arising from professional malpractice lawsuits against another partner. (A partner who loses a malpractice suit for his or her own mistakes, however, doesn't escape liability.)

As attractive as they are, limited partnerships and limited liability partnerships (and limited liability companies, which we'll discuss in Section C) are not cheap to create. The filing fee is just $70, but California also charges a minimum annual tax of $800 for both types of limited partnerships. The tax is due in the first quarter of operations, whether or not you're making a profit.

2. Pass-Through Taxation

Similar to a sole proprietorship, a partnership (general or limited) is not a separate tax entity from its owners; instead it's what the IRS calls a "pass-through entity." This means the partnership itself does not pay any income taxes; rather, income passes through the business to each partner, who pays taxes on an individual share of profit (or deducts a share of losses) on an individual income tax return (Form 1040, with Schedule E attached). However, the partnership must also file what the IRS calls an "informational return"—Form 1065—to let the government know how much the business earned or lost that year. No tax is paid with this

return. Just think of it as the feds' way of letting you know they're watching.

3. Personal Liability for Business Debts

Since a partnership is legally inseparable from its owners, just like a sole proprietorship, general partners are personally liable for business-related obligations. What's more, in a general partnership, the business actions of any one partner bind the other partners, who can be held personally liable for those actions. So if your business partner takes out an ill-advised high-interest loan on behalf of the partnership, makes a terrible business deal, or gets in some other business mischief without your knowledge, you could be held personally responsible for any debts that result.

EXAMPLE: Jamie and Kent are partners in a profitable landscape gardening company. They've been in business for five years and have earned healthy profits, allowing them each to buy a house, decent wheels, and even a few luxuries—including Jamie's collection of garden sculptures and Kent's roomful of vintage musical instruments. One day Jamie, without telling Kent, orders a shipment of exotic poppy plants that he is sure will be a big hit with customers. But when the shipment arrives, so do agents of the federal drug enforcement agency who confiscate the plants, claiming they could be turned into narcotics. Soon thereafter criminal charges are filed against Jamie and Kent, resulting in several newspaper stories. Though the partners are ultimately cleared, their attorney fees come to $50,000 and they lose several key accounts, with the result that the business runs up hefty debts. As a general partner, Kent is personally liable for these debts even though he had nothing to do with the ill-fated poppy purchase.

Before you get too worried about personal liability, keep in mind that many small businesses don't face much of a risk of racking up large debts.

For instance, if you're engaged in a low-risk enterprise such as freelance editing, landscaping, or running a small band that plays weddings and other social events, your risk of facing massive debt or a huge lawsuit is pretty small. For these types of small, low-risk businesses, a good business insurance policy that covers most liability risks is almost always enough to protect owners from a catastrophe such as a lawsuit or fire. Insurance won't cover regular business debts, however. If you have significant personal assets like fat bank accounts or real estate and plan to rack up some business debt, you may want to limit your personal liability with a different business structure, such as an LLC or a corporation.

4. Partnership Agreements

By drafting a partnership agreement, you can structure your relationship with your partners pretty much however you want. You and your partners can establish the respective shares of profits (or losses) each will receive, what the responsibilities of each partner will be, what should happen to the partnership if a partner leaves, and how any number of other issues will be handled. It is not legally necessary for a partnership to have a written agreement. The simple act of two or more people doing business together creates a partnership. But only with a clear written agreement will all partners be sure of the important—and sometimes touchy—details of their business arrangement.

In the absence of a partnership agreement, California's version of the Revised Uniform Partnership Act (RUPA) kicks in as a standard, bottom-line guide to the rights and responsibilities of each partner. For example, if you don't have a partnership agreement, then California's RUPA states that each partner has an equal share in the business's profits, losses, and management power. Similarly, unless you provide otherwise in a written agreement, a California partnership won't be able to add a new partner without the unanimous consent of all partners. (California Corporations Code § 16401.) But you can override many of the legal provisions contained in the California RUPA if you and your partners have your own written agreement.

What a Partnership Agreement Can't Do

Although a general partnership agreement is an incredibly flexible tool for defining the ownership interests, work responsibilities, and other rights of partners, there are some things it can't do. These include:

- freeing the partners from personal liability for business debts
- restricting any partner's right to inspect the business books and records
- affecting the rights of third parties in relation to the partnership—for example, a partnership agreement that says a partner has no right to sign contracts won't affect the rights of an outsider who signs a contract with that partner, and
- eliminating or weakening the duty of trust (the fiduciary duty) each partner owes to the other partners.

There's nothing terribly complex about drafting partnership agreements. They're usually only a few pages long, and cover basic issues that you've probably thought over to some degree already. Partnership agreements typically include at least the following information:

- name of partnership and partnership business
- date of partnership creation
- purpose of partnership
- contributions (cash, property, and work) of each partner to the partnership
- each partner's share of profits and losses
- provisions for taking profits out of the company (often called partners' draws)
- each partner's management power and duties

Partnership Agreement #1

Alison Shanley and Peder Johnson make the following partnership agreement.

Name and Purpose of Partnership

As of September 22, 200X, Alison and Peder are the sole owners and partners of the Vermont Fly-Fishing Company. The Vermont Fly-Fishing Company shall be headquartered in Rutland, Vermont, and will sell fly-fishing equipment by mail order.

Contributions to the Partnership

Alison and Peder will make the following contributions to the partnership:

Alison Shanley	cash	$10,000
	desk, miscellaneous office furniture	1,000
	Total contribution:	$11,000
Peder Johnson	cash	$7,000
	computer system	2,000
	Total contribution:	$9,000

Profit and Loss Allocation

Alison and Peder will share business profits and losses in the same proportions as their contributions to the business.

Management of Partnership Business

Alison and Peder will have equal management powers and responsibilities.

Departure of a Partner

If either Alison or Peder leaves the partnership for any reason, including voluntary withdrawal, expulsion, or death, the remaining partner shall become the sole owner of the Vermont Fly-Fishing Company, which shall become a sole proprietorship. The remaining owner shall pay the departing partner, or the deceased departing partner's estate, the fair market value of the departing partner's share of the business as of the date of his or her departure. The partnership's accountant shall determine the fair market value of the departing partner's share of the business according to the partnership's book value.

Mediation of Disputes

Alison and Peder agree to mediate any dispute arising under this agreement with a mutually acceptable mediator.

Amendment of Agreement

This agreement may not be amended without the written consent of both partners.

Alison Shanley	Peder Johnson
Signature _____ _____	Signature _____
Date _____	Date _____
Address _____	Address _____
_____	_____
Social Security # _____	Social Security # _____

Partnership Agreement #2

Christine Wenc, Simon Romero, and Brendan Doherty agree to the terms of the following agreement.

1. **Name of Partnership.** Christine, Simon, and Brendan are partners in the Wenc & Romero Partnership. They created the partnership on July 12, 200X.

2. **Partnership Purpose.** The Wenc & Romero Partnership will provide newspaper clipping services to clients.

3. **Contributions to the Partnership.** Christine, Simon, and Brendan will contribute the following to the partnership:

   Christine: $1,000 cash; one Macintosh computer (value $1,500); and one monitor (value $500).
   Simon: $1,000 cash; one fax machine (value $400); one laser printer (value $1,200).
   Brendan: $500 cash; various office equipment (value $500).

4. **Profits and Losses.** Christine, Simon, and Brendan shall share profits and losses as follows:

Christine	40%
Simon	40%
Brendan	20%

5. **Partnership Decisions.** Christine, Simon, and Brendan will have the following management authority:

Christine	2 votes
Simon	2 votes
Brendan	1 vote

   No partner may accept a new client without the agreement of the others.

6. **Additional Terms to Be Drafted.** Christine, Simon, and Brendan agree that in six months they will sign a formal partnership agreement which covers the items in this agreement in more detail, and the additional following items:
   • each partner's work contributions
   • provisions for adding a partner
   • provisions for the departure of a partner, and
   • provisions for selling the business.

7. **Amendments.** This agreement may not be amended without the written consent of all partners.

Christine Wenc
Signature_____ Date _____

Simon Romero
Signature_____ Date _____

Brendan Doherty
Signature_____ Date _____

- how the partnership will handle departure of a partner, including buy-out terms
- provisions for adding or expelling a partner, and
- dispute resolution procedures.

These and any other terms you include in a partnership agreement can be dealt with in more or less detail. Some partnership agreements cover each topic with a sentence or two; others spend up to a few pages on each provision. Of course, you need an agreement that's appropriate for the size and formality of your business, but it's not a good idea to skimp on your partnership agreement.

More information on partnerships. *The Partnership Book,* by Denis Clifford and Ralph Warner, is an excellent step-by-step guide to putting together a solid, comprehensive partnership agreement. Also, *How to Create a Buy/Sell Agreement,* by Anthony Mancuso and Bethany K. Laurence, explains how to draft terms that will enable you to deal with business ownership transitions. (Both books are published by Nolo.)

If you think you may need more than the simple partnership agreements provided in this book but don't want to spend more time on it, there are more detailed partnership agreement forms on CD (as well as many other resources for running your business) in *Quicken Legal Business Pro 2004.* You can learn more about all of these resources at www.nolo.com.

Take a look at the short sample partnership agreements on the following pages to see how a very basic partnership agreement can be put together. You'll also find a blank partnership agreement in Appendix C and on the CD-ROM that comes with this book. These samples are about as basic as it gets—the bare minimum—and you'll almost surely want to use something more detailed for your business.

C. Limited Liability Companies (LLCs)

Like many business owners just starting out, you might find yourself in this common quandary: On the one hand, having to cope with the risk of personal liability for business misfortunes scares you; on the other, you would rather not deal with the red tape of starting and operating a corporation.

Fortunately for you and many other entrepreneurs, you can avoid these problems by taking advantage of a relatively new form of business called the limited liability company, commonly known as an LLC. LLCs combine the pass-through taxation of a sole proprietorship or partnership (business taxes are paid on each owner's individual income tax returns) with the same protection against personal liability that corporations offer. And now that California no longer requires LLCs to have at least two members, solo business owners also have the option of forming an LLC.

However, professional services businesses may not use the LLC structure in California. "Professional services" are "any type of professional services that may be lawfully rendered only pursuant to a license, certification, or registration authorized by the Business and Professions Code, the Chiropractic Act, or the Osteopathic Act" or the Yacht and Ship Brokers Act. (Cal. Corp. Code §§ 13401(a), 13401.3.)

If you're a professional services provider and want a business structure with limited personal liability for the principals, all is not lost. You may recall from Section B1 above, that accountants, lawyers, and architects may form limited liability partnerships (LLPs). If you want limited personal liability with another type of professional services business, you'll need to use the corporate business structure, which we'll discuss in Section D.

1. Limited Personal Liability

Generally, owners of an LLC are not personally liable for the LLC's debts. (There are some exceptions to this rule, discussed below.) This protects the owners from legal and financial liability in case their business fails, or loses a lawsuit and can't pay its debts. In those situations, creditors can take all of the LLC's assets, but they generally can't get at the personal assets of the LLC's owners. Losing your business is no picnic, but it's a lot better to lose only what you put into the business than to say goodbye to everything you own.

> **EXAMPLE:** Callie forms her own one-person mail-order business, using most of her $25,000 in savings to establish a cool website and buy mailing lists. Callie realizes that she'll have to buy a significant portion of her sales inventory up front to be able to ship goods to her customers on time, so she plans to buy those items on credit. While she is willing to risk her $25,000 investment to pursue her dream, she is worried that if her mail-order business fails, she will be buried under a pile of debt. Callie decides to form an LLC so that if her business should fail, she'll only lose the $25,000; no one will be able to sue her personally for the business debt that she owes. She feels more secure going into business knowing that even if her business fails, she can walk away without the risk of losing her house or her car.

Keep in mind that, like a general partner in a partnership, any member of a member-managed LLC can legally bind the entire LLC to a contract or business transaction. In other words, each member can act as an agent of the LLC. (Some LLCs are managed by managers, instead of by members. In manager-managed LLCs, any *manager* can bind the LLC to a business contract or deal.)

While LLC owners enjoy limited personal liability for many of their business debts, this protection is not absolute. There are several situations in which an LLC owner may become personally liable for business debts or claims. However, this drawback is not unique to LLCs. The limited liability protection given to LLC members is just as strong as (if not stronger than) that enjoyed by the corporate shareholders of small corporations. Here are the main situations in which LLC owners can still be held personally liable for debts:

- **Personal guarantees.** If you give a personal guarantee on a loan to the LLC, then you are personally liable for repaying that loan. Since personal guarantees are often required by banks and other lenders, this is a good reason to be a conservative borrower. Of course, if no personal guarantee is made, then only the LLC—not the members—are liable for the debt.
- **Taxes.** The IRS or the California Franchise Tax Board may go after the personal assets of LLC owners for overdue corporate federal and state tax debts, particularly overdue payroll taxes. This is most likely to happen to members of small LLCs who have an active hand in managing the business, rather than to passive members.
- **Negligent or intentional acts.** An LLC owner who intentionally, or even carelessly, hurts someone will usually face personal liability. For example, if an LLC owner takes a client to lunch, has a few martinis and injures the client in a car accident on the way home, the LLC owner can be held personally liable for the client's injuries.
- **Breach of fiduciary duty.** LLC owners have a legal duty to act in the best interest of their company and its members. This legal obligation is known as a "fiduciary duty," or is sometimes simply called a "duty of care." LLC owners who violate this duty can be held personally liable for any damages that result from their actions (or inactions). Fortunately for LLC owners, they normally will not be held personally responsible for any honest mistakes or acts of poor judgment they commit in doing their jobs. Most often, breach of duty is found only for serious indiscretions such as fraud or other illegal behavior.
- **Blurring the boundaries between the LLC and its owners.** When owners fail to respect the separate legal existence of their LLC, but instead treat it as an extension of their personal affairs, a court may rule that the owners are personally liable for business debts and liabilities. Generally this is more likely to

occur in one-member LLCs; in reality it only happens in extreme cases. It can easily be avoided by opening a separate LLC checking account, getting a federal employer identification number, keeping separate accounting books for your LLC, and funding your LLC adequately enough to be able to meet foreseeable expenses.

2. LLC Taxation

Like a sole proprietorship or partnership, an LLC is not a separate tax entity from its owners; instead it's what the IRS calls a "pass-through entity." This means the LLC itself does not pay any income taxes; instead, income passes through the business to each LLC owner, who pays taxes on the individual share of profit (or deducts his share of losses) on an income tax return (for the feds, Form 1040 with Schedule E attached). But a multiowner LLC, like a partnership, does have to file Form 1065—an "informational return"—to let the government know how much the business earned or lost that year. No tax is paid with this return.

LLCs give members the flexibility to choose to have the company taxed like a corporation rather than as a pass-through entity. In fact, partnerships now have this option as well. (See Form 8832, Entity Classification Election, in Appendix C.)

You may wonder why LLC owners would choose to be taxed as a corporation—after all, pass-through taxation is one of the most popular features of an LLC. The answer is that, because of the income-splitting strategy of corporations (discussed in Section D2a, below), LLC members can sometimes come out ahead by having their business taxed as a separate entity at corporate tax rates.

For example, if the owners of an LLC become successful enough to keep some profits in the business at the end of the year (or regularly need to keep significant profits in the business for upcoming expenses), paying tax at corporate tax rates can save them money. That's because federal income tax rates for corporations start at a lower rate than the rates for individuals. For this reason,

many LLCs start out being taxed as partnerships, and when they make enough profit to justify keeping some in the business (rather than doling them out as salaries and bonuses), they opt for corporate-style taxation.

LLCs face significant taxes and fees at the state level. California charges a minimum annual tax of $800, which is due in the first quarter of operations, whether or not you're making a profit. (We discuss LLC taxes in more detail in Chapter 9, Section D.)

3. LLCs vs. S Corporations

Before LLCs came along, the only way all owners of a business could get limited personal liability was to form a corporation. Problem was, many entrepreneurs didn't want the hassle and expense of incorporating, not to mention the headache of dealing with corporate taxation. One easier option was to form a special type of corporation known as an S corporation, which is like a normal corporation in most respects, except that business profits pass through to the owner (as in a sole proprietorship or partnership), rather than being taxed to the corporation at corporate tax rates. In other words, S corporations offered the limited liability of a corporation with the pass-through taxation of a sole proprietorship or partnership. For a long time, this was an okay compromise for small-to-medium-sized businesses, though they still had to deal with many of the corporate aspects that S corporations retained. (We'll talk more about these below.)

Now, however, LLCs offer a better option. LLCs are indeed similar to S corporations in that they combine limited personal liability with pass-through tax status. But a significant difference between these two types of businesses is that LLCs are not bound by the many regulations that govern S corporations.

Here's a quick rundown of the major areas of difference between S corporations and LLCs. Keep in mind that we'll discuss corporations, including S corporations, in more detail in the next section.

- **Ownership restrictions.** An S corporation may not have more than 75 shareholders, all of whom must be U.S. citizens or residents. This means that some of the C corporation's main benefits—namely, the ability to set up stock option and bonus plans and to bring in public capital with an IPO—are pretty much out of the question for S corporations. And even if an S corporation initially meets the U.S. citizen or resident requirement, its shareholders can't sell shares to another company (like a corporation or an LLC) or a foreign citizen, on pain of losing S corporation tax status. In an LLC, any type of person or entity can become a member—a U.S. citizen, a citizen of a foreign country, another LLC, corporation, or limited partnership.

- **Allocation of profits and losses.** Shareholders of an S corporation must allocate profits according to the percentage of stock each owner has. For example, a 25% owner has to receive 25% of the profits (or losses), even if the other owners want a different division. Owners of an LLC, on the other hand, may distribute profits (and the tax burden that goes with them) however they see fit, without regard to each member's ownership share in the company. For instance, a member of an LLC who owns 25% of the business can receive 50% of the profits if the other members agree (subject to a few IRS rules).

- **Corporate meeting and record-keeping rules.** For S corporation shareholders to keep their limited liability protection, they have to follow the corporate rules—issuing stock, electing officers, holding regular board of directors' and shareholders' meetings, keeping corporate minutes of all meetings, and following the mandatory rules found in the corporation code. By contrast, LLC owners don't need to jump through most of these legal hoops—they just have to make sure their management team is in agreement on major decisions and go about their business.

- **Tax treatment of losses.** S corporation shareholders are at a disadvantage if their company goes into substantial debt—for instance, if it borrows money to open the business or buy real estate. That's because an S corporation's business debt cannot be passed along to its shareholders unless they have personally cosigned and guaranteed the debt. LLC owners, on the other hand, normally can reap the tax benefits of any business debt, cosigned or not. This can translate into a nice tax break for owners of LLCs that carry debt.

4. Forming an LLC

Before you decide the LLC is the best thing since easy cheese, you should be aware that an LLC is generally not as cheap to start as a partnership or sole proprietorship. To form an LLC, you must file Articles of Organization with the California Secretary of State. While the filing fee itself isn't terribly expensive ($70), the California Franchise Tax Board requires that you pay a minimum annual LLC tax of $800 when you start your LLC.

Many brand-new business owners aren't in a position to pay this kind of money right out of the starting block, so they start out as partnerships until they bring in enough income to cover these costs. Since California lowered its corporate start-up fees in 2000, some entrepreneurs are tempted to start out as corporations, which are now cheaper to start than LLCs. However, keep in mind that the added expenses of running a corporation (legal and accounting fees, for example) can often make a corporation more expensive in the long run than an LLC.

⚠ Some LLCs must comply with securities laws. LLCs that have owners who do not actively participate in the business may have to register their membership interests as securities or, more likely, qualify for an exemption to the registration requirements. For information about the federal securities laws, visit the Securities and Exchange

Commission's website at www.sec.gov and click on "Information for: Small Business."

For more on LLCs. *Form Your Own Limited Liability Company*, by Anthony Mancuso (Nolo), gives detailed information on LLCs, including step-by-step instructions and forms for creating one in every state. For a briefer treatment, consult *Nolo's Quick LLC*, also by Anthony Mancuso. It offers an overview of LLCs as well as comparisons to other business structures, but does not include any start-up forms.

D. Corporations

For many, the term "corporation" conjures up the image of a massive industrial empire more akin to a nation-state than a small business. In fact, a corporation doesn't have to be huge, and most aren't. Stripped to its essentials, a corporation is simply a specific legal structure that imposes certain legal and tax rules on its owners (also called shareholders). A corporation can be as large as IBM or, in many cases, as small as one person.

One fundamental legal characteristic of a corporation is that it's a separate legal entity from its owners. If you've already read this chapter's sections on sole proprietorships and partnerships, you'll recognize that this is a major difference between those unincorporated business types and corporations. Another important corporate feature is that shareholders are normally protected from personal liability for business debts. Finally, the corporation itself—not just the shareholders—is subject to income tax.

Publicly traded corporations are a different ball game. This section discusses privately held corporations owned by a small group of people who are actively involved in running the business. These corporations are much easier to manage than public corporations, whose shares are sold to the public at large. Any corporation that sells its stock to the general public is heavily regulated by state and federal securities laws, while corporations that sell shares, without advertising, only to a select group of people who meet specific state requirements are often exempt from many of these laws. If you plan to sell shares of a corporation to the general public, you should consult a lawyer.

1. Limited Personal Liability

Generally, owners of a corporation are not personally liable for the corporation's debts. (There are some exceptions to this rule, discussed below.) Limited personal liability is a major reason why owners have traditionally chosen to incorporate their businesses: to protect themselves from legal and financial liability in case their business flounders or loses an expensive lawsuit and can't pay its debts. In those situations, creditors can take all of the corporation's assets (including the shareholders' investments), but they generally can't get at the personal assets of the shareholders.

EXAMPLE: Tim and Chris publish *Tropics Tripping,* a monthly travel magazine with a focus on Latin America. Because they both have significant personal assets, and because they will have to borrow a lot of capital to start up their magazine, they form their business as a corporation to protect their personal assets in case their magazine fails. They do great for a few years, but suddenly their subscription and advertising revenue starts to suffer when a recession plus political unrest in several Latin American countries reduce interest in travel to that area. Hoping the situation will turn itself around, Tim and Chris forge ahead—and go deeper into debt as it proves impossible to pay printing and other bills on time. Finally, when their printer won't do any more print runs on credit, Tim and Chris are forced to call it quits. *Tropics Tripping*'s debts total $250,000, while business assets are valued at only $90,000— leaving a $160,000 debt to creditors. Thankfully for Tim and Chris, they won't have to use their personal assets to pay the $160,000, because as owners of a corporation, they're shielded from personal liability.

Corporations aren't the only option. With the advent of limited liability companies, corporations aren't the only business entities that provide limited liability status for all owners. (See Section C on LLCs, above.)

Forming a corporation to shield yourself from personal liability for business obligations provides good, but not complete, protection for your personal assets. Here are the principal areas where corporation owners still face personal liability.

- **Personal guarantees.** If you give a personal guarantee on a loan to the corporation, then you are personally liable for the repayment of that loan. Since banks and other lenders often require a personal guarantee, this is a good reason to be a conservative borrower. Of course, if no personal guarantee is made, then only the corporation—not the shareholders—is liable for the debt.

- **Taxes.** The IRS or the California Franchise Tax Board may go after the personal assets of corporate owners for overdue corporate federal and state tax debts, particularly overdue payroll taxes. This is most likely to happen to owners of small corporations who have an active hand in managing the business, rather than to passive shareholders.

- **Negligent or intentional acts.** A corporate owner whose negligent (that is, careless), or perhaps even intentional, actions end up hurting someone can't hide behind the corporate barrier to escape personal liability. Shareholders are subject to personal liability for wrongs they commit—such as attacking a customer or leaving a wet floor in a store—that result in injury.

- **Breach of fiduciary duty.** Corporate owners have a legal duty to act in the best interest of the company and its shareholders. This legal obligation is known as a "fiduciary duty," sometimes simply called a "duty of care." An owner who violates this duty can be held personally liable for any damages that result from those actions (or inactions). Fortunately for corporate owners, run-of-the-mill mistakes or lapses in judgment aren't usually considered breaches of the duty of care. Most often, breach of duty is found only for serious indiscretions such as fraud or other illegal behavior. For example, if a corporate officer falsified some financial data in order to seal a deal with a client, that officer may be held personally liable for any damages that result from that breach of duty to the company.

- **Blurring the boundaries between the corporation and its owners.** When corporate owners ignore corporate formalities and treat the corporation like an unincorporated business, a court may ignore the existence of the corporation (in legal slang, it may "pierce the corporate veil") and rule that the owners are personally liable for business debts and liabilities. To avoid this, it's important for corporate owners not to allow the legal boundary between the corporation and its owners to grow fuzzy. Owners need to scrupulously respect corporate formalities by holding shareholders' and directors' meetings, keeping attentive minutes, issuing stock certificates, and maintaining corporate accounts strictly separate from personal funds.

Don't be fooled into thinking that incorporating will solve all your liability problems. Limited personal liability can prevent you from losing your home, car, bank account, and other assets—but it won't protect you from losing your investment in your business. A business can quickly get wiped out if a customer, employee, or supplier wins a big lawsuit against it and the business has to be liquidated to cover the debt. In short, even if you incorporate to protect your personal assets, you should purchase appropriate insurance to protect your business assets. (Insurance is discussed in

Chapter 8.) But remember, insurance won't help if you simply can't pay your normal business debts.

2. Corporate Taxation

The words "corporate taxes" raise a lot of fear and loathing in the business world. Fortunately, the reality of corporate taxation is usually less depressing than the hype. Here are the basics—think of it as Corporate Tax Lite. If you decide to incorporate, you'll likely want to consult an accountant or small business lawyer who can fill you in on the fine print. (See Chapter 13 for information on finding and hiring a lawyer.)

The first thing you need to know is that you'll be treated differently for tax purposes, depending on whether you operate as a regular corporation (also called a C corporation) or you elect S corporation status. An S corporation is the same as a C corporation in most respects, but when it comes to taxes, C and S corporations are very different animals. A regular, or C, corporation must pay taxes, while an S corporation is treated like a partnership for tax purposes and doesn't pay any income taxes itself. Like partnership profits, S corporation profits (and losses) pass through to the shareholders, who report them on their individual returns. (In this respect, S corporations are very similar to LLCs, which also offer limited liability along with partnership-style tax treatment.) These two types of corporations are explained in more detail just below.

a. C Corporations

As a separate tax entity, a regular corporation must file and pay income taxes on its own tax return, much like an individual does. After deductions for such things as employee compensation, fringe benefits and all other reasonable and necessary business expenses have been subtracted from its earnings, a corporation pays tax on whatever profit remains. In small corporations where all of the owners of the business are also employees, all of the corporation's profits are often paid out in tax-deductible salaries and fringe benefits—leaving no corporate profit and thus no corporate taxes due. (The owner/employees must, of course, pay tax on their salaries on their individual returns.)

Fringes and Perks

Like employee salaries, corporations can deduct many fringe benefits as business expenses. If a corporation pays for benefits such as health and disability insurance for its employees and owner/employees, the cost can usually be deducted from the corporate income, reducing a possible tax bill. (There's one main exception: benefits given to an owner/employee of an S corporation who owns 2% or more of the stock can't be deducted as business expenses.)

As a general rule, owners of sole proprietorships, partnerships, and LLCs can deduct the cost of providing these benefits for employees, but not for themselves. (These owners can, however, deduct a portion of their medical insurance premiums, though it's technically a deduction for the individuals, not a business expense.)

The fact that fringe benefits for owners are deductible for corporations may make incorporating a wise choice. But it's less likely to be a winning strategy for a capital-poor start-up that can't afford to underwrite a benefits package.

Initial rates of corporate taxation are comparatively low (15%–25%) (See "Marginal Tax Rates for Corporations," below.) Corporations that keep some profits in the business from one year to the next—rather than paying out all profits as salaries and bonuses—can take advantage of these low tax brackets. This practice, sometimes called income-splitting, basically involves strategically setting salaries at a level so that money left in the business is taxable only at the 15% or 25% corporate tax rate (which applies to profits up to $50,000 or $75,000). Since any amount of "reasonable" compensation to employees is deductible, corporate owners have lots of leeway in setting salaries to accomplish this.

Marginal Tax Rates for Corporations

The following chart shows tax rates for corporations. For example, if a corporation's taxable income was $75,100, it would pay 15% of its first $50,000 of income, 25% of the next $25,000, and 34% on its remaining $100 in income. The corporation's marginal tax rate—the tax rate a corporation would pay on the last dollar of its income—would be 34%.

Taxable Income	Tax Rate
0 to $50,000	15%
$50,001 to $75,000	25%
$75,001 to $100,000	34%
$100,001 to $335,000	39%
$335,001 to $10,000,000	34%
$10,000,001 to $15,000,000	35%
$15,000,001 to $18,333,333	38%
Over $18,333,333	35%

Keep in mind that these corporate rates don't apply to professional corporations, which are subject to a flat tax of 35% on all corporate income.

EXAMPLE: Alexis and Matt run Window to the Past, Inc., a glass manufacturing business that specializes in custom work for architectural renovations. Toward the end of the year, they calculate that year's profit to be approximately $145,000. They decide to give themselves each a $50,000 bonus out of the profit (on top of their $40,000 salaries). Because both salaries and bonuses are tax-deductible business expenses, this reduces Window to the Past's taxable income to $45,000. The resulting corporate profit of $45,000 will be taxed at only 15%, the lowest rate. (If Alexis and Matt had left all the profits in the business, the profits over $75,000 would have been taxed at 34%, and profits over $100,000 would have been taxed at a whopping 39%.) Of course, the bonuses Alexis and Matt give themselves increase their personal incomes, which will be taxed on their individual returns. Still, their personal tax rates are lower than the high corporate rates of 34% and 39%.

This income-splitting strategy is available only to shareholders who also work for the corporation. If they're not at least part-time employees, then shareholders won't be in a position to earn salaries or bonuses, and will be able to take money from the corporation only as dividends. This brings us to the vexing problem of double taxation, routinely faced by larger corporations with shareholders who aren't active employees. Unlike salaries and bonuses, dividends paid to shareholders cannot be deducted as business expenses from corporate earnings. Since they're not deducted, any amounts paid as dividends are included in the total corporate profit and taxed. And when the shareholder receives the dividend, it is taxed at the shareholder's individual tax rate as part of personal income. As you can see, any money paid out as a dividend gets taxed twice: once at the corporate level, and once at the individual level.

You can avoid double taxation simply by not paying dividends. This is usually easy if all shareholders are employees, but probably more difficult if some shareholders are passive investors anxious for a reasonable return on their investment.

b. The Un-Corporation: S Corporations

Unlike a regular corporation, an S corporation does not pay taxes itself. Any profits pass through to the owners, who pay taxes on income as if the business were a sole proprietorship, a partnership, or an LLC. Yet the business is still a corporation. This means, of course, that its owners are protected from personal liability for business debts, just as shareholders of C corporations and owners of LLCs.

Until the relatively recent arrival of the LLC (discussed in Section C), the S corporation was the business form of choice for those who wanted limited liability protection without the two-tiered tax structure of a C corporation. Today, relatively few businesses are organized as S corporations, since S corporations are subject to many regulations that do not apply to LLCs. (See Section C above for an outline of the differences between S corporations and LLCs.)

3. Forming and Running a Corporation

Unlike sole proprietorships and partnerships, you can't clap your hands twice and conjure up a corporation. In addition to tax complexity, a major drawback to forming a corporation—either a C or an S type—is time and expense. Now that California has reduced the up-front fees for incorporating, however, most of the expense involves legal and other professional fees that are almost always incurred in forming a corporation. To incorporate, you must file Articles of Incorporation with California's Secretary of State, along with a filing fee of $100. (Significantly, the minimum annual tax of $800 is no longer due in the first business year for corporations created on or after January 1, 2000.) You will have to file a Statement by Domestic Stock Corporation every year, beginning within 90 days of filing your Articles of Incorporation. (These requirements are covered in detail in Chapter 7.) And if you decide to sell shares of the corporation to the public—as opposed to keeping them in the hands of a relatively small number of owners—you'll have to comply with lots of complex federal and state securities laws. Finally, to protect your limited personal liability, you need to act like a corporation, which means adopting bylaws, issuing stock to shareholders, maintaining records of various meetings of directors and shareholders, and keeping records and transactions of the business separate from those of the owners.

Corporations must comply with securities laws. Corporations must either register their shares with the Securities and Exchange Commission or qualify for an exemption to securities registration requirements. For a brief overview of

securities law, read the "Corporations FAQ" found in the Corporations Section of Nolo's Small Business Law Center at www.nolo.com. And for information about small business exemptions to the federal securities laws, visit the Securities and Exchange Commission's website at www.sec.gov and click on "Information for: Small Business."

More on running corporations. For more information on the many complexities of running a corporation, read either *How to Form Your Own California Corporation* or *The Corporate Minutes Book,* both written by Anthony Mancuso and published by Nolo.

E. Choosing the Best Structure for Your Business

Although there are many differences between the various types of business organizations, most business owners choose an operating structure based on one major legal issue: the personal liability of owners for business debts. While the issue of personal liability can have a huge impact on successful small businesses a few years down the road, business owners who are just starting out on a shoestring often care most about spending as little money as possible on the legal structure of their business. This is certainly an understandable approach; far more new businesses die painful deaths because they don't control costs than because they lose costly lawsuits. In short, for many new small businesses, incorporating or organizing as an LLC is as unnecessary an expense as a swank downtown office or a gleaming chrome espresso machine in the lunchroom.

That said, owners of any business that will engage in a high risk activity, rack up large business debts, or have a significant number of investors should always insist on limited personal liability, either with an LLC or a corporation. This is even more true if the business can't find or afford appropriate insurance.

Analyzing Your Risks

Starting a business is always risky. In some businesses, however, the risks are particularly extreme. If you're planning to launch an investment firm or start a hazardous waste management company, there is little doubt that you'll need all the protection you can get, including limited personal liability as well as adequate insurance. Other businesses are not so obviously risk laden, but still could land you in trouble if fate strikes you a blow. Here are a few red flags to watch for when analyzing how risky your business is:

- using hazardous materials, such as dry cleaning solvents or photographic chemicals, or hazardous processes, such as welding or operating heavy machinery
- manufacturing or selling edible goods
- driving as part of the job
- building or repairing structures or vehicles
- caring for children or animals
- providing or allowing access to alcohol
- allowing activities that may result in injury, such as weightlifting or skateboarding, and
- repairing or working on items of value, such as cars or antiques.

If you've identified one or more serious risks your business is likely to face, figure out whether business insurance might give you enough protection. Some risky activities, such as job-related driving, are good candidates for insurance and don't necessarily warrant incorporating. But if insurance can't cover all of the risks involved in your business, it may be time to form an LLC or a corporation.

Keep in mind that insurance will never insulate you from regular business debts. If you foresee your business going into serious debt, an LLC or corporation may be the best business structure for you.

(For more information on risk management and insurance, see Chapter 8.)

If you decide that your personal liability is worth the extra cost, you still need to decide whether to form a corporation or an LLC. Many business owners who want limited liability protection realize that incorporation normally makes sense only if a business needs to take advantage of the corporate stock structure to attract key employees and investment capital. No question, corporations may have an easier time attracting capital investment by issuing stock privately or publicly. And some businesses may find it easier to attract and retain key employees by issuing employee stock options. But for businesses that never go public, choosing to operate as an LLC rather than a corporation normally makes the most sense, if limited liability is your main concern. If the corporate stock structure isn't something you want or need for your business, the simplicity and flexibility of LLCs offer a clear advantage over corporations.

☑ Chapter 2 Checklist

- ☐ Identify the number of owners of your business.

- ☐ Analyze your business's risks and decide how much protection from personal liability you'll need.

- ☐ Determine how you'd like the business to be taxed (as a pass-through entity or as a corporation).

- ☐ Decide if your business would benefit from the stock structure of a corporation (by being able to distribute stock options and sell stock).

- ☐ Choose a business structure.

- ☐ If you will structure your business as a partnership, draft and sign a partnership agreement.

- ☐ If you will structure your business as an LLC or corporation, file articles with the California Secretary of State and draft bylaws (corporations) or an operating agreement (LLCs).

Picking Winning Business Names That Won't Land You in Court

There's a lot of room for personal and professional creativity when picking a business name, but there are also legal requirements and pitfalls that you absolutely need to understand. In particular, it's important for all business owners to understand the basics of trademark law, which establishes and protects the legal right to use a particular name for businesses, products, or services.

If you choose a business or product name that's too similar to a competitor's name, for instance, you could find yourself accused of violating the competitor's trademark (called "infringing" or "unfairly competing") and be forced to change your business name and possibly pay money damages. Having to change a business name can be a serious blow to a business that has worked hard to build name recognition among its customers—not to mention the cost of changing signs, stationery, preprinted invoices, and the like.

But suppose you plan to open a local business so small that you don't even expect to compete with businesses in the next county, much less in another state or country. You probably wonder if the arcane world of trademark law really affects you. Just 20 years ago the answer would have clearly been no—you didn't really have to worry too much about national or global name conflicts back then. As long as a quick search of your phone book didn't reveal any obvious local conflicts and you didn't call your business "Ford," "IBM," or some other famous name, you were fine. But in today's world of the Internet, mail order, and rapidly growing national chains, "local" obviously isn't what it used to be. Even if you're opening just a tiny bookstore in a small town, if you inadvertently choose the same name as an Internet store that sells books, you may very well be accused of infringing the online store's trademark—even if the online store's headquarters are on a different continent.

One good way to figure out how concerned you need to be about trademark law is to consider the consequences of having to change your business name. If a name change would be cheap and easy and wouldn't seriously confuse your customers, then don't lie awake nights worrying about picking a name that's absolutely bulletproof. However, if changing your name would be messy or expensive, you'll want to take the time and trouble to be sure the name you plan to use doesn't already belong to someone else.

Have we convinced you that paying attention to the law of business names is important? Good. Now we'll explain how to choose a name that won't land you in legal hot water and how to secure the maximum legal protection for it. We'll also cover some nonlegal aspects of naming your business, including tips and advice on how to choose the most effective name for your particular business.

Watch out for other legal issues. Besides watching out for trademark conflicts, business owners also need to comply with other legal rules. Many businesses must comply with fictitious business name requirements. (See Chapter 7, Step 3.) Typically this means you'll need to register a fictitious business name statement (or similar document) with your county clerk and possibly publish it in a local newspaper. And for corporations, LLCs, and limited partnerships, the California Secretary of State must approve your business name before it will accept Articles of Incorporation, Articles of Organization or a Statement of Limited Partnership.

Getting the Terms Straight

One reason the law of business names often seems confusing is that it is riddled with lots of arcane and often overlapping legal jargon. For example, local, state, and federal agencies often use different terms to describe the same or very similar legal concepts. Here's a brief rundown of the terms you need to know, all of which are discussed in greater detail in the rest of this chapter.

- The term **legal name** means the official name of the entity that owns a business. The legal name of a sole proprietorship is simply the full name of the owner—for example, John Potter. If a general partnership has a written partnership agreement that gives a name to the partnership, then that name is the legal name. Otherwise, the legal name of the general partnership is simply the last names of the owners. (Many sole proprietorships and partnerships present their businesses to the public under names that are different from their legal names—see fictitious business names, below.) And for corporations, LLCs, and limited partnerships, legal names are the names registered with the California Secretary of State.

- A **trade name** is simply the name that a business uses with the public, which may or may not be the same as the name of the business owner or the business's legal name. John O'Toole's Classic Cars, Amoeba Records, and Nolo are examples of trade names. You see trade names on business signs, in the telephone book, and on invoices. In many transactions, such as opening a bank account or applying for a loan, you'll need to provide the owners' names, the legal name of the business (if different), and the trade name of the business (if different).

- The term **fictitious business name** is used when the trade name of a business is different from its legal name. For instance, if John O'Toole named his sole proprietorship Turtle's Classic Cars, the name "Turtle's Classic Cars" would be a fictitious business name because it

does not contain the owner's last name, "O'Toole." A fictitious business name is sometimes called a **DBA** name. DBA stands for "doing business as," as in "John O'Toole, doing business as Turtle's Classic Cars." Corporations and LLCs may also have to file fictitious name statements if the name they hold out to the public differs from the legal name they registered with the state. For example, if the owners of Southern Colusa County Auto Mechanics Ltd. Liability Co. decide to operate a repair shop under the fictitious name "Grease Monkeys," they'll have to file a fictitious business name statement.

- When a business incorporates, it must choose and register a **corporate name** with the California Secretary of State. Similarly, a limited liability company (LLC) must register an **LLC name** and a limited partnership (LP) must register an **LP name** with the California Secretary of State. Corporate, LLC, and limited partnership names must have the Secretary of State's approval before they will be registered. If a corporation, LLC, or limited partnership operates under the same name that's registered with the Secretary of State, then its name will be both its legal name and its trade name.

- A **trademark** (sometimes called simply a mark) is any word, phrase, design, or symbol used to market a product or service. Technically, a mark used to market a service, rather than a product, is called a service mark, though the term "trademark" is commonly used for both types of marks. Owners of trademarks have legal rights under both federal and California law, which give them the power in some cases to prevent others from using their trademarks to market goods or services.

- **Business name** tends to be a catchall term that can refer to any of the names used by a business—the name of a business itself, a corporate name, a fictitious business name, or the name of a business's product or service.

Business Names and Trademarks Often Overlap

Many trade names double as trademarks and service marks for products and services of the business. For instance, when McDonald's (trade name) advertises McDonald's French fries, the trade name "McDonald's" also becomes a trademark because it is used to identify the maker (or brand) of French fries. And when the company puts up a sign in front of its restaurant, the term "McDonald's" becomes a service mark, identifying who's providing the fast food service of that restaurant. In other words, any time you use your trade name to identify a product, service, or business location, you're using the trade name as a mark—either a trademark or a service mark. As you can see, a name can wear a bunch of different hats: it can be a trade name, a legal name, and a trademark (or service mark) all in one.

Legal Name	Trade Name	Trademarks/Service Marks
McDonald's Corporation	McDonald's	McDonald's French fries Big Mac Mayor McCheese Golden arches symbol
Microsoft Corporation	Microsoft	Microsoft Word Windows 2000 Internet Explorer "Where do you want to go today?" slogan
Nolo Press/Folk Law, Inc.	Nolo	Nolo Scales symbol "Law for all" slogan
Trader Joe's Company	Trader Joe's	Trader Joe's Baked Tortilla Chips Trader Giotto's Italian Roast coffee beans Trader Darwin's vitamins
Ronco, Inc.	Ronco	Popeil Pocket Fisherman Dial-O-Matic Food Slicer
Kraft Foods, Inc.	Kraft	JELL-O Gelatin Cheez Whiz Tang Instant Breakfast Drink "It's the cheesiest" slogan for Kraft Macaroni & Cheese "Good to the last drop" slogan for Kraft Maxwell House Coffee

A. An Overview of Trademark Law

In a nutshell, trademark law—which is really a catchall term referring to a large body of statutes, regulations, and court decisions—prevents a business from using a name or logo that is likely to be confused with one that a competing business already uses. This general rule applies both to the name of a business and to the names of any of its products or services.

Allowing businesses to have exclusive use of certain names helps consumers to identify and recognize goods in the marketplace. When you buy Racafrax brand of wood glue, for instance, you'll know that it will be similar in quality to the Racafrax glue you bought last time. By contrast, if any company was allowed to call its glue "Racafrax Glue," customers would never know what they were getting. And because customers would never know when they were using the Racafrax company's glue, the Racafrax company wouldn't be able to build customer trust or goodwill, even if its glue was the best available. In this way, consumers and businesses alike benefit from trademark protection.

This section will give you a rundown of what's protected by trademark law and how to determine and protect your rights to the names you use. This will help you understand what steps you should take as part of forming your business to avoid infringing others' rights (and opening yourself up to lawsuits). And it will also give you the legal basics you'll need to protect your business name and to figure out whether your rights are being infringed by others down the road.

Trademark Protects More Than Names

In this chapter, we talk mostly about how trademark applies to business names. But the rules apply to a lot more; logos, designs, slogans, and packaging features can also be protected by trademark. For example, Nike's slogan, "Just Do It," and American Express's mantra, "Don't leave home without it," are protected by the law of trademark. For more information on using trademarks in other aspects of your small business, read *Trademark: Legal Care for Your Business and Product Name*, by Stephen R. Elias (Nolo).

Pick a name that won't bring legal trouble. The main reason to learn the basics of trademark law is not so you can successfully defend your name in court against another business that tries to use it. Even if you were to win a complex and expensive court fight, you'd be a huge loser when it comes to time, worry, and legal fees. Far better to avoid disputes in the first place by choosing a safe name that has a very low likelihood of leading to customer confusion and, therefore, an infringement lawsuit.

1. What Is a Trademark?

The definition of "trademark" is simple: any word, phrase, logo, or other device used to identify products or services in the marketplace. This includes the names of products or services themselves and often the name of the business that's selling them. Using a name in public commerce to identify goods or services for sale is enough to make it a trademark; there is no registration requirement. However, registration with the U.S. Patent and Trademark Office will greatly strengthen your power to enforce your rights to the trademark. For example, if you federally register your trademark, you can stop any subsequent user in your field from using the same or a confusingly similar mark anywhere in the United States. (Trademark registration is covered in Section E.)

Keep in mind, however, that a key part of the definition of a trademark is that it must be used in public to identify goods or services for sale. So if you don't use the name of your business or product or service in public in conjunction with something you're trying to sell, it isn't considered a trademark. For example, if a software company called ZZP Web Masters markets bookmarking software for the Internet called "WebWorm," then the name WebWorm is a trademark. If the only marketing done for WebWorm is an ad that reads, "Manage your bookmarks with WebWorm," then the business name ZZP Web Masters will not be a trademark because it's not used in public to sell WebWorm. But an ad that reads, "WebWorm: The best bookmarking software on Earth, by ZZP Web Masters," includes two trademarks: the product name WebWorm and the trade name ZZP Web Masters.

By the same token, a name that appears only in nonpublic documents—for example, an internal memo or a product sample that isn't available to the public—isn't a trademark.

For practical purposes, many if not most business names are also considered trademarks, since most businesses do use their names to promote or sell their products or services.

Trademarks vs. Service Marks

You've probably heard the term "trademark," which applies to names, logos, and slogans that identify products (such as Chia Pet), a whole lot more than the term "service mark," which is used when a name identifies a service (such as H&R Block Tax Preparation Services). Because the legal rules for trademarks and service marks are virtually identical, the term "trademark," or sometimes just "mark," is commonly used for both types of marks. But since the two terms do refer to technically different things, you should be aware of the distinction, especially if your businesses will primarily provide services.

---

a. Trademark Rights

The power of a trademark comes from the fact that you may be entitled to exclude others from using the same mark. If you were the first to use a trademark, then you own certain rights to it and can take legal action against others who use it illegally. In legal terms, if others "infringe your trademark" by using it in a way that's likely to confuse your customers or that has "diluted" your trademark, you can take them to court and force them to stop using it, and maybe even to pay damages.

For example, if ZZP Web Masters had been selling WebWorm for two years and then another company started selling a similar product called "WebWorm," ZZP Web Masters could sue the other company and force it to stop using the product name "WebWorm." If ZZP Web Masters could prove that its business suffered because of the infringement, it might also be entitled to some financial compensation (damages) from the other company. (We'll discuss when use of a similar trademark can cause customer confusion or trademark dilution in Sections 2 and 3, below.)

So far, so good—you're probably even wondering why everyone says trademark issues are such a bear to deal with. Here's why: Just because you own a trademark doesn't mean you can always prevent someone else from using it (and likewise, another owner of a trademark can't always prevent you from using that mark). Unlike a copyright, which generally gives the same level of protection to all owners, a trademark gives widely varying degrees of protection to the owner, depending on a variety of circumstances. So, as we explain below, the key legal point isn't so much whether you own a trademark but whether it qualifies for trademark protection—and if so, how much.

b. Strong vs. Weak Marks

The general rule is that distinctive business names such as Yahoo! and Mountain Dew receive the strongest legal trademark protection. Below we define "distinctive" in more detail, but for the moment, it's important that you understand why distinctive names get more protection. The theory is that distinctive names such as Pepsi or Cisco make strong connections in the minds of consumers and play a big role in their buying choices. The opposite is considered to be true for names that aren't very distinctive, such as Quality Vitamins or Brite Paint.

Since distinctive names are thought to play such a big role in helping consumers choose among brands, it follows that the more distinctive a name is, the more likely it is that customers will be confused (in legal theory at least) by more than one business using the name. To avoid this confusion, the law gives more protection to distinctive names, and less or none to names that are merely ordinary and descriptive.

A truly distinctive trademark (also called a "strong trademark") is one that clearly distinguishes the product or service it represents from others. Memorable, unusual names such as Xerox or 3M are additional good examples of distinctive marks. While there's no magic formula for what makes a trademark distinctive, strong marks tend to be surprising or fanciful names that often have nothing to do with the business, product, or service. Still more examples of distinctive marks include Chia Pet, Velcro, and Comet (cleanser).

On the flip side, a weak trademark consists of ordinary, descriptive words that merely describe aspects of the product or business, such as durability ("Sturdy Knapsacks"), location ("The Edge of Town Tavern"), or other qualities ("Speedy Dry Cleaners," "Tasty Vegetables"). Also, trademarks that include personal names are usually considered to be ordinary marks and therefore weak. (But, as we explain below, weak trademarks can become stronger with use.)

An additional reason why ordinary, descriptive trademarks aren't strongly protected, at least at first, is to make sure that competitors aren't unfairly prevented from using common words to describe their own products. For example, a food delivery service company called "Galloping Gourmet" wouldn't be able to monopolize the word "gourmet" and stop a deli from using the name "Tom's Gourmet Sandwiches."

c. How Trademarks Can Grow Stronger

A weak trademark can eventually offer good protection if it becomes distinctive and therefore stronger through use. Called "acquiring a secondary meaning" in legalese, this is particularly likely to occur when a product or service with a weak mark becomes a lasting success, making it likely that the public will associate the mark with the product or service being sold. For example, as the designer clothing brand Tommy Hilfiger has become popular worldwide, its previously weak trademark has grown stronger as customers have come to associate the ordinary name with a particular company. Examples of the weak-to-strong phenomenon include Burger King, Tom's Natural Toothpaste, Ben & Jerry's Ice Cream, and The Yellow Pages.

d. Unfair Competition Laws

What if your weak trademark never becomes strong? Just because you have a weak trademark doesn't mean that others are free to use your business name. Because of a legal doctrine called unfair competition, you may be able to prevent others from using your descriptive name, as long as you used it first. While unfair competition law is a separate body of law from trademark law, it can have the same effect. It's based on the same idea—that it's not fair for another business to rip off your business's good reputation.

For example, if you've been selling dry cleaning services in Bakersfield under the name Jean's Quick Cleaners, and someone else in the same city opens Jeanne's Quick Cleaners, you could claim unfair competition and convince a court to prevent the newcomer from using that name. As you can see, unfair competition law can have the same result as trademark law: It can prevent another business from using a name identical or confusingly similar to yours, if you used the name first. Keep in mind, however, that your right to stop trademark infringement is stronger than your right to stop unfair competition, so it will be easier to prevent someone from using your business name if it's trademarked.

2. When Do Trademarks Conflict?

As you surely know, plenty of businesses share the same name, or at least part of the same name, without violating each other's trademark rights. Examples include United Airlines and United Van Lines; Ford Motor Company and Ford Modeling Agency; and Scott Paper Products and Scott Sunglasses. This is perfectly legal, because trademark infringement occurs only when the use of a mark by two different businesses is likely to cause customer confusion. (An exception to this rule, called "dilution," is explained in Section 3, below.) If customers aren't likely to be confused, then both businesses may legally use the same mark. But if customer confusion is likely, then the rightful owner of the mark can prohibit the other businesses from using it, and can sue for damages (financial compensation) for any unauthorized use.

Dual uses of the same or similar mark can cause customer confusion if it's unclear which company actually makes a product or service, or if customers will be misled as to the source of the product. Customer confusion can happen in a number of different ways. Sometimes dual uses of a mark lead customers to believe that a certain company made a product when it actually did not. Or a customer may see trademarks being used in two different places and think that the companies are jointly owned or somehow affiliated, which may not be true.

Determining whether two marks legally conflict (in other words, whether customer confusion is likely) is one of the trickiest bits of trademark law. In making this determination, courts deem the following factors to be particularly important:

- how strong (distinctive or well known) the original trademark is
- how much the products or services really compete against one another, and
- how similar the trademarks are in appearance, sound or meaning.

We'll look at each of these in more depth in the next few sections. As you read on, keep in mind that trademark conflict is a legal question—which means that legal rules, as opposed to common sense, will dictate the outcome.

a. How Strong Is the Mark?

As we discussed above, distinctive (strong) marks receive the most protection because, in legal theory, they are more likely to stick in consumers' minds and play a role in their buying choices. Since strong trademarks tend to stick in customers' minds, so the theory goes, customer confusion is likely if more than one company uses a strong trademark. To protect consumers from such confusion, courts will typically prohibit more than one company from using a strong trademark. In addition to protecting consumers, prohibiting multiple uses of a strong trademark prevents businesses from stealing customers or getting a free ride off another business's good reputation by using its established trademark.

For example, the very strong and well-known trademark Microsoft is firmly implanted in millions of people's minds. If a company called itself Microsoft Consulting, plenty of people would be confused about whether Bill Gates had anything to do with that consulting company. If Bill Gates sued Microsoft Consulting for trademark infringement, he would have a very good chance of winning.

Trademark law doesn't give much, if any, protection to weak trademarks because they don't trigger a strong association in customers' minds between the mark and a particular product or service (or so the legal thinking goes). For that reason, courts are less inclined to find that customer confusion is likely when more than one business uses a weak trademark. Note that this is true even if customer confusion does in fact exist. For example, if Smith Jewelry and Smith Hardware exist in the same town, customers may wonder if they're owned by the same family. Nonetheless, trademark law won't protect the name of either business, since the name Smith is so common. (However, unfair competition law may protect the hardware-store Smiths if the jewelry-store Smiths started getting into the hardware business, making the businesses direct competitors.)

b. Do the Products or Services Actually Compete?

If the products or services that share the same trademarks are in completely unrelated fields or industries, or if they're sold in different geographical regions (and not on the Internet), there's obviously far less chance that customers will be confused. In other words, the less products or services actually compete, the less likely it is that there will be a trademark violation. For example, a pizza joint named Rocket Pizza probably won't be confused with a record store named Rocket Records, even if they exist in the same city. And an auto shop named Armadillo Repairs in Portland, Maine, most likely won't run into any trademark conflicts with Armadillo Auto Repairs in San Diego. Because they are so far apart and serve purely local customers, chances are slim that customers would confuse the two companies.

> **EXAMPLE:** You open a coffee shop in Weed, California, and name it Pam's Coffee Stop. A year later, you're driving through Barstow and notice a small café also named Pam's Coffee Stop. After thinking about it, you decide that there's little chance of a trademark violation by either business. The trademark is ordinary and descriptive and therefore weak, plus the shops are so far away from each other that they're not competitors. But this gets you wondering what you'd do if a big national chain started using the name and moved into your area. The answer is, you would retain the right to use the name because you were the first to use it in your area (as long as the national chain hadn't registered the name with the U.S. Patent and Trademark Office before you first used it). But the chain could prevent you from expanding into other areas of the country if this ever became your goal.

New marketing techniques, new competitors. As we mentioned at the beginning of this chapter, with the arrival and widespread use of the Web, the fast expansion of mail-order catalog businesses, and ever more frequent travel, the old rule that small, local businesses don't have to worry about trademarks from other geographical regions has largely gone out the window. Today even small, local businesses commonly establish websites, hundreds of thousands of businesses send out catalogs, and some local restaurants and hotels seek to reach a national (or even worldwide) pool of tourists. The upshot is that many formerly local businesses that just a few years ago never would have been confused with each other are now competitors, which of course increases the likelihood of customer confusion and trademark infringement if their names are the same. (Be sure to read Section B below on new trademark issues and considerations in today's ever smaller world.)

Of course, there are plenty of gray areas where two businesses aren't in head-to-head competition, but use the same marks for products that are similar enough to make a customer stop and think, for example, "Is a Parker calendar made by the same company as Parker pens?" Even though a company with the same name may not be stealing business from a competitor, it may be unintentionally taking advantage of that company's goodwill and getting a free ride from its advertising.

Whether infringement exists in these gray areas often depends on how strong the original trademark is (as discussed above). If the original trademark is weak, there's probably not much goodwill or reputation to rip off (few customers would be confused by the similar name), so a court wouldn't be likely to find infringement. But if the original trademark is strong, there's a greater likelihood that the newer trademark will rip off the older one's reputation, making it likely for the court to agree that there's been an infringement.

> **EXAMPLE:** Your pet products company begins selling a toy that looks like a cross between a dog and a weasel, which you name the Garden Weasel. Soon after your toy hits the market, the makers of the nationally marketed Garden Weasel 5-in-1 garden tool contact you, claiming that you are infringing their trademark. Since you feel that the products are unrelated enough to minimize the chance of customer confusion (the products don't compete with one another), your first thought is to stick with the Garden Weasel name.
>
> Think again. The Garden Weasel trademark is distinctive (memorable and unusual) and therefore strong. If you are sued—and you may well be—defending the lawsuit is likely to cost you tens or possibly even hundreds of thousands of dollars that you almost surely can't afford. And if the Garden Weasel mark is strong enough, you may lose the suit, even though the products don't compete. A better approach would probably be to tweak your name a bit, to something like the Lawn Weasel or the Garden Ferret, for instance.

c. Sight, Sound, and Meaning Test

Obviously, dual use of identical trademarks can cause customer confusion, as we discussed above. But what about merely similar trademarks? If two marks look alike, sound alike, or have the same meaning, a court could decide that they conflict with each other, just as if they were identical.

Small or superficial differences between two trademarks may not be enough to prevent customer confusion. The difference in spelling, for example, does not make the name "Ekzon" sufficiently different from "Exxon" to avoid trademark problems. And even though they're expressed in two different languages, the names "Le Petit Fleur" and "The Little Flower" have the same meaning, which increases the likelihood that some customers could confuse the two.

> **EXAMPLE:** You open an auto lubrication business and name it Jiffy Oil. A few weeks later, you receive a stern letter from the attorneys of Jiffy Lube, a national chain of auto lubrication businesses. The letter informs you that the name "Jiffy Oil" infringes on the rights to the trademark "Jiffy Lube," since customer confusion is likely because the names are very similar, are used to describe an almost identical service, and mean pretty much the same thing. They demand that you change your business's name or be taken to court. You'd be wise to comply. The "Jiffy Lube" trademark, though a descriptive term (for fast lubrication), has become a very strong mark over time—customers have come to recognize it as a specific brand of service. And because your shop is a direct competitor of Jiffy Lube, the chance of customer confusion is high.

3. The Dilution Exception

As we've mentioned several times, there is a big exception to the rule that one trademark infringes another only where there is the likelihood of customer confusion. Even when customer confusion is improbable, courts will stop a business from using a trademark that's the same as or similar to someone else's if the use has diminished—or "diluted"—its distinctiveness. This legal protection kicks in only when a mark is so well known that even if you were to use it in a different context than the original trademark, lots of people would think of the original trademark. For example, a court might stop an athletic shoe manufacturer from using the trademark Exxon or a gas station from calling itself Nike. Even though customers would not be likely to confuse an oil company with a shoe maker, this sort of copying is a legal no-no, since allowing others to use the very famous trademark can chip away at its distinctiveness and slowly reduce its legal strength.

B. Trademark Issues Online

As in many other legal areas, the traditional principles of trademark law are scrambling to keep up with the fast clip of technological change. The Internet has changed many of the rules regarding trademark issues, just as it has created some entirely new ones. This section outlines a number of Net-related concerns about trademarks and business names.

1. The Web Has Changed the Rules

As described in the previous section, one of the touchstones of trademark infringement is whether or not the two trademarks in question are likely to cause customer confusion. In the pre-Internet world, a small, local business didn't have to worry too much about name conflict as long as no one in their area had a similar name. But geographical distance is irrelevant in cyberspace.

Particularly if you plan to put your business online, you'll have to consider not only the trademarks of businesses already on the Web, but also those of businesses located anywhere the Web reaches—which, of course, is just about everywhere. If you create a Web page for a small home-based business, your business is no longer local in character. You're essentially launching a national or worldwide business that can compete with businesses everywhere, whether or not those businesses are online.

For example, if you create a website for your antique restoration business, Dalliance Designs, you could be competing with every antique resto-

ration business in the country. If one of these owns the trademark "Dalliance Designs," your effort to share the market with that business opens a potentially ugly can of legal worms.

The Web has changed trademark rules for everybody—even businesses that don't go digital. As more and more small businesses launch websites introducing themselves in a keystroke to consumers all over the globe, your purely local, offline business might find itself in competition with businesses several time zones—or even continents—away. Although courts are still chewing over many trademark issues raised by online commerce, it is already clear that, in some circumstances at least, a Web business with the same name as yours poses just as great a threat of a trademark lawsuit as does a real-life, bricks-and-steel business across the street.

EXAMPLE: Jarrod is a mechanic who opens a small machine shop in a rural area of California. He's lived in the area for 30 years, and knows every business for miles around. Nevertheless, as part of choosing a name for his business, Jarrod carefully checks the phone book and the county register for fictitious business names and ultimately settles on his first choice, Checkers Tool and Die.

All goes smoothly for a few months, until a customer compliments Jarrod on his slick-looking website. This leaves Jarrod totally confused since he hates computers and has only a vague notion of what the Web is. But in talking with his customer about this mysterious website, Jarrod realizes that a machine shop in Florida is also using the name "Checkers Tool and Die," and sells a number of specialized parts via an online catalogue. This doesn't particularly worry Jarrod until his customer (a lawyer, naturally) goes on to explain that if the distant business can prove it owns the trademark to "Checkers Tool and Die" and convince a court that it shares the same market as Jarrod, it might be able to force Jarrod to stop using the name.

Although at least one customer has been confused, Jarrod doesn't really expect the Florida outfit to go after him—after all, his business is small and local, provides primarily repair services (with parts as a sideline) and doesn't sell on the Web. Nevertheless, even the possibility of legal trouble worries him—especially because he'd like to open a retail machine parts shop next to his repair shop. After learning that the Florida outfit has been using the name Checkers Tool and Die for years and seems to be putting lots of energy into expanding its website, Jarrod decides to be safe and spend the time and money necessary to change the name of his business to White Mountain Tool & Die before he expands.

2.   Domain Name Conflicts and Cybersquatting

Besides making sure that your business name won't create trademark trouble, if you plan to create a website for your business, you'll also need to choose a domain name that's legally safe. A domain name (such as nolo.com) is part of a website's URL (such as http://www.nolo.com/index.html), which functions as its Internet "address." Later in this chapter we discuss the process of choosing and registering a domain name; for now, we'll focus on the trademark issues that can surround domain names.

The first thing you should understand is that, generally speaking, your domain name will function as a trademark if you conduct business at your site—that is, if you offer products or services for sale. This is true whether or not you register your domain name with the U.S. Patent and Trademark Office (PTO). Registering your domain name with the PTO will strengthen your power to enforce your trademark rights to it, but using it for a commercial purpose is all that's technically necessary to establish your trademark rights. For instance, amazon.com is the domain name for a huge

website that sells books and videos—and the name amazon.com also serves as a trademark. This means that trademark law prohibits anyone else from using the name amazon.com for a business.

Keep in mind, however, that if your domain name is generic such as software.com or books.com, it won't qualify for much trademark protection. This rule applies to generic business or product names such as lawyer, building supplies, or pet food: the law will generally not allow you to establish any trademark rights to these generic terms. But as we discussed earlier (in talking about weak trademarks), even generic domain names can grow stronger with use. Consider etrade.com, which has become almost synonymous with online stock trading. Originally, the name wouldn't have deserved much trademark protection since it wasn't distinctive at all—anyone can slap an "e" on the beginning of a word. Now, however, the mark has acquired "secondary meaning" and is probably entitled to trademark protection.

For most business owners, the best way to make sure their customers will find them online is simply to tack ".com" onto their regular business names. However, while trademark law will allow two or more companies to use the same name as long as it won't confuse customers, the technical limitations of the Web won't allow for two identical domain names. In other words, Ford Trucks and the Ford Modeling Agency won't both be able to use ford.com as a domain name. Since each website must have its own unique address, you may be out of luck if someone is already using your business name plus .com as a domain name. As you can imagine, this is where things can get sticky.

a. Dealing With Domain Name Conflicts

If you're starting a brand-new business that you haven't named yet, choose a name that also can be used as a domain name. That way, you can register it as a domain name right away and sidestep the whole issue of what to do if your domain name is already taken. You'll need to decide for yourself how important it is to you to have a domain name that's the same as your business name. If it's really important, then you may have to work hard to come up with a business name that's good for business, available as a domain name, and available as a trademark. If it's not that important, then your naming process will be somewhat easier—but you may regret it down the road when your business name can't be registered as a domain name.

A few possible scenarios may arise when someone is using your business name as a domain name. One is that you may simply have missed your chance to get that domain name yourself—even though you have trademark rights to it—and will either have to choose a different name or buy it from whoever registered it first. These are likely to be your only options if your mark isn't nationally famous and customers aren't likely to be confused by another business using your name.

> **EXAMPLE:** Gene and Beth run a bookstore in San Diego called Lexicon. After about a year of planning, they decide to launch a website—but are disappointed to find out that the domain name lexicon.com was already taken. By doing a search on the Web and going to the lexicon.com website, Gene and Beth discover that the owner of lexicon.com is a freelance editor in Chicago. Since Gene and Beth's bookstore doesn't have any national exposure, they probably won't be able to force the editor in Chicago to give up the name—the editor's site probably would not confuse customers into thinking there was some association with their bookstore.

On the other hand, you may be able to assert your trademark rights against someone who is using your trademark as a domain name if:

- his or her use of the trademark is likely to cause customer confusion, or

- your trademark is distinctive and nationally known—even if the other party's use of it is not likely to cause customer confusion. (Recall from Section A above that laws against trademark dilution protect famous marks from use by others, even if customer confusion is not likely.)

> **EXAMPLE:** Assume that Gene and Beth's bookstore, Lexicon, already had a well-established national mail-order catalog business and the name Lexicon was familiar to a national audience. In this situation, they might be able to assert their trademark rights in court and force the Chicago editor to give up the lexicon.com domain name.

You will have to weigh carefully the pros and cons of attempting to force someone to give up a domain name based on a potential trademark infringement. On the one hand, the possibility of prevailing and getting the domain name you want may make this course worth it. On the other hand, remember that lawsuits cost time and money, and can easily exceed $10,000 in legal and court fees (and sometimes ten times that amount). You may be better off simply choosing a different domain name or even buying the name from the other party.

⚠️ **Come to your own defense.** Your trademark rights can become weakened if you fail to defend your trademark when you know or should know that it's being infringed. For this reason, it's probably a good idea to go after a website or any other business or individual that infringes your trademark. For more in-depth information on defending your trademark and dealing with infringers, see *Trademark: Legal Care for Your Business and Product Name,* by Stephen R. Elias (Nolo).

b. Dealing With Cybersquatters

You may find that the domain name you want has already been registered by someone who wants to sell it back to you at a profit. For instance, say you own a well-known car racing magazine called *Auto Racing Today*. When you are ready to launch a website, you discover that the domain name autoracingtoday.com is already registered by another business, which offers to sell the name back to you for $250,000 (actually a modest amount compared to similar sales). This practice, known as "cybersquatting," became a real problem in the late 1990s before businesses realized the importance of reserving domain names as soon as possible.

A 1999 federal law known as the Anti-Cybersquatting Consumer Protection Act makes cybersquatting illegal and provides remedies for those who suffer harm from it, including getting the domain name back and possibly receiving money damages. To win a cybersquatting lawsuit, you'll have to sue the cybersquatter in federal court and prove that:

- the cybersquatter acted in bad faith by registering the name solely to make a profit by selling it back to you
- your mark was distinctive at the time the domain name was registered
- the domain name is identical or confusingly similar to your trademark, and
- you were the first to use the trademark in commerce.

An alternative to a lawsuit is to use a procedure set forth by ICANN (short for International Corporation for Assigned Names and Numbers), the international group now in charge of Internet domain name policy. ICANN's process for resolving cybersquatting disputes is known as the Uniform Domain Name Dispute Resolution Policy (UDRP), and typically will cost far less and take less time than a lawsuit. You'll have to prove that:

- the domain name is identical or confusingly similar to your trademark
- the registrant has no legitimate interests in or rights to the domain name, and

- the domain name was registered or is being used in bad faith, or both.

Another advantage of the ICANN procedure is that it can be used in international domain name disputes, while a lawsuit based on the Anti-Cybersquatting Act can only be brought against domain name registrants in the United States. For more information, visit ICANN's website at www.icann.org.

3. Using Meta Tags That Conflict With Trademarks

Meta tags are keywords—embedded in the HTML source code of Web pages—that search engines like Yahoo! or Excite look for when conducting a search. For instance, if you did a Yahoo! search for the term "digital video," the search engine would check the meta tags of all the pages on the Web, and return to you the ones that contained the key words "digital video." Assuming that sites such as *DV Magazine* and Sony Electronics would have included the term "digital video" in their meta tags, your search would bring up those sites and those of whoever else used that meta tag.

When choosing meta tags for your site, be careful not to use someone else's trademark without their permission—doing so may subject you to a trademark infringement lawsuit. It's becoming common for trademark owners to sue others who use their trademarks as meta tags to deceptively lure browsers to their sites. For example, a site called Calvin Designer Label used the words "Playboy" and "Playmate" as meta tags so that anyone searching for those words would be directed to the Calvin page. When *Playboy* magazine sued, a federal court found Calvin Designer Label liable for infringement and ordered it to stop using *Playboy*'s trademarks as meta tags.

On the other hand, there may be instances in which it's legal to use someone else's trademark in your meta tags—even without their permission. Generally, this is more likely if the use is for a legitimate descriptive purpose. For example, in another *Playboy* case, the famous magazine sued Terri Welles, a former Playmate, for using the terms "Playmate of the Year" and its abbreviation "PMOY" at her website, www.terriwelles.com, and within the site's meta tags. Ms. Welles had won the title Playmate of the Year in 1981, and was using her site to promote herself for her modeling career. A court found that her use of "Playmate of the Year" and "PMOY" was permissible, since she had earned the title and was using it legitimately to describe herself. Her case was also strengthened by the fact that her site offered numerous disclaimers that it was not endorsed by or affiliated with *Playboy* magazine.

Remember also that an owner of a weak, descriptive trademark doesn't have much (if any) power to stop you from using part or all of that trademark. For instance, you could safely include the words "house" and "garden" in the meta tags of your home design website without being afraid that *House & Garden* magazine would sue you. The same goes for using the word "news" for your current events site, without fear of a lawsuit from *U.S. News & World Report* magazine. Of course, using actual trademarked phrases like "U.S. News & World Report" or "House & Garden" as meta tags would probably get you into trouble.

Unfortunately, there's no clear test for determining whether it's permissible to use someone else's trademark as a meta tag. The only way to get a definitive answer may be through a lawsuit, something you probably don't want to risk. Proceed with caution when using any trademarks owned by others in your website or in its meta tags, and definitely avoid any deceptive use of trademarks to lure browsers to your site.

C. Name Searches

By now you get the picture that a dispute over business names can be thorny. To avoid potential trademark hassles later on, you need to do some digging before you finally settle on a name for your business. The main way to accomplish this is to conduct a name search to find out whether another business is already using a name that's identical or similar to the one you want to use. The information in this section will help you figure out how to go about researching your chosen name, and what to do once you've found one that you'll be able to use—and protect—as a trademark.

Searching domain name availability. It's easier to find out whether a name is available as a domain name than to figure out whether it's being used as a trademark. To find out if a domain name is available, simply go to one of the many domain name registrars online (a good list is available at www.internic.com). Once you enter the name you want, the registrars tell you whether it's available and, if not, who has registered it.

The scope of your search will depend largely on the size and geographical scope of your business and your plans for its future. If you plan from day one to sell a product nationally—whether via catalog, through retailers, or online—you'll obviously need to worry about trademarks across the country. If, on the other hand, you're starting a small home-based service business, don't plan to advertise, and are relatively certain you won't expand geographically, a search of names in your county, and perhaps state, may be all you need (though we recommend that you always search widely so that you at least know what's out there).

Keep in mind that the extent of your search encompasses not only how widely you search geographically, but also how deeply you search—in terms of looking not only for identical names, but also for those that are merely similar or have a slight resemblance to yours. Searching for the exact name (also called a "direct hit" search) is quick and cheap, but risks missing look- and sound-alikes. A more in-depth search, such as one that looks for names with slight variations in spelling, is safer, but can get quite complicated and expensive.

1. Sources of Name Information

Name research can be difficult because there is no one place to look. In large part, this is because a business can—and millions do—establish a trademark simply by using it. Since millions of marks aren't registered with the government, in addition to checking federal and state trademark databases you'll want to check many other sources of information, such as business directories and phone books, for unregistered trademarks. You should check some or preferably all of the following resources for name conflicts, depending on how extensive a search you need.

a. The World Wide Web

We recommend this one first because it is huge, fast, and free. By using several of the Web's search engines, such as Yahoo!, Lycos, or Google, you can quickly see whether someone else on the Web is using a specific term and how it is being used. Search engines are easy to use; simply enter the terms you're looking for (often called a "query") and the engine will scan the Web and retrieve any sites that contain the terms in your query. Consult the "help" area of the particular search engine you're using for more detailed instructions on how to construct your queries.

Another easy way to check trademarks online is to go to a domain name register online and put in variations of the name you want to use. (Go to www.internic.com for a list of registrars.) If another company has reserved a domain name that contains your proposed trademark, chances are you won't be able to use it as a trademark. If the domain name qualifies as a trademark—which essentially means it is being used to sell a product or service online—then, as described earlier in this chapter, you won't be able to use it as a trademark if your use would be likely to confuse customers.

b. Phone Directories

Don't overlook the phone book as a valuable source of local name information. If you find someone who's using the name you want in your local area and your businesses are similar, there's no reason to waste money searching the federal trademark register or other government databases. However, if your businesses are different enough, you might be able to use the name.

c. Industry Sources

Trade publications and business directories can be great sources of business name information (and they can also give you good ideas for names). You can also call trade associations and chambers of commerce to ask if they can provide lists or directories of businesses in the area.

d. Federal Trademark Database

All those starting a business, no matter how tiny and local, should search the federal trademark database to determine whether the name they want to use has already been registered by a similar business in the United States. The most important reason to do this is to avoid being sued for "willful infringement." If you use a trademark already registered at the federal level (even if yours is a tiny, local business), you can be sued for knowingly violating someone else's trademark—even if you didn't actually check the federal database and had no idea it was there. Searching the federal database can be complicated, and there are a few different ways to go about it—including hiring a trademark search firm to do the work for you. (Search options for the federal trademark database are discussed below in Section 2.)

e. California Secretary of State Databases

The California Secretary of State maintains databases of registered names of corporations, limited partnerships, and LLCs. Be aware, however, that these databases do not overlap, even though they're all maintained by the Secretary of State. In other words, you need to check each database separately.

To find out whether a name appears in the corporate, LLC, or limited partnership database, you can contact the Secretary of State by mail, by phone, or in person. Inquiring by phone costs a small fee—$4 in 2004—and requires a prepaid account. The phone number for the Secretary of State's office is 916-653-6814.

More information about checking name availability is available online at www.ss.ca.gov. Click on "California Business Portal" and proceed to the "Business Filings" information for your business type: corporation, LLC, or other form. (See Appendix A for local office locations of the Secretary of State.)

f. California's Trademark Unit

The California Secretary of State also maintains a state trademark registry at its Trademark Unit. This database is a good one to check—and you can search by phone for free. You're allowed to have two names checked per phone call. To contact California's Trademark Unit call the Secretary of State's Office at 916-653-6814.

You may also want to check some or all other states' trademark registries. You can check them by calling the states yourself and finding out their individual rules for searching the state trademark register, or you can hire a trademark search firm to do the work for you. (Search firms and types of searches are discussed below, in Section 2.)

g. County Fictitious Business Name Databases

Each county maintains a database of fictitious business names (FBNs) that have been registered in that county. If you register a fictitious business name statement with your county (discussed in Chapter 7), you'll be asked to check the county's FBN database to see if any other business in the county has already registered that name. But even if you won't be using an FBN—because you'll use your own name or your corporate, limited partnership, or LLC name—it's a good idea to check the FBNs used by other businesses. In all counties these databases can be searched in person for free, or you can submit a name by mail and have it checked by a staff person at the county clerk's office for a small fee (from $5 to $30 or so, depending on the county). You can check any and all county databases for a name even if you don't plan to register an FBN statement there. (A list of California county clerks and contact information appears in Appendix A.)

State and county agencies usually check only exact matches. These agencies won't tell you whether a similar name is included in that database. If, for example, the county clerk's office tells you that "The Dog House" does not appear in its fictitious name database, you might be surprised later to find that "The Dawg Haus" has been in business for years. In short, you may have to do a more extensive search than the one provided by the state or county office.

County and state databases have limits. Just because a name doesn't appear in any county or state name databases, that doesn't mean another business doesn't already own that trademark. Use of the name, not registration, is what creates trademark ownership. Plenty of businesses own trademarks that they have never registered, so it's important to check for unregistered trademarks using the resources discussed above. And many businesses won't bother registering at the state level, but will register a federal trademark. If you plan to invest time and money in establishing your trademark, it's essential that you do a federal trademark search, too.

> **EXAMPLE:** Tom and Jen, both veterinarians in California, search their county's fictitious business name database for the name "Critter Care," which they want to use for the animal hospital they're planning to open. They don't find anyone else using the name in their area, so they believe they can use it. But just to be safe, Jen decides to check the California state trademark directory for the name. She finds out that a California corporation has already obtained state trademark protection for the name "Critter Care." Since that corporation was doing business under its own name and not a fictitious one, it didn't have to register with any county fictitious name databases. (Tom and Jen also would have found the name by checking the Secretary of State's corporate name database.)

2. Searching the Federal Trademark Database

As discussed above, to avoid a charge of willful infringement it's a very good idea to check the federal trademark registry, maintained by the U.S. Patent and Trademark Office (PTO). Only the tiniest of microbusinesses should even consider skipping this step, and then only after careful thought and consideration. The Internet and other communication technologies have simply created too many potential trademark conflicts, even for small businesses.

If possible, begin your search with the free trademark database on the PTO's website. The PTO's database consists of all federally registered marks and all marks for which registration is pending. To start, go to the PTO's Trademark Electronic Business Center at www.uspto.gov/web/menu/

tmebc/index.html and choose "Search." Then follow the instructions you see on the screen.

If using the Internet isn't feasible for you, visit your local Patent and Trademark Depository Library (PTDL) and use its research materials. (A list of PTDLs is included in Appendix A.) If a PTDL isn't convenient, a large public library or special business and government library near you should carry the federal trademark register, which contains all federal trademarks and service marks arranged by categories of goods and services.

Another option is to hire a professional search firm to do the work for you. You can order a complete search of registered and unregistered marks through Trademark Express, Thompson and Thompson, CCH Trademark Research Corporation, or one of the PTDLs that offer electronic search services for very reasonable fees (for example, see the Sc[i]3 website at www.sci3.com).

If you decide to hire a search firm, the cheapest and easiest type of national search is a direct-hit search, which will reveal whether another business has registered an identical name with the PTO. You can often hire one of the companies mentioned above to do a direct-hit search for you for less than $50. But while direct-hit searches are quick and cheap, they usually won't turn up trademarks that are similar, but not identical, to the name you're considering. For example, if you want to name your softball training center "The Strike Zone," a direct-hit search may not turn up a trademark for "The S. Zone." And as discussed above, any mark that looks like, sounds like, or means the same as your name could present a trademark conflict.

More extensive national searches take a lot more time and money, but may be necessary if you plan for your business to reach a wide audience and want to eliminate any risk of infringing someone else's existing trademark. For an in-depth search, it may make the most sense to hire a search firm; expect a fee of roughly $200 to $350 for a professional, comprehensive search. If you do decide to hire search services, you're likely to save money if you do some quick, preliminary searches on the Internet yourself—to rule out some of your choices.

For more information on national trademark searches. See *Trademark: Legal Care for Your Business and Product Name*, by Stephen R. Elias (Nolo).

3. Analyzing Your Search Results

If, after your search, you determine that the name you've chosen does not already belong to someone else (or that someone else isn't using a similar name), you can go ahead and use it. Assuming you really are the first user of the name, you'll own the trademark, which will give you the right to stop others from using it in certain situations. But since registering a trademark conveys important additional rights and protections, you may want to register your name with the PTO, and maybe with the State of California as well. (The basics of trademark registration are discussed in Section E, below.)

But what if your search (or a search done by a professional firm) turns up an identical or similar name to the one you want to use? If the name is a famous trademark, it's probably time to pick a new name. Remember that if using your business name diminishes a famous trademark's distinctiveness or disparages its reputation for quality, the owner of the famous trademark may stop you from using your name, even if its customers aren't likely to be confused between its products and yours.

Be sure to check domain names. If your Internet business will be important to you, pick a name that can also be used as a domain name. You can check whether a domain name is available at any domain name registrar—you can find a list of registrars at www.internic.com.

Even if the name isn't famous, if it has been registered for official trademark protection, especially at the federal level, consider that as a huge "No Trespassing" sign that should be taken seriously. Owners of federally registered trademarks have the right to use their trademarks anywhere in the country, and it is easy for them to sue and recover damages. If your search shows that the name is being used but isn't registered at the federal or state levels, then you might have a bit more leeway— but not much more. Since use, not registration, conveys trademark rights, you still need to be very careful not to infringe that owner's rights.

That being said, there are a few instances when taking a name that is already being used by someone else is okay. If the name is being used for a company that provides a very different product or service than the one you plan to sell, then you may have good reason to move forward with your plans to use the name. This is especially true if the two businesses serve only local markets and are hundreds of miles apart.

For example, just because a tiny clothing store in Newport Beach calls itself Nature's Calling doesn't mean that you, in Humboldt County, can't use Nature's Calling for your plumbing business. But if you wanted to start a clothing store in your town called Nature's Calling, and one already exists in Newport Beach, then you should at the very least do more research before using it. If a federal trademark register search indicates that the Newport Beach store has registered the mark "Nature's Calling," your subsequent use is a clear legal no-no. But even if the name is not registered and the Newport Beach store seems like a local outfit, it could have plans to expand its territory—or, as is even more likely, to create a website. Neither of these actions would necessarily prohibit your use of the name on your original store, but they could prevent you from using it more widely. The bottom line is that even if you feel certain that your business is different enough from that of the trademark owner to allow you to use the name, you should proceed only with lots and lots of caution.

How would you feel? If you are uncertain as to whether your proposed trademark would infringe an existing trademark, use a variant of the Golden Rule: How would you feel if you owned the existing trademark and someone started to use it? Ask a few friends the same question. If any of the answers are "Pissed off," consider choosing a different name or at least invest a few hundred dollars in a consultation with an experienced trademark lawyer.

Other resources on name and trademark issues. For more help understanding the nuances of different types of trademarks, picking a bulletproof name, and searching and registering trademarks, by far the best source of sophisticated information is *Trademark: Legal Care for Your Business and Product Name,* by Stephen R. Elias (Nolo). And you'll find lots of free information on trademarks and business names in the Trademark and Copyright area of Nolo.com's Legal Encyclopedia, at www.nolo.com.

D. Choosing and Registering a Domain Name

Assuming that your business will create a website—something we definitely recommend—you'll need to choose a domain name and register it.

Keep in mind that when you register a domain name, you're securing the right to use that address for your website. You'll still need to find a company to host your site, which means keeping your website files on their servers. Depending on the size of your site, you can expect to pay anywhere from $20 to more than $100 per month. (If you or one of your associates is computer savvy, you can set up your own server for considerably less money over the long haul.) To find a Web host, look in your phone book under categories such as "Web Hosting" or "Computers—Internet Services."

1. Picking a Great Domain Name

The best domain names are often the simple ones: memorable, clever, and easily spelled. But names that are straightforward and descriptive won't qualify for much trademark protection. Many good domain names—for instance, coffee.com, drugs.com, and business.com—are not eligible for trademark protection because they are the names of whole categories of products or services. Likewise, domain names that use surnames or geographic names are unlikely to get trademark protection. (Of course, it's possible for a generic name, such as etrade.com, to become famous and develop "secondary meaning," as we discussed in Section A2, above.)

Many of these generic names, however, are potentially powerful because of the way people find information on the Internet, so consider carefully whether it will benefit you more to choose a domain name that's distinctive and protectable or easy to find and not protectable. One good strategy may be to choose to use one of each, such as peets.com and coffeebeans.com. But even if you come up with a domain name or names that are brilliant from a marketing standpoint, remember that your domain name is at risk if it legally conflicts with any of the millions of commercial trademarks that already exist.

You may want to register several domain names. In addition to your business name, you may want to register the names of your products or services, or other related names. For example, if you design and sell gourmet aprons, and your primary domain name is kitchenstuff.com, you might also want to register aprons.com so that customers who are looking for aprons and enter "aprons.com" into their browsers will land at your site. Remember, names of your products or services may be as important as your business name from a marketing perspective. It's also a good idea to register common misspellings of your primary domain name and of the names that reflect the nature of your products or services. It will, of course, cost more for multiple registrations, but the increased traffic may be worth it.

One potential problem in picking a domain name is that millions of names are already taken. For example, if your business name is Flaky Cakes, you may find that FlakyCakes.com already belongs

to someone else, so you'll have to use a different domain name or change your business name if it's important to you that your business and domain names are the same.

If you do find a domain name that's available, make sure the one you pick doesn't conflict with someone else's trademark. At the risk of being a little repetitive, let's review this crucial point. Remember, your domain name will probably function as a trademark just as your regular business name will—assuming you conduct business at your site. (This is true whether or not you register it with the U.S. Patent and Trademark Office. Registering your domain name with the PTO will strengthen your enforcement rights, but using it for a commercial purpose is all that's technically necessary to establish your rights to it.) It follows that you are not allowed to use a domain name that's likely to cause customer confusion between your company and another, whether that company is online or off.

New Web Extensions Should Ease Domain Name Congestion

In 2000, the Internet Corporation for Assigned Names and Numbers (ICANN) approved seven new generic top-level domains for use on the Internet: .biz, .info, .name, .pro, .aero, .coop, and .museum. As of early 2004, all but .pro are active. (Check with RegistryPro, the .pro registry operator, at www.registrypro.com, for updates on when it will be operational.) Each domain name registry has different rules, and some, like .museum or .coop, have eligibility requirements. As long as you are eligible, you can sign up for a domain name in one of these new domains at any approved registrar online—check at www.internic.com for a list.

2. Registering Your Domain Name

Once you've found a domain name that's legally safe, go online to a domain name registrar to register it. (A list of approved registrars is available at www.internic.com.)

What's the Difference Between a Registry and a Registrar?

When educating yourself about domain names, you might get confused by the terms "registry" and "registrar." Basically, a registry is the official list of names included in a particular domain. For instance, the new .biz registry consists of all of the names that people have signed up for in that domain—mainstreetpets.biz, mariospizza.biz, stellarjewelers.biz, etc. A registrar, on the other hand, is an entity that is authorized to add new people or businesses to a registry. For example, the registrar Alldomains.com can register a domain name for you in several different registries—.com, .biz, .info and so on.

Registries typically are operated by one official company, often called a registry operator. For example, the .biz registry is operated by NeuLevel, Inc. However, over 100 registrars are authorized to sign new customers to the .biz registry (and most other registries as well). In other words, you don't need to sign up for a .biz domain name at NeuLevel, Inc.—you can sign up with any approved registrar. The same is true for the other domain registries. You can find a list of approved registrars at www.internic.com.

At the registrar's site, you'll be prompted to enter your proposed domain name to see if it's already been registered. If it has, you'll need to choose a different name (or pursue other options; see Section B2 above). If the domain name is not already registered, then you'll be allowed to proceed and register the name. Fees will vary depend-ing on what options you choose, but all are quite affordable.

Once you've chosen your options, simply enter information about your business and provide credit card information. Most registrars also allow you to provide credit card information by phone.

As simple a process as registering a domain name is, there are some real pitfalls to watch out for. In particular, be careful what information you use when registering the name—especially who is listed as the domain name registrant and the administrative contact. Why? If you're not careful, you could find out that you have no control over your domain name.

Your domain name is a business asset, and the people or companies who are listed in the domain name registration will have varying degrees of authority in managing it. Be particularly careful who you list in the following positions:

- **Registrant.** Think of the registrant as the legal owner of the domain name. Use your business's legal name—definitely not your Web host.
- **Administrative contact.** The administrative contact should be someone in your business who has authority to make policy decisions, particularly with regard to the domain name. Your Web host should not be listed here.
- **Technical contact.** This is the person whom the registrar may contact with technical issues. It's okay for your Web host to be listed here.

If your Web host handles domain name registration or renewal, make sure it uses the contact or registrant information you want. Otherwise, it may cost you many times the original registration fee to get the registration back in your rightful name. Register.com, for instance, charges a $200 fee to transfer the registrant from one name to another—even if it was never your intention to have your Web host or someone else listed as the registrant in the first place. (One way to avoid this fee is simply to transfer the domain name to another registrar such as NetworkSolutions.com, making sure to use the correct names when you transfer the registration.)

Some Web hosts will offer you discounted or free website hosting if you use their company name as part of your domain name. (For example, this would make your business domain name http://aol.members.com/mybiz instead of www.mybiz.com.) This is tempting, but not necessarily in your long-term best interests. If the Web host holds your domain name hostage, you can't switch hosts or otherwise manage this often-crucial part of your business without changing your domain name at least in part.

That's pretty much it. In about five minutes, you can go from You to You.com. Other than remembering to renew (how often depends on the renewal period that you choose), there's not much else to it.

Apply for federal trademark registration.
In addition to applying for protection for your business name, you should also try to register your domain name with the PTO. While you don't need to register to establish your rights to your domain name, registering it will strengthen your power to enforce your rights to it against infringers. It will also prevent someone else from registering the same name, which could save a lot of headaches in the future.

For more information on domain names.
Check out Nolo's free Internet Law Center at www.nolo.com. Also read *Domain Names: How to Choose & Protect a Great Name for Your Website,* by Stephen R. Elias and Patricia Gima (Nolo), an excellent book that goes into far more detail in this area than is possible here.

E. Trademark Registration

By now you should understand that registering your trademark will strengthen your rights to it and make it easier to protect the name in case of a dispute. Registration is simply the process of notifying the state or, more commonly, the U.S. government that you're using a particular trademark. When registration is complete, the trademark gets placed on an official list of registered names commonly called a trademark register.

The U.S. Patent and Trademark Office (PTO) maintains two registers, the Principal Register and the Supplemental Register. When people refer to a federally registered trademark, they're generally talking about marks on the Principal Register. Trademarks that appear on the Principal Register get the most protection, and the penalties can be harsh for those who improperly use a name that appears on it. The Supplemental Register, on the other hand, is reserved for weaker, less distinctive trademarks that don't qualify for the Principal Register. The main function of the Supplemental Register is to provide notice of a mark's current use to anyone who does a trademark search. After five years on the Supplemental Register, a mark may qualify to be moved to the Principal Register if it's been in continuous use during that period.

The PTO provides registration forms and instructions. These are available from a number of sources, including the PTO's website at www.uspto.gov. For simple trademarks such as business names (as opposed to trademarks for special packaging or product design—called "trade dress" in the biz), the instructions will probably be easy enough to follow. (You can also fill in and submit the form online at the PTO's Trademark Electronic Business Center. For detailed instructions on filing online see "Federally Registering a Trademark Online," below.)

California (and most other states) maintain just one register for all trademarks. State registration doesn't give as many benefits as federal registration, so it generally makes most sense to register federally for the widest scope of protection. Some trademarks, however, don't qualify for federal registration because they aren't used in national, international, or territorial commerce—in other words, they're only used within the state. These marks can only be registered at the state level. Although use of a trademark on the Internet almost guarantees the right to apply for federal registration, if you are only using the mark within California, state registration may be the only option.

The process of registering a trademark with the state of California is similar to the federal system's procedure. State trademark registration forms are available from the Trademark Unit of California's Secretary of State, or you can download them from the Web at www.ss.ca.gov. (Click on "California Business Portal" and proceed to "Trademarks and Service Marks" under "Business Filings.") Contact California's Trademark Unit at 916-653-4984 for more information.

Federally Registering a Trademark Online

If You Haven't Yet Used Your Trademark:
Go to the PTO's Trademark Electronic Business Center at www.uspto.gov/web/menu/tmebc/index.html and choose "Filing." To file electronically (you'll need to pay with a credit card), click eTEAS. Or, to complete the application online, print it out, and send it in, click printTEAS. (You'll need to print out your completed application and mail it to the PTO with a check.) Then follow the instructions provided. Choose the "intent-to-use" (ITU) option, since you haven't yet used your trademark in commerce, and provide a drawing or image of the mark. Be prepared to respond to the trademark examiner's questions and concerns within the deadlines assigned to you.

If You Have Already Used Your Trademark Commercially:
Go to the PTO's Trademark Electronic Business Center at www.uspto.gov/web/menu/tmebc/index.html and choose "Filing." To file electronically (you'll need to pay with a credit card), click eTEAS. Or, to complete the application online, print it out, and send it in, click printTEAS. (You'll need to print out your completed application and mail it to the PTO with a check.) Then follow the instructions provided. Choose the "actual use" option, since you are already commercially using the mark. Provide the information as requested: a drawing or image of the trademark, samples of how the trademark is actually being used, the first date the trademark was commercially used anywhere, and the first date the trademark was used outside your state. Be prepared to respond to the trademark examiner's questions and concerns within the deadlines assigned to you.

F. Winning Names for Your Business, Products, and Services

Now that you have a general idea of the legal hurdles you need to clear and the snags and traps to watch out for, let the naming begin! Despite the trademark hassles involved, choosing names for your business and its products or services remains one of the more fun parts of starting your business. It gives you a chance to use your creative juices to come up with a name that is both marketable and infused with your individual personality (or the collective personalities of all the business partners). A business name can help you establish the overall vibe of your business, from strictly professional to downright funky, to a dozen things in between.

Besides legal restrictions and personal preferences, the traditions and realities of your particular industry or business will probably have a lot to do with what kind of business name you choose. Good, memorable business and product names range from the clever (SuperFantastic Bubble Plastic, Garden Weasel, Liquid Paper) to the straightforward (24-Hour Fitness, Fruit Roll-Ups, Jenny Craig Weight Loss Centers) to sometimes even the cryptic (Yahoo!, Chia Pet, Floam). In part because there really are so many different kinds of businesses and so many approaches to choosing a distinctive name, it's impossible to give any kind of specific advice on choosing a great name. There are, however, a few things that are helpful to keep in mind when choosing your business names.

- Especially for small local businesses that don't plan to expand geographically, straightforward, informative names often work better than fancy ones. For example, if you plan to open a shop selling aquarium supplies and tropical fish in Oakland, East Bay Aquariums & Fish may be a far more effective name than The Lure of the Ocean. Also, choosing an ordinary name—especially one with a geographic identifier—will make you less likely to infringe on someone else's trademark since humble, descriptive names qualify for less trademark protection (unless they are already famous; see Section A2,

above). Of course, you have to make sure no one else is already using your proposed ordinary name in your immediate area.

- Think about how your customers will locate your business and your products. If you don't expect customers to seek out or remember your company as a whole, but only its products, it's silly to focus much attention on the business name (which you may never use as a trademark). For instance, while millions of people know the product The Clapper and its commercial jingle ("Clap on! Clap off! The Clapper!"), few know or care who its makers are.

- Before you finally commit to a name, get some feedback from potential customers, suppliers, and others in your support network. They may come up with a downside to a potential name or suggest an improvement you haven't considered. Doing this type of homework is especially important if you will market your goods or services to customers who are members of several different ethnic groups. You obviously don't want to choose a name or symbol and learn later that it offends or turns off a key group of customers. For example, one organization we know couldn't figure out why it got such a cold shoulder from Mexican-Americans. The answer turned out to be that the shape, size, and type used on its signs were similar to a "No Trespassers—Keep Out" sign widely used in Mexico. And virtually everyone with email has by now seen a widely circulated humor piece on a number of advertising translation blunders—such as Kentucky Fried Chicken's "finger lickin' good" slogan translated in China as "Eat your fingers off."

- Niche businesses are often identified by their trade names, even when the focus is on the products. This means that it is wise to pay particular attention to picking a memorable name if you will try to capture a particular, small field. The publisher of this book, Nolo, is a good example. Even though book buyers in other fields usually identify books they want by title or author, Nolo customers have come to recognize its name, often going into a bookstore and asking where the Nolo books are. In other words, Nolo has come to mean "self-help law" to many customers familiar with it, in contrast to the name HarperCollins—a large publisher of books on many topics—which might not evoke anything particular in most book customers' minds.

- In certain service businesses in which an owner's personal attention and savvy is important (for example, architecture or accounting), it is common to use the owner's name, as in Charles Schwab. In other service and retail businesses, it is more common to use creative names—Kinko's and Fuddrucker's come to mind—and not only for the business itself, but sometimes for its products, too.

EXAMPLE: Jerri and Orlando operate a car wash named Storm, which develops a good deal of name recognition in the city. Besides relying on the reputation of their trade name, they come up with clever names for various service packages (such as Sunday Shower, Typhoon Tuesday, and the Everyday Squall Special) in hopes that those names will catch on as well.

- Be sure your trade or business name will still be appropriate if and when your business grows. If you open Berkeley Aquariums & Fish, will it be a problem (or an advantage) if you want to open a second store in San Rafael? Especially if you plan to sell products on the Internet, you should think twice about giving your business a geographical identifier. Similarly, if you start a business selling and installing canvas awnings using the name Sturdy Canvas Awnings, your name might be a burden if you decide to also start making other products such as canvas signs. On the other hand, the name Sturdy Canvas would let you move into all sorts of canvas products, such as duffel bags, canvas signs, and drop cloths.

Think national even if you act local. As discussed throughout this chapter, even though you may plan to open just one local office or store, it's a good idea to be sure your name is safe from trademark conflicts on a statewide or even national basis (and, if appropriate, from domain name conflicts). Then, if your business takes off, you won't bump into someone else who already uses the name in another area or online.

Chapter 3 Checklist

☐ Become familiar with the basics of trademark law, including what types of trademarks qualify for maximum legal protection.

☐ Draft lists of business, product, and domain names that could work.

☐ If you plan to do business online, check to see whether your proposed business names are available as domain names. (Ideally, your domain names will be the same as your business or product names.)

☐ If the online aspect of your business will be important to you, narrow your list of names to those that are available as domain names.

☐ Do a trademark search of the names on your list.

☐ If any names are already being used as trademarks, eliminate the ones that are either already famous trademarks or would lead to customer confusion if you also used the name.

☐ Choose between the names that are still on your list.

☐ Register your business and product names as domain names whenever possible.

☐ Register your business and product names as trademarks.

Choosing a Legal and Lucrative Business Location

For many types of businesses, location can mean the difference between feast or famine. Other enterprises will do more or less the same whether they're located in downtown San Francisco or in a deep crevasse on Mars. Not only does the importance of location vary greatly from business to business, but what makes a location desirable for one business might not work for another. Since there's no universal definition of what makes a location good for business, it's important for every business owner to figure out how location will (or will not) contribute to the success of the business—and to choose a spot accordingly.

That being said, there are some basic issues to consider when choosing a business location. For starters, make sure the location makes economic sense. It's obviously important that the rent for your business space fits into your overall budget. And, of course, the location that you choose needs to be legally acceptable for whatever you plan to do there. Especially if you are planning to work from home or in a nonbusiness area, you'll need to check zoning laws to see if they prohibit your type of business. This chapter will help you figure out how to find a suitable place that meets all the needs of your business and complies with your local laws.

➡ Planning to work from home? If you plan to use your home as your office, you can skip directly to Section D, which discusses special issues for home businesses. Working from home can be a much simpler arrangement than renting a separate space, but it can also put you in violation of zoning and other laws that regulate residential and business spaces. Section D covers these laws and legal issues, such as the home-office tax deduction.

A. Picking the Right Spot

Your first task is to figure out how important location is to your business. For some businesses, the classic "location, location, location" advice definitely applies. But for others, location may be a lot less important than getting affordable rental space. And for plenty of businesses, location is practically irrelevant: wholesalers, service businesses that do all their work at the customer's location (like roofers or plumbers), mail-order companies, and Internet-based businesses can set up shop practically anywhere without jeopardizing the bottom line. Especially if you can pass on your rent savings to your customers, picking a spot in an out-of-the-way area might be to your advantage. In other words, if location isn't that crucial to your business, don't blow all your start-up money on an expensive space in a thriving location.

If, on the other hand, you determine that location will be important to your business success, you'll need to figure out the best place to locate so that lots of customers can find you. It's one thing to know that you need a good location, but it can be harder to figure out what makes a location good. Ask yourself these questions:

- Will customers come on foot?
- Will customers drive and, if so, where will they park?
- Will more customers come if you locate near other similar businesses?
- Will the reputation of the neighborhood or even of a particular building help draw customers?

As you struggle to answer these and similar questions, here are a few more things you'll want to consider.

1. Planting Yourself in Rich Soil

The key to picking a profitable location is to figure out what factors will increase customer volume for your unique business, and then to concentrate on finding a location that achieves as many of them as possible. For example, if you're opening a coffee shop, you may assume your customer volume will be highest if there's lots of pedestrian traffic nearby during the hours you plan to be open. Furthermore, if you envision your cafe to be a mellow place to sit and read, you'd probably prefer a university area or shopping district full of people with time to kill, rather than an area buzzing with busy businesspeople. If, on the other hand, you plan to open a small coffee shop with no tables—just fast, high-volume service—a busy downtown office district might be the right spot.

Audrey Wackerley, owner of RetroFit, a vintage clothing store in San Francisco:

When we first opened we got a space in the perfect neighborhood, with lots of thrift stores, coffee shops, and other walk-in type businesses on a strip with lots of foot traffic (plus, it was only a few blocks from my apartment). But we were on a cross street a few doors around the corner from Valencia Street, the main strip. We did okay, but nothing like the shops on Valencia itself. Finally we got a good deal on a storefront on Valencia Street, and we moved. Our business practically tripled! We do pay a bit more for the better space, but our boost in sales more than makes up for it.

Keep in mind that different types of businesses attract customers in different ways. One key distinction is foot traffic versus automobile traffic. An auto repair shop, for example, will obviously draw customers in radically different ways than the coffee shop. For the auto shop, the choicest locale is a well-traveled street, where it will be seen by many drivers who will easily be able to pull into the lot. For an urban coffee shop, on the other hand, a popular location might be in an area where there are lots of people passing on foot. But of course no rule is absolute, and even some coffee shops thrive because commuters stop for "to go" coffee and baked goods every morning.

Also think about whether it would benefit your business to be around similar businesses that are already drawing the type of customers that you want. A women's clothing store, for example, would no doubt profit from being near other clothing shops, since many women shopping for clothes tend to spend at least a few hours in a particular area. The point is, the perfect location for any business is a very individual matter. Spend some time figuring out the habits of the customers you want to attract, then choose a location that fits.

2. Keeping Rent Within Your Budget

One obvious and important factor in finding a business space is how much you can afford. Chances are that you have found or will find a fabulous spot that you can only dream about because the monthly rent is so high. While it's okay to dream, don't be foolish enough to overpay for a space that you can't afford. And keep in mind the factors discussed above—you won't want to spend a fortune for a spot on an exclusive commercial strip unless it's really going to pay off.

As part of your business planning (discussed in detail in Chapter 5), determine how much rent you can afford each month and stick to it. One good way to find out how much rent is reasonable for an area is to call a commercial broker or agent and have a chat about how much space generally goes for in the locations you're considering. Brokers and agents are great sources of information on the going rates for rent in various neighborhoods. They'll generally give you an average figure for what commercial space costs per square foot per year in a given area; once you have this figure, you can compare it to the costs of any potential spaces you're considering. But keep in mind that agents and brokers are self-interested professionals who may benefit from higher rents. In other words, don't necessarily accept the figures they give you at face value.

Remember that square footage rates are generally given in cost per year, so once you multiply the rate by the square footage of a space, you'll need to divide it by 12 to determine the monthly rent.

EXAMPLE: Jennifer and Oliver are planning to open a theater in a certain neighborhood of their city. They call a few real estate brokers out of the phone book whose ads indicate they handle commercial space leasing. All the brokers say that commercial space in the area they like generally goes for $10 per square foot. (Jennifer and Oliver know that this is an annual figure, which works out to about 83 cents per square foot per month.) A few weeks later, Jennifer and Oliver notice a building for rent, and call the agent for more information. The agent tells them that the monthly rent is $1,800, and that the space is 2,400 square feet. Jennifer and Oliver do the math and see that this rent is slightly less than the going rate for the area:

$1,800 per month
x 12 months per year = $21,600 per year

$21,600 per year
÷ 2,400 square feet = $9 per year per square foot

They figure that if the space rented out for the going rate, $10 per square foot, they'd have to pay $2,000 per month for the space.

$10 per square foot per year
x 2,400 square feet = $24,000 per year

$24,000 per year
÷ 12 months per year = $2,000 per month

They're not quite ready to enter a lease, but the fact that this space is somewhat of a bargain ($9 per square foot) puts it near the top of their list.

While being realistic about your rent is important, don't sabotage your business by picking a cheap, but bad, location. Even the best-run business will fail if its customers can't find it or don't want to go to an unsafe neighborhood This may seem obvious, but sometimes new business owners become blind to common wisdom when pre-sented with an opportunity to rent a super-cheap space. Even if they've already determined that location will play a key role in their success, they either believe that the savings in rent will make up for slow sales or convince themselves that they'll be the pioneers in a new area that is sure to swell into a hot business district by the middle of next week. While this does occasionally happen (bless those brave pioneers), it's generally a poor idea to move into a dead or unsafe section of town, since it almost certainly won't bloom fast enough to support your business in its financially vulnerable start-up days.

Unless you have a sound reason to believe that you'll get enough customers in your oddball location, don't let the lure of low rent tempt you into a bad business decision. At least in popular urban areas, rent can be the highest overhead expense for many new businesses.

3. Getting the Right Physical Features

When picking your space, your biggest consideration might not be where it is but what it is. Ask yourself whether the building facilities are appropriate or adaptable for your business. For example, if you're planning to open a coffeehouse, you might fall in love with a beautiful brick warehouse space in a funky shopping district. But if the place doesn't have at least minimal kitchen facilities, you should probably forget it. Unless you can convince your landlord to put in the needed equipment—plumbing, electrical work, and the rest (discussed below)—it's highly unlikely that laying out the cash to do it yourself will be worth it.

Sure, some improvements might be relatively cheap, such as putting up a wall or two or adding new light fixtures. But if the building lacks something major that is essential to your business operation, take it as a sign that the place isn't right for you—even if it has loads of other great qualities. You'll have to decide for yourself which features your business absolutely can't live with, or live without.

EXAMPLE: Charlotte and Sandra plan to open an alternative health store that will offer products such as medicinal herbs, aromatherapy products, and yoga supplies. They also plan to offer services such as aromatherapy sessions and consultations with nutritionists and herbalists. Since they have high hopes for the service side of their business, Charlotte and Sandra know that their physical space needs to be comfortable and appealing to customers. After looking at a number of storefront spaces in their chosen neighborhood (near the university, of course), they find one that seems just perfect—until they notice the lack of windows. Except for the glass front door, the place has almost no natural light. Even though not having windows doesn't absolutely prevent them from doing business, Charlotte and Sandra decide that given their expected customer base (and their own feelings), they need a brighter space.

Another consideration that's important for many businesses these days is having modern phone and other data lines. Anyone who spends much time on the Web knows that old, slow lines can seriously impact your productivity (and drive you crazy to boot). Old lines can also slow down your faxes and may even result in dropped telephone connections—not exactly a good thing for business. When you're considering a specific space, ask the agent or the landlord for information on the phone and data lines into the space, such as whether it's connected to a fiber optic network or is wired for DSL or a T1 line (high-volume Internet connections). Also, find out if the landlord has sold the rights to the risers (wire conduits) in the building to a single telecommunications provider such as MCI or AT&T—if so, you could be stuck with that provider.

In addition to high-tech communications wiring, don't overlook plain-old electrical power as an important consideration in choosing a business space. Make sure that any space you're looking at has enough power for your needs, both in terms of the number of outlets and the capacity of the circuits. If you'll mostly be running computer equipment, a copier, a coffee machine, and the like, chances are that any reasonably equipped commercial space will have enough power for you. But if you'll be running machinery or other electricity-hungry equipment, make sure to find out from the landlord how much juice the circuits can handle and whether a generator is available during power outages. Also, if you'll keep sensitive computer equipment at your office, ask the landlord how many hours of air-conditioning are included in the terms of your lease, and negotiate longer hours if necessary.

Another common need for many businesses is adequate parking. If a significant percentage of your customers will come by car and there isn't enough parking at your chosen spot, it's probably best to look elsewhere. In fact, the city might not allow you to operate there if parking isn't adequate. (See Section B on zoning laws regarding parking.)

Check local planning or health department requirements. For instance, if you're starting a small food manufacturing business to produce energy bars, you may need to rent a space with a certain number of vents, a fire-resistant roof, and walls of proper material and adequate thickness. Contact your city or county departments of planning, health, fire, or other appropriate agency to find out about any requirements you might be required to meet.

B. Complying With Zoning Laws

A certain spot may be good for your business, but if it's not properly zoned for what you plan to do, forget it. Local zoning laws (often called "zoning ordinances" or "land use regulations") prohibit certain activities from being conducted in particular areas. To use an obvious example, a nightclub wouldn't be allowed to operate in a district zoned for residential use. Sure, only a fool would try to open a disco on a quiet residential street—but there are less obvious zoning no-nos that you must observe.

Zoning ordinances typically allow certain categories of businesses to occupy different districts of a city or county. For example, mixed commercial and residential uses might be allowed in one district while another district allows heavy industry and warehouses. So if you open your small jewelry-making business in a space zoned for commercial use, you could be in for a real headache if zoning officials decide you're a light-industrial business that's not allowed to operate in a commercial district. Similarly, you may not be allowed to run a commercial business—particularly one that's open to the public—in an industrial zone.

Besides regulating the types of businesses allowed in certain areas, zoning laws also regulate specific activities. Depending on your area, you might be subject to laws regulating parking, signs, water and air quality, waste management, noise, and the visual appearance of the business (especially in historic districts). In addition to these regulations, some cities restrict the number of a particular type of business in a certain area, such as allowing only three bookstores or two pet shops in a certain neighborhood. Finally, some zoning laws specifically regulate home businesses. (Home-office regulations are discussed separately in Section D, below.)

Expect Zoning Laws on Parking Spaces and Business Signs

Local zoning laws commonly require a business to provide parking, and they also may regulate the size and type of business signs. Be prepared for officials from your city or county to look into both these issues. If there's already a parking problem in your proposed area, you may have to come up with a plan for how to deal with the increased traffic your business will attract.

Also be ready for zoning officials to get really nitpicky about your business sign. Many local laws limit the size of business signs (no signs over 5 feet by 3 feet, for instance), their appearance (such as whether they're illuminated, flashing, colorful, or made of neon), and their placement (flat against the building, hanging over the sidewalk, or mounted on a pole). There are even some regulations attempting to limit the use of foreign language on signs. Be sure to find out what your local regulations are before spending money on having signs made.

More often than not, zoning laws are enforced for the sake of the other people and companies in the neighborhood. (This is particularly true of home-based businesses.) While some areas are strict about their zoning laws, most of the time you won't have a zoning official knocking unannounced on your door unless neighbors have complained or you're in flagrant violation of the laws. Since enforcement is often triggered by complaints, it's a good idea to get to know your neighbors and develop good relationships with them.

Never sign a lease for a business space without first knowing that you'll legally be able to do business there. (However, it's okay to sign a contingent lease, with a clause stating that the lease won't be binding if you don't get zoning approval.) Being forced to move your business is a headache, but not nearly as catastrophic as having to pay rent on a lease for a space that you can't use.

Never assume that you'll be allowed to do a certain activity simply because the previous tenants of the space did it. For all kinds of reasons, some businesses get away with zoning violations, even for long periods of time. But new occupants are sometimes scrutinized more carefully than already existing businesses. It may not be fair, but a new business may be told it can't do what an old one had long been doing.

It's also possible that the previous tenants were operating outside the zoning restrictions—but with an official okay. For example, the previous occupants might have had a zoning variance (an exception to zoning laws) for their particular business—one that won't necessarily be extended to you. And lots of times when zoning laws change, businesses that are already in place are allowed to keep doing what they were doing, even if the activity violates the new zoning law (a system referred to as "grandfathering"). When a tenant with a grandfathered exception leaves and new occupants come in, however, the new business usually has to abide by the new, more restrictive zoning law.

1. Finding Out What Laws Apply to Your Business

How do you find out whether a given location is properly zoned for your business and whether you need to get any approvals? The answer varies from area to area. In some cities and counties, zoning approval is part of the tax registration process (discussed in Chapter 7). In San Diego, for instance, when you apply for your business tax certificate you must also pay a Zoning Use Clearance fee to have your business approved for the location listed on your application. And the city of Oakland won't accept your new business application without prior approval of your business location by the city's zoning division. Other cities such as San Francisco don't require proof of zoning approval before issuing a tax registration certificate—but that doesn't mean you should take the zoning laws any less seriously. Whether or not you're required to deal with your local zoning department before starting your business, you'll still be subject to its monitoring and enforcement on an ongoing basis.

If your city doesn't include zoning approval as part of its start-up requirements for new businesses, you'll need to do some detective work. Generally this involves talking with your local zoning officials. Most zoning agencies are part of city or county planning departments. Look under "Planning" or "Zoning" in the government section (blue pages) of your white-pages phone book. If your business will be located in a city, you probably only need to worry about city zoning ordinances. Businesses in rural areas should contact the county zoning or planning offices.

Getting zoning approval typically begins with filling out a form issued by the city planning department on which you provide information about your proposed location and what you plan to do there. In some cities, you may be required to submit detailed building plans to show exactly how you intend to use the space in question. Your application may be evaluated simply upon the information you provide in the form, or the zoning department may send out an inspector to more closely examine the potential business space. Once the zoning department has all the information it requires to make a decision, it will either approve your application without limitations, approve it with certain conditions, or deny it altogether.

There's a world of difference in how strict zoning officials are from area to area. Many zoning departments aren't terribly rigid about enforcement, mostly responding to complaints from neighbors or other citizens about businesses that create a nuisance or other trouble. In a few areas, however, zoning agents relish sniffing out minor infractions and enforcing their zoning ordinances to the letter.

If you're considering going ahead with your business despite what you consider to be a minor zoning problem, do your best to find out how strict the zoning police are in your area. Start by asking other local businesspeople about their experiences. If they tell you that there's little enforcement other than responding to complaints, you can breathe a little easier about what might be a minor infraction, such as including tennis-racket stringing (which officials might consider a light-industrial activity) at your sports shop in an area zoned only for commercial use. Even so, it never pays to engage in a prohibited activity that is fundamental to your business, in case zoning officials make you stop the activity. While tennis rackets could be strung elsewhere, a health club wouldn't want to have to locate its juice bar two blocks away.

But no matter how mellow your zoning department, at the very least you need to know what the rules are for your proposed location. Ignoring the rules while counting on lax enforcement is just plain dumb.

2. Dealing With Snags in Zoning Approval

If your zoning board has a problem with any of the activities you plan to conduct at your chosen location, you have a few options, usually ranging from making appropriate changes to your business to giving up on that location and finding a new one. Obviously, some zoning conflicts are simply not fixable—you'll never be allowed to open a nightclub on a quiet cul-de-sac. But the good news is that a creative (and, when necessary, assertive) business owner can often persuade zoning officials or the zoning appeals board to work out an acceptable accommodation that will allow the business to use the desired location.

For borderline situations, one approach is simply to advocate an interpretation of the zoning law that's favorable to you *before* you get an official "No." Communicate with zoning officials and try to persuade them to give you their seal of approval.

If the zoning officials have already denied your application, it's often possible to appeal their decision, usually to a higher authority within the zoning agency, such as a board of appeals. If you're successful, the zoning board may grant you a "variance," which is basically a one-time exception to the local zoning laws. Or the board may give you a "conditional use permit," which essentially gives you approval to operate your business as long as certain conditions are met, such as restricting the maximum occupancy to a certain number or providing additional parking spaces.

When lobbying for an exemption from a zoning requirement, be aware that you're asking for special treatment, so make your case as persuasive as possible. If your business will be valuable to the community, present evidence of that fact. Proof can include demographic data about the area, testimony from community leaders, or statements from other local businesspeople. Your goal is to show that the value of allowing your business in the area is greater than the trivial zoning conflicts that may exist. If you can compromise in some other area, offer to do so.

EXAMPLE: Carolyn wants to open a small printing shop, Nelson's Press, on a commercial strip where storefront space is cheap and plentiful. Before signing a lease, she applies for zoning approval. The local zoning board rejects her application because Carolyn's proposed location is zoned commercial, while her print shop would technically be a light-industrial business. Carolyn decides to try to get an exception, because her printing operation will be small (only one small offset printing press) and would be an asset to the neighborhood, which needs new businesses.

She submits detailed plans of her business to the zoning board, showing the business's small scope and including specific protocols for dealing with toxics such as ink. She also submits letters from other business owners in the neighborhood, documenting how commerce in the area has languished for years and arguing that a new business would help revitalize the strip. Many of the business owners also note that a local printer would be convenient for the existing area businesses, which currently have to go across town for their print jobs. A few weeks later, Carolyn gets a conditional use permit allowing her to proceed with her printing business, as long as she doesn't expand her business with additional presses and follows a number of standard rules governing the chemicals she'll use in printing.

Zoning and Home Businesses

Just as business owners seeking commercial office spaces, owners of home businesses need to make sure they don't violate their local zoning rules. As home businesses have become a nationwide phenomenon, more and more local governments have adopted specific provisions in their zoning laws regarding home-based businesses.

Mercifully, most of the rules are straightforward and fair—with some exceptions, of course. If you're unlucky and find that you're subject to prohibitive municipal ordinances or private land use restrictions, you'll need to take a hard look at whether you should set up shop in your home after all. But more often, you'll find that you'll need to jump through a simple hoop or two and pay a modest fee to run your business from home. (We discuss zoning rules for home businesses in Section D, below.)

C. Commercial Leases

Chances are that you'll rent rather than buy a space for your business. After all, most small start-ups don't have the funds to purchase real estate, and it's usually not a good idea to saddle your business with high interest payments anyway. But just because you've rented plenty of apartments or flats over the years, don't assume that you know the score when it comes to leasing business space.

Practically and legally speaking, there are lots of differences between commercial leases and residential leases. Commercial leases are not subject to most consumer protection laws that govern residential leases—for example, there are no caps on deposits or rules protecting a tenant's privacy. Also, commercial leases are generally subject to much more negotiation between the business and the landlord, since business owners often need special features in their spaces, and landlords are often eager for tenants and willing to extend special offers. While a residential tenant will usually just take an apartment or flat more or less as-is, a business will often need to modify the existing space—for example, by adding cubicles, raising a loading dock, or rewiring for telephones and computers.

Since company owners must negotiate modifications suitable for their own operations, commercial leases are relatively flexible creatures. Of course, your bargaining power will vary a great deal from situation to situation. For example, getting a landlord to accept your demands would probably be a lot easier for a long-term lease in a largely vacant office building than for a six-month lease in a hot commercial area. Likewise, local landlords are often more willing to make concessions than huge property management companies or real estate investment trusts.

When negotiating a commercial lease, keep in mind that the success or failure of your business may ride on certain terms of the lease. The amount of the rent is an obvious concern, as is the length of the lease. (You probably don't want to tie yourself to a five- or ten-year lease if you can help it, in case your business grows faster than you expect or the location doesn't work out for you.) But other, less conspicuous items spelled out in the lease may be just as crucial to your business's success. For instance, if you expect your shoe repair business to depend largely on walk-in customers, be sure that your lease establishes your right to put up a sign that's visible from the street. Or, if you are counting on being the only sandwich shop inside a new commercial complex, make sure your lease prevents the landlord from leasing space to a competitor. If you are starting a new Web company that you expect to grow quickly, make sure there's room for expansion.

The following checklist includes many items that are often addressed in commercial leases. Pay attention to terms regarding:

- rent, including allowable increases and method of computation
- whether the rent you pay includes insurance, property taxes, and maintenance costs (called a gross lease) or whether you will be charged for these items separately (called a net lease)
- the security deposit and conditions for its return
- the length of the lease (also called the lease term) and when it begins
- whether there's an option to renew the lease or expand the space
- how the lease may be terminated, including notice requirements, and whether there are penalties for early termination
- exactly what space is being rented, including common areas such as hallways, rest rooms, and elevators, and how the space is measured (some measurement practices include the thickness of the walls)
- specifications for signs, including where they may be placed
- whether there will be improvements, modifications (called buildouts when new space is being finished to your specifications), or fixtures added to the space, who will pay for them, and who will own them after the lease ends (generally, the landlord)

- who will maintain the premises
- whether the lease may be assigned or subleased to another party, and
- whether disputes must be mediated or arbitrated as an alternative to court.

Beware the Americans With Disabilities Act. The Americans With Disabilities Act (ADA) requires all businesses that are open to the public or that employ more than 15 people to have premises that are accessible to disabled people. Make sure that you and your landlord are in agreement about who will pay for any needed modifications, such as adding a ramp or widening doorways to accommodate wheelchairs.

For more on leasing office space. For lots of detailed information on finding a space and negotiating a lease, see *Leasing Space for Your Small Business,* by Janet Portman and Fred S. Steingold (Nolo).

D. When Your Home Is Your Office

It's not an exaggeration to say that the explosion of home-based businesses has radically reshaped the small-business landscape. By most accounts, the number of home-based businesses in the United States exceeds 30 million and is growing strong. Along with the boom in home businesses, whole new industries have emerged such as major office supply chains, home office networking equipment dealers, home business consultants, and a host of magazines, websites, and other media dedicated to home business issues. No question about it, home businesses—and the industries that have grown around them—are here to stay.

While growing phenomenally, the home business sector has achieved a new level of respect. Entrepreneurs of all stripes and funding levels have discovered that setting up shop in a home can be a cost-efficient, flexible way to get a business venture off the ground. While many businesses eventually move into company digs, an increasing number are staying put at their founders' homes. "Home business" no longer means Tupperware parties or shady multilevel marketing schemes. Even the most professional, reputable, and aggressively growth-minded companies are joining the ranks of home-based businesses.

It's no secret why the idea of starting a business from home is so attractive to so many. The convenience of working at home is a major draw, especially to parents who want to cut commute times and increase time with the family. Not having to pay rent for an external office helps the bottom line of any business—especially important in the start-up days. And thanks to fast, affordable Internet connections and wireless networks, it's never been easier to exchange documents, do research, send email, teleconference, and otherwise be connected to the world from home.

In addition to communications and networking, a number of other technologies have advanced in leaps and bounds to help home businesses get firmly established. Prosumer—a hybrid of professional and consumer—imaging products such as digital cameras, scanners and printers, and easy-to-use Web development software, allow home businesses to create professional-looking brochures, websites, and other marketing materials. With all this new technology, home businesses can develop a much more professional image than was possible a decade ago.

Before you hang out your shingle, however, it's important to realize that a home business isn't immune from a number of the requirements that affect businesses in general. Similar to a business operated from a commercial office space, a business run from home must comply with zoning requirements in your area. And there are several special tax rules for home businesses, as well as insurance issues, that you should understand. We discuss them in this chapter.

Is Your Business Right for a Home Office?

While many types of businesses lend themselves to being run out of a residence, others don't. Make sure you've considered whether using your home as your office is a good idea. Ask yourself questions such as:

- How will you deal with customers and suppliers? Will they be able to easily park and pick up or unload material if necessary?
- Will customers take you and your company seriously if you work out of your house?
- Will your business require a lot of space for performing services or storing supplies?
- Can you work productively in your home, considering distractions like kids, the couch, the refrigerator, and the TV?
- If you rent, will your landlord approve of your business?

Businesses that require nothing but a small office and don't generate much coming and going—such as graphic design, accounting, and Web development businesses—and businesses in which most of the dirty work is routinely done off-site—such as construction and plumbing—are particularly well-suited for home offices.

Kimberly Torgerson, owner of Your Word's Worth, a freelance editing and writing service in Berkeley:

Setting up my home office was much harder than navigating the licensing agencies to start up my business. Where to put the fax? How to get the monitor set up just right? How to organize a spaghetti tangle of cables? Someday I'd like to get a sleeker setup, with everything in a tailored niche, but for now I put money into upgrading equipment, not furniture.

1. Zoning Restrictions on Home Offices

As with leased office spaces, you need to make sure that the business activities you plan to do in your home are acceptable to your local zoning officials. You may also have to apply for a special "home occupation permit" before you begin. (Zoning laws typically refer to home offices as "home occupations.")

Since your home is most likely in an area zoned for residential use only (some loft-type or urban apartments might be zoned for mixed use), the types of businesses allowed by your neighborhood ordinances will likely be pretty limited. A few areas actually forbid home businesses altogether. But most cities and counties allow home offices that have little likelihood of causing noise or pollution, creating traffic, or otherwise disturbing the neighbors. Writers, artists, attorneys, accountants, insurance brokers, and piano teachers are examples of businesspeople commonly allowed to work from home. Typically not allowed are retailers, automotive repair shops, cafes or bars, animal hospitals or breeders, or any type of adult-oriented business.

Watch out for private land-use restrictions. If you live in a condo, a co-op, a planned subdivision, or a rental property, you are likely subject to private land use restrictions in addition to your local laws. Condo regulations, for instance, often contain language restricting or sometimes even prohibiting business use of the premises. Or your apartment lease might forbid business from being conducted on the property. Be sure to check the documents governing your property to see if there are any such rules.

To find out how your city or county deals with home offices, call the planning department and ask for any available information on home occupations. Some areas have special pamphlets with information explaining home office restrictions and how to obtain any necessary permits. In other places, all that's available might be a grainy photocopy of the municipal code, which you'll have to decipher yourself. If there's no approval or permit process for home businesses in your area, it's generally up to you to comply with your area's zoning code.

Keep in mind that the best way to avoid trouble with zoning officials is to do your best to decrease your business's impact on the neighborhood. As long as you're not in flagrant violation of the zoning laws regarding home businesses, you'll probably be fine as long as your neighbors are happy.

Assuming that your local zoning laws do allow your type of home business, they are likely to impose some restrictions, such as allowing only residents of your home to be employees, restricting the number of customers that may come to your house, limiting the percentage of your home's floor space that can be used for business, and prohibiting signs outside of your house that advertise the business.

In addition to these general limitations, cities often impose restrictions upon specific types of home businesses. For instance, while a city might forbid any type of home business from having a neon sign, it might also have a special rule for landscapers that doesn't allow landscaping supplies to be kept at the home office. Be sure to find out if there are special rules for your type of business in your city.

If you find out that your city will allow your type of home business in your area, you may have no further need to contact the zoning office. Many cities do not require any special permit, as long as the home business complies with all of the rules and restrictions contained in its planning code (such as the rules discussed above). Some cities, however, require all home business owners to get a "home occupation permit." Obtaining such a permit is usually a simple matter of filling out a form provided by the planning department and paying whatever fee may be required. If your business meets the restrictions your city imposes, your permit will be issued.

If you don't meet all of your city's rules for having a home occupation, or your area just isn't zoned for your type of home business, you may be out of luck and simply won't be allowed to run your business from home. In some locales, however, a home business that meets most but not all

of the city's restrictions may be allowed to operate, but only after obtaining a home occupation permit. In San Diego, for instance, no permit is required for home businesses that meet all of the city's criteria: no business signs, no nonresident employees on premises, and so on. But if the home business deviates from the criteria, the city may allow the business to proceed, but only with a home occupation permit. Acceptable deviations in San Diego include having one employee or having one client who visits your home office by appointment, and using more than one vehicle for business.

Below, we've listed some home occupation restrictions and permit fees for a few of California's larger cities. It's a good general guide to the types of regulations home businesses face across the state. There are, of course, exceptions to these rules and they are subject to change, so be sure to check with your city for its specific laws regulating home occupations.

City	Home Office Restrictions	Required Permit for Home Offices	Fees for Home Offices
Fresno	• all employees must be residents of home • business may not use more than one room of home • business may not use space outside the main home structure (for example, no business activities in the garage) • business vehicle may not weigh more than one ton, and must be stored in an entirely enclosed garage	None	None
Oakland	• any employees must be residents of home • sign may not be larger than one square foot, must be nonmoving, and may be lit only if indirectly without flashing lights • if business is conducted in garage, garage door must be closed • any vehicle with sign advertising business may not be visible from the edge of the property	Same zoning approval requirements as all other businesses ($10 fee for zoning clearance)	$10 zoning clearance fee (applies to all businesses, not just home occupations)
Los Angeles	• may conduct business between 8 a.m. and 8 p.m. • one client per hour allowed on premises during business hours • no business signs allowed	None	None
Sacramento	• only three employees or partners allowed; two must be residents of home • only one customer or client per hour • only one truck weighing up to one ton allowed • no signs allowed	Home Occupation Permit	$45 one-time fee
San Francisco	• no more than 1/4 of home's floor space may be used for business • all employees must be residents of home • no inventory may be kept on premises	None	None
San Jose	• all employees must be residents of home • only two clients allowed on premises at one time • clients allowed only between 9 a.m. and 9 p.m. • only one vehicle under 10,000 pounds may be kept at residence	None	None

Keep in mind that the zoning agency is probably not the only land-use regulatory agency in your area. While your activity might be okay with zoning officials, operating out of your home may not pass other departments' requirements. For example, if you're starting a catering business, chances are your county health department won't let you work out of your home kitchen. You may be allowed to convert your garage or another separate structure into a professional kitchen—but of course, that requires securing building permits and passing county health inspections in addition to zoning compliance or permission. (For more information on permits for your specific business activities, see Chapter 7 on start-up requirements.)

Let your neighbors in on your business plans. Getting to know your neighbors can be a huge help in avoiding problems with zoning officials. For instance, if your business requires people to be coming and going from your house or packages to be delivered daily, your neighbors might jump to the nutty conclusion that you're a drug dealer and report you to the city. Even though you can show your drug of choice is vitamin C, the city might unearth technical zoning violations that never would have otherwise turned up. In short, communicating with your neighbors and dealing with their concerns about issues such as parking and noise will greatly reduce the likelihood that the zoning police will come knocking on your door.

2. The Home Business Tax Deduction

If your office is located in your home, you may be able to claim a portion of your home expenses—such as rent, depreciation, property taxes, utilities, and insurance—as a special deduction when reporting federal taxes. (This deduction will also flow through to your state tax return.) The IRS's general rule is that if your business qualifies (discussed below), you can deduct a pro rata share of home business expenses. "Pro rata" simply means a share that's proportional to the percentage of home space that you use for your business.

Before we tackle the nitty gritty requirements, let's look at basics. First, the IRS definition of "home" is pretty broad, generally including any type of dwelling in which you can cook and sleep. This includes houses, condos, apartment units, mobile homes, boats, and wherever else you reside. Both renters and owners are eligible for taking the home tax deduction.

Moving on to the meat of the criteria, the IRS has two requirements for any business owner who wants to deduct expenses for using part of a home as a business.

1. You must *regularly* use part of your home *exclusively* for a trade or business (see Section a, below), and

2. You must be able to show that you:
   - use your home as your principal place of business (see Section b, below), or
   - meet patients, clients, or customers at home (see Section c, below), or
   - use a separate structure on your property exclusively for business purposes (see Section d, below).

First, we'll look at each of these criteria a bit more closely. Then we'll offer some guidance on how to figure out which expenses are in fact deductible. (For information on how businesses in general are taxed, see Chapter 9.)

Many expenses are automatically fully deductible. Many taxpayers mistakenly believe that they need to qualify for the home business deduction before they can claim any expenses associated with a home-based business. But in fact, you can deduct business expenses necessary for your business whether they're incurred in your home or anywhere else, even if you don't qualify for the home business deduction. For instance, you can always deduct the portion of your home long-distance phone bill that you spend on business-related calls. Other deductible business expenses might include office supplies, furniture, and equipment that you use in your home office, and the cost of bringing a second telephone line into your home for business use. As used in this section, "home business expenses" will refer to expenses that can only be claimed with the home business deduction.

a.   Exclusive and Regular Use for Business

The IRS will allow you to deduct home business expenses only for space in your home that is 100% dedicated to business use. For example, a graphic designer who sometimes sits at the kitchen table to do illustrations can't claim business deductions for using the kitchen—assuming the kitchen is also sometimes used for nonbusiness purposes like cooking and eating. A spare room, however, that's set up as an office space and used only for business would probably meet the exclusive use test. But if the room contains a bed for the occasional overnight guest or doubles as storage space for clothing, technically, it wouldn't qualify.

The regular use test is generally pretty easy to pass. As long as you use your home business space for business on a frequent, continuing basis, rather than for a once-in-a-while garage sale or lemonade stand, you'll probably make the cut.

> **EXAMPLE 1:** Stacey runs a hat-making business. She makes the hats in an extra room of her house where she has a sewing machine and all her supplies, as well as a computer and a file cabinet containing her sales and other financial information. Since the only use of that room is for the hat-making business, it will meet the IRS's criteria of exclusive use. And since Stacey has made and sold hats for a couple years, with consistent monthly sales, she'll have no trouble proving that she uses the space regularly for business.

> **EXAMPLE 2:** Parisha has a full-time job at a plant nursery, but also does occasional freelance work in photography. She has a darkroom in her basement that she uses to develop photos for her assignments. Her darkroom is dedicated to her photography business, but she spends most of her time working at the plant nursery and has only done one photo shoot in the last six months. Parisha would be ill-advised to claim her darkroom expenses as a home-office deduction, since she doesn't regularly use it for business.

b.   Principal Place of Business

In addition to fulfilling the exclusive and regular use requirements, your home business space must also be the main place where you do business—with two exceptions explained below. Thankfully, since 1999, the principal place of business rule has been fairly easy to satisfy. Before 1999, business owners often had to use an imprecise formula to balance how "primary" their various places of business were. Now, however, the rule is simple. Your home office will qualify as the principal place of business if you:

- use the office to conduct administrative or management activities, and
- do not have an office or other business location outside your home set up to conduct these activities.

This rule is just as straightforward as it sounds. As long as you use your home office to keep track of your business files, do your bookkeeping and accounting, maintain your client databases, or conduct whatever other type of administration is required, and you don't have a space away from home set up for these activities, your home office will be considered your principal place of business.

If your home office doesn't qualify as your principal place of business under the test described above, you can still qualify for the home-office deduction if:

- you regularly meet clients or customers at home, or
- you use a separate structure on your property for your home office.

In these two cases, it doesn't matter whether your home office or separate structure is your principal work space. But remember: The rule still applies that your home office space must be used exclusively and regularly for business.

Tips on Establishing Home Business Use

Home business owners should make an effort to clearly establish their home offices as places of business.

Here are some ways you can accomplish this.

- Take pictures of your home office that show its business character.
- Draw a diagram showing the floor plan of the house with the home office clearly defined. Include room dimensions if possible.
- Keep a log of the times you work in the office.
- Keep a record of all client meetings at your office—including whom you met, when, and the subject of the meeting. Recording client visits to your home office is especially important if you also have an outside office.
- Have your business mail sent to your home.
- Get a separate phone line for the business.

---

c. Figuring Deductible Home Business Expenses

Once you've determined that you do in fact qualify for the home business tax deduction, you'll need to figure out exactly how much you can deduct. Obviously, you can't deduct all of your housing costs—only the expenses attributable to business purposes qualify.

At the outset, you'll need to determine a "business percentage" for your home—simply, the percentage of your home that is used for business. You can calculate this percentage in one of two ways: the "square footage" method or the "number of rooms" method. Either approach is acceptable to the IRS.

The square footage method simply divides the square footage of the business space by the square footage of the whole house. For instance, if you use 250 square feet for business, and your entire house takes up 1,000 square feet, then your business space uses 25% (250 ÷ 1,000) of your home.

The number-of-rooms method is just as simple: If your house has five similarly sized rooms, and you use one of them for business, then the business uses 20% (1 ÷ 5) of your home.

Once you have calculated a space percentage for your business, use it to calculate the portion of your home expenses that is deductible to the business. Home expenses fall into one of three categories, with different deductibility rules for each.

Unrelated expenses. Expenses that are unrelated to your business space are not deductible at all. For example, you can't deduct the cost of repainting your bedroom or replacing your dining room window.

Direct expenses. You can fully deduct expenses that directly affect your business space such as the cost of installing new carpeting, replacing a broken window, or repairing the heating vent in your office space. (Note that direct expenses for a day care center may not be fully deductible. For more information, see IRS Publication 587, *Business Use of Your Home.*)

Indirect expenses. Expenses that affect the whole house—called indirect expenses—are deductible, but only partially, based on the percentage of your home that is used for business. For instance, you can deduct a percentage of the cost of a new foundation, a new water heater, mortgage interest, real estate taxes, and utility bills.

To calculate the portion of indirect expenses attributable to your business, you generally multiply the indirect expense by your business percentage. Rent, for example, is an easy expense to prorate. If your business uses 25% of your home, and your rent is $800 per month, then $200 per month is a deductible home business expense (25% x $800). The same simple approach generally works for calculating the deductible business portion of many other indirect expenses such as homeowner's insurance, mortgage interest, home utilities, and repairs.

If you own your home and you qualify for the home business tax deduction, one indirect expense that you may deduct is the depreciation of your home. Depreciation of your home is an allowance for the wear and tear inflicted upon it. And the home business depreciation deduction is simply a deduction for the business portion of this. Calculating this deduction is slightly more involved than the indirect expense deductions mentioned above. We offer an overview below of how to calculate the depreciation deduction; detailed instructions are included in IRS Publication 587, *Business Use of Your Home.*

Keep in mind that depreciation is calculated for the building only—not the land. Property tax assessments usually show the breakdown of home value versus land value. First you'll need to calculate the portion of the cost of your home that can be depreciated. This amount is called the "depreciable basis." Calculate the depreciable basis by multiplying the percentage of your home used for business by the smaller of the following (remember not to include the value of the land, only the home itself):

- the adjusted basis of your home (its cost, plus the cost of permanent improvements, minus casualty losses or depreciation deducted in earlier tax years) on the date you began using it for business, or
- the fair market value of your home when you began using it for business.

The result of this calculation—the depreciable basis—is the portion of the home's value attributable to the business. (The IRS explains adjusted basis in its Publication 551, *Basis of Assets.*)

Then, calculate the actual deduction that your home business will be able to claim. To oversimplify, this deduction is calculated by multiplying your depreciable basis by a certain percentage, set by the IRS. The percentage and specific depreciation method to use will depend on when you started your home business.

There are many more details involved than we can cover here, so we recommend you at least consult the IRS publications before tackling the depreciation deduction on your own. (See Recommended Reading icon below.) Or consider handing the job over to an experienced business accountant.

Get tax information from the horse's mouth. The IRS offers examples and detailed instructions in two publications: Publication 587, *Business Use of Your Home,* and Publication 946, *How to Depreciate Property.* These publications are available online at www.irs.gov/formspubs/index.html.

Tax Issues When You Sell Your Home

Homeowners with home businesses face a couple of tax issues if they end up selling their homes: capital gains taxes and depreciation recapture. These concepts are widely misunderstood, with the result that many home business owners don't claim their rightful share of deductions for fear of the tax implications. Don't make this mistake. Not only are the rules relatively easy to understand, they're quite favorable to home business owners.

No Tax on Proportional Gain

Before 2002, a home business owner who sold a home at a profit had to pay capital gains tax on the portion of the home used by the business. This was a widely cursed exception to the general IRS rule that exempted home sellers from capital gains taxes on gains up to $250,000 ($500,000 for married couples), as long as they owned and lived in the home for at least two of the last five years. For home business owners, even if the profit from the home sale was within the exempt limits, capital gains taxes would be due on the portion allocated to the home business. One way around this was to stop claiming home business deductions—which is exactly what many home business owners did, kissing goodbye hundreds or thousands of dollars in potential tax savings.

Mercifully, in December 2002, the IRS reversed itself with a new regulation. Now, when you sell your home at a gain, you do not need to allocate a portion of that gain to your home business. You can go ahead and claim all the home business tax deductions you're entitled to, without worrying that you'll be stuck with capital gains taxes for your home business portion. You'll only have to pay capital gains taxes if you exceeded the limits of $250,000 gain ($500,000 for married couples), which would apply whether or not you had a home business.

An important exception to the IRS's 2002 rule is that home businesses located in a separate structure will continue to be subject to capital gains taxes. So if you run your business from a separate, freestanding garage or shed for example, you'll be stuck paying the gains taxes when you sell your home. To avoid this, stop claiming the home business tax deduction two years before you sell your home.

Providing relief to many, the eased rule is retroactive to tax years 1999, 2000, and 2001. A home business owner who didn't claim home business deductions for fear of the capital gains issue can amend tax returns for the past three years to reap the rewards of the deductions.

Recaptured Depreciation Tax

The IRS's 2002 rule change does *not* change what's known as "depreciation recapture," however. As in the past, home business owners who sell their homes must still pay taxes on the depreciation deductions they've taken over the years. In other words, if you claim depreciation deductions for a home business, the total of those deductions will be taxed—"recaptured," if you will—when you sell your house.

> EXAMPLE: Mariana teaches ballet lessons to children and has been using a room in her home as a dance studio for five years. She sells her house at a gain of $200,000. Her home studio takes up 10% of her home. Under current IRS rules, she will not be subject to capital gains taxes for the 10% of her home used for business activities. However, Mariana must pay depreciation recapture tax on the total depreciation deductions she's taken in the five years of operating her home teaching studio.

This rule isn't really so bad when you consider the depreciation recapture rate is only 25%. Most business owners pay much more than this on income—self-employment tax at a rate of 15.3%, plus their federal personal tax rate of 15%, 28%, or higher, plus state tax rates—so that depreciation deductions can easily offer savings of 40% or more each year. The bottom line is that it's worth it to take the depreciation deductions since you'll almost certainly save more in cumulative savings over the years than you'll end up paying when you sell your home.

For more on the home office deduction.
For more detailed information on tax deductions for home businesses, read *Tax Savvy for Small Business,* by Frederick W. Daily (Nolo).

3. Insurance and the Home Business

While lots of home-based business owners might not have to worry too much about insurance in their very early days, there are a few special issues to watch out for if you plan to run a business from home. In a nutshell, don't expect your homeowner's or renter's policy to automatically cover you for business-related losses, including theft or damage of business property and personal injury claims related to your business. Not having additional coverage can be a real catastrophe if your computer system is stolen or destroyed in an earthquake, or if a client trips and falls over your garden hose on the way up your front walk.

Potentially even worse, your regular homeowner's or renter's policy might be voided entirely—even for home-related claims—if the insurance company finds out you are running a business in the home without their knowledge. Some companies require you to tell them about any home business (and may bill you for added coverage) or they'll invalidate your policy. Compared to the risks of having the whole policy yanked out from under you, paying some extra premium dollars will probably be well worth it.

(For more information on small business insurance, see Chapter 8.)

Chapter 4 Checklist

☐ Determine how much rent you can afford.

☐ Decide what neighborhood would be best for your business.

☐ Find out what the average rents are in the neighborhoods you're considering.

☐ Identify the features and fixtures your business space will need.

☐ Make sure any spaces you're considering are or can be properly zoned for your business.

☐ Examine any commercial lease carefully before signing and negotiate the best deal you can.

☐ If working from home, make sure your business activities won't violate any zoning restrictions on home offices.

☐ Become familiar with the rules on home-office deductions before claiming them on your tax return.

☐ Be sure your home office is adequately insured. (Insurance is further discussed in Chapter 8).

Drafting an Effective Business Plan

If you think only Type A personalities compose business plans, think again. Talk to a random sample of successful business owners—even the most laid-back—and you'll be amazed at how many took the time to put their business plans into writing. If you're truly determined to succeed, you'll follow their example because without a plan, you're leaving far too many things to chance. Just as a blueprint is used to ensure that a building will be structurally sound, a business plan will help you make sure that your business will be able to stay afloat.

The purpose of a business plan is simple: to bring together in one document the key elements of your business. These include the products or services you'll sell, what they'll cost to produce, and how much sales revenue you expect during your first months and years of operation. Most important, your plan will help you see how all the disparate elements of your business relate to one another, which will allow you to make any necessary alterations to increase your business's potential to turn a profit.

Business plans are often written by business owners who want to borrow money or attract investment. This is good as far as it goes—lenders and investors do want to understand as much as possible about how a business will work before deciding whether to back it financially. Unless you're prepared to show them a well-thought-out plan for making your business profitable, you won't have much chance of convincing them to finance your project.

But creating a business plan is a good idea even if you don't need to raise start-up money. The planning process often brings up issues and potential problems that you hadn't thought of before. And the discipline involved in developing financial projections like a break-even analysis and a profit and loss forecast will help you decide whether your business is really worth starting, or whether you need to rethink some of your key assumptions. As any experienced businessperson will tell you, the business you decide not to start (often because its business plan doesn't pencil out) can play

a greater role your long-term success than the one on which you bet your economic future.

This chapter will explain how to create a thorough business plan. If you've already written one, you may want to skip this chapter—or you might want to use the information here to double-check your plan. Of course we remember you have no time to waste, so we will keep our focus on the essential elements and spare you the fluff.

For more help on the business of business plans. Nolo offers a couple of resources for those in need of setting up or revising business plans. *How to Write a Business Plan,* by Mike McKeever is a comprehensive guide explaining how to write a business plan—including how to evaluate the profitability of your business idea; estimate operating expenses; determine assets, liabilities, and net worth; and find potential sources of financing. And *Business Plan Pro 2004* is software that offers a fast, easy way to generate the plan you need to launch or expand your business.

A. Different Purposes Require Different Plans

All good business plans have two basic goals: to describe the fundamentals of the business idea, and to provide financial calculations to show that it will make good money. But, depending on how you intend to use it, a business plan can take somewhat different forms.

- If you will use your plan to borrow money or interest investors, write it with an eye towards selling your vision to skeptical people. Generally, you should include a persuasive introduction and a request for funds, in-depth market research information, an evaluation of your main competitors, your key marketing strategies, and a management plan. In addition, your plan should contain detailed financial information—including your best estimates of start-up costs, revenues, and expenses. Finally, since your plan will be submitted to people who don't know you well, the writing should be polished and the format clean and professional.

- If your plan will primarily be for your own use—that is, if you don't need to raise money—don't worry so much about making a sales pitch or slick presentation (although you'll probably want to do a quick market and competitive analysis). But don't skimp when it comes to doing your numbers. You'll need to include estimates of start-up costs, revenues, and expenses. The last thing you want is to experience the very real misery of realizing too late that your business never had a chance to make a solid profit.

Plan to get the help you need. Not all businesspeople are great writers. But excellent writing skills can be a big help in creating a compelling business plan. Consider paying a freelance writer with small business savvy to help you polish your plan. Similarly, if you are challenged by numbers, find a bookkeeper or accountant to provide some help with the math.

B. Describing Your Business and Yourself

The first several sections of your plan should describe the beauty of your business idea. If you will show your plan to potential lenders, investors, or colleagues, you'll want to show them right up front that you've hit upon a product or service that customers really want. In addition, you'll want to show that you are exactly the right person to make this fine idea a roaring success. Your goal is to have them say, "Wow! What a great business idea! And yes, I see exactly why Carlos Burns is the ideal person to make it a big success."

To accomplish these goals, you should include the following in your plan:

- a statement of the purpose of your business

- a detailed description of how the business will work
- an analysis of your market
- an analysis of your competitors
- a description of your marketing strategy, and
- a résumé setting forth your business accomplishments.

Again, depending on how you intend to use your business plan, you may be able to skip some of these elements. For example, if you don't need to raise start-up money and are writing a plan mostly for your own use, you may decide to skip the résumé of your own business accomplishments. But think twice before you leave out too much. Any new business will need to introduce itself to loads of people—suppliers, contractors, employees, and key customers, to name a few—and showing them part or all of your business plan can be a great way to do it.

1. State Your Business's Purpose

What will your product or service be? And why does the great big world—or your small town or narrow niche market—need the product or service you want to offer? The first paragraph of your plan should address this question as directly and compellingly as possible. For example, if you're planning to open a pet-grooming salon, you might start with the proposition that in today's increasingly busy world, pet owners need and want to keep their pets clean and groomed, but often don't have time to do it themselves. Similarly, if you want to start a sea kayaking guide service, you might start with the proposition that more and more people are participating in this exciting sport, but need equipment, planning, training, and logistical help to do it in other parts of the world.

A statement of business purpose doesn't need to be complicated or lengthy. In fact, some of the best simply state the obvious. If the need for your business will be clear to lenders or investors (for example, a sandwich shop in a fast-growing office area), one paragraph may be all you need. But if the value of your business idea isn't so readily apparent (for example, an innovative software company), you will want to say more. Show how your business will solve a real problem or fill an actual need. And explain why customers will pay you to accomplish the task.

2. Describe Your Business

Once you've stated the need that your business will fill, describe exactly how you'll go about filling it. Don't write a bunch of fluffy text about how brilliant your entrepreneurial idea is. Instead, outline in detail exactly how your business will operate. While the degree of detail may vary depending on what kind of business you're starting and who will be reading your business plan, your description should include specifics such as:

- how you will provide the product or service
- where you will buy key supplies
- how customers will pay you
- how many employees you will have and what they will do
- your hours of operation, and
- your business location (if possible, include details about how your customers will find you).

Keep in mind that even the smallest, simplest business involves a swarm of pesky details. While you're writing your business description, don't assume there's anything obvious about your business, even if it's a tiny one-person operation. For example, if you plan to start a pet-grooming business, how many different types of services will you offer: Shampooing? Flea bathing? Nail cutting? Hair trimming? Teeth cleaning? Will you charge separately for each individual service, sell them in packages, or both? How will you attract customers and regularly stay in touch with the best ones? How will you accommodate animals with special needs such as allergies or behavioral problems such as aggressiveness? How will people drop off and pick up their pets? Will your business need insurance in case an animal is injured or dies while in your care?

 A little repetition is okay. The description of how your business will operate is likely to be the longest section of your plan and will probably discuss topics that are also covered elsewhere. No problem. For example, you should discuss the key issue of how you will establish and keep a competitive edge in your big-picture business description and in your marketing strategy section. (See Section 5, below.)

Use the process of writing your business description as an opportunity to change or refine your business idea. When you write and rewrite this section, you'll probably come up with ideas and questions you haven't yet thought through. If so, great—this gives you an opportunity to fill in the gaps before you actually open for business. And even if you discover a flaw so big that you decide not to start the business after all, your business plan has done its job. While undoubtedly disappointing, it's far better for your business to fail on paper than in real life.

3. Define Your Market

Who will buy your product or service? Even the most innovative business will fail if it doesn't quickly find enough customers to make a profit. In this section, your task is to demonstrate to a potential investor or lender (or convince yourself) that there are indeed customers out there, ready and willing to buy your product or service. Use whatever data you can get your hands on to demonstrate this. And don't neglect your imagination— unconventional arguments are fine as long as they are convincing. Here is a brief list of points you may wish to make:

- Similar businesses have been successful. For example, if several fitness clubs with Internet access are all the rage in L.A., you might explain why this is a good indication that your similar business would succeed in Sacramento, where the market is currently dominated by less-cutting-edge gyms.

- Marketing surveys or demographic reports point to a growing need for your product or service. For instance, to buttress your contention that there will be a need for your new line of paralegal training materials, point to U.S. government reports listing paralegals as one of the fastest-growing occupations.

- Media reports confirm the popularity of and demand for your business. For example, include newspaper clips or transcripts of television news reports on the surge of demand for antibacterial air fresheners as evidence that your germ-killing Sani-Scent™ will sell.

- Your conversations with potential customers show a need for your business. It's often a good idea to carry out an informal survey of your most likely customers and include the results. For example, if you will run a business repairing and reconditioning acoustic guitars and similar stringed instruments, you might include results of a survey of guitarists and other musicians on what kind of repair services they need, as well as quotes from them saying that they'd use your services.

In addition to claiming that there is a solid market for your business, do your best to define and describe exactly who makes it up. If you're opening a bar with live entertainment, for instance, you might identify your market as primarily childless, urban 21- to 35-year-olds who tend to have more disposable income and leisure time than others. Similarly, if you're planning an antique restoration service, you might identify your target market as professionals and others in the 40–70 age range with household incomes of $100,000 or more. The better you can show that you know exactly who your market is, the more confident lenders and investors will be that you can actually find these people and sell to them.

Include a profile of your target customer. Explain why and how this fictional person would need your product or service. Do your best to flesh out a believable person, right down to the color of his or her socks. Creating a typical customer gives a face to an otherwise abstract market definition and gives your market analysis more impact.

4. Analyze Your Competition

Just because you have a great business idea doesn't mean you'll be successful—other businesses may have already cornered the market or be poised to do so. For example, lots of small-business owners who ran successful movie-rental businesses were wiped out when chains like Blockbuster rolled out thousands of megastores. It's often all too easy for a bigger, better-capitalized outfit to copy your best features and pull the rug out from under your business. Use this section to explain why your business really will have few direct competitors—or, if competitors will abound (as is far more likely), to show how your business will develop and keep an edge. Don't be shy about detailing competitors' strengths as well as weaknesses as part of showing why your business will better meet customers' needs.

In discussing the competition, it's important to put yourself in the shoes of a customer who is comparing your business to a competitor's. From the customer's perspective, what factors are most important in choosing which business to patronize? Some obvious considerations are quality of products or services, convenience (access), reliability, and price. Your competitors will probably excel in some of these areas and be weaker in others. The same will probably be true of your business. The trick is for you to find a spot, or niche, among the competition, and offer a combination of elements—such as price and convenience—that no one else offers.

! Think twice before competing on price. No matter how efficient your business is and how little you charge, someone will always charge less. Given the purchasing power and other efficiencies of big business, few small operators can successfully compete on pricing alone. Far better to look for another edge—quality, uniqueness, or customer convenience, to mention a few.

EXAMPLE: John wants to open a business to sell and service classic cars. In developing his business idea, he discovers that there are about a dozen existing companies within a 20-mile radius of his proposed location that already provide some or all of the services he envisions. Before finally committing to opening the business, he needs to identify and create a convincing competitive edge. One day, talking to a friend, he realizes that his edge could be a better system for finding parts. If he could locate new and used classic car parts nationwide, rather than just in his region, he would have a huge advantage over other shops. John begins by developing a database of websites that specialize in classic and reproduction car parts, organized by make and model. By using these online dealers—plus other dealers nationwide who aren't online,

but whom John will get to know as he attends regional trade shows and does more national business—John will be able to get parts faster than any of his competitors. Putting some extra energy into the parts aspect of his business gives John a key marketing hook to convince his knowledgeable (and often finicky) customers that his business really is a step ahead.

Businesses With Specialized Knowledge Are Hard to Copy

The business owner who knows the most about how to beat out competitors usually wins. But what is business knowledge, and how can you exploit it? In the broad sense, it's anything a business knows how to do that can give it a meaningful edge over competitors. Common examples include:

- the ability to buy products for resale cheaper than competitors
- a great location
- a unique, hard-to-duplicate product
- excellent customer service, and
- superior customer accessibility—longer hours or better parking, for example.

Consider the example of Laura and Brad's import business. They were importing clothing from Guatemala, but with competition from hundreds of other small importers, it was hard to make a dime. Leaving Brad to manage the business for a few weeks, Laura spent some time working with a dozen weavers in a small Guatemalan town. They focused on creating specially woven and dyed Guatemalan fabric suitable for luxury window coverings. Realizing that the high end of the import business was an underexploited niche, Laura quickly created a product with a hard-to-copy look and a solid profit margin. In short, she transformed a not particularly savvy, barely profitable import business into a highly intelligent, highly profitable one.

5. Describe Your Marketing Strategy

By now you've shown that there are people out there who will buy your product or service from you instead of from your competitors. Great, but your job isn't done. Investors and others interested in supporting your business will want to know how you'll reach your customers in a cost-effective way. The answer to this question is, in a nutshell, your marketing strategy.

Any marketing strategy worthy of the name should be based on the particular characteristics of the market you're trying to reach, with the goal of reaching as many customers as possible for the least expense. For instance, if you're trying to reach a very tiny group of people, such as left-handed ophthalmologists, or even a slightly larger audience, such as digital video editors, it makes no sense to spend the big bucks required for television advertising. On the other hand, if your market consists of all children between the ages of six and ten, TV advertising might be an efficient way to reach them.

In describing your plan for reaching your customers, explain what methods you will use, such as radio or newspaper advertising, Web marketing, or directory listings such as trade directories or the Yellow Pages. If you plan to use nontraditional guerrilla marketing tactics such as putting up posters all around town or staging publicity stunts, explain exactly what you plan to do. And no matter what kind of marketing strategy you outline, be sure to explain why you think it will work.

Small businesses that don't have much of a marketing budget shouldn't be shy about their smaller-scale plans. Even if you don't plan to spend much (if any) money on marketing or advertising, you should have a plan for how you'll reach your first customers. In your business plan, simply explain what this strategy is. The following example shows how a small business with a minimal advertising and marketing budget might explain its strategy.

EXAMPLE: Turtlevision's Marketing Strategy

We plan to keep our marketing costs very low, at least for the first year or two. Rather than spending money on traditional advertising, Turtlevision's strategy will be to list services in local video-related directories and use various online communities to promote the business. In addition, the plan for the early days of Turtlevision is to offer services at a discount to various nonprofit organizations to develop a strong portfolio and to generate good word of mouth. For example, Turtlevision is currently providing discounted services to the nonprofit Film Foundation to stream a monthly short film and video series on the Web. The hope is that recommendations from our satisfied customers will give Turtlevision a start in the right direction.

Spam is bad. No matter how delectable you find the potted meat product, do not fool yourself into believing that sending out masses of unsolicited emails (a practice known as "spamming") will be good for your business. Most Web-savvy entrepreneurs already know what nutritionists have told us for years—spam is bad for you. At the very least, it's bad for any goodwill that may exist for your business. No one likes getting junk email, no matter what fabulous deal it may offer. Be a good Net citizen and use more savory marketing tactics than spam.

 Marketing without advertising can be successful. Especially in niche or local markets, people often make purchasing decisions based on the recommendations of people they respect, not on ads. If you doubt this, think about how you chose your dentist, plumber, or the company that recently fixed your roof. Chances are good that you got a recommendation from someone you trusted. To be the beneficiary of positive word of mouth, you need to run an excellent business. Assuming you do, there are loads of cost-effective ways to let potential customers know about your great service. For a book full of great ideas, read *Marketing Without Advertising,* by

Michael Phillips and Salli Rasberry (Nolo). Its subtitle, *Inspire Customers to Rave About Your Business to Create Lasting Success,* explains exactly why every small businessperson should read it.

6. Describe Your Business Accomplishments

Above and beyond demonstrating the beauty of your business idea, you'll want to show that you're the right person to run it. Do this by creating a résumé showing your business accomplishments. Here you have the chance to highlight all of your relevant experience and training, as well as any other personal information likely to inspire confidence in you as a businessperson.

Prospective lenders and investors will want to know the following things about you:

- **Do you understand the business?** Emphasize that you understand the basic tasks of the business inside and out. Surprisingly, lots of people start small businesses in areas in which they are amateurs. (For example, a person who isn't mechanically inclined but who loves German cars may want to open a VW repair shop.) Lack of hands-on experience will likely be a red flag to investors, who know a nonexpert boss can't roll up his or her sleeves and help out in emergencies. Do your best to show them otherwise.
- **Can you manage people?** All sorts of organizations, including small businesses, fail because their leaders—no matter how technically competent—can't work well with others. Bad people management is one of the surest ways to create a poor workplace atmosphere, one with low morale, mediocre productivity, and high turnover. If you have successfully worked with, and preferably led, people, emphasize this experience.
- **Do you understand money?** A surprising number of people who open small businesses don't know how to manage—or

make—money. Even though their business idea is a good, competitive one and their employees are energetic, they make such poor financial decisions that their businesses don't prosper. Knowing this, people who will consider funding your business will want to see if you or another key person in your business has money management skills. If you do—even if your experience was in a very different business—emphasize it.

C. Making Financial Projections

In addition to describing how your business will work, including how it will reach plenty of customers and fend off competitors, you'll also need to do some number-crunching to show that it will in fact turn a profit. All the rosy descriptions in the world won't make it a success if the numbers turn up red.

Projecting the finances of your business may seem intimidating or difficult, but in reality it's not terribly complex. Basically, it consists of making educated guesses about how much money you'll need to spend and how much you'll take in, then using these estimates to calculate whether your business will be sufficiently profitable.

Predicting and planning the finances of your business are important not only to attract investors, but also to demonstrate to you and your family that your business idea will fly. If your first projections show your business losing money, you'll have an opportunity while still in the planning stage to make sensible adjustments, such as raising your prices or cutting costs. If you neglect to make financial projections, you won't realize your plan is a money loser until you actually start losing money. At that point, it may be too late to turn things around.

Nonetheless, many new entrepreneurs avoid crunching their numbers, often due to fear that their estimates will be wildly off-base and yield useless results. This is a poor reason to avoid forecasting your finances. If you do your best to make realistic predictions of expenses and revenues and accept that your guesstimates will not be absolutely correct, you can learn a great deal about what the financial side of your business is likely to look like in its early months and even years of operation. Even a somewhat inaccurate picture of your business's likely finances will be much more helpful than no picture at all.

For a basic understanding of your business's projected financial situation, you'll need to make the following estimates and calculations, all of which are discussed in detail in the rest of this chapter:

- **a break-even analysis.** Here you use income and expense estimates for a year or more to see whether, in theory at least, your business will be able to turn a profit. If you have trouble projecting a solid profit, you might need to consider abandoning your idea altogether.

- **a profit/loss forecast.** Here you'll refine the sales and expense estimates that you used for your break-even analysis into a formal, month-by-month projection of your business's net profit for at least the first year of operations.

- **a start-up cost estimate.** As the name suggests, this is simply the total of all the expenses you'll incur before your business opens. These costs should be included in your business plan to give a true picture of how much money you'll need to get your business off the ground.

- **a cash flow projection.** Even if your profit/loss forecast tells you that your business will have higher revenues than expenses, that doesn't mean that you'll always have enough cash available on key dates such as when rent is due or when you need to buy more inventory. A cash flow projection lays out how much cash you'll have—or how much you'll be short—month by month. This lets you know if you'll need to get a credit line or set up other arrangements to make sure funds are available.

Get to Know Your Numbers

The calculations involved in accounting aren't terribly complex. The main reason people get confused is not that they're bad at math—it's that they don't understand what the numbers mean. It's important that you take a little time early on to learn what your key financial numbers are, and how they relate to one another. To help you keep the numbers straight, keep in mind this formula (see Section D2, above, for an explanation of "costs of sale" and "fixed costs"):

$$
\begin{array}{rl}
& \text{sales revenue} \\
- & \text{costs of sale (variable costs)} \\
= & \text{gross profit} \\
- & \text{overhead (fixed costs)} \\
= & \text{net profit} \\
- & \text{taxes} \\
= & \text{after-tax profit}
\end{array}
$$

You'll have a much easier time understanding all the various financial calculations involved in accounting—including break-even, profit/loss, and cash flow analysis—once you're familiar and comfortable with this basic formula.

To make these financial forecasts, you could use accounting software, a simple spreadsheet program such as *Excel*—or even a calculator and some blank ledger sheets. With accounting software, most of your calculations can be done automatically with the click of a button, which can be very helpful when you're in the planning stages and trying out lots of different numbers.

If you plan to use software for bookkeeping and accounting once your business is started, you might as well also use it to prepare your financial projections. Accounting software is relatively easy to figure out and will definitely save you lots of time in the long run. *Quickbooks, Quicken Home & Business, MYOB Accounting* and *Peachtree Accounting* are very popular and priced within reach of just about any budget. Magazines such as *Home*

Office Computing, MacWorld, and *PC World* are good sources of information on other programs.

Once you start shopping for accounting and bookkeeping software, you'll probably also find special business plan software. Most of these programs, however, provide you with only a word processing function and some empty spreadsheets to fill in. Most real accounting software includes the same kinds of spreadsheets, and usually a lot more. Chances are the word processing program you already have is a lot more powerful than whatever is offered with a business plan program.

The rest of this chapter will walk you step by step through each of these financial forecasts. When you're done, you should be able to tell whether your business will actually make enough money to pay the bills and turn a profit. Assuming the answer is yes, you'll also see whether you need to obtain start-up money from investors or lenders and if so, how much. Finally, once your business is up and running, you can refer back to your forecasts to see how your performance is measuring up.

D. Break-Even Analysis

Your break-even point is the point at which the income you'll bring in just covers your expenses. Expenses include the costs of providing your product or service (also known as variable costs, since they change depending on how many products or services you provide), plus your overhead, which includes rent, salaries, and utility bills (commonly called fixed costs).

Because break-even analysis offers a glimpse of your ultimate profitability, it's a great tool for weeding out losing business ideas. For example, if you see that you'll need to achieve a highly optimistic sales number just to cover your costs, you should rethink your entire business plan. Maybe you'll figure out a way to adjust parts of your business so that you can realize a profit from lower sales. If not, it might be best to ditch your less-than-brilliant business idea.

To find your break-even point, first make a best-guess estimate of your sales revenue for the products or services you plan to sell. Then predict how much profit you'll make on each sale (by subtracting the costs of the sale from the revenue it will generate), and figure out a "gross profit percentage"—how much of each sales dollar exceeds the cost of the product or service itself. Finally, estimate what your fixed costs (such as rent and insurance) will be. After a few calculations, you'll see whether the profit you'll make on each individual sale (also called gross profit) will cover your fixed costs.

Before we go into the details of calculating your break-even point, let's look at a very simple example to illustrate the overall process. All the calculations are explained in more detail below; for now, just focus on the process as a whole.

EXAMPLE: Michele is starting a business selling her own handmade jewelry. To calculate her break-even point, she makes her very best estimate of how much jewelry she thinks she could sell in a year. She figures she could sell an average of 20 pieces a month at $20 apiece, making her yearly income $4,800. Then she figures out how much she'd make on each sale, above the cost of materials. (For this super-simplified example, let's leave the cost of her time out of the equation.) Since the materials for each piece cost Michele $5, she'd be making $15 on each sale. In other words, her gross profit would be $15 per piece. Next she calculates her gross profit percentage, which is her gross profit ($15) divided by her selling price ($20). This puts her gross profit percentage at 75%, which means that .75 of each sales dollar exceeds of the cost of the piece of jewelry itself. Next Michele would figure out what her fixed costs would be—the cost of her tools and the monthly fee for her booth at a local arts and crafts mall. She figures that these fixed costs total $50 per month, or $600 per year.

To calculate her break-even point, Michele will divide her annual fixed costs ($600) by her gross profit percentage (.75) to arrive at $800. This means that just to cover the costs of the materials, and her tools and booth, Michele must bring in $800 per year; anything above that amount will be her pre-tax profit. Since she earlier estimated that she could sell $4,800 worth of jewelry per year, Michele figures that she'll easily reach her break-even point—and make a $4,000 profit as well.

Before we explain exactly how to do the calculations, we'll quickly discuss two items that you need to understand before actually crunching your numbers: making financial estimates and categorizing your expenses.

1. Making Estimates

When you estimate your income and expenses, your estimates should extend over enough time to catch up with seasonal fluctuations. Depending on your type of business, your revenue and expenses may vary wildly from month to month. For example, if you plan to manufacture custom snowboards, most of your sales will be in the late fall and early winter months, while the opposite would be true if you made surfboards. A good way to account for this is to make estimates for each month of the year, then add them up to get a yearly figure. We recommend covering at least a one-year period, which is enough time to account for normal ups and downs, but not so long as to be overly speculative.

2. Categorizing Your Expenses

Your business expenses break down into two categories: fixed expenses (fixed costs) and variable expenses (variable costs). This division is not only important for your break-even analysis, it's also a standard method of categorizing expenses for accounting and tax reporting. Here's the difference.

- **Fixed costs.** Commonly referred to as "overhead," these include all regular expenses not directly tied to the product or service you provide. Rent, utility bills, phone bills, payments for outside help such as bookkeeping services, postage, and most salaries (except in service businesses) are common fixed costs.

- **Variable costs.** These costs—sometimes also called product costs, costs of goods, or costs of sale—are directly related to the products or services you provide and include inventory, packaging, supplies, materials, and sometimes labor used in providing your product or service. They're called "variable" precisely because they go up or down depending on the volume of products or services you produce or sell. (In the case of services, one of the biggest variable expenses is almost always the wages or salary of the service provider—see "Salaries and Labor Costs—Fixed or Variable?" below.)

Salaries and Labor Costs—Fixed or Variable?

Whether you'll categorize labor expenses as fixed or variable costs often depends on the type of workers you pay and the kinds of products or services you're selling. Salaries or wages of the managers and employees who are necessary to keep your business going (you or your bookkeeper, for example) are usually best seen as fixed costs. But salaries or wages for employees who create the products or provide the services you sell may be more appropriately treated as variable costs. For example, an ad agency that pays six freelance copywriters to service clients' accounts should treat their paychecks as variable costs.

To figure out whether a labor cost should be designated as fixed or variable, ask yourself: If I sell one, ten or 100 more products or services this week, will my labor costs go up? If not, you're probably looking at a fixed cost. For instance, suppose you're trying to decide whether your receptionist's salary should be categorized as a variable cost or a fixed cost. If you produce and sell 100 more Mr. Hankey dolls, will your reception costs go up? Probably not. So your receptionist's salary should be part of your overhead. But if you have to hire five temporary employees to handle the phones at Christmastime to handle the spiking demand for Mr. Hankeys, their wages should be classified as variable costs. (Hint: Money paid to workers who are temps or independent contractors are usually categorized as variable costs, because those payments are usually tied to providing a product or service.) Of course, if you sell more products or services regularly, you'll probably decide to expand your business and increase your overhead, because you'll have to hire more support staff, managers, and other necessary employees just to get along. At that point, you might revisit your allocation of fixed and variable costs.

3. Estimate Your Sales Revenue

Start your break-even analysis by making your best estimate of annual sales revenues. Your estimate will obviously depend on several different variables, such as your type of business, what you plan to charge for each product or service you'll offer, and how successful you'll be at selling products and services.

Though at first it may seem overwhelming to project revenues based upon so many untested variables, it is essential that you take the plunge and try out some numbers. Even though your estimates won't be anywhere near 100% accurate, they'll force you to focus and refine key elements of your business idea and may even help you spot big potholes in your plan. And besides, you need these estimates to move ahead with your break-even calculations, so get over it and start estimating.

One good way to estimate how much money you'll be bringing in is to compare your business to similar ones. Retail businesses, for example, often measure annual sales revenue per square foot of retail space. Thus, if you plan to open a pet supply store, you'll want to find out the annual sales revenue per square foot of other pet supply shops. While direct competitors probably won't share this information, industry trade publications almost always provide it. Attending industry trade shows where you can meet and talk to people who own similar businesses in other parts of the country is another good way to gather valuable information.

EXAMPLE: Inga is planning to open a used bookstore in San Francisco called Inga's Book Haus. She plans to sell mostly used books, which generally have a high profit margin, but she'll also stock a limited selection of new books at the front of the store to attract more customers. She'll sell some miscellaneous trinkets like postcards and magnets as well.

To figure out how much sales revenue she can realistically expect for Inga's Book Haus, Inga calls up a couple friends who happen to be in the book business. One who works at a nearby used bookstore confides to Inga that the store sells approximately $450 worth of books per square foot per year. Another friend owns a new and used bookstore in a Pasadena; she tells Inga that they bring in about $400 annually per square foot. Neither of these stores is exactly like the one Inga envisions; the one in San Francisco doesn't sell any new books, and the one in Pasadena does a healthy trade in textbooks, which Inga doesn't expect at her store. To round out her information, Inga also looks into some trade publications and does a bit of sleuthing at local new-and-used bookstores, examining their prices and how busy they seem to be. Ultimately she decides that an annual income of $350 per square foot is realistic. She has her eye on a few storefronts, all around 1,200 square feet, so she estimates her annual revenues to be $420,000.

Basing your projected revenue on the numbers of similar companies also works for nonretail businesses such as wholesaling or manufacturing companies—but, it can be somewhat tricky to find a solid basis for comparison. Unlike retail businesses, sales per square foot wouldn't really apply. If you're not already well acquainted with your field, you'll have to do some research. Study similar businesses to find out how many employees they have, how wide their distribution is, and how much annual income they earn. Base your income projections on similarly sized businesses with a comparable range of distribution.

If yours is a service business, your estimate of sales revenue will depend on how many billable sales you'll be able to make each month. A big part of this calculation is how many hours you and any employees will work and how much you'll be paid per hour by your clients. But don't overlook the fact that all of your time won't be billable—you won't be providing services every hour you're at work. For example, if you run a landscaping business, a sizable portion of your time will not be spent performing landscaping work, but managing your accounts, maintaining your equipment, and

soliciting new clients. You'll need to make a realistic assessment of how much of your time will be taken up by these nonbillable activities and how much time you'll spend providing actual services to clients to get an accurate picture of how much money will be flowing in.

4. Calculate Your Average Gross Profit Percentage

Your next task is to figure your average gross profit percentage. That may sound complex, but basically it's just a figure that represents how much of each sales dollar will be left over after paying for the costs of the products or services themselves. There are a number of steps involved in calculating this figure, but none involve anything more than simple math (addition, subtraction, multiplication, and division). Once you know your average gross profit percentage, you'll easily be able to figure out how much money you'll need to bring in to cover all the costs of your business.

In a nutshell, to figure your average gross profit percentage you'll need to:

1. Figure out your gross profit for each major category of your products or services.
2. Determine an average gross profit for your business overall, including all your products and services.
3. Divide your average gross profit by your average selling price.

In case you're wondering what the difference is between "gross profit" and "average gross profit," here's a quick explanation. (The details will be covered as we go through the calculations below.) When you sell an individual product, the money that you earn above the cost of the item itself (called your variable cost, or sometimes cost of goods) is called gross profit. For instance, if your pet store sells a doghouse for $200, and you bought the doghouse for $110, then what's left over for you after the sale is $90—your gross profit. If your business sells more than one kind of product, you'll need to calculate an *average* gross profit for your total product line in order to get a realistic figure. The average gross profit for your pet store would include all of your products—cat scratching posts, pet food, play toys, and so on— including their sale prices and what they cost you.

The next few subsections take you through the process of calculating your business's average gross profit.

a. Figure Your Gross Profit by Category

As described above, your gross profit is the amount of money you make on each sale, above what it costs you to provide the product or service—that is, the variable cost, or cost of sale. Gross profit is determined simply by subtracting the variable cost of your product or service from its sales price.

Variable costs are generally fairly easy to estimate. If you're selling products bought from a wholesaler, your variable costs may be as simple as what you pay for the products themselves. If you'll assemble the products, then include your costs for the parts and labor needed to put them together. Also remember to include items like packaging or freebies in your variable costs. If you only sell services, variable costs basically include what you pay to whomever provides the services (you or perhaps an employee), not including time spent on administrative tasks and managing accounts, which is generally considered to be a fixed, not variable, cost. It can sometimes be tricky to figure out the variable costs of a service business. Do your best to separate out the costs that are not associated with individual projects—those are your fixed costs.

> **EXAMPLE:** Turtlevision, a digital video editing service, pays its staff editor $50 per hour for 80 hours per month of editing work. In addition, Turtlevision pays an office assistant $15 per hour for 100 hours per month of administrative work. Turtlevision's monthly variable costs

would include the editor's salary of $4,000, but not the salary paid to the office assistant, which is not tied to any particular client or project.

One kink in figuring out your business's gross profit is that your selling prices and variable costs may vary a great deal from product to product (or service to service). For instance, say you buy cat collars for an average of $4, and sell them for an average price of $10 (your gross profit per cat collar would be $6). Doghouses, on the other hand, cost you an average of $110, and you sell them for an average price of $200 (your gross profit per doghouse would be $90).

To account for these differences, you should categorize your products or services and figure an average gross profit for each category. There are a few steps to follow, but hang in there—each one is pretty simple.

First, estimate the average selling price and average variable cost for products or services with roughly similar selling prices and variable costs. For instance, you might group all your animal collars together—for cats, dogs, and ferrets—since their selling prices ($9 to $13) and variable costs ($3 to $5) aren't too different. Don't lump together products or services with considerably different selling prices or variable costs. As a general rule, the more tightly you define your categories, the more accurate your estimates will be.

After you've estimated the average selling price and average variable cost for each category, subtract the average variable cost from the average selling price for each category, and you'll have an average gross profit dollar figure for each category.

	Animal collars	Bird-houses	Dog-houses
Average selling price	$11	$60	$200
− Average variable cost	4	30	110
= Average gross profit	$7	$30	$90

The next step is to figure out a gross profit percentage for each category. A gross profit percentage tells you how much of each dollar of sales income is gross profit. To calculate each category's gross profit percentage, divide the average gross profit figure by the average selling price.

Animal collars category:

	Average gross profit	$ 7
÷	Average selling price	$ 11
=	Gross profit percentage	63.6%

Using the above example, it follows that if you sold $1,500 in cat collars, 63.6% of that—$954— would be gross profit, or the amount left over after paying costs of sale. As you can see, converting your gross profit into a percentage allows you to quickly figure out how much of your income will be left over after variable costs have been covered.

b. Calculate Your Average Gross Profit

After you've found the gross profit percentage for each category, you'll be able to determine your average gross profit for your business as a whole.

First, estimate your annual sales revenue per category. Earlier you estimated your total annual sales revenues; now divide that figure as best you can into your estimates for each category. For example, if you estimated total annual revenues of $100,000 for your pet supply business, divide that among your categories, such as collars, birdhouses, and doghouses—say $25,000 in collar sales, $40,000 in birdhouses, and $35,000 in doghouses. Base your division on your best sense of which categories and products will make up a big part of your business, and which will have a smaller share. Then, for each product category, multiply the estimated sales revenue by the category's gross profit percentage (arrived at above) to arrive at your total gross profit dollars per category.

Animal collars category:

	Estimated sales revenue	$25,000
x	Gross profit percentage	63.6%
=	Total gross profit	$15,900

Finally, add together the gross profit dollar amounts for each category to arrive at a total annual gross profit for your business. Divide the total annual gross profit figure by the total annual sales that you estimated for all products or services. The result will be an average gross profit percentage for your business.

Let's look at how this process works with Inga's Book Haus.

EXAMPLE: As you may recall, Inga plans to sell new and used books, plus some peripheral items such as postcards and refrigerator magnets. Since the profit margins for new books, used books, and trinkets are different, Inga figures a gross profit percentage for each of these categories. (Inga might want to establish separate categories for hardback, paperback, and coffee-table books, but we'll keep things simple.)

To accomplish this, first Inga estimates an average variable cost for each category. In addition to the cost of the merchandise, she includes the cost of free bags, bookmarks, and wrapping paper for gifts. For instance, used books cost her an average of $3, and she figures the bookmarks and bags that go with each sale will cost her an average of 10¢. So her total average variable cost in the used book category is $3.10. She doesn't include fixed costs, like rent or salaries, here.

Next, Inga fills in an average selling price for each product category. Her average selling price for used books, for example, is $7. She then subtracts the average variable cost (arrived at above) from the average selling price to get an average gross profit figure for each product category. Subtracting her average variable cost for used books ($3.10) from her average selling price for used books ($7) leaves her with an average gross profit for used books of $3.90.

Used book category:

Average sales price	$ 7.00
− Average variable cost	3.10
= Average gross profit	$ 3.90

Inga does the same calculations for new books, which also shows an average gross profit at $3.90, and trinkets, which has an average gross profit of $1.40.

To determine the gross profit percentage, she'll simply divide the gross profit by the selling price in each category to get a gross profit percentage for each category. Dividing her average gross profit for used books ($3.90) by her average selling price ($7) gives Inga a gross profit percentage of 56% for used books, a good percentage. That means that for every dollar she'll bring in from used books, 44 cents per dollar will be eaten up on Inga's costs, leaving 56 cents per dollar to cover fixed costs and go towards a net profit. Her gross profit percentage for new books is 33%, and for trinkets it's an impressive 70%, as shown below.

New book category:

Average gross profit	$ 3.90
÷ Average selling price	$12.00
= Gross profit percentage	33%

Trinkets category:

Average gross profit	$ 1.40
÷ Average selling price	$ 2.00
= Gross profit percentage	70%

Using the gross profit percentages and estimated sales revenues for each category, Inga can calculate the gross profit dollar figure for each category. For example, her estimated annual sales of used books is $300,000. (Remember from Section 3 that Inga estimated her total annual sales revenue to be $420,000. She thinks used books will account for a little over ⅔ of her sales.) By multiplying $300,000 by the used book category's gross profit percentage (56%), she estimates an annual gross profit of $168,000. Adding up the gross profit figures for each category, Inga figures that her total gross profit will be $215,000. Finally, by dividing this

amount by her annual estimated revenues of $420,000, she easily determines her total gross profit percentage, which is 51.2%.

	New books	Used books	Trinkets
Average variable cost per product	$ 8.00	$ 3.00	$ .50
+ bookmarks, bags	.10	.10	.10
= Average total cost	$ 8.10	$ 3.10	$ .60
Average selling price	$12.00	$ 7.00	$2.00
− Average total variable cost	8.10	3.10	.60
= Average gross profit	$ 3.90	$ 3.90	$1.40
Average gross profit	$ 3.90	$ 3.90	$1.40
÷ Average selling price	12.00	7.00	2.00
= Gross profit percentage	33%	56%	70%
Average sales	$100,000	$300,000	$20,000
x Gross profit percentage	33%	56%	70%
= Annual gross profit	$ 33,000	$168,000	$14,000

Annual gross profit	
New books	$ 33,000
+ Used books	168,000
+ Trinkets	14,000
= Total annual gross profit	$ 215,000
÷ Total annual sales	$ 420,000
= Average gross profit percentage	51.2%

5. Estimate Your Fixed Costs

You're done with the hard part—compared to calculating your gross profit percentage, fixed costs are a breeze. Simply estimate your monthly fixed expenses, including items like rent, utility bills, office supplies, uncollectable debts—basically, any anticipated costs that don't depend on the product or service you sell. Since many of these costs recur monthly, it's usually easiest to estimate them per

DRAFTING AN EFFECTIVE BUSINESS PLAN

month and total them for one year. It's also a good idea to throw in a little extra—say 10% or so—to cover miscellaneous expenses that you can't predict. Once you've arrived at a total, you'll know that you'll need to make at least this much gross profit (and probably a healthy chunk more) to keep your business afloat.

EXAMPLE: Here is a list of Inga's monthly estimates for fixed costs.

Rent	$3,500
Wages for part-time clerks	2,500
Utilities	800
Telephone	700
Office equipment	700
Insurance	500
Advertising	700
Accounting	300
Electronic payment system fees	300
Misc.	1,000
Total fixed expenses per month	$11,000
Annual total fixed expenses (monthly expenses x 12)	$132,000

Don't forget you have to eat. Notice that Inga has chosen not to list a salary here as an expense. She, like many sole proprietors, figures that her savings, help from friends and family, and some extra crumbs the business may produce should be enough to live on for the short term. Once she figures out how much profit the business will bring in regularly, she'll decide how much profit she can expect to take out of the business and add that number to her fixed costs. Leaving out payments for your own living expenses in your break-even analysis, however, can be dangerous, at least if you're planning to live off your business's profits from the get-go. If this is your plan, you should add to your fixed costs the minimum amount you'll need to take out of the business to cover your living expenses. Then, if you can't project your income to be higher than your fixed costs when the amount you'll need for living expenses is included, you'll know you can't plan on

living off the company. This may be a clue that your business is not a good bet.

Keep fixed costs as low as reasonably possible. If your business is slow to get started—and lots of businesses take months or even years to become solidly profitable—high fixed costs can quickly eat up your savings. Rather than committing yourself to high overhead, it's usually better to keep expenses low, allowing increases only when your income justifies spending more. For example, few businesses really depend on a pricey physical location for their success. If your business won't depend on a big casual walk-in trade, don't overpay for a trendy zip code. Operating from a low-cost warehouse district, an older office building, or even your garage may work just fine, at least at the beginning.

6. Calculate Your Break-Even Point

Once you have estimated your fixed costs (from Section 5, above) and your average gross profit percentage (from Section 4, above), it's easy to figure out how much revenue you'll need to break even. Remember, your gross profit percentage represents how much of each dollar of revenue is actual profit, left over after paying for the product or service itself. To figure out your break-even point, you'll divide your estimated annual fixed costs by your gross profit percentage. The result will be your break-even point—the amount of sales revenue you'll need to bring in just to cover your costs.

EXAMPLE: The break-even point for Inga's Book Haus will equal her annual fixed expenses divided by her average gross profit percentage.

Annual fixed expenses	$132,000
÷ Average gross profit percentage	51.2%
= Break-even point	$257,813

If you're having trouble understanding how this equation works, you're not alone. Conceptually, it's a little tricky to see how dividing your fixed costs by your gross profit percentage yields your break-even point. Think of it this way: However much money your business brings in, some of it will be eaten up by the cost of the product or service itself (your variable costs), leaving you a reduced amount left over to pay your bills. How much is left over is determined by your gross profit percentage—this number tells you just how much will be left over, on average, from each dollar, after paying for your product or service itself (your variable costs). When you divide your estimated annual fixed costs by your gross profit percentage, the resulting number (the break-even point) is the exact amount that's enough to cover all of your costs.

EXAMPLE: Let's look at another extra-simplified example to illustrate this concept. Remember Michele, from earlier in the chapter, who was going into business selling jewelry? Her gross profit percentage was 75%, meaning that for every dollar she brought in, 25¢ would be eaten up by the cost of the jewelry materials, leaving Michele 75¢ to cover her fixed costs. Michele's fixed costs were $600 per year. So, you're wondering, why isn't Michele's break-even point $600? Because if Michele earned exactly $600 in a year, only 75% of that would be available to cover her fixed costs—the other 25% would have already been eaten up by the costs of her jewelry, and she wouldn't be able to pay all of the $600 in fixed costs. To account for this, Michele needs to divide her fixed costs ($600) by her gross profit percentage (75%) to arrive at the higher amount that she'll need to bring in to cover both her fixed costs and her variable costs. Dividing $600 by .75 results in $800, her break-even point; if Michele brings in $800, 25% of it will go towards the cost of the product, and the rest ($600) is just enough to cover her fixed costs.

7. Analyze Your Result

If your estimated revenue exceeds your break-even point, great—but that's not the same thing as saying you are free to put the excess money in your pocket. Again, remember that every dollar you bring in doesn't come for free; you had to pay something for the products or services that brought in that money. The portion of excess sales revenue that's really yours (ignoring taxes for the moment) is equivalent to (you guessed it) your gross profit percentage of that excess revenue. In order to determine how much of the excess revenue is pretax profit, multiply the excess by your gross profit percentage. The result is your estimated net profit.

EXAMPLE: Earlier, Inga estimated her annual sales revenue to be $420,000—over $160,000 more than she needs to break even.

Estimated revenue	$420,000
− Break-even point	257,813
= Excess revenues	$162,187

To figure out how much of her excess revenue will be actual pretax profit, Inga multiplies it by her gross profit percentage.

Excess revenues	$162,187
x Gross profit percentage	51.2%
= Net profit	$83,040

Inga is happy to see her projections show a profit. But she needs to remember that none of her estimates included any payments to herself, meaning she'll probably need to take some of that net profit just to meet her living expenses.

If, on the other hand, your break-even point is higher than your expected revenues, you'll have some decisions to make. You'll have to decide whether certain aspects of your plan can be amended in order to come up with an achievable break-even point. For instance, perhaps you could find a less expensive source of supplies, do without an employee, or save rent by working out of your home.

But don't change your numbers without a very good reason. When confronted by a break-even point that exceeds your estimated revenues, you may be tempted to tweak and squish your numbers into a profitable forecast, even if those numbers aren't realistic. Unless you really do have a good reason to think you can break even at a lower point, this is a temptation to guard against. For example, to have your plan pencil out in the black, you might boost your sales estimates in hopes that you'll somehow be able to pull it off. But can you really sell 50,000 Sausage Shooters™, 3,000 books on medieval dentistry, or 2,000 Tori Spelling mini-tees per month?

Generally speaking, when trying to pencil out a more profitable break-even point, it's best to focus on your costs. The most reliable way to tilt a business from the red to the black is to reduce what you will pay out, not to make a more optimistic projection of what you'll take in.

E. Profit/Loss Forecast

If your break-even analysis shows that, based on realistic estimates of revenue and expenses, your business will turn a profit, your next job is to use these figures to create the profit/loss forecast component of your business plan. Similar to a break-even analysis, a profit/loss forecast (sometimes called a P & L forecast) uses your estimates for sales revenue and variable costs to calculate your gross profit, then subtracts your fixed expenses from gross profit to arrive at net profit. If you use accounting software, it will generate a P & L statement automatically once you enter monthly sales and expense estimates.

The main difference between a P & L and a break-even analysis has to do with timing. A break-even analysis looks at profit and loss on a yearly basis, while your P & L forecast calculates monthly net profit. A P & L also differs from a cash flow projection, which we discuss in Section G, in the kinds of income and expenses that it includes. A cash flow

forecast looks at all sources of income and expenses, including loans, transfers of personal money into the business, start-up costs, and all other types of cash inflows and outflows. A P & L, on the other hand, is only concerned with money earned from normal business operations. For this reason, a P & L forecast will tell you whether your business operations are generating enough income to cover your expenses, something you can't glean from a cash flow forecast.

Here's how to translate your break-even figures into a profit/loss forecast. Start by breaking down your annual sales estimate into monthly amounts. If you expect significant seasonal fluctuations in sales, account for them here.

Next, figure your gross profit for each month. The easiest way to do this is to multiply each month's sales revenue by the gross profit percentage for your business as a whole, which you calculated earlier. (If you rounded off your gross profit percentage, you'll get a slightly different gross profit figure here than you did in your break-even analysis.)

Enter your monthly fixed expenses by category, and add them together to get monthly totals. Then, for each month, subtract your total fixed expenses from your gross profit and enter the result in the net profit row. If the result is a negative number, it means your expenses are more than your gross profit. Put parentheses around the result; in accounting symbols, a number in parentheses is a negative number.

⚠ Not a complete picture. Other income and costs such as loans and start-up expenses aren't included in your P & L statement, which reflects only money earned and spent as part of providing your products or services. For the full picture of all money that comes into and goes out from your business—including start-up costs, loans, taxes, and other money that isn't earned or spent as part of your core business operation— you'll need to do a cash flow analysis. (Predicting your cash flow is covered in Section G, below.)

EXAMPLE: Here's Inga's one-year profit/loss forecast for her bookstore:

Inga's Book Haus Profit/Loss Forecast: Year One Total

	Jan	Feb	Mar	April	May
Sales Revenues	$30,000	$35,000	$35,000	$35,000	$35,000
Gross Profit (51.2%)	**15,360**	**17,920**	**17,920**	**17,920**	**17,920**
Fixed Expenses					
Rent	3,500	3,500	3,500	3,500	3,500
Salaries	2,500	2,500	2,500	2,500	2,500
Utilities	800	800	800	800	800
Telephone	700	700	700	700	700
Office Equipment	700	700	700	700	700
Insurance	500	500	500	500	500
Advertising	700	700	700	700	700
Accounting	300	300	300	300	300
Fees for electronic payment system	300	300	300	300	300
Miscellaneous	1,000	1,000	1,000	1,000	1,000
Total Fixed Expenses	**11,000**	**11,000**	**11,000**	**11,000**	**11,000**
Net Profit (Loss)	**$4,360**	**$6,920**	**$6,920**	**$6,920**	**$6,920**

June	July	Aug	Sept	Oct	Nov	Dec	Year Total
$35,000	$35,000	$35,000	$35,000	$35,000	$35,000	$40,000	$420,000
17,920	**17,920**	**17,920**	**17,920**	**17,920**	**17,920**	**20,480**	**$215,040**
3,500	3,500	3,500	3,500	3,500	3,500	3,500	$42,000
2,500	2,500	2,500	2,500	2,500	2,500	2,500	$30,000
800	800	800	800	800	800	800	$9,600
700	700	700	700	700	700	700	$8,400
700	700	700	700	700	700	700	$8,400
500	500	500	500	500	500	500	$6,000
700	700	700	700	700	700	700	$8,400
300	300	300	300	300	300	300	$3,600
300	300	300	300	300	300	300	$3,600
1,000	1,000	1,000	1,000	1,000	1,000	1,000	$12,000
11,000	**11,000**	**11,000**	**11,000**	**11,000**	**11,000**	**11,000**	**$132,000**
$6,920	**$6,920**	**$6,920**	**$6,920**	**$6,920**	**$6,920**	**$9,480**	**$83,040**

A completed P & L will outline your business's profitability month-by-month. If your expenses are higher than revenues for a month or two, don't panic—most start-up businesses lose money for at least a few months—but you will need to figure out how to make it through these lean months (for example, by getting a start-up loan). More important in the big picture is whether you can see a trend toward stable profitability. If not, you may need to revisit parts of your plan (or possibly scrap your idea all together). But as mentioned earlier, resist the temptation to inflate your sales estimates; a more realistic approach is to lower your costs. Once you have a P & L that shows consistent profits each month, based on realistic estimates, you're ready to move forward.

F. Start-Up Cost Estimate

If your profit/loss forecast shows your projected income will be higher than expenses each month, great—but you haven't yet accounted for an important category of expenses: business start-up costs. The worst part about start-up costs is that you need to pay them before your business is actually making any money. That's why you should have a firm grasp on what you really need to spend to successfully start your business and a plan for where that money will come from. Of course, potential lenders or investors will want to

see that you've accounted for these costs in your planning. But it's also important that you understand for yourself how high this initial financial hurdle will be so that you can figure out how to clear it. Obviously, you don't want to start a business with high start-up costs but low projected profits, since it will take you far too long to recover your initial investment.

⚠️ **Buy only what your business really needs.** Too many new small business owners weigh down their new enterprises with unneeded start-up costs. Unless a particular item is absolutely necessary to generate revenue, don't buy it—or, if you do, spend as little as possible on it. Sure, you need a desk, but unless customers will see it (and sometimes even if they will), repainting a door and laying it across a couple of secondhand filing cabinets at a net cost of $40 makes a lot more sense than paying $800 for a new one.

Compared to the projections we just went through, estimating your start-up costs is a breeze—just list them and add them up. Include items like business registration fees and tax deposits you need to pay up front, rent and security deposits you'll have to pay before business starts, costs of any initial inventory, office supplies, equipment, and anything else you'll have to cover before your business starts bringing in money.

EXAMPLE: Inga makes a list of the start-up expenses she expects to pay before she'll start selling books.

Initial inventory	$20,000
Rent deposit (security deposit and last month's rent)	7,000
Office supplies, stationery	500
Fax machine	500
Business registration fees	200
TOTAL	$28,200

If you don't have enough cash to pay all of your start-up costs out of pocket, you'll either need to come up with the money or figure out a way to spread the costs over the first few months of business when you'll have at least some cash flowing in. For instance, maybe you could lease, rather than buy, needed equipment.

The next (and final) financial projection we'll do as part of your business plan—a cash flow projection—will help you plan and manage your incoming and outgoing cash so that you can cover needed expenses when they come due.

G. Cash Flow Projection

To round out the collection of financial information in your business plan, you should include a cash flow projection. While your profit/loss forecast may show that your business should make enough sales at a high enough price to cover your estimated expenses, a cash flow projection analyzes whether the cash from those sales, as well as from other sources, such as loans or investments, will come in fast enough to pay your bills on time. Cash flow management is important once your business is up and running, especially if you plan to stock a good-sized inventory or extend credit to customers. A high sales volume won't be enough to cover your expenses if your customers are slow to pay you and your checking account is empty.

Cash flow projection is also important in your planning stages in order to show how you intend to survive the first few lean months of business— particularly after you figure in your start-up expenses. If you'll have more than enough cash to cover your expenses for the first months of business, then you're one of the lucky few. More likely you'll be pressed to figure out how to cover a cash deficit for at least the first few months, and maybe longer. One way to do this is to put off or cut some expenses. Another is to get a loan or sell part of your business to investors, or to hit up your family or friends for a loan. The important thing is to do your best to predict your cash needs in advance, both to give yourself ample time to come up with a plan for getting the cash, and to inspire more confidence in lenders or investors.

Your cash flow projection will use many of the same figures you developed for your profit/loss forecast. The main difference is that you'll include all cash inflows and outflows, not just sales revenues and business expenses. Also, you'll record costs in the month that you expect to incur them, rather than simply spreading annual amounts equally over 12 months. Inflows and outflows of cash that belong in your cash flow analysis include loans, loan payments, and start-up costs. Once you're turning a profit, you'll also include tax payments in your cash flow analysis, but for now let's assume that you'll be free from taxes for your first year.

For each month, simply start your projection with the actual amount of cash your business will have on hand. Next, fill in your projected cash-ins for the month, which should include sales revenues, loans, transfers of personal money—basically any money that goes into your business checking account. Add these together along with the cash you have at the beginning of the month to get your total cash-ins for the month.

Next enter all your projected cash-outs for the month, such as your fixed expenses and any loan payments. Remember also to include costs of products and materials you use in your products or services—your variable costs. Add together all your cash-outs to obtain a total for the month. Subtract total monthly cash-outs from total monthly cash-ins and the result will be your cash left at the end of the month. That figure is also your beginning cash balance at the start of the next month; transfer it to the top of the next month's column, and do the whole process over again.

EXAMPLE: Inga projects her cash flow for her first year in business. She starts her projection one month early to account for the money she must spend before she opens her bookstore. In her cash-in section, she figures in $15,000 that she will put into the business: $9,000 of her own savings and an interest-free loan from her sister of $6,000. In her cash-out section, she includes what she'll pay for the initial setup of the business, as well as that month's

Inga's Book Haus Cash Flow Projection: Year One

	Dec	Jan	Feb	Mar	Apr	May
Cash at Beginning of Month	$0	($17,200)	($16,540)	($8,920)	($3,400)	$4,220
Cash-ins						
Sales Paid	0	30,000	35,000	35,000	35,000	35,000
Loans and Transfers	15,000	0	0	0	0	0
Total Cash-ins	**15,000**	**12,800**	**18,460**	**26,080**	**31,600**	**39,220**
Cash-outs						
Start-up Costs	28,200	0	0	0	0	0
Books & Other Products	0	14,640	17,080	17,080	17,080	17,080
Rent	3,500	3,500	3,500	3,500	3,500	3,500
Salaries	0	2,500	2,500	2,500	2,500	2,500
Utilities	0	800	800	800	800	800
Telephone	0	700	700	700	700	700
Office Equipment	0	1,400	0	2,100	0	0
Insurance	0	3,000	0	0	0	0
Advertising	0	700	700	700	700	700
Accounting	0	300	300	300	300	300
Electronic Payment System Fees	0	300	300	300	300	300
Loan Payments	0	500	500	500	500	500
Misc.	500	1,000	1,000	1,000	1,000	1,000
Total Cash-outs	**32,200**	**29,340**	**27,380**	**29,480**	**27,380**	**27,380**
Cash at End of Month	**($17,200)**	**($16,540)**	**($8,920)**	**($3,400)**	**$4,220**	**$11,840**

	June	July	Aug	Sept	Oct	Nov	Dec
	$11,840	$17,360	$21,980	$29,600	$34,420	$42,040	$49,660
	35,000	35,000	35,000	35,000	35,000	35,000	40,000
	0	0	0	0	0	0	0
	46,840	52,360	56,980	64,600	69,420	77,040	89,660
	0	0	0	0	0	0	0
	17,080	17,080	17,080	17,080	17,080	17,080	19,520
	3,500	3,500	3,500	3,500	3,500	3,500	3,500
	2,500	2,500	2,500	2,500	2,500	2,500	2,500
	800	800	800	800	800	800	800
	700	700	700	700	700	700	700
	2,100	0	0	2,800	0	0	0
	0	3,000	0	0	0	0	0
	700	700	700	700	700	700	700
	300	300	300	300	300	300	300
	300	300	300	300	300	300	300
	500	500	500	500	500	500	500
	1,000	1,000	1,000	1,000	1,000	1,000	1,000
	29,480	30,380	27,380	30,180	27,380	27,380	29,820
	$17,360	$21,980	$29,600	$34,420	$42,040	$49,660	$59,840

rent and a $500 allowance for unexpected expenses. Inga also includes in her cash-out section a $500 payment each month to her sister for the loan.

Notice that Inga's cash-outs look a bit different than her expenses in her profit/loss forecast, even though they add up to the same totals. The reason is that Inga's cash-out section of her cash flow projection reflects that some expenses are paid in lump sums, rather than monthly, such as her insurance, which is paid twice a year. She also breaks up her estimates for office expenses into lump payments, as she doesn't expect to spend equal amounts each month.

Also notice that Inga's estimated paid sales (as opposed to sales on credit) for the year come to the same total as her estimated annual sales revenue. That's because for her first year at least, Inga doesn't plan to take credit cards or checks, only cash and ATM purchases. That way all her sales will be paid immediately.

Inga's happy to see that by the end of April she should have cash left in the bank after all her expenses are paid (though she hasn't yet provided for money for her living expenses). Still, she needs to close the cash deficits that she predicts for her first three months in business. Based on her cash flow projection, an extra $17,200 up front would keep her cash flow (barely) in the black. She decides to apply for a loan of $15,000 and try to juggle expenses to cover the remaining $2,200 shortfall.

Once you've completed a year's worth (or more, if you want) of a cash flow projection, you'll have a blueprint for your business's financial situation from month to month. If any months are projected to have a cash deficit, you'll need to tweak your plan to make sure you can cover all of your important expenses. As usual, this means you'll have to juggle, reduce, or cut costs. A cash flow projection that shows difficulty in paying all your bills won't only scare investors away, it may mean that your plan needs serious revision. On the other hand, if your cash flow projection shows that you'll be in the black every month, then you'll be in a good position to show your numbers to potential sources of money—and to get your business under way.

⚠ **Credit transactions complicate the picture.** Cash flow analysis is concerned with when your business receives or spends money, not when sales or purchases are made. This means that you'll need to account for delayed payments if you do any sales or purchases on credit.

📖 **For more on business plans.** Mike McKeever's *How to Write a Business Plan* (Nolo) offers more detail on how to complete your cash flow analysis, including how to deal with credit transactions.

H. Putting It All Together

Congratulations! You've finished the descriptive and financial aspects of your business plan. While you kick back and enjoy a cold one, think about how you want to put all the information together. If you put the plan together for your own information, then you might want to simply review it, edit anything that needs fixing, print it out, and put it into a binder for your reference. If you plan to present the information as part of a loan request or as a package for investors to review, you might want to do some extra polishing. As mentioned earlier, consider hiring a writer to help you develop the information into a well-written, persuasive document. The bottom line is to package the information as needed for your specific purposes.

☑ Chapter 5 Checklist

☐ Decide how you will use your business plan: to attract investors or for your own use as a blueprint for your business.

☐ Draft sections of your business plan that describe your business in detail.

☐ Put together financial projections for your business, including a break-even analysis, a profit/loss forecast, and a cash flow analysis.

☐ Have a friend or business associate look over your plan—both the descriptive elements and the financial analysis—and make edits or suggestions.

☐ Edit your plan and prepare a final draft. Assemble the various sections of the plan into a final document, and package it as necessary for however you intend to use the plan.

■

Pricing, Bidding, and Billing Projects

Pricing is a crucial factor in any business strategy, yet many fledgling business owners have little idea how to go about setting prices that are both competitive and profitable. This chapter explains how to develop your pricing strategy and introduces you to some standard methods for setting prices, whether your business sells services or products.

In addition, this chapter offers guidance for business owners who need to make bids to get work. Service businesses typically fall into this category, though sometimes product-based businesses also need to bid for jobs. We'll go through some general tips for the process and include an outline for what typical proposals include.

On a cautionary note, be aware that antitrust laws forbid business competitors to fix, or even merely discuss, prices. For this reason, you won't find newsgroups or bulletin boards online where other businesses in a certain industry offer specific information on their pricing. Both online and off, pricing discussions among businesses in the same industry are not just taboo, they're illegal. (For more on antitrust issues, a decent resource online is AntiTrust.org; check out the "Common Sense Guidelines" at www.antitrust.org/guidelines.html.)

Directly sharing pricing information with competitors is illegal, but publishing general information about pricing guidelines is not. Good thing, since pricing is what we're going to discuss first, in Section A, below.

Product sellers can skip ahead. Business owners who plan only to sell products don't need to deal with service-pricing or service-billing issues. If you don't plan to offer services, skip ahead to Section C where we discuss pricing for businesses that sell products.

A. Pricing and Billing for Service Businesses

Two major components of running a service-based business are setting prices and figuring out how to bill clients. Having rates that are well thought out is a key factor in soliciting clients with confidence. And if you know the best way to bill clients, you can manage your projects for maximum profitability, and establish yourself as a true professional. This section explains these two essential tasks for service businesses. Once you understand what drives the pricing and billing processes, you'll find them much easier.

1. Setting Hourly Rates

Those who work as freelancers or own service-based businesses often find it difficult to figure out what rates to use. Many people can't understand how to assign value to their time. Remember that your service rates are not just a measure of the value of your time—they also need to cover your overhead and yield your profits. There's no single formula to put a price on your services, but there are a couple of common approaches. One formula is based on adjusting the number of billable hours so that revenue equals salary, overhead, and profit. And some businesses base their rates on what the market will bear. Let's take a look at each of these approaches.

a. Billable Hours Formula

Many service businesses use a fairly simple formula to calculate their hourly rate. To keep it simple, we'll look at this formula as if you're a solo freelancer without any employees:

	Desired annual salary
+	Annual fixed costs (or overhead)
+	Desired annual profit
÷	Annual billable hours
=	Hourly rate

The gist of the formula is that it adds together all the money you want to bring in each year and divides that total by the number of hours you plan to work each year. The result is the hourly rate. This simple formula can be adjusted depending on the specifics of your business.

Let's take a closer look.

- **Desired salary:** This is straightforward. How much would you like to earn annually? We're just talking salary here—we add in your desired profit later.
- **Fixed costs:** This is also a simple concept. How much will you spend each year on rent, utilities, office equipment, computers, and other items of overhead? As discussed in Chapter 5, fixed costs are independent of individual projects or services. You pay them regardless of how much business you're doing.
- **Desired profit:** You're in business to make a profit, not just to bring home a paycheck. A typical profit goal is 20% above salary and overhead (or fixed costs).
- **Billable hours:** There's no single way to estimate this. Basically, the fewer billable hours you estimate, the higher your hourly rate will be; the more billable hours, the lower your hourly rate. A common way to approach this estimate is by calculating the number of potentially billable hours in a year. With 52 weeks in the year and a 40-hour workweek, there are 2,080 potentially

billable hours each year. Reduce that total by the number of nonbillable hours you expect to have—vacation, administrative work, or selling, for example. Just use your best estimate here. Very generally, the percentage of your time that is billable will probably be 50 to 80 percent. Much below that won't be very profitable, and higher than that usually isn't realistic. Use this percentage to determine how many billable hours you'll probably have each year. For instance, if 70 percent of your time will be billable, you will have 1,456 billable hours (2080 hours x 70%).

Now add together your desired salary, fixed costs, and desired profit. Then divide that total by your billable hours. The result will be the hourly rate you'll need to charge to cover your fixed costs and bring in your desired salary and profit.

EXAMPLE: Samantha is starting a translation service and wants to figure out her hourly rate. She sets a salary for herself of $30,000 per year and estimates her annual fixed costs to be approximately $25,000. This totals $55,000 for salary and overhead. A 20 percent profit brings the total to $66,000. Samantha thinks she'll have to spend a good amount of time doing sales and getting her business off the ground, so she figures only about 60% of her time will be billable, resulting in 1,248 available billable hours. By dividing her salary, fixed expenses, and profit ($66,000) by 1,248 billable hours, Samantha sees that her hourly rate should be $52.88. She rounds that up to $55 per hour.

Salary:	$30,000.00
+ Fixed costs	25,000.00
Total salary & fixed costs	55,000.00
+ 20% profit	11,000.00
Total salary, fixed costs & profit	66,000.00
÷ Billable hours	1,248
= Hourly rate	$ 52.88

b. Setting Market-Based Rates

Another way to set your hourly rate is to throw the formula out the window and simply set your rate for what the market will bear. Be aware that this might not yield a profitable hourly rate, because you're not basing your rate on the actual numbers you'll need to achieve. On the other hand, this approach may be more likely to deliver a rate that customers will accept.

If you base your rates on the market, use any market information you can get to guide you, including what competitors charge, industry standards, and your own experience of using various rates. If you constantly fail to snag clients once you provide a quote, that's a sign your rates may be too high. On the flip side, if you get every job you bid on, you could probably get away with nudging, or even shoving, your rates upward.

It is legal to research and use competitors' rates. The antitrust laws mentioned earlier are intended to protect consumers by maintaining competition in the marketplace. The laws are supposed to prevent anticompetitive agreements among competitors to set prices at a certain level. On the other hand, setting your rates to position your business among similar businesses is perfectly legal, so long as you obtained your competitors' pricing information from another source, not directly from them. After all, researching the market and setting prices accordingly is the essence of competition.

2. Billing Options

Service business owners and freelancers typically use a variety of billing options to accommodate different types of projects and clients. Common billing options include flat fees, hourly billing, or retainer arrangements. We'll look at each of these below.

a. Flat Fees

With flat-fee billing, you and your client agree to a total fee for a specific project. In the right situation, it is efficient and professional to charge your client a flat fee for your services. The fee should roughly reflect the number of hours you'll work multiplied by your hourly rate. Contractors typically discount their hourly rates for larger projects.

Billing per project makes clients happy because they know up front what their costs will be. Project-based billing can also benefit you. A flat fee encourages efficient project management and reduces the hassle of tracking and billing for your hours (though you should always keep track for your own records).

However, flat fees aren't the best idea for every project. You will feel underpaid if it takes much more work to finish a project than you expected, and the customer will feel overcharged if a project takes much less time than you estimated. If you want to bill per project, you and the client should both understand and agree on the project's exact scope. In fact, you should reach this agreement even before you quote a fee. Once the client accepts your fee, the project details should be outlined in a contract. Payment terms can vary, but contractors typically require a deposit up to one-half of the total fee on signing the project contract.

Sometimes it's not possible to pin down a project with specificity at the outset. Some clients simply don't want to hammer out all details. Other times, a short deadline makes it difficult or impossible to carefully consider all aspects of the project before you start work. In these cases, you ask for trouble if you set a flat fee.

Suppose, for instance, that a client calls and needs a new section developed for a website ASAP. The owners of the site desperately want you to start immediately, but you have only a vague idea of the work involved. A flat fee here would be a really bad idea. The project could take much longer than you expect, leaving you to do the work for an unfairly low flat rate.

If the project isn't carefully outlined before you start, forget the flat fee; hourly billing is probably the safest way to go.

b. Hourly Billing

Billing clients by the hour is pretty straightforward: You keep track of how many hours you work and bill the client accordingly. As explained above, you should use this type of billing (also called "time and materials billing") in situations in which the project isn't well defined.

While billing by the hour will protect you from being underpaid for a poorly defined project that takes more time than you thought it would, the client will never be happy if you present a huge, unexpected bill. Even when you choose hourly billing for a project without a clear scope, do your best to work efficiently, communicate with the client, and avoid handing over a surprising bill.

Keep in mind that it's up to you to demonstrate your value to the client—including why your hourly rate is justified and how you spent your hours. Even if you can't define the project specifically enough to set a flat rate, do your best to estimate how long the project will take, and try to keep your hours within your estimates.

Charging for Outsourced Services

Sometimes service businesses need to hire another contractor (typically called a subcontractor) to get a job done for a client. You can charge your client for the subcontractor's work in different ways. You can simply charge your standard hourly rate for all work completed, whether your company did the work or a subcontractor did. This approach can work for or against you, depending on what you pay the subcontractor. Under a common second approach, businesses mark up the cost of the subcontractors by 15 or 20% and bill the client accordingly.

Sometimes the client will hire and pay the sub directly, without a markup. This can work if that piece of the work is discrete, or distinct from the rest, and the client is responsible for supervising the sub's work and has appropriate liability insurance. However, many contractors prefer to choose and supervise all workers on the same project, for many reasons: They like to have total control over the project, they like to choose subcontractors whose work they trust, they usually make a fair profit on the subcontractor, and it simplifies the project as well as the contractor's potential liability to the subcontractor and the client.

In any case, let your client know in advance whether you plan to use subcontractors on a project, especially if the subcontractor is a highly skilled specialist and the rate you bill for the subcontractor will be higher than your standard rate.

EXAMPLE: Glenn is a construction contractor with a standard hourly rate of $55 per hour. When hired for a remodeling project, Glenn tells his client he will need to hire a few subcontractors over the course of the project who may have rates higher or lower than his. Glenn and the client come to the understanding that they'll agree to all subcontractors and their rates before Glenn hires them. When it's nearly time to bring in a plumber, Glenn tells his client he'd like to hire Khalsa, whose rate to the client will be $69 per hour. Khalsa's own rate is $60 per hour, but Glenn marks up the rate by 15% to $69 so that he can make a reasonable profit for managing Khalsa on the project.

Set reasonable increments when billing. For instance, will you bill the client a full hour for work that takes you 20 minutes to finish, or for a five-minute phone conversation? We don't recommend this, because clients think it's unfair. Many people use increments of 15 or 30 minutes for billing purposes. It can be good public relations to show some short phone calls on the bill with no charge attached. That makes the client feel better about the times you round up to the nearest 15 minutes for other tasks.

c.   Retainer Arrangements

In a traditional retainer arrangement, the client pays an ongoing fee, usually monthly, to keep the contractor "on call" for certain services. Retainer arrangements are usually best for clients with predictable needs—for example, regularly updating a law firm's website, providing maintenance services for an apartment building, sewing and tailoring costumes for a theater, or doing public relations for a ski resort. As with flat-rate billing, always define the amount and scope of services expected of you under a retainer arrangement.

In some professional businesses, especially law offices, a "retainer" is requested at the outset that is really a deposit, or a prepayment of fees and costs, usually under a written fee agreement. Lawyers also sometimes use the traditional monthly-fee retainer described above.

B. Bidding and Creating Proposals

Sometimes it is not possible to sell a service or product just by offering it to the public for a certain price. Many service businesses (and some businesses selling products) must submit a bid or a proposal on a project to be considered for the job. (The terms "bid" and "proposal" are often used interchangeably.) If the client accepts the bid, then a contract is typically written and signed to confirm the sale.

Since a bid can make or break a sale, you should take care when putting one together, both with the contents of the bid and its physical appearance. Often, the hardest part of bidding is breaking down the project into smaller parts so that you can make good estimates of how much work, time, and materials it will require. Once that's done, it is usually quite easy to write the proposal. This section outlines how to put together a bid to help ensure your chances of success.

When you don't need to get it in writing. Businesses selling products usually don't need to worry about bids or proposals. If you don't need to learn about the bidding process, skip ahead to Section C, where we discuss pricing for businesses selling products.

When a proposal becomes a contract. A proposal usually converts to a contract when a client accepts your terms. In practice, however, you should suggest that you sign a separate contract to finalize the agreement with the client. This is partly because it's an opportunity to make sure the client truly understands what you said in your proposal. It's also a good idea because there are things you should cover in a contract that you wouldn't necessarily put in a proposal, such as who provides the insurance, how you will handle extras or change orders, specifics of each side's remedies for breach of contract, which state's laws apply, and whether you will mediate or arbitrate any disagreements. In Chapter 10, we'll look specifically at how to use contracts in your business.

1. Get All the Information You Need

You won't be able to make an effective bid on a project until you thoroughly understand all the details involved. Ask the prospective client as many questions as necessary to flesh out the full scope of the project. A prospective client who's putting a project out to bid among competitors may already have a sheet of specifications, but if you have any questions, be sure to ask them.

Often, the client will want to be involved in certain aspects of the project, so it's important you both agree who will take a primary role in various tasks or duties. Hash out the breakdown of duties and the workflow right at the beginning.

2. Break Down the Project and Make Estimates

In the next step, break down the project into manageable components and estimate how much time, labor, and materials you'll need for each one. This is generally the best way to make accurate estimates.

For instance, your head will spin if you try to estimate how long it will take you to complete an entire landscape design project. But once you break the project into parts—grading, spreading gravel, paving, planting trees, and so on—making estimates for the individual bits won't seem nearly as overwhelming.

Multiply the number of hours you expect the project to require by your hourly rate. It's common for freelancers to lower their hourly rates a bit if the project is a large one. This is reasonable, because it's usually more profitable for a freelancer to work consistently on one project than to work piecemeal on several smaller projects.

However, sometimes freelancers are tempted to lower their estimates out of fear. After adding up all the hours needed for a large project and multiplying this by their normal hourly rate, they think the fee looks too high and start slashing it to make it more acceptable to the client. Guard against this temptation. It's fine to reduce your hourly fee slightly when you anticipate efficiencies on a large-scale project, but don't sell yourself short just to get the job. Not only will you regret it after you've worked long hours on the project for an unreasonably low fee, but you'll fail to earn respect from clients if you don't ask for the compensation you are worth.

3. Consider Expenses

Who will be responsible for expenses incurred during the project? The answer varies from project to project; there are no hard and fast rules. Typically, contractors are responsible for covering their own normal expenses of doing business. (However, this is not always true. Attorneys, for example, commonly bill clients for copies and telephone calls.) Clients usually bear printing and production costs, as well as any costs that aren't typical to the contractor's business—such as travel, international phone calls, or equipment rental fees.

In any case, you and the client should agree in advance who will cover which expenses. In addition, make sure to address whether there are any limits on reimbursable expenses or whether the client must approve expenses in advance.

Also nail down the matter of how you will bill the client for expenses. For example, travel expenses are quite often billed to clients. It's wise to make a specific breakdown of the expenses that will be covered—such as airfare, rental car, lodging, taxi, train, parking, and food.

Proposing reasonable limits on client expenses. Even if your client has deep pockets and seems willing to cover whatever expenses you incur, you should offer some limits on reimbursable expenses. This will help to head off any potential conflicts or unpleasant surprises over reimbursement bills. It also shows the client that you care about giving a good deal.

You can handle payments for expenses a number of different ways. For example:

- Set an amount that the client will pay, regardless of the amount actually incurred. For instance, you and the client can agree that the client will pay $1,000 to cover all travel costs. If your actual costs are lower, the extra money will be yours; if higher, you'll eat the difference.

- Bill the client for actual expenses incurred. You can do this with or without a cap. For instance, you could agree that the client will reimburse you for all actual travel costs. Or you could agree the client will reimburse you for actual travel costs up to $500.
- Set a per diem rate for certain expenses. "Per diem" simply means "per day." Food is typically billed at a set per diem rate—say, $35 or $50 per day.

EXAMPLE: Samantha is working on a bid for a translation project that will require her to travel to Brazil three times during the course of the project. Her client, Bahia Travel Company, says it will cover travel expenses and asks Samantha to draft a proposal specifying the terms. Samantha drafts the following terms regarding travel expenses that she will include in her proposal:

"Samantha will be responsible for all expenses involved in the project, except for travel-related expenses, which Samantha will bill to Bahia Travel Company monthly, as follows:

Airfare: Billed as actually accrued, including all taxes, not to exceed $1,500 per round-trip ticket. Tickets will be economy class.

Rental car: Billed as actually accrued, including insurance and taxes, not to exceed $50 per day.

Lodging: Billed as actually accrued, including all taxes, not to exceed $75 per night.

Food: Billed at $40 per day.

Taxi: Billed as actually accrued.

Parking: Billed as actually accrued."

4. Write Your Proposal

Once you've finalized all the important details of the project, it's time to put together your proposal. Your goal is to present all important information clearly and professionally, and to demonstrate you have a solid plan for getting the job done right.

While proposals should always be professional and somewhat formal in tone, do not be afraid to let your personality show. If you feel stiff, you won't usually have a better bid, just a more stilted one.

Most project proposals are two to three pages long, though there's no hard and fast rule here. You should use as much space as it takes to outline the project details with adequate—but not excruciating—detail. An outline for a project proposal might go something like this:

- **Project overview.** Describe the big picture of the project, including a description of the client and an overview of the project.
- **Project objectives.** Include detailed information about the project, including all the different components of the project and how they fit together.
- **Proposed approach.** Describe how you would approach the project and how you would achieve the client's goals. Be specific, and don't assume that the client knows anything about how you do your work.
- **Specific responsibilities.** Outline your understanding of your specific responsibilities.
- **Deliverables.** This is a term for the specific products that your work will yield. For instance, deliverables might include a 20-page written report, a set of tax documents, or a 100-page travel guide.
- **Timetable.** Scheduling is always an important part of project management, so you should always outline when you expect certain parts of the project will be completed.
- **Fee and payment terms.** In stating your fee, you don't have to explicitly state your hourly rate or how you arrived at your amount. Simply make it clear that your fee is based on your understanding of the project requirements as outlined in the rest of the proposal.
- **Expenses.** Outline whatever agreement you and the potential client have regarding who will cover which expenses.
- **Conclusion.** Wrap up the proposal. Strive for a professional tone that expresses your en-

thusiasm for the project. While some proposals serve as the project contract once the client has accepted them, you will usually state here that you expect to sign a separate formal contract.

C. Pricing for Businesses Selling Products

As with pricing services, there are different ways to figure out what to charge for the products that your business sells. Of course, your cost of acquiring or making the products will play a big part in your pricing decisions. But you may have difficulty deciding on an appropriate markup. This section walks you through a few issues to consider when pricing goods.

⚠ **Don't discuss pricing strategy with competitors.** Antitrust laws forbid you to fix prices with your competitors and even to share price information or discuss prices with them. Steer clear of this potentially serious legal trouble.

1. Establish an Overall Strategy

Before deciding how much you'll charge for your widgets, think about and adopt an overall pricing strategy for your business. Keep in mind that the very same widget might be sold for 99¢ at your local 99¢ store, $5 at a chain retailer, and $25 at a swank boutique. The price can vary so much because each of these stores has its own pricing strategy—and you should, too.

The concept is simple: Will your business use a high-end, middle-end, or low-end strategy? Each strategy can be profitable if you work within its logic. Here's a quick description of how each strategy typically works:

- **High-end** shops can charge high prices so long as they offer something in return, such

as a great selection of hard-to-find or highly specialized products, extraordinary customer service, an exclusive atmosphere, or simply top-notch quality.

- **Middle-range** shops charge average prices and succeed on the basis of other factors such as selection, customer service, and convenient hours and locations. None of these factors are exceptional enough to justify high-end prices, but they're attractive enough to draw customers who aren't necessarily looking for the very lowest price.

- **Low-end** shops succeed by forgoing some amenities such as a reliable selection or a convenient location. They attract customers by offering the lowest prices. Customers might have to paw through bins of merchandise or drive across town to a cold, cheerless warehouse store, but they'll do it because they know they'll get a bargain.

Whichever strategy you choose, it's important that you stick with it and use it consistently. You will confuse customers and push them to your competitors if you offer a confounding mix of high-end and low-end items in the same store.

2. Research Markup Data

Once you've got a pricing strategy in place, decide how much you'll mark up your products for sale. You can set your prices appropriately after you do some research to figure out how much other similar businesses mark up their goods.

One easy source of markup information is simply the manufacturer's suggested retail price (MSRP, also called the suggested list price). If you buy a line of floor lamps that cost you $15 per unit and the MSRP is $45, then you know the manufacturer is recommending a markup of 200% of cost. You don't have to follow the recommendation—the days of strict adherence to MSRPs are over—but you'll get a good idea of what may be typical in the marketplace for that item.

In addition to using MSRPs, ask your manufacturers and suppliers for information they may have on average markup rates. Your suppliers can be a valuable source of this kind of information, beyond setting MSRPs for each product.

What's Up With Markup?

Markup is the amount that's tacked on to the cost of an item to arrive at its selling price. For instance, a wristwatch that cost $25 to the retailer may be marked up by $37.50 for a selling price of $62.50. What can be confusing is that markup rates are sometimes expressed as a **percentage of cost**, and other times as a **percentage of selling price**.

For example, the markup percentage for the wristwatch is 150% of cost or 60% of selling price. What does this mean? The percentage of cost calculation works like this: The cost of the watch ($25) is multiplied by 150%, resulting in a $37.50 markup, which is added to its original cost ($25) to arrive at the selling price of $62.50.

Here is the percentage of selling price calculation: The selling price ($62.50) is multiplied by 60%, resulting in the same $37.50 markup we arrived at with the percentage of cost calculation. As you can see, these two different ways of expressing a markup percentage yield the same result.

When you search markup rates, be sure you know which type of percentage you're dealing with: percentage of cost or percentage of selling price. If you apply a percentage of selling price markup rate to the item cost, or use the percentage of cost markup with the item's selling price, you'll end up with the wrong result. For instance, if you mistakenly calculate the wristwatch markup by multiplying the item cost ($25) by the percentage of selling price markup rate (60%), you'll end up with a markup of $15, and a selling price of just $40.

You can find good information about industry standard markup rates in many sources. Trade associations and journals may give you valuable data. Directories and guidebooks are also available on many industries. These books tend to be expensive ($100 and up) but are often treasure troves of valuable industry info. Hoover's Inc. is a company that specializes in providing comprehensive market data; its website (www.hoovers.com) offers a wealth of information and publications for sale. Many of the titles offered at Hoover's are from Plunkett Research, another firm specializing in market data. Plunkett has its own website at www.plunkettresearch.com.

Don't stop there. Do your own research, and look specifically for info pertaining to your type of business. Search online, visit the library of a local business school, ask local trade associations, and generally do some sleuthing to turn up the data you need.

✓ Chapter 6 Checklist

☐ Never discuss the topic of pricing with competitors—basically, anyone in the same industry as you.

☐ Service businesses should set hourly rates carefully, either using a formula or basing their rates on market conditions. However you set your rates, remember that you'll need not only to earn a salary but also pay for your overhead and make a profit.

☐ Those in service businesses should become familiar with various ways to bill clients and understand which methods are best for specific situations.

☐ Any business owners who will have to bid for work should learn how to put together a professional proposal.

☐ Those who sell products need to develop an overall pricing strategy to guide their pricing decisions.

☐ Owners of businesses who sell products should research the market to understand what typical markup rates are used by others in the same industry.

Federal, State, and Local Start-Up Requirements

B y now you've finished hammering out the details of how you plan to operate your business. In a perfect world, you could hang up your "open" sign and start selling your products or services at a nice profit. Sorry! In the real world of California business, things are not quite that easy. Before you can legally begin your business, you need to take care of a number of pesky requirements with governmental agencies from the city to the federal level. Although none of these requirements are difficult or even terribly time consuming, lots of entrepreneurs get stymied at this point because it's so hard to find one centralized source of information that explains what to do. They're left to ferret out each bureaucratic requirement one by one and hope they've found all of them by the time they start doing business.

For example, your city tax office can tell you what forms you must file there, but won't tell you how to obtain a California seller's permit in order to sell retail goods. And while the state Board of Equalization can tell you everything you need to know about getting a seller's permit, it won't explain how to obtain a federal employer identification number, which is required for most businesses. The process of finding out what you need to do and how to go about doing it can feel like putting together a jigsaw puzzle without knowing how many pieces it should have or how it should look when completed.

To help you figure out what you need to do and where you need to do it, we've pulled together all the basic start-up requirements for California businesses in this chapter. We will guide you through the bureaucratic maze and explain the typical registration requirements that apply to most businesses. (Businesses with employees have to meet a few extra requirements—we explain them in Chapter 12.) There are far more regulations for specific small businesses than we could possibly cover here—particularly at the state and city levels. However, this chapter explains the basic regulatory structure that every businessperson will have to

deal with, and points out which agencies typically deal with certain types of requirements. By the time you finish reading this chapter, you'll know a number of registration requirements that you will have to meet, plus you'll have a good idea of where to check for other requirements that may apply to you, depending on what type of business you're starting and where you'll be conducting it.

Sure, dealing with city and state bureaucrats can be a mind-numbing endurance contest. But once the mystery is taken out of the registration process and you have a clear idea of which requirements may apply to you, you'll be able to tackle the bureaucracy with a minimum of time and stress.

One-Stop Shopping for Information on Government Requirements

One of the few centralized sources of small business start-up information is an online clearinghouse called CalGOLD. It's maintained by the California Environmental Protection Agency (CalEPA), but the information it offers isn't restricted to environmental permit issues. When you enter your type of business and the city and county in which it's located, this interactive site will pull up a comprehensive list of registration requirements and contact information for the agencies that administer them. The Web address is www.calgold.ca.gov.

Jennifer Mahoney, owner of an illustration service in Northern California:

I'm lucky enough to have a technical skill to combine with a regular drawing skill that puts me in a market niche among illustrators. Lacking any entrepreneurial "uncles," it took me a while to get a clue about the business world, like finding untapped markets, understanding agreements, getting paid, handling copyright issues, and finding out how many regulatory bodies need a portion of my modest income. It all felt like groping in the dark: Where are all the rules written down? I'm doing well for myself now, supporting my family, but I wish it hadn't taken me so long to figure out.

![] **Slower going for corporations, LLCs, or limited partnerships.** Although starting up a company that offers limited liability—a corporation, LLC, or limited partnership—isn't rocket science, the process is more complex than starting a sole proprietorship or general partnership. While this chapter outlines the basic start-up requirements for businesses that offer limited liability, you will also need to understand some additional formalities and requirements. For example, if you plan to create one of these types of businesses, you may need to comply with federal and state securities laws. In Section A, below, we give you a brief overview of the extra formation step (Step 1) you'll have to take to set up a business with limited liability. Once you have formed your corporation, LLC, or limited partnership, you'll be ready to use the information in this chapter on permits, licenses, and tax-filing requirements. As we mention in Section A, Nolo offers several self-help products that give in-depth, detailed information about starting and running these limited liability business types.

Here are the general start-up steps we walk you through below:

Step 1: File organizational documents with the California Secretary of State (corporations, LLCs, and limited partnerships only).

Step 2: Obtain a federal employer identification number (FEIN).

Step 3: Register your fictitious business name with your county.

Step 4: Obtain a local tax registration certificate (also known as a business license).

Step 5: Obtain a State of California seller's permit.

Step 6: Obtain specialized vocation-related licenses or environmental permits if necessary.

"Why Am I Filling Out All These Forms?"

Why do you have to sort your way through a tangled bureaucracy to start a small business? At the most basic level, there are three purposes to the various business permit and license requirements.

- **To identify you.** No matter what kind of business you run, society has an interest in making sure that you are accountable for your actions. That's why businesses that don't use their owners' names as part of their business names must register a fictitious business name statement with the county in which their business is headquartered. That way, a member of the public who has a problem with Racafrax Designs or Acme Sandblasting can easily find out who the owners are, complain to them, and, if necessary, sue them.

- **To protect the public.** Government agencies issue permits and licenses to ensure that your business offers safe products or services that won't harm people or the environment. For example, if you open a food service business, your city's department of health understandably wants to make sure that your kitchen is sanitary, and will likely require that you obtain a permit, license, or other official approval before you can start serving snacks.

- **To keep track of your finances for tax purposes.** Several of the registration requirements are based on the government's nasty habit of taxing everything that moves (and lots of things that don't). To be sure that they collect every possible tax and fee, local, state, and federal governments use various registration requirements to keep tabs on your business.

A. Step 1: File With the Secretary of State

Sole proprietors and partnerships can skip this step. Only corporations, LLCs, and limited liability partnerships need to file organizational documents with the state. If you're starting a sole proprietorship or partnership, skip ahead to Step 2, discussed in Section B, below.

Unlike sole proprietorships or partnerships, businesses with limited liability don't just pop into existence as soon as their owners start selling products or services. You need to take the first step of explicitly creating a corporation, LLC, limited partnership, or limited liability partnership by filing registration papers with the California Secretary of State. For corporations, the necessary papers are called Articles of Incorporation; for LLCs they're called Articles of Organization. Limited partnerships must file a Certificate of Limited Partnership (LP-1). Limited liability partnerships file a Limited Liability Partnership Registration form. Samples of all four types of organizational documents appear in Appendix C, but this book does not contain the rest of the forms or information necessary to create one of these business types. We've provided the samples for your reference only; to create these business forms you'll need to do additional reading or consult other resources (see "Additional Resources From Nolo," below.)

When you file your organizational documents with the Secretary of State, you will be registering your corporate, LLC, or limited partnership name at the same time. The Secretary of State must approve all names before they can be registered, however; otherwise, your papers will be rejected. Your name won't be approved if another California business of the same legal structure (corporation, LLC, or limited partnership) has already taken that name. A California corporation may not use a name that's used by an existing corporation, an LLC may not use a name that is used by another California LLC, and so on.

If you file your organizational papers without checking on your business name, you run the risk of having to redo the papers with a new name and refile them. To save time and headaches, before you file your papers check your potential names with the Secretary of State to see if they are available, then reserve one of them. That way, when you file your organizational documents, your business name is sure to be accepted.

Checking and reserving a name by phone both involve a small fee—in 2004, the charge was $4 to check availability and $10 to reserve—and require a prepaid account. The Secretary of State's phone number is 916-653-6814; follow the prompts for each division. More information is available online at www.ss.ca.gov. Click on "California Business Portal" and proceed for your type of business.

Generally, the office will reserve the first name on your list that is available for 60 days.

You may also be able to do a name search in person at one of the California Secretary of State offices (addresses appear below). Call ahead to find out if that office will allow you to search in person. No matter how you search, we highly recommend that you reserve a name once you find one that's available.

California Secretary of State Offices

Sacramento Headquarters
1500 11th Street   916-657-5448
Sacramento, CA 95814

Fresno Branch
1315 Van Ness Avenue, Suite 203   559-445-6900
Fresno, CA 93721

Los Angeles Branch
300 S. Spring Street, Room 12513   213-897-3062
Los Angeles, CA 90013

San Diego Branch
1350 Front Street, Suite 2060   619-525-4113
San Diego, CA 92101

San Francisco Branch
2 Rincon Center
121 Spear Street, Suite 420   415-904-2344
San Francisco, CA 94105

Additional Resources From Nolo

Nolo's Quick LLC: All You Need to Know About Limited Liability Companies and Form Your Own Limited Liability Company (includes forms on disk), by Anthony Mancuso, offer guidance on creating an LLC and legal and tax information about this form of business. Also, a software package, *LLCMaker*, and *Your Limited Liability Company: An Operating Manual*, both by Anthony Mancuso, offer detailed information on how to manage LLCs in compliance with various state and federal laws.

On the corporate side, *How to Form Your Own California Corporation*, by Anthony Mancuso, takes you step by step through the requirements for forming a corporation in California. It also explains limited liability partnerships. And *The Corporate Minutes Book: Legal Guide to Taking Care of Corporate Business*, also by Anthony Mancuso, provides forms and instructions for running a corporation and handling corporate meetings and documentation.

For more information on limited partnerships, see *The Partnership Book*, by Denis Clifford and Ralph Warner.

Just because your name is accepted by the Secretary of State doesn't mean you're free to use it. As discussed in Chapter 3, trademark and unfair competition laws may prevent you from using a name used by another business, including businesses that aren't included in California's corporate, LLC, or limited partnership name databases. For instance, the name of a general partnership wouldn't be registered in California's corporate name database, but may have been in use for years. Or the name you've chosen may have been taken by a corporation in another state, which means it would not appear in California's database. To avoid running afoul of trademark and unfair competition laws, it's a good idea to do a trademark search before choosing any name for your business, or for its products or services. (Be sure to read Chapter 3 for a full discussion of the legal issues surrounding business names.)

B. Step 2: Obtain a Federal Employer Identification Number

Sole proprietors and partners don't need to explicitly "create" their business by registering with any state office; once they're engaged in business activity, their businesses more or less exist by default. (See Chapter 2 for more information about creating all types of businesses, including sole proprietorships and partnerships.) If you're starting a sole proprietorship or a partnership, getting a federal employer identification number from the Internal Revenue Service should be your first registration task, mainly because you can get one before you've registered with any other agency or filled out any other forms.

Corporations and LLCs must also apply for a federal employer identification number, but they have to file their organizational documents with the state first (see Step 1, above).

1. What an FEIN Is and Who Needs One

A business's federal employer identification number (alternately called an FEIN, an EIN, or an employer ID) is roughly equivalent to a Social Security number for an individual. It's a number the government uses to identify your business, and you'll use it over and over again on most of your important business documents, including your business's local tax registration forms, your federal tax return, and any applications for business licenses.

Some of you are probably saying, "But I don't plan to have employees—why do I need an employer ID number?" Blame the IRS for the confusing terminology. Although it's called an "employer" ID number, FEINs are required for most businesses, even those that don't have employees. The one exception is sole proprietors with no employees, who can use their own Social Security number instead of an FEIN. Partnerships, LLCs, and corporations need FEINs whether they have employees or not.

2. Applying for an FEIN

Thanks to a mail-in and phone system, getting an FEIN is easy—and free. Simply fill out and submit IRS Form SS-4, according to the instructions just below. (This book contains two copies of Form SS-4: one in Appendix C, which you can tear out and use, and one on the CD-ROM, along with the IRS's instructions for completing the form.) If you submit the form by mail you'll get your FEIN in about four weeks.

Better yet, by using the IRS's free Tele-TIN phone-in system you can file by phone, get your number the same day, and then send in Form SS-4. To do this, simply call the appropriate Tele-TIN number for your location (listed on the SS-4 form) and relay the information from your completed SS-4 form to the IRS representative, who will then give you your FEIN over the phone. Enter the FEIN in the upper right corner of the SS-4, sign and date the form, then mail or fax it to the Tele-TIN service center within 24 hours of the phone call.

A blank copy of Form SS-4 appears below.

Form SS-4
(Rev. December 2001)
Department of the Treasury
Internal Revenue Service

Application for Employer Identification Number

(For use by employers, corporations, partnerships, trusts, estates, churches, government agencies, Indian tribal entities, certain individuals, and others.)

▶ See separate instructions for each line.   ▶ Keep a copy for your records.

EIN

OMB No. 1545-0003

Type or print clearly.

1 Legal name of entity (or individual) for whom the EIN is being requested

2 Trade name of business (if different from name on line 1)

3 Executor, trustee, "care of" name

4a Mailing address (room, apt., suite no. and street, or P.O. box)

5a Street address (if different) (Do not enter a P.O. box.)

4b City, state, and ZIP code

5b City, state, and ZIP code

6 County and state where principal business is located

7a Name of principal officer, general partner, grantor, owner, or trustor

7b SSN, ITIN, or EIN

8a **Type of entity** (check only one box)
- ☐ Sole proprietor (SSN) _____
- ☐ Partnership
- ☐ Corporation (enter form number to be filed) ▶ _____
- ☐ Personal service corp.
- ☐ Church or church-controlled organization
- ☐ Other nonprofit organization (specify) ▶ _____
- ☐ Other (specify) ▶

- ☐ Estate (SSN of decedent) _____
- ☐ Plan administrator (SSN) _____
- ☐ Trust (SSN of grantor) _____
- ☐ National Guard   ☐ State/local government
- ☐ Farmers cooperative   ☐ Federal government/military
- ☐ REMIC   ☐ Indian tribal governments/enterprises
- Group Exemption Number (GEN) ▶ _____

8b If a corporation, name the state or foreign country (if applicable) where incorporated

State

Foreign country

9 **Reason for applying** (check only one box)
- ☐ Started new business (specify type) ▶ _____
- ☐ Hired employees (Check the box and see line 12.)
- ☐ Compliance with IRS withholding regulations
- ☐ Other (specify) ▶

- ☐ Banking purpose (specify purpose) ▶ _____
- ☐ Changed type of organization (specify new type) ▶ _____
- ☐ Purchased going business
- ☐ Created a trust (specify type) ▶ _____
- ☐ Created a pension plan (specify type) ▶ _____

10 Date business started or acquired (month, day, year)

11 Closing month of accounting year

12 First date wages or annuities were paid or will be paid (month, day, year). **Note:** *If applicant is a withholding agent, enter date income will first be paid to nonresident alien. (month, day, year)* . . . . ▶

13 Highest number of employees expected in the next 12 months. **Note:** *If the applicant does not expect to have any employees during the period, enter "-0-."* . . . . ▶

Agricultural	Household	Other

14 Check **one** box that best describes the principal activity of your business.
- ☐ Construction ☐ Rental & leasing ☐ Transportation & warehousing
- ☐ Real estate   ☐ Manufacturing   ☐ Finance & insurance
- ☐ Health care & social assistance ☐ Wholesale–agent/broker
- ☐ Accommodation & food service   ☐ Wholesale–other   ☐ Retail
- ☐ Other (specify)

15 Indicate principal line of merchandise sold; specific construction work done; products produced; or services provided.

16a Has the applicant ever applied for an employer identification number for this or any other business? . . . . . ☐ Yes   ☐ No
Note: *If "Yes," please complete lines 16b and 16c.*

16b If you checked "Yes" on line 16a, give applicants legal name and trade name shown on prior application if different from line 1 o r 2 above.
Legal name ▶   Trade name ▶

16c Approximate date when, and city and state where, the application was filed. Enter previous employer identification number if known.
Approximate date when filed (mo., day, year) | City and state where filed | Previous EIN

Third Party Designee   Complete this section **only** if you want to authorize the named individual to receive the entity's EIN and answer questions about the completion of this form.

Designees name

Designees telephone number (include area code)
(   )

Address and ZIP code

Designees fax number (include area code)
(   )

Under penalties of perjury, I declare that I have examined this application, and to the best of my knowledge and belief, it is true, correct, and complete.

Applicants telephone number (include area code)
(   )

Name and title (type or print clearly) ▶

Applicants fax number (include area code)
(   )

Signature ▶   Date ▶

For Privacy Act and Paperwork Reduction Act Notice, see separate instructions.   Cat. No. 16055N   Form **SS-4** (Rev. 12-2001)

Keep Your Business Names Straight on Form SS-4

Although most of the information you'll have to put on the form is pretty basic, you need to be careful—and consistent—about names. Here are some tips to help you get the job done.

Line 1   asks for the legal name of the entity that is applying for the FEIN. Sounds simple enough, but it can get a little tricky.

Sole proprietors should enter their full individual name—first, last, and middle initial. Do not enter any fictitious business name (FBN) you use or plan to use. (A fictitious business name is a name you use for your business that doesn't contain your legal name. FBNs are explained in more detail in the next section.)

A partnership should use the legal name of the partnership as it appears in the partnership agreement. For example, say Gene Cook and Beth Lynch own a partnership that they refer to as "Cook and Lynch, Partners" in their partnership agreement. This is the name they should write on Line 1. If you own a partnership but don't have a written partnership agreement, insert the name you plan to use for all official business and on all government forms—either a business name that contains each partner's last name or the trade name that you will present to the public (also known as your fictitious business name or your "DBA name," discussed below). (See Chapter 3 for the full spiel on the various types of business names.)

An LLC should enter the official company name as it appears in its articles of organization. A corporation should use its legal name as it appears in its articles of incorporation.

Line 2   asks for the trade name of the business. This is the same as asking for your fictitious business name or your "doing business as" (DBA) name. You can leave this line blank if you plan to do business under the name you entered in Line 1. For example, if Gene Cook and Beth Lynch plan to do business under the name Cook and Lynch, Partners, and they entered that name in Line 1, they can leave Line 2 blank. Similarly, if a sole proprietor named Stacey Stickler will use just her name to identify her landscape design services, she, too, can leave Line 2 blank.

But when your company's legal name doesn't match its trade name, you should enter the trade name on Line 2. For example, if Stacey Stickler decides to do business as Stickler's Landscape Design—she should enter that on Line 2. And a partnership that wants to do business under any name other than its legal name would do the same thing. For example, if "Cook and Lynch, Partners" want to do business under the trade name "CooLyn Enterprises," they will enter "Cook and Lynch, Partners" on Line 1 and "CooLyn Enterprises" on Line 2. (You'll find more on trade names and fictitious business names just below.)

While it may seem like we're splitting hairs, this is actually quite important. Think about it: the FEIN form introduces you and your business to the IRS, and identifies you in an official way. Using the correct name will help you avoid snafus with the IRS and other government agencies. For example, if the Cook and Lynch partnership goes back and forth between calling its business "Cook and Lynch" and "CooLyn Enterprises" on government documents, then Cook and Lynch will almost surely experience a raft of bureaucratic headaches.

C. Step 3: Register Your Fictitious Business Name With Your County

As discussed in Chapter 3, any trade name that doesn't contain the legal names of the owners (for sole proprietorships or general partnerships) or doesn't match the company's corporate, limited partnership, or LLC name on file with the state is called a fictitious business name (FBN). Fictitious business names are sometimes called assumed names or "DBAs" for "doing business as"—as in, "Spikey Andrews, doing business as Coffee Corner" or "Alibi Corporation, doing business as Ferryville Bait and Tackle." In this chapter and the rest of the book, we'll use the term fictitious business name for any business name that doesn't contain the legal name of the business owner.

California requires every business that uses a fictitious business name to file a fictitious business name statement with the county clerk in the county in which its primary business site is located. You'll find information on who needs to register in Section 2, below.

Counties keep track of business names for a couple of reasons. One is to prevent customer confusion between two local businesses that use the same name. (Before a business owner can register a fictitious business name, the owner will be required to search the county database of registered names to make sure the name isn't already being used.) Another reason is to give customers a quick way to find out who the owner of a company is without having to hire a private investigator. This allows customers to easily contact the owners to make a complaint or to take legal action against them. Requiring owners to register their business names makes it harder for fly-by-night businesses to operate anonymously and defraud customers.

1. The Importance of Filing an FBN Statement

Do not neglect or put off registering your fictitious business name. Without proof of registration, many banks will not open an account under your business name. Also, if you don't register your name, it won't appear in any county fictitious name databases. This means that another business will be less likely to find out you're using it—and may start using the name itself. Even though you have other legal avenues to stop another business from using a name that you used first (see Chapter 3), you don't want to create customer confusion between the two businesses and get into a name dispute with another business. If you lose a dispute over a name, at the very least you'll have to redo stationery, signs, and anything else that contains the name, such as T-shirts or maybe even your company logo.

2. Who Needs to Register?

The rules for registering fictitious business names depend on which business structure you use:

Sole proprietorships. A sole proprietor who includes his or her last name in the business name—such as O'Toole's Classic Cars—does not need to file an FBN statement. But it is not enough to include only initials, a nickname, or part of a name. For example, a business called J.R.'s Classic Cars would have to file a fictitious name statement indicating that it really is John O'Toole's business.

If your business name falsely implies that additional owners are involved, you must file a fictitious business name statement. If Jason Todd were a sole proprietor, for example, and named his business Jason Todd and Sons, or Jason Todd & Associates, he would have to file an FBN statement, even though he included his last name in his business name.

Partnerships. If a partnership includes the last names of all the partners—for example, Lawrence

Anderson and Nancy Fawcett name their business "Anderson and Fawcett Metal Designs"—they don't have to file a statement. Otherwise, an FBN statement will be required. For example, if three partners—Lynch, Cook, and Briggs—did business only under the name "Lynch & Cook," they would have to file an FBN statement.

Corporations, LLCs, and limited partnerships. A corporation, LLC, or limited partnership does not need to file an FBN statement unless it operates under a name different from its official name as stated in its articles of incorporation, articles of organization or certificate of limited partnership. For example, an LLC that registered with the Secretary of State under the name "Landmark Lanes, LLC" wouldn't have to file an FBN statement as long as it conducted business under that name. Any other trade name, "Landmark Bowl," for instance—or even "Landmark Lanes" without the "LLC" tacked onto the end—would be considered fictitious and would have to be registered. The same is true for corporations: If "Inc." is included in the corporation's name in the articles of incorporation, but not in the company's trade name, an FBN statement must be filed.

3. Filing With Your County

The law governing fictitious business names (California Business and Professions Code §§17900 to 17930) applies to the whole state, but is administered by each county. The result is a mammoth exercise in governmental inefficiency, with each county in California issuing different forms and charging different fees for registering an FBN. (In Appendix C and on the CD-ROM, we provide a form that includes all the information required by state law for FBN statements.) Logically, each county should accept this form, but, of course, some clerks will insist that you use a specific form provided by a particular office.

Your first step should be to call your county clerk's office to find out its requirements and fees.

Many counties allow you to order the FBN registration form by phone; others require you to request it in writing, with a self-addressed stamped envelope. Unless you live a good distance from the nearest county clerk, it may be easiest just to go to the office and complete the form in person. If you'd rather handle the process by mail, call and ask if the office will accept our standard form and, if so, how many copies you must submit and what fees you must pay. If the clerk's office requires filers to use a specific county form, use that form. The clerk will tell you how to obtain one. Many counties allow you to order the form by phone; others require you to send a written request for it along with a self-addressed stamped envelope. (You'll find a list of county clerks' offices and contact information in Appendix A.)

a. Searching the County Database

In most counties, you'll be instructed to search the county database of registered fictitious business names before submitting your statement, to make sure no one else has already registered the name you want to use. Typically, you can search a county's database (often an easy-to-search computerized system) for free if you go to the office in person. Sometimes, you can pay a fee for a staff person to do the search for you. If you want the clerk's office to do the search, you must usually submit the request and fee by mail.

b. Completing and Submitting an FBN Statement

If the name you've chosen is free to use, simply fill out the FBN statement and submit it to your county clerk along with the appropriate fees. The following instructions are for the standard form (on the next page) that we've included in Appendix C and on the CD-ROM.

<table>
<tr><td colspan="1">

Office of the County Clerk

Address _____

City _____

☐ First Filing   ☐ Renewal Filing
</td>
<td colspan="1">

Fees

$ _____ for 1 FBN and registrant

$ _____ for each additional FBN filed on same statement and doing business at same location

$ _____ for each additional registrant
</td>
<td colspan="1">

FILING STAMP ONLY

File Number: _____
</td></tr>
</table>

FICTITIOUS BUSINESS NAME STATEMENT

THE FOLLOWING PERSON(S) IS (ARE)

1 Fictitious Business Name(s)

1

2

3.

Articles of Incorporation Number (if applicable)
AL#

2 Street Address & City of Principal Place of Business in California (P.O. Box alone not acceptable)   Zip Code

3 Full Name of Registrant   if corporation—incorporated in what state

Residence Street Address   City   State   Zip Code

3a Full Name of Registrant   if corporation—incorporated in what state

Residence Street Address   City   State   Zip Code

3b Full Name of Registrant   if corporation—incorporated in what state

Residence Street Address   City   State   Zip Code

4 This Business is conducted by:
( ) an individual   ( ) a general partnership   ( ) joint venture   ( ) a business trust
( ) co-partners   ( ) husband and wife   ( ) a corporation   ( ) a limited partnership
( ) an unincorporated association other than a partnership   ( ) other—please specify _____

5 ( ) The registrant commenced to transact business under name or names listed on (date): _____
( ) Registrant has not yet begun to transact business under the fictitious business name or names listed herein.

6 If registrant is not a corporation or a limited liability company sign below:

_____   _____
SIGNATURE   TYPE OR PRINT NAME

_____   _____
SIGNATURE   TYPE OR PRINT NAME

_____   _____
SIGNATURE   TYPE OR PRINT NAME

6a If registrant is a corporation or a limited liability company sign below:

_____
COMPANY NAME

_____
SIGNATURE & TITLE

_____
TYPE OR PRINT NAME AND TITLE

This statement was filed with the County Clerk of _____ County on date indicated by file stamp above.

NOTICE—THIS FICTITIOUS NAME STATEMENT EXPIRES FIVE YEARS FROM DATE IT WAS FILED IN THE OFFICE OF THE COUNTY CLERK.
A NEW FICTITIOUS BUSINESS NAME STATEMENT MUST BE FILED PRIOR TO THAT DATE. The filing of this statement does not of itself authorize the use in this state of a fictitious business name in violation of the rights of another under federal, state, or common law (SEE SECTION 14400 et seq., Business and Professional Code).

This form should be typed *or* printed *legibly in* black ink.

Item 1: Insert the fictitious business name or names you will use. If you enter more than one, such as "Loaded for Bear Publishing" and "Bear Bones Comics," be sure to number them to make it clear that they're separate names. You're only allowed to register business names used at the same address on a single FBN statement. For instance, if the same owners use more than one fictitious business name at the same location, such as "Snak Central Cafe" and "Turtle Tavern" all under one roof, both names can be registered on one statement. Business names used at different locations— or by different owners at the same location—must be registered on separate FBN statements.

Item 2: Enter the street address of the business. P.O. boxes aren't acceptable. If you're working from home, just enter your home address.

Item 3: Enter the legal name and residence address of the person, people, LLC, or corporation that's registering the fictitious business name. Partnerships should enter this information for each general partner. For LLCs and corporations, use the name in the articles of organization or incorporation that were filed with the Secretary of State and the business's principal address (again, no P.O. boxes). LLCs and corporations should also indicate the state in which they organized or incorporated (probably California) and enter their articles of organization or incorporation number.

Item 4: Indicate what type of business entity you are operating—most likely a sole proprietorship, general partnership, LLC, or corporation. For corporations and LLCs, some counties, such as Los Angeles, require you to attach a certified copy of the articles of organization or incorporation. Check with your county for its requirements.

Item 5: Enter the date you started your business or check the box that indicates you haven't opened for business yet. State law requires you to file an FBN statement within 40 days of using a fictitious business name, though this rule isn't strictly monitored.

Item 6: Enter the appropriate signatures. The following people may sign for each specific business type:

Sole proprietorship:	Sole proprietor
Partnership:	General partner
LLC:	Officer or manager
Corporation:	Officer

Whoever signs for an LLC or corporation must indicate his or her title.

You can submit the form in person or by mail. Depending on the county, the fee is generally between $10 and $40 for registering one business name and one business owner. You can also pay an additional fee, around $5 or so, to register additional business names to be used at the same business location or additional owners. In other words, the more owners a business has, the more expensive it is to file an FBN statement.

c.   Publishing Notice of Your FBN Statement

Once you've filed your name and paid the necessary fees, you are free to start doing business under that name—but there is one more catch. Within 30 days of your filing date, you must have your FBN statement published in an approved newspaper in the county in which you filed it. Most county clerks will provide a list of acceptable publications for posting your FBN statement, though by state law any newspaper of general circulation in the county will suffice. (Really, no one reads these notices anyway.) Publishing your statement is dead simple; just take a copy of your completed statement to your publication of choice, which will have a standard format to present the required information.

⚠ Searching usually isn't enough. Ironically, the county clerk's requirement that you search its database of registered FBNs may well do more harm than good. Why? Because lots of people who find that no one in the county has registered a certain name are misled into believing that the name is free to use.

The truth of the matter is that only the tiniest of businesses can feel safe after doing only a county-wide search of a name they want to use. If someone else is using the name in a neighboring county, or even in a different state or country, you may well run into legal trouble, depending on your geographical scope and the products or services you sell. Particularly with the explosion of e-business, geographical distance is becoming irrelevant as the World Wide Web turns businesses on opposite sides of the globe into neighbors.

To avoid being accused of unfair competition or trademark infringement, it is wise to check neighboring counties' FBN databases, look into California and other state registries of corporate and LLC names, or even do a full international trademark search. Failing to do an appropriate search puts you at risk not only of lawsuits, but also of having to change your name after you start your business when you may already have stationery, business signs, and invoices printed up. Be sure to read Chapter 3 on trademark and business name issues for more information on choosing and researching a name that won't get you into legal trouble.

💡 Obscure publications often charge the lowest fees. As long as a newspaper is on the approved list or doesn't otherwise violate your county's rules, there's nothing wrong with picking the cheapest one.

The published notice must run once a week for four consecutive weeks. Within 30 days after the last publication, an affidavit (sometimes called Proof of Publication) must be filed with the county clerk to show that publication has been completed. Many newspapers that provide publication services will automatically send in the affidavit for you after your ad has completed its run. Make sure to find out whether the publication you use will do this (and double check after four weeks to make sure it actually has done it). If not, you'll have to get the affidavit from the publication yourself and submit it to the county clerk within the 30-day deadline. If the affidavit isn't filed in time, you may have to start the process all over again.

💡 Save your ad receipt. For practical reasons, you may need to prove that you completed your fictitious business name filing requirements, including publication, before your ad has actually run for four weeks. Banks, for instance, want to see that you have met fictitious name rules before they allow you to open an account in that name. Fortunately, a receipt from the newspaper showing that you have paid for publication, along with a copy of the FBN statement certified by the county clerk, is generally sufficient to prove that you've met all the registration requirements, even though the ad hasn't yet run for four weeks. So be sure to get a certified copy of your FBN statement back from the county clerk when you submit it, as well as a receipt from the newspaper when you pay for publishing the statement.

4. After You File

Legally, your FBN statement must be renewed every five years. You (or someone at your business) should keep track of your expiration date—five years after the date of initial filing. The county clerk will not notify you when your renewal date approaches. Also, you must renew your FBN statement if there is any change in the facts in the statement (except for changes of residence of an owner). If you don't file a new FBN statement when facts change, your FBN statement will expire in 40 days. If you no longer want your FBN registered, your FBN statement will expire as soon as you file a statement of abandonment, which usually costs anywhere from $10 to $40.

Changes to Your Business That Require a New FBN Statement

You'll have to file a new FBN statement in these circumstances:

- business name change
- business address change
- change of business ownership (unless a withdrawing partner files a statement of withdrawal), or
- change of business type (for example, you change your partnership to an LLC).

D. Step 4: Obtain a Local Tax Registration Certificate

Most cities require all businesses (including home businesses) to register with that city's tax collector, regardless of business type, structure, size, or name. Businesses located in rural, unincorporated areas must usually register with the county clerk rather than a city tax collector.

Depending on where you register, the locality may use different names for the process: tax registration, business tax application, business license application, or tax certification, for example. We use the terms "tax registration" and "tax registration certificate" in this book—and we recommend that you don't use the term "business license" when you really mean "tax registration certificate" (or whatever term is used in your locality for tax registration). True licenses, which are discussed in Section F, below, are typically administered at the state level. Certain businesses must obtain them if they engage in regulated activities, such as selling alcohol or cutting people's hair. Getting such a license often involves taking a test or otherwise proving you're qualified to do a certain activity.

Some businesses need more. Your tax registration certificate is not the same as a specialized license your business might need—such as a permit from the local health department for handling food, from the Federal Communications Commission for broadcasting over the radio waves, or from a regional air management district for emitting particles into the air. (Section F, below, discusses these specialized licenses and permits.) Whether or not you need one of these licenses or permits, you'll still need to get a tax registration certificate.

Why do you need to register with your local tax collector? Because just like the federal and state governments, your local government wants a cut of your business income. The tax registration requirement is basically your local government's way of keeping track of your business so that it will be able to collect any taxes it owes. Cities and counties have been known to tax businesses with even more flair and creativity than the feds or the state. Localities tax businesses based on criteria such as net profit, gross income, number of employees, total payroll, number of vehicles, number of machines, and sometimes even seating capacity. In addition, most cities categorize businesses and use different tax structures for each category. Oakland, for instance, taxes media firms at $1.20 per $1,000 of gross receipts, recreation/entertainment businesses at $4.50 per $1,000 of gross receipts, and limousine companies at $75 per vehicle.

For the privilege of registering to pay local taxes, you'll generally have to pay an annual fee, which varies a lot from city to city. Usually the annual fee depends partly on how much tax your business is expected to owe the following year, based on city (or county) tax rates. If the fee is based on estimated taxes, at least part of the registration fee may be a nonrefundable administrative fee—in that case, the other part of the fee will go toward paying your estimated taxes or will be returned to you if your taxes turn out to be lower than expected. In Oakland, for instance, registering your business with the city costs $30, but you must also pay your estimated tax based on your business category and your estimated income for the next year. The estimated tax portion—but not the $30 fee—will be credited towards your tax bill for the next year.

For your city's requirements, call your city tax collector; look under "Tax Collector" in the city government section of your white pages. The tax collector's office will be able to provide you with the forms necessary to register in your city, as well as any breakdown of business categories and tax tables. If you're doing business outside city limits, call your county clerk, usually listed under "County Clerk" in the county government section of the phone book.

E. Step 5: Obtain a State Seller's Permit

Those who sell merchandise must get a seller's permit from the California Board of Equalization (BOE), which is in charge of collecting taxes from businesses that do retail sales. The permit allows your business to collect sales taxes from customers to cover any sales tax that you'll owe to the BOE.

You'll pay any taxes you owe annually, quarterly, or monthly, depending on your sales volume. Businesses that will owe $100 or less per month in sales taxes can pay yearly; those that will owe $101 to $300 per month will have to pay quarterly; those that will owe $301 to $1,200 per month will need to pay monthly; and businesses that will owe more than $1,200 per month will need to use a special prepayment plan. Businesses that will owe $20,000 or more per month in sales taxes are subject to special electronic filing requirements. (We discuss collecting, reporting, and paying state sales taxes more fully in Chapter 9.) This section explains how to get a seller's permit, so you can get on with your business.

Kimberly Torgerson, owner of Your Word's Worth, a freelance editing and writing service in Berkeley, California:

It took me much less than 24 hours to get started as a freelance editor and writer; I wandered into the Berkeley business licensing office, talked with the helpful folks there, paid some fees, and bought a used computer. My biggest challenge starting out was convincing my mother that my business was real.

1. Who Needs a Seller's Permit?

Any business—whether it's a sole proprietorship, LLC, corporation, or any other type—must have a seller's permit if it sells any tangible goods to the public. Tangible goods are things you can touch, like furniture or food. Businesses that sell only services are exempt from the seller's permit requirement.

If you plan to sell tangible goods, you'll need a seller's permit whether or not those sales will be taxable. While a seller's permit is required if you sell tangible goods, taxes are due on those sales only if the tangible goods are sold to a final user within the state. In other words, you'll need a seller's permit even to conduct nontaxable sales of tangible goods—such as to a wholesaler or to an out-of-state customer. This means you need to get a sales permit before you begin to sell tangible goods; when the sales are made, you'll distinguish the taxable ones from the nontaxable ones. When it comes time to report and pay sales taxes to the state, you'll be taxed only on the taxable sales. (We cover reporting and paying sales taxes in more depth in Chapter 9.)

Unfortunately, it's sometimes tricky to figure out whether a permit is required (or whether a sale is taxable), mostly because distinguishing service sales (no permit required) from product sales (permit required) can be tough. For instance, graphic designers were for years subject to confounding BOE rules that treated their work as tangible merchandise. Many designers assumed that they operated a service, not a retail business, and thus never collected or paid sales tax. Several were socked with hefty back taxes and fines because the BOE considered them to be selling tangible goods, rather than providing services. After years of efforts by the Graphic Artists Guild and other groups, the BOE finally clarified the sales tax regulations in 2002, resulting in clearer—and, many say, fairer—treatment of the intangible nature of many graphic artists' work.

As you can see, the rules don't always comply with common sense, so you shouldn't make assumptions about how the BOE will treat your busi-ness when it comes to seller's permits and sales taxes. If you can't figure out whether your business needs a seller's permit, check out the BOE's pamphlets (listed below). Or, check out the regulations themselves, posted online at www.boe.ca.gov/sutax/staxregs.htm.

If you want a more definitive answer as to whether your specific business needs a seller's permit, you can call the BOE at 800-400-7115 and speak with an agent. When describing your business to an agent, give as much detail as you can about what you'll be doing—but not so much information that you invite an audit! It's a good idea not to identify yourself or arouse too much bureaucratic interest in your business.

Keep track of service and product sales separately. Many businesses both perform services and sell products. A metalsmith, for instance, both repairs jewelry and sells raw materials, such as precious metals and gemstones. If a business sells both labor and goods, it will need a seller's permit. Plus, to assure proper tax reporting, that business will need to keep its labor sales separate from sales of goods, since sales of services aren't taxed. (Chapter 11 explains simple bookkeeping and how to account for taxable sales separately from tax-exempt sales.)

Commonly Requested BOE Publications

In addition to the application forms for seller's permits, the BOE offers hundreds of free publications, including regulations and tax tips for particular businesses.

Some of the more popular BOE pamphlets are:

Pamphlet 22, *Tax Tips for the Dining & Beverage Industry*

Pamphlet 24, *Tax Tips for Liquor Stores*

Pamphlet 25, *Tax Tips for Auto Repair Garages and Service Stations*

Pamphlet 32, *Tax Tips for Purchasers from Mexico*

Pamphlet 35, *Tax Tips for Interior Designers and Decorators*

Pamphlet 37, *Tax Tips for the Graphic Arts Industry*

Pamphlet 76, *Audits and Appeals*

Pamphlet 80B, *Electronic Funds Transfer Program*

Commonly requested regulations include:

Regulation 1501, *Service Enterprises Generally*

Regulation 1502, *Computers, Programs, and Data Processing*

Regulation 1574, *Vending Machine Operators*

Regulation 1602, *Food Products*

Regulation 1668, *Resale Certificates*

Many of these publications are available in Chinese, Spanish, Korean, and Vietnamese.

There are a number of different ways to get BOE publications.

- You can use one of the BOE's order forms to order information by mail. An order form is included in Appendix C; you can also download an order form from the BOE's website at www.boe.ca.gov.

- If you already know which publication you want, you can call the BOE at 800-400-7115 and order it 24 hours a day by leaving a message. Or call during business hours so that you can ask an agent which publication you need.

- All publications are also available in person at any of the BOE's field offices, which are listed in Appendix C, in the California Seller's Permit Application.

- Finally, a limited selection of the BOE's publications can be downloaded directly from the Web, at www.boe.ca.gov.

2. Obtaining a Seller's Permit

To obtain a seller's permit, a sole proprietor or partnership must submit Form BOE-400-MIP to the Board of Equalization. LLCs and corporations must use Form BOE-400-MCO, which is only slightly different. A sample copy of BOE-400-MIP appears on the next two pages. This book contains both BOE-400 forms for you to fill out and use. (Tear-out forms are in Appendix C; digital copies are on the CD-ROM.) The BOE's instructions are included with the forms.

You'll need a seller's permit for each location where you sell goods, but you don't need to apply separately for each one. If you'll sell goods from more than one location, just include the address of each location with your application, and the BOE will issue as many permits as you need from the single application.

Most of the items on the BOE-400 form are self-explanatory, but we'll go through a few details for both kinds of forms.

Note that you will need to include a photocopy of each owner's driver's license or California ID card with your application. Generally this rule applies to everyone who signs the application, including sole proprietors, general partners, LLC members, and corporate officers.

BOE-400-MIP (FRONT) REV. 18 (1-03)

APPLICATION FOR SELLER'S PERMIT AND REGISTRATION
AS A RETAILER (INDIVIDUALS/PARTNERSHIPS)

STATE OF CALIFORNIA
BOARD OF EQUALIZATION

Use additional sheet(s) to include information for more than two partners

SECTION I: OWNERSHIP INFORMATION

	FOR BOARD USE ONLY			

1. PLEASE CHECK TYPE OF OWNERSHIP

☐ Sole Owner   ☐ Husband/Wife Co-ownership

☐ General Partnership   ☐ Limited Partnership
Provide documents if filed with Secretary of State.

☐ Limited Liability Partnership *(registered to practice law, accounting or architecture) Provide documents filed with Secretary of State.*

Enter Federal Employer Identification Number (FEIN), if any

TAX	IND	OFFICE	NUMBER
SR			

BUSINESS CODE   AREA CODE

APPLICATION PROCESSED BY   VERIFICATION:
☐ DL   ☐ Other

OWNER OR PARTNER

2. PARTNERSHIP NAME *(if applicable)*

3. Did you include a copy of your partnership agreement? ☐ Yes ☐ No

4. FULL NAME *(first, middle, last)*

5. SOCIAL SECURITY NUMBER

6. DRIVER LICENSE NUMBER *(attach verification)*

7. RESIDENCE ADDRESS *(street, city, state, zip code)*

8. RESIDENCE TELEPHONE NUMBER
(   )

9. NAME, ADDRESS & TELEPHONE NUMBER OF A PERSONAL REFERENCE WHO DOES NOT LIVE WITH YOU

CO-OWNER OR PARTNER

10. FULL NAME *(first, middle, last)*

11. SOCIAL SECURITY NUMBER

12. DRIVER LICENSE NUMBER *(attach verification)*

13. RESIDENCE ADDRESS *(street, city, state, zip code)*

14. RESIDENCE TELEPHONE NUMBER
(   )

15. NAME, ADDRESS & TELEPHONE NUMBER OF A PERSONAL REFERENCE WHO DOES NOT LIVE WITH YOU

SECTION II: BUSINESS INFORMATION

16. BUSINESS NAME [DBA] *(complete if different than entity name)*

17. BUSINESS ADDRESS *(street, city, state, zip code) [do not list P.O. Box or mailing service]*

18. BUSINESS TELEPHONE NUMBER
(   )

19. MAILING ADDRESS *(street, city, state, zip code) [if different from business address]*

20. BUSINESS FAX NUMBER
(   )

21. DATE YOU WILL BEGIN BUSINESS ACTIVITIES *(month, day & year)*

22. TYPE OF ITEMS SOLD

23. NUMBER OF SELLING LOCATIONS *(if 2 or more, attach list of all locations)*

24. TYPE OF BUSINESS *(check one that best describes your business)*

☐ Retail   ☐ Wholesale   ☐ Mfg.   ☐ Repair   ☐ Service   ☐ Construction Contractor

CHECK ONE
☐ Full Time   ☐ Part Time

25. OWNERSHIP CHANGES

Are you buying an existing business? ☐ Yes ☐ No   If yes, complete items 26 through 30 below.

Are you changing from one type of business organization to another (for example, from a sole owner to a general partnership or from a general partnership to a limited liability company, etc.)? ☐ Yes ☐ No   If yes, complete items 28 and 29 below.

Other: _____

26. PURCHASE PRICE
$

27. VALUE OF FIXTURES & EQUIPMENT
$

28. FORMER OWNER'S NAME

29. SELLER'S PERMIT ACCOUNT NUMBER

30. IF AN ESCROW COMPANY IS REQUESTING A TAX CLEARANCE ON YOUR BEHALF, PLEASE LIST THEIR NAME, ADDRESS, TELEPHONE NUMBER AND THE ESCROW NUMBER

31. DO YOU MAKE INTERNET SALES?
☐ Yes ☐ No   If yes, answer 32.

32. WEBSITE ADDRESS

Continued on Reverse

— tear at dotted line —

BOE-400-MIP (BACK) REV. 18 (1-03)

33. IF ALCOHOLIC BEVERAGES ARE SOLD, PLEASE LIST YOUR ALCOHOLIC BEVERAGE CONTROL LICENSE NO. AND TYPE

34. NAME, ADDRESS & TELEPHONE NUMBER OF BUSINESS LANDLORD

35. NAME, ADDRESS & TELEPHONE NUMBER OF PERSON MAINTAINING YOUR RECORDS

36. NAME & LOCATION OF BANK OR OTHER FINANCIAL INSTITUTION *(note whether business or personal)*	CHECKING ACCOUNT NUMBER(S)
	SAVINGS ACCOUNT NUMBER(S)
37. NAMES & ADDRESSES OF MAJOR SUPPLIERS	PRODUCTS PURCHASED

SECTION III: SALES AND EMPLOYER INFORMATION

38. PROJECTED MONTHLY SALES *(if unknown, enter an estimated amount)*

Total gross sales $ Taxable sales $

39. INFORMATION CONCERNING EMPLOYMENT DEVELOPMENT DEPARTMENT *(EDD)*

Are you registered with EDD? .... ☐ Yes ☐ No

If no, will your payroll exceed $100 per quarter? .... ☐ Yes ☐ No

If yes, you must apply with EDD.

Number of employees   (See pamphlet DE 44, *California Employer's Guide*)

I received pamphlet DE 44, *California Employer's Guide*. .... ☐ Yes ☐ No

CERTIFICATION

All owners and partners must sign below.

I am duly authorized to sign the application and certify that the statements made are correct to the best of my knowledge and belief.
I also represent and acknowledge that the applicant will be engaged in or conduct businesses as a seller of tangible personal property.

NAME *(typed or printed)*	SIGNATURE	DATE
NAME *(typed or printed)*	SIGNATURE	DATE
NAME *(typed or printed)*	SIGNATURE	DATE
NAME *(typed or printed)*	SIGNATURE	DATE

FOR BOARD USE ONLY
Furnished to Taxpayer

REPORTING BASIS	FORMS	PUBLICATIONS
SECURITY REVIEW	☐ BOE-8 ☐ BOE-400-Y	☐ PUB 73 ☐ PUB DE 44
☐ BOE-598 $ _____ ☐ BOE-1009 BY	☐ BOE-467 ☐ BOE-519 ☐ BOE-1241-D	
APPROVED BY REMOTE INPUT DATE BY	REGULATIONS ☐ REG. 1668 ☐ REG. 1698 ☐ REG. 1700	RETURNS
☐ Permit Issued Date _____		

a. BOE-400-MIP (for Sole Proprietorships and Partnerships)

Section I, Item 1: Indicate whether your business is a sole proprietorship (sole owner), a husband/wife co-ownership, or a partnership. If you and your spouse are co-owners, either as a partnership or as a sole proprietorship at which one spouse occasionally works without pay, the BOE wants you to check the husband/wife co-ownership box. But if one spouse is a sole proprietor and the other is either an official employee or not involved in the business at all, check the sole proprietorship box. (See Chapter 2, Section A, on different business structures and how a spouse of a business owner can sometimes participate in a sole proprietorship.)

> **EXAMPLE 1:** Chris and his wife Amy are starting a small business selling chili peppers that they grow on their ranch in the Central Valley. Since they will both actively work in the business, they will be partners for tax purposes. When filling out their application for a seller's permit, they check the "Husband/Wife Co-ownership" box.

> **EXAMPLE 2:** Tim is starting a business selling imports from Brazil and other South American countries. His wife Abby will do some work for the business, but won't share in management decisions. If Tim decides to hire Abby as an employee and pay employment taxes, he should check the "Sole Proprietorship" box on his seller's permit application. But if he doesn't want to pay employment taxes, he could simply allow Abby to volunteer for the business without being classified as an employee. In that case, Tim would check the "Husband/Wife Co-ownership" box on the seller's permit application.

Items 2 and 3: Partnerships should enter the partnership name in Item 2. The BOE's instructions (included with the BT-400-MIP form) state that partnerships should include a partnership agreement, if one exists, with the application. If you do send a partnership agreement along with the application, check the box in Item 3. The instructions go on to explain that if the partnership agreement states that business assets are held in the name of the partnership, any delinquent accounts will be collected first from partnership assets, then from the partners' personal assets. This doesn't change anything about the personal liability of partners for partnership debts. It simply clarifies the BOE's collections procedure for partnerships that use this language in their partnership agreements.

Section III, Item 38: Estimate your monthly revenue, dividing it into total gross sales and taxable sales. Generally, taxable sales include tangible items (products) sold to the final user. Nontaxable sales include sales of services and sales of tangible items to resellers. (See Chapter 9, Section G, for a detailed discussion of sales taxes.)

Item 39: If you have employees, you must register with the Employment Development Department (EDD). (See Chapter 12 on registering with the EDD and other requirements for hiring employees.) Sole proprietors and partners are owners—not employees. Your spouse, if involved in the business, may be treated as an employee or a partner, or may be nonclassified. (See Chapter 2, Section A, on husband/wife businesses and the status of your spouse as a partner or employee.) Then check the applicable box.

Certification Section: Be sure that all owners sign.

b. BOE-400-MCO (for Corporations and LLCs)

Section I: Enter basic information about your business, including the type of business entity (generally, a corporation or an LLC), its FEIN, full legal name, and state incorporation or LLC number. Then enter the requested information for each of the owners of the corporation or LLC. If your

LLC has designated officers, such as a president, secretary, and treasurer, check the "LLC or Corporate Officer" box for those individuals. Otherwise, LLC owners should just check the "LLC Member" or "LLC Manager" box. (For more on member-managed versus manager-managed LLCs, see Chapter 2.)

Section III, Item 45: Estimate your monthly revenue, dividing it into total gross sales and taxable sales. Generally, taxable sales include tangible items sold to the final user. Nontaxable sales include items sold to resellers or sales of services. (See Chapter 9, Section G, for a detailed discussion of sales taxes.)

Item 46: Virtually every corporation will have at least one employee, which means it must register with the Employment Development Department (EDD). (See Chapter 12 on registering with the EDD and other requirements for hiring employees.) If your LLC has any employees (as opposed to members), it must register with this department.

Certification Section: Only one corporate officer or LLC member should sign.

Submit your application for a seller's permit about 30 days prior to your first sale. After you apply, it generally takes two to three weeks until you get your permit. If you want a permit right away, some BOE field offices will issue one on the same day if you apply in person. (Field office addresses and phone numbers are listed in Appendix C, in the California Seller's Permit Application.)

Sole proprietorships and partnerships don't have to pay a fee for the permit. However, if you have a blemished history with a previous seller's permit—for instance, if you were late with your tax payments to the BOE—you may be required to post a deposit. Corporations and LLCs that sell retail goods are also often required to post a security deposit, which generally amounts to half a year's estimated sales tax. If your business is diligent about paying its taxes, the BOE should refund the deposit after three years.

Businesses with higher revenues must report more often and pay larger deposits. No one wants to tie up a big deposit with the State of California or pay taxes more often than is necessary. To avoid this, your best bet is to make a low estimate of expected revenues. Since no one knows how much you'll really sell (including you), it is usually possible to get the BOE to accept a modest number. This is especially likely to be true if your business will primarily provide services—and you emphasize that fact to the BOE.

c. BOE-410-D (for Swap Meets, Flea Markets, and Special Events)

Swap meet and flea market vendors need seller's permits too. Even though you're only selling junk from your backyard or garage, you're not exempt from seller's permit requirements. The BOE requires a flea market vendor to get a seller's permit unless the vendor is an "occasional seller," who is defined as follows: "A person who has cleared their garage of used items *accumulated for their own use* and who sells *only* those items would usually qualify as an occasional seller, provided they make sales no more than twice in a 12-month period."

The BOE requires flea market operators to ask individual vendors, including you, for your seller's permit number and other information. (The BOE form for this purpose, BOE-410-D, is included in Appendix C and on CD-ROM.) If you're a vendor, fill it out and give it to the coordinator of whatever sale you're participating in; don't send it to the BOE.

F. Step 6: Obtain Special Licenses or Permits

Depending on the nature of your business, you might be finished with your list of bureaucratic tasks. But before you run off to rev up your cash register, cool your jets—you may be surprised to find out that even your simple little business is subject to an extra regulation or two. Some business activities are prohibited until you obtain a license or permit to engage in them, and some business locations require special approval from the local planning department. These extra requirements are especially likely to apply to your business if it has any potential for harming the environment or hurting the public, but they also apply in lots of seemingly risk-free situations.

Figuring out what additional permits or licenses you might need can be confusing, because there are literally hundreds of independent agencies from the local to the federal level that regulate various businesses. Obviously you don't want to waste your time calling each and every one of them to find out whether your business is subject to its rules. This section will help streamline the process by first outlining the basics on what types of activities are generally regulated, and by whom. This should help you figure out whether your business is likely to face a special regulation. Then we'll direct you to a few resources that will help you make sense of the crazy patchwork of local, state, and federal regulations that might apply to your business.

Regulations have different focuses. Very generally speaking, local regulations tend to focus on the location of your business and whether it poses a nuisance or a threat to public safety. State and federal regulations typically focus more on the type of work you do and your qualifications to do it.

1. Zoning and Local Permits

Local business regulations usually deal with the physical location of the business and the safety of the premises and equipment. City zoning laws, for instance, regulate which activities are allowed in particular locations. If a certain location is zoned exclusively for residential use, there isn't enough parking to support your business, or there are too many similar businesses nearby, the zoning board

might not approve your business location. Even if your business activities are acceptable for the time being, you might not be allowed to put up the sign you want or put in additional seating once your business takes off.

If your business doesn't comply with zoning laws, you'll either need to get a permit known as a conditional use permit, or be granted an exception to the law (sometimes called a variance). Your city or county planning department is generally in charge of zoning laws. Contact them to find out whether your business complies with local rules, and, if not, how to request a conditional use permit or a zoning variance. (Chapter 4 discusses zoning laws and picking a business location.)

Audrey Wackerley, owner of RetroFit, a vintage clothing store in San Francisco:

Getting the right permits turned into a total hassle for our clothing store. After we'd been in business for a year and a half, a cop walked in our store and said we needed a "second-hand" permit. We had never even heard of one! It's not like we hadn't really made an effort to get all the permits we needed. Before we opened, we spent hours in all these different buildings downtown, waiting in endless lines (it's a lot like going to the DMV), asking a million questions to find out what permits we needed to open our store. We had a business license, a seller's permit, a sign permit...we thought we had everything we needed. But all of a sudden this cop said he'd shut us down if we didn't get the second-hand permit within five days. Five days! The permit cost $700, which was a real stretch for us right then. But what could we do? We had to scramble to get the money together and buy that stupid permit. The cop also let us know that we needed a separate jewelry permit to sell jewelry, but getting the second-hand permit was enough of an ordeal. We just decided to stop selling jewelry.

Assuming your business has met zoning requirements, it still might need to be approved by other city agencies, such as the fire or police departments, the building inspector, or the department of public health. To ensure compliance with local laws, such as health and fire codes, noise laws and environmental regulations, you may need one or more permits from these agencies. When you register with your local tax collector, you may receive information on these agencies and which types of businesses need to contact them. Your county clerk might also be able to direct you to information about regulatory agencies in your area.

San Francisco's Permit Agencies

To give you an idea of the types of local regulations that apply to businesses, here's a partial list of agencies in San Francisco and the types of businesses that they regulate.

Health Department: preparers, servers, manufacturers, and marketers of food; laundries

Police Department: billiard parlors, dance halls, massage parlors, street peddlers, taxicabs, valet parking services

Fire Department: garages, storage facilities, service stations, theaters, handlers of hazardous chemicals or gases

Public Works Department: apartments and hotels.

---

2. State and Federal Regulations

The State of California keeps track of how you conduct your business. For instance, the state wants to make sure that your cosmetologists are competent and that your carpenters do safe work. The state regulates these business activities through licensing. Businesses are more likely to need a state license or permit if they are highly specialized or if they affect the public welfare. In other words, if there's a risk that poor handling of your business activities might harm the public,

chances are good that a state license is required. Common examples of state-licensed businesses are bars, auto shops, health care services, and waste management companies.

Don't assume that your business is so simple or straightforward that you don't need a special license. You'd be amazed at how many activities the state regulates: to name a few, locksmiths must be licensed by the Bureau of Security and Investigative Services; people who train guide dogs must be licensed by the State Board of Guide Dogs; and furniture makers must be licensed by the Bureau of Home Furnishings. If you think some of these regulations sound far-fetched, take a look at a list of California's regulatory agencies—you'll quickly see that we're not making this stuff up.

The federal government doesn't regulate as heavily as local and state offices, but you may need a federal permit or license to engage in certain activities, including:

- operating a common carrier such as a trucking company (Interstate Commerce Commission)
- constructing or operating a radio or television station (Federal Communications Commission)
- manufacturing drugs or meat products (Food and Drug Administration)
- manufacturing alcohol or tobacco products, or making or selling firearms (Bureau of Alcohol, Tobacco and Firearms), and
- providing investment advice or counseling (Securities and Exchange Commission).

3. License and Permit Information Resources

Fortunately, there are resources that offer help with license and permit questions. Unfortunately, recent budget cuts forced several business assistance offices to close. Note that many of the phone numbers and other contact information you'll find at California government websites are no longer in service.

If you aren't sure what regulations might apply to your business, consult the resources listed below for help figuring out what you need to do to keep your business in full compliance.

- **CalGOLD.** The state Environmental Protection Agency (CalEPA) has an impressive interactive website that offers information on all the government requirements—not just environmental ones—a start-up business needs to know about. The site, located at www.calgold.ca.gov, requires you to enter your business type and location (city and county), then returns a list of all the licenses and permits you'll need from the local to the federal level, as well as contact information for the agencies that administer them. You won't find any detailed information about these requirements, but it still is very helpful to see them all at a glance. On the down side, this website is like any other automated information source, in that it can only handle very standard information requests. For example, if you're not sure how to categorize your business, this site won't be of much help.

- **Small Business Development Centers (SBDCs).** In California—and nationwide—networks of SBDCs offer valuable and free assistance to small businesses on a range of issues, including permit and license questions. For a list of SBDCs around the state, go to the Commerce and Economic Development Program's website at http://commerce.ca.gov. Then click on "Business and Community Resources" and proceed to the Small Business section.

- **_The California Permit Handbook_ and the _License Handbook._** Both these guides are available online for free. While the _Permit Handbook_ has not been revised since 2002, it still contains useful information about the environmental permit process. The _License Handbook_ identifies state licensing requirements and offers information about the offices that are responsible for licensing, including contact information. However, keep in mind that many of the resources listed in both these guides have changed, moved, or been eliminated. Among these is the California Office of Permit Assistance (COPA), which no longer exists.

Keep in mind that while the Web is a potentially awesome resource for navigating the permit requirements in your area, many state and local governments are still lagging in posting this kind of practical information. Don't waste your precious time searching endlessly through a state website trying to find the information you need. If it's not readily available at the site, chances are it's either not there or is so hopelessly buried that it's not worth your time to ferret it out. In these situations, it may well be better to just get on the phone or even go to the state office in person.

☑ Chapter 7 Checklist

☐ File organizational documents with the California Secretary of State (corporations, LLCs, and limited partnerships only).

☐ Obtain a federal employer identification number (FEIN).

☐ Register your fictitious business name with your county.

☐ Obtain a local tax registration certificate.

☐ Obtain a seller's permit from the California Board of Equalization to sell retail goods and collect state sales tax.

☐ Obtain specialized vocation-related licenses or environmental permits if necessary.

■

Risk Management and Insurance

In Chapter 2, we looked at the different business structures that exist and how they relate to liability issues. As discussed, creating a corporation or an LLC generally protects business owners from personal liability. If the corporation or LLC loses a lawsuit or otherwise finds itself in debt, only the business will be liable for that debt, not the owners. But in a partnership, each partner is 100% personally liable for all the business's debts and obligations. True, these debts should normally be shared among the partners, and one partner can sue the others to force them to pay up. But this not a very satisfying option if the other partners are broke or have disappeared.

Shielding owners (or employees, which we'll discuss more below) from personal liability is a totally different issue from shielding the business itself. In fact, when an individual owner or employee avoids personal liability, you can usually assume that the business will be stuck with it. The owners and employees might be happy they are not personally liable, but there's not much to cheer about when the business assets are wiped out to satisfy a judgment.

The bottom line is that a successful lawsuit against a business can be devastating, whether or not the owners are personally liable for the damages. No matter who ultimately faces liability, every business should consider where risks lurk and how to avoid them. In our litigious society, you must take liability issues seriously and take active steps to protect your business and yourself.

While the world of possible lawsuits is limited only by lawyers' imaginations, most claims arise from predictable—and often preventable—situations. If you analyze the true risks that face your business and employees, you can learn to recognize where your business is truly vulnerable and reduce the likelihood of ending up in court.

This chapter outlines the typical risks your business might face, and offers guidance on how to reduce them. We'll look at who and what may be at risk—including the owners, the staff, and the business itself. Then we'll offer risk management strategies and techniques to reduce your exposure to liability.

The encouraging news is that there are things you can do to protect yourself and your business. Hiring carefully, training thoroughly, having solid personnel policies in place, maintaining a safe working environment, and purchasing insurance are important risk management techniques that all businesses should use. It's crucial to do as much as you can *before* any legal issues arise.

Get advice on possible liability claims.
Liability issues typically involve gray areas, so the only way to absolutely determine whether someone will be held responsible for a particular act is to find out in court—an expensive way to get an answer. Use the information in this chapter as a foundation for understanding what can go wrong, and do your best to reduce your risks, but consult an attorney if you fear possible legal trouble. And run, don't walk, to an attorney if you receive an official document such as a court order, a subpoena, or a written complaint that signals the start of a lawsuit.

A. Who Might Sue or Be Sued?

Pretty much anyone you deal with in your business can sue you or the business, and vice versa. What you want to do is ward off claims by understanding your risks and taking steps to avoid problems. This section lists what could possibly go wrong for a business, divided according to which people are involved. You can read it as a checklist now, or come back later to make sure you've covered the most likely risks for your business.

The most likely kind of claim or lawsuit that could be brought by or against your business will be over a contract or agreement of some sort. That's because businesses routinely buy, rent, make, sell, or provide products or services—and all of those transactions involve contracts, whether written or oral. Most small businesses find their main problems are money related, whether it's getting paid by reluctant customers or insurers or meeting their own financial obligations by paying their suppliers, landlord, or employees. Problems like these are called "contract" claims, because they stem from contractual agreements.

A less likely but extremely serious risk can also arise when someone in or around your business gets injured—financially or personally—by some act not related to a contract. For example, if one of your employees injures someone by being negligent, typically the business will be liable. A lot of your risk management efforts will be directed at preventing these kinds of claims—called "torts" in legalese—because they can be very costly to you and your business.

1. Co-owners

If you are a co-owner of your business, you and the other co-owners have many obligations toward one another. That's because mismanaging the business, whether on purpose or unintentionally, can damage the owners' investment and may expose all owners to liability.

Claims between and among owners can arise from one owner:

- lying—for instance, about cash flow or complaints
- self-dealing—working for personal interests instead of the business's
- stealing the business's money or taking business assets for personal use

- handing out profits incorrectly
- selling property for less than it's worth
- conspiring—for example, to defraud or push out one of the co-owners
- failing to live up to the business agreement—for instance, by not contributing the amount of time and money agreed
- mishandling company funds
- mistreating the employees
- making bad deals
- producing bad products or providing poor service
- defrauding lenders, customers, landlords, or suppliers
- failing to pay payroll and income taxes
- violating laws and regulations of various kinds: safety or securities regulations, local ordinances, employment laws, and antitrust laws
- failing to properly hire, train, and supervise employees, or
- failing to observe formalities, such as recording corporate minutes or keeping personal money separate from business money.

There are many possible claims involving those who venture into business together. For example, even if you've done nothing wrong personally, a partner could sue you for your share of partnership debts, which may result in an expensive verdict or settlement. If your co-owner is your spouse, and you get divorced, the business could get mired in the tussle over marital assets. Or if you and your co-owners decide to stop being in business together, you could sue each other over mismanagement, unfair competition, wrongfully expelling a partner, or other irregularities in splitting up.

2. Business Contacts

As we mentioned above, business contracts are a common source of claims and problems. Lenders, suppliers, landlords, and customers could sue you—just as you could sue them—over contracts. For instance, your landlord could claim rent was in arrears or that you damaged the premises. Or you could sue your landlord for failing to make promised repairs or improvements. You could take over a lease or a contract and find that you are obligated for more than you agreed to take on. Customers could claim that your goods are shoddy and your return policy inadequate. Or you could have a supplier who gives you substandard goods.

Injuries outside of contractual agreements are the other main risk. Claims can be based on acts that were either intentionally bad or just unintentionally unfortunate. Customers could be accidentally injured on your premises, or by your products. You or another partner could physically assault, harass, or make racially derogatory remarks about a supplier or customer. Your customers could claim that you were not careful enough in hiring, training, and supervising the employees—who subsequently hurt someone or something. You could have a claim if a business contact assaults your employee or steals your property. The people who hire your former employee could claim you gave a falsely positive recommendation. (Employees' claims against owners are a distinct category, discussed below in Section 3c.)

employee. An injured person nearly always looks for a way to sue the employer, who usually has assets, including insurance. An employer who has to pay an injured person for harm caused by an employee could theoretically sue the employee for reimbursement, but it's not worth the trouble if the employee has no money.

A rare but important problem is that employees sometimes steal customer lists or a secret process or invention, and then go into business in competition with their former bosses. An employee with a head full of business information and years of experience in the field can be a formidable competitor, even without stealing trade secrets or a customer list.

For more information on restricting business information. The laws controlling how much and how long you can effectively restrict a former employee or associate from going into competition with you can be tricky. For guidance, see *How to Create a Noncompete Agreement,* by Shannon Miehe, and *Nondisclosure Agreements: Protect Your Trade Secrets & More,* by Richard Stim and Stephen Fishman (both published by Nolo).

3. Employees

Many businesses simply can't operate without employees to help. But while these extra minds and bodies may be essential to the business, they can also be the targets and sources of liabilities and lawsuits.

a. Owner's Claims Against Employees

A business owner may sometimes be compelled to sue an employee. Theft and property damages are common impetuses—although it may not be cost-effective to take a pilfering employee to court for small reimbursements or money owed for small repairs.

In almost every case, someone who is injured by your employee will choose to sue you—not the

---

Risks Facing Employees

Employees may have to pay an injured person for damages for injuries they cause at work by:

- failing to act reasonably and carefully—for example, working without enough sleep when they need to stay alert
- acting with reckless disregard for the safety or interests of others—for example, removing safety equipment from a machine or ignoring warnings on it, or
- hurting someone deliberately or breaking the law.

If the person injured is a coworker, the legal relief is usually limited to workers' compensation benefits.

b. Owner's Responsibility for Claims Against Employees

A business owner's responsibility for harm done by an employee is an area of potentially very serious liability. There are two different ways an employer may be held responsible for the harmful acts of an employee: when the employer is at fault in some way, and when the employer isn't at fault at all. This is surprising, but unfortunately true.

In general, an employer is liable for everything an employee does "within the course and scope of employment," because the employee acts as the employer's agent. This means that for legal purposes, it is as if the employer directed an employee's every move, simply by authorizing the employee to act. For instance, the U.S. Supreme Court recently held that a real estate corporation was "vicariously liable" for its salesman's illegal discrimination when he refused to accept a biracial couple's offer to buy a house. (*Meyer v. Holley*, 537 U.S. 280 (2003).) The ruling expressly held that the corporation's sole owner was not personally liable. This effectively protected the corporation owner's other assets by limiting liability to the corporation itself—exactly why some business owners choose to incorporate.

An employer obviously should be held responsible when the employer tells the employee to do something, and the employer knows that act will probably cause harm. An employer who knows or should know that the employee is harming someone or something will also be held culpable.

In addition, an employer is often legally responsible for an employee's acts—even when the employer did not direct the employee to do the act that caused the trouble and didn't know that the employee was doing it—if the employer *should have* done something to prevent the situation from arising. For example, an employer may be liable for carelessness in hiring, training, or supervising an employee who causes some harm on the job. This can be true even when the harm happens after work hours or away from the work premises, as long as there is some connection to the job.

 For more in-depth information on employers' potential liabilities. See *The Employer's Legal Handbook,* by Fred S. Steingold, and *Everyday Employment Law: The Basics,* by Lisa Guerin and Amy DelPo (both published by Nolo).

Liability for Independent Contractors

An independent contractor is someone who works for you but is not a regular employee. (For a discussion of the differences between an independent contractor and an employee, see Chapter 12, Section A.)

Employer liability for an independent contractor's acts is a complex area. Because a typical independent contractor works offsite, using his or her own equipment, without direct supervision, a business owner usually has little control over how the work is done. Nonetheless, the employer may still be liable to anyone who is hurt by the finished product that the independent contractor produces—for instance, if the employer uses the product at the business site or sells it to the public.

Fortunately, independent contractors often have insurance, so an employer who is sued can in turn sue the independent contractor for mistakes. For more information, see *Hiring Independent Contractors: The Employer's Legal Guide,* by Stephen Fishman, and *The Employer's Legal Handbook,* by Fred S. Steingold (both published by Nolo).

c. Claims by Employees Against Owners

Employment-related claims may pose a major liability risk to businesses with employees. Lawsuits alleging wrongful termination, sexual harassment, or other types of illegal discrimination are a serious risk to all businesses—and possibly to individual owners, managers, and employees. Here's an extremely brief and simplified outline of the types of workplace-related suits commonly faced by businesses.

 For more information on employee lawsuits. See *The Employer's Legal Handbook,* by Fred S. Steingold; *Dealing with Problem Employees: A Legal Guide,* by Amy DelPo and Lisa Guerin; *Everyday Employment Law: The Basics,* by Lisa Guerin and Amy DelPo; and *Federal Employment Laws: A Desk Reference,* by Lisa Guerin and Amy DelPo (all published by Nolo). You can also get lots of free information online from the legal encyclopedia under the heading Employment Law at www.nolo.com.

1. Wrongful Termination

In California, every employee without a written employment contract has a job only as long as both the employer and the employee agree to continue the employment. An employee can quit at any time, for any reason or no reason, and the employer can fire the employee any time, for any or no reason. This is a legal doctrine called "employment at will."

There are major qualifications to that general rule, however, that may open an employer to a lawsuit for firing a worker. For instance, an employer can't fire someone for an illegal reason, such as wrongful discrimination (discussed below), in retaliation for union organizing, or whistleblowing—reporting the employer's wrongdoing to a government agency. In these cases, the employees could sue their former employers for wrongful termination.

And employees who have written contracts setting out conditions of termination—an increasingly rare breed—can sue a business on a claim that the company did not have "good cause" to terminate the employment. This is a "breach of contract" claim. Most businesses avoid these claims by making it clear in writing that all their employees are at-will.

 For more on potential liability for firing workers. See *Everyday Employment Law: The Basics,* by Lisa Guerin and Amy DelPo (Nolo).

2. Defamation

A business that gives out false and damaging information about a former employee may be sued for harming that individual's reputation—also called defamation.

Defamation may rear its head to business owners and managers who are asked to give references for former employees. In California, there is a legal defense called a "privilege" that protects people who give job references in good faith or when negative information is true. However, if sued for defaming a former employee, it would still cost time and money to defend yourself in court.

Another problem is that, while you may believe something to be true, it is always possible to argue about the truth of subjective evaluations and personal experiences. To combat this, some managers refuse to comment at all about any former employee, except to confirm that the employee worked for the business and when. While this may be a wise policy for problem former employees, it also limits the opportunity to pass along good information about good workers. It's best to use discretion.

Another time for business owners and managers to beware of the possibility of defaming a worker is during the firing process, when emotions often run high. It's always wise to keep termination discussions brief—and tied to specifics about an individual's work performance.

3. Sexual Harassment

Sexual harassment is any unwelcome sexual conduct on the job that creates an intimidating, hostile, or offensive work environment—and by now you're surely aware that it can expose a business to liability. Some courts categorize harassing behavior as either "quid pro quo" or "hostile environment." In quid pro quo—literally, "do this for that"—a worker is confronted with demands for sexual favors to keep a job or get a promotion. Hostile environment harassment is found when sexual jokes, pictures, innuendoes, or comments are allowed to persist in the workplace.

A business can help avoid these types of claims by putting a strong sexual harassment policy in place and strictly enforcing it—along with offering periodic training for all employees on how to recognize and report sexual harassment on the job.

For in-depth information on liability for sexual harassment. See *Sexual Harassment on the Job: What It Is & How to Stop It,* by William Petrocelli and Barbara Kate Repa (Nolo).

4. Illegal Discrimination

Federal law prohibits discrimination in employment based on race, skin color, gender, religious beliefs, national origin, disability, or age. And state and local ordinances may also protect additional characteristics, such as medical condition, political activities and affiliations, and sexual orientation. That makes it illegal to use any of these factors in decisions about hiring, promoting, making job assignments, firing, or paying workers. It is even a bad idea to ask questions about those parts of an applicant's background before the business gives the offer to hire. Most businesses use clear job descriptions, review standards, and termination guidelines to avoid claims of discrimination. And, of course, epithets or hostility on the job based on these protected characteristics should not be tolerated.

But discrimination law can get more subtle and complicated, making it necessary to pay attention to reality rather than blindly enforce workplace policies. An apparently neutral job requirement may disproportionately harm members of a protected group. For instance, in California, black male employees have successfully challenged grooming codes requiring all workers to be clean-shaven, on the basis of medical evidence that black men are disproportionately likely to suffer from a skin disorder giving them painful ingrown hairs after shaving.

A growing number of discrimination complaints these days are filed by employees who have disabilities. A federal law, the Americans With Disabilities Act, requires an employer to make "reasonable accommodations" for an employee who has a disability but is otherwise able to do the job—as long as the employee requests an accommodation and the business can provide it without suffering hardship. The accommodation may be buying a special chair, computer, or other equipment, or installing a safety bar in the restroom. It may be allowing the employee to reduce work hours to undergo chemotherapy, or reassigning an employee to a job that requires less lifting or standing.

How far the employer must go to accommodate the employee varies on the facts of each situation. The employer need not always provide the most expensive accommodation or the one the employee requests first or most stridently. At a minimum, the employer and the employee should discuss and negotiate what accommodations are possible and reasonable.

The Americans With Disabilities Act also requires many businesses and buildings to be made accessible to people with disabilities. Not complying with that law is another form of illegal discrimination.

Another growing area of discrimination claims arises from bringing religion into the workplace. Employees may complain that they are being harassed by evangelical coworkers or upset by required prayers at business meetings. But if the business forbids all religious practice, employees may claim that they have a right to practice their religion at work, including praying and proselytizing. Employers often handle this by restricting religious and personal postings to a designated bulletin board, and prayer groups to nonwork times. However, a business should generally accommodate employees' religious practices, including religious garb and religious holidays.

For more on illegal discrimination in the workplace. See *Federal Employment Laws: A Desk Reference,* by Lisa Guerin and Amy DelPo (Nolo).

5. Privacy

The flip side of bringing an employee's personal beliefs into the workplace is that many employees do not want an employer to know about their lives outside the office. A manager who inquires about whether an employee went to church on Sunday may be both invading privacy and appearing to discriminate based on religious beliefs.

Various forms of employer testing may also involve privacy concerns for workers. In California, a business may legitimately require a drug test prior to offering a job. The employer may also require drug testing on the job if there are specific and significant reasons why drug testing is necessary, such as when employees handle dangerous machinery or drive on the job. However, many potential legal hazards can be addressed simply by having a rule that forbids being "under the influence" of any substance at work. An employee can be held responsible for truly dangerous or inappropriate behavior without requiring an invasive or humiliating test. Keep in mind that some prescription and over-the-counter drugs also may temporarily affect an employee's mood or concentration.

For more on drug testing and privacy issues in the workplace. See *Everyday Employment Law: The Basics,* by Lisa Guerin and Amy DelPo (Nolo).

6. Personal Injuries

An employee who is injured on the job cannot usually sue the employer or another employee for damages because state workers' compensation laws provide insurance benefits to cover those injuries. State or private disability insurance may also help compensate an injured employee.

For more information on workers' compensation laws and disability insurance. See *The Employer's Legal Handbook,* by Fred S. Steingold (Nolo).

4. Outsiders

People you never expect to come into contact with your product or service could be injured by it. And you or your employee might get into an auto accident in a company car, or on company business, and sue or be sued. You might also commit a crime that results in harming someone.

B. Risk Management Strategies

"Risk management" refers to actively addressing, managing, and reducing risks for any business. It is a rapidly growing field, partly because of the widespread and realistic fear of lawsuits. Your first goal is not to win a lawsuit, but to avoid a claim altogether. Your second goal is to resolve any claim as quickly and cheaply as appropriate, without a lawsuit. Only as a last resort should you venture to court, because that is usually very expensive and the outcome is always a gamble.

Insurance is part of a risk management program, but beware that it does not in itself constitute risk management. Sometimes the protection of insurance is adequate, but in some cases insurance may be either too expensive or simply unavailable for particular activities. (We discuss insurance in Section C, below.)

Here's one example of risk management: Many commercial and industrial sites have residual contamination from solvents, metals, and chemicals. If you buy the property, you may legally have to pay for environmental cleanup, even though the mess wasn't your fault. So, before you purchase, you should consider some ways to manage your risk.

Here are some possibilities.

- You could evaluate the likelihood and extent of contamination with scientific sampling by an engineering firm that also provides an estimate of the probable cost of cleanup. Then you would weigh whether the purchase is worth the additional costs.
- You could try to get protection through contracts—for instance, you could try to purchase insurance directly, or to negotiate a reimbursement agreement or an agreement to purchase environmental insurance from the seller.
- You could ask the relevant government agencies for a "comfort letter," in which they promise—or at least come close to promising—that their lawyers will not go after innocent landowners. Your bank may require this letter as a condition of a loan.
- You could look into a federal "brownfields" program, which gives you certain immunities from future surprise liability if you clean up urban industrial land.

See how many options there are to manage that one potentially expensive risk?

1. Find Out What Can Go Wrong

A good place to start your risk management program is to outline what you are trying to protect. Most businesses will have a similar list: its people, its physical and financial assets, and its reputation. Keeping these items in mind, you can move ahead to anticipating potential threats to them.

In addition to general risks, find out what can go wrong in your field. Talking with an insurance agent who is familiar with your type of business is one of the best ways to assess the possible risks you face. Talking with people who own or work in similar businesses is also useful, especially outside your local area; if they don't compete with you, it's more likely you can trust what they tell you. Reading trade magazines and the newspapers will keep you abreast of the kinds of lawsuits being brought. And finally, ask your employees what risks they see and what problems are waiting to

happen. They may be one of your best sources for ideas to prevent problems.

Liability Lurks All Around You

There is a sea of laws and regulations controlling safety, land use, business, employment, and other matters that business owners must abide—and ignorance of them is no excuse. You never know when you will be hauled up short for parking too many cars on the street, having an unsafe workplace, or causing an environmental disaster. You should have a pretty good idea, though, of the kinds of laws that apply to you, especially if you are in a heavily regulated industry such as manufacturing, food preparation, or professional services. There can be harsh penalties (including prison time) if, for example, you fail to report a workplace death to the appropriate agency.

Finally, it should be no surprise that you can also get in trouble by breaking various criminal laws. Businesses traditionally have special problems with failing to pay taxes, with property crimes such as theft, fraud, and arson, and with antitrust laws that prohibit forming monopolies.

2. Focus on Prevention

Once you've identified the main ways that your business is vulnerable, brainstorm ways to protect against these risks.

a. Setting a Solid Foundation

Most obviously, you should choose your partners, lenders, landlords, business sites, vendors, agents, and employees carefully. In particular, investigate in depth any deal that seems too good to be true—including the sales pitches of people who encourage you to set up in a franchise or buy expensive equipment.

Next, if you will be a joint owner of the business, get a clear understanding with your coowners about all aspects of your business: what you want to accomplish, what you expect from one another, and how or when you might split up or buy out. Money is usually the first big issue; control is next. You would be wise to have your business formation agreement in writing, whether it's a simple one-page partnership agreement or a detailed operating agreement for an LLC. If possible, co-owners should agree to mediate disputes that do arise. Mediation is generally quicker, simpler, and cheaper than a lawsuit, which is why the business community has adopted it enthusiastically.

It goes without saying that you should operate your business on the up-and-up. That includes:

- filing all the required papers and getting the right permits
- telling the truth on all documents and to everyone with whom you deal
- keeping track of company funds, inventory, and important documents
- paying your debts
- delivering what you promise
- observing business formalities, such as keeping your personal money separate from business accounts
- maintaining safety standards, and
- complying with all applicable laws, especially by paying your income and payroll taxes quarterly.

Owners must make sure their businesses comply with bureaucratic requirements. Applying for permits and licenses, filing reports, paying taxes, and so on are necessary evils for all businesses, and failing to do so may, in some cases, expose the owners to personal liability. (We cover the preliminary bureaucratic hurdles in detail in Chapter 7.) Even if a manager or another employee is in charge of filling out and filing the paperwork, ultimately it's your responsibility as an owner to make sure your business is in compliance. Check in regularly to make sure that paperwork is getting done.

Risk management can affect your decisions about what your business actually does. You may need to change or eliminate certain activities that are uninsurable or too risky. What is too risky may depend on the law and the availability of insurance—especially for construction, manufacturing, and professional services.

b. Covering Employee Issues

Employees make businesses vulnerable. Every business owner who hires employees should be very concerned about workplace-related liability issues and take steps to decrease the risks from possible claims and lawsuits. Lay the groundwork to hire carefully, train thoroughly, supervise adequately, have solid personnel policies in place, and maintain a safe working environment.

If you are unsure what your employment policies should be and what laws you must follow, check the Small Business Compliance section of the U.S. Department of Labor website (www.dol.gov) and the California Department of Industrial Relations by phone at 800-963-9424 or at its website at www.dir.ca.gov.

You can also consult a personnel specialist or HR manager, or review other employers' personnel manuals to see what's covered. Websites such as The Human Resources Learning Center (www.human-resources.org) and Nolo's Legal Encyclopedia (www.nolo.com) also provide good free information.

 For in-depth information on employment matters. See *The Employer's Legal Handbook,* by Fred S. Steingold; *Dealing with Problem Employees: A Legal Guide,* by Amy DelPo and Lisa Guerin; *Everyday Employment Law: The Basics,* by Lisa Guerin and Amy DelPo; *Create Your Own Employee Handbook,* by Lisa Guerin and Amy DelPo; and *Federal Employment Laws: A Desk Reference,* by Amy DelPo and Lisa Guerin (all published by Nolo).

With many workplace issues, the most effective risk management technique is to implement effective policies and training programs. For instance, straightforward hiring and firing policies, including a written policy that employment is "at will," help protect you against claims of discrimination and wrongful termination. A solid orientation and annual training program for employees on sexual harassment and other discrimination issues will significantly reduce your liability exposure in those areas. Every business with employees should have written, posted policies to clarify what behavior is expected and what will not be tolerated.

Similarly, workplace safety issues can be addressed through training programs and posted materials. You can ask consultants who know your type of business to evaluate your workplace for compliance with the Occupational Safety and Health Administration (OSHA)—the agency that establishes and oversees workplace safety standards. Workplace safety will be an ongoing consideration and expense.

Beyond establishing and communicating personnel and other policies, your business needs to have enforcement mechanisms in place. The toughest written sexual harassment or safety policy won't protect a business from a major lawsuit if there's no one to complain to who has power to change the situation, or if complaints go uninvestigated and policies unenforced.

An "open door" policy and a safe channel to launch complaints are very helpful. Employees who understand that their employers are taking care of their concerns are less likely to become frustrated and sue.

3. Deal With Problems

When a problem does arise, stay as calm as possible while you get as much information as you need to decide what to do. You won't do yourself or your business any good with an unconsidered response.

If a problem comes up in an area that is addressed in a written contract, a calm meeting or phone call is a good idea, followed up by a letter summarizing the meeting or conversation. Any meeting with a problem employee should be witnessed by at least one person who is neutral. If

you are out of your depth, contact an expert such an accountant, a lawyer, a doctor, an employment law specialist, or a mediator. Keep employment matters confidential.

For in-depth information on many business problems. See *Legal Guide for Starting and Running a Small Business* and *The Employer's Legal Handbook*, by Fred S. Steingold; *Dealing With Problem Employees: A Legal Guide*, by Amy DelPo and Lisa Guerin; and *Tax Savvy for the Small Business*, by Frederick W. Daily (all published by Nolo). There are also numerous articles on lawsuits and personal injuries at the free online legal encyclopedia at www.nolo.com.

You can ask the employee to agree in advance to refer serious issues to a mediator and then, if they can't be resolved within a reasonable time, to an arbitrator. A mediator is someone who helps people come to an agreement, while an arbitrator makes a binding decision. Many employers have such an agreement in their personnel manuals, which every new employee reads and signs.

It helps morale if the employer pays the costs of mediation and arbitration. After all, the employee probably has very little spare money, and a one-day mediation can commonly cost anywhere from $500 to $3,000. Some community mediation groups will take on small business claims for free or a nominal cost.

Finally, realize that you might end up paying something to settle a claim or to defend yourself, whether or not you feel responsible for what went wrong. As we discussed in Chapter 2, owners of sole proprietorships and partnerships are personally liable for all business debts, including damages stemming from a lawsuit against the business. It doesn't matter much whether these owners are personally named or found liable in a lawsuit, or whether only the business itself is either way, they'll be personally responsible for paying the damages. This fundamental rule regarding sole proprietorships and partnerships is a major reason why many business owners choose to create an LLC or corporation.

If your small business is an LLC or a corporation (or if you are a limited partner in the business), then you, and owners like you, will ordinarily not be personally responsible for any damage awards against the business. Only business assets can be used to satisfy those debts. Of course, that could wipe out your business.

⚠ **Personal guarantees may bind you.** As a practical matter, most suppliers and banks require a personal guarantee from small business owners on contracts and loans. This means that there will be personal, individual liability on claims arising from those contracts. Similarly, business owners will personally sign the document that creates their business, so the co-owners can sue one another personally on claims that arise out of starting, running, or winding up the business.

All business owners—even owners of corporations and LLCs—may face personal liability in certain situations. Those who recklessly or intentionally cause harm may be found personally liable for injuries caused by their actions. The same is true for business owners who don't carefully investigate a deal before making a business decision.

Paying for What Goes Wrong

If you have been prudent, and if the business is reasonably successful, there will be some extra money in the bank for emergencies. There may be business assets, such as machinery or a building or inventory, that you can sell or pledge to raise money—subject, of course, to agreement by your co-owners. You may also have some insurance that applies. An insurance company has to pay for an attorney to defend you against a claim your policy covers. It will likely also pay some, maybe most, of any eventual settlement or judgment against you if the claim is covered by your policy. (We discuss insurance in more detail below.)

C. Insurance

Insurance coverage is a powerful tool in risk management. However, there's no requirement that you obtain property or liability insurance for your business, unless:

- you or your employees use a company or personal vehicle for business purposes, in which case California law requires you to have liability coverage
- you have one or more employees, which in California means you must purchase workers' compensation and unemployment insurance (see Chapter 12), or
- your lender requires it as a condition for getting a loan.

But just because you don't have to get insurance doesn't mean you shouldn't. Even if you form a corporation or an LLC which shields your personal assets from business liabilities (see Chapter 2), it won't protect you from losing your business if disaster strikes. Careful as you may be, fate sometimes deals an unforeseen blow. If you face unexpected trouble, you'll be thankful you've taken steps to protect yourself.

There is an art to insuring your business: You want to get the maximum protection from insurance without blowing your whole bankroll on policies for every conceivable risk. Once you start to look, you'll find every imaginable type of insurance policy out there, although your business will probably need only a few of them at most. The two most common and generally useful types of policies are property insurance and liability insurance. We'll explain the basics of these and introduce you to many other kinds of policies that cover specific risks involved in your business. We'll also shine some light on the process of shopping for and buying the policies you need.

💡 **Caring for your policy.** Treat your insurance policy like the precious, and possibly irreplaceable, document that it is. Store it carefully. Keep an old policy even after you change insurance providers. A claim could come up that arises from a long-ago event, and that document may be your only way to track down an insurer that you had in the past. Believe it or not, if the insurance company or its successor is still in business and you have a copy of the old policy to prove it covered that event, the insurance company should provide the protection you paid for at the time.

1. Property Insurance

We've mostly looked at liability issues in this chapter, but other types of losses can also be devastating to a business. Property insurance can cover your business for damages or loss to your business property due to theft, fire, or other causes. There is a good deal of variation among policies on what property and what risks are covered and what the coverage is. Be sure you're absolutely clear on these terms when you choose a policy.

You'll want to make sure that your property insurance covers the premises themselves as well as the business's assets that are kept there, including:

- fixtures to the property, such as lighting systems or carpeting
- equipment and machinery
- office furniture
- computers, telephones, and other office machines, and
- inventory and supplies.

Most basic property insurance policies will cover these items.

If you rent your business space. Your lease may require you to get a specific amount or type of property coverage. Be sure to check your lease for any insurance requirements before you purchase a policy.

If you purchased your business property. You almost certainly paid for title insurance, which protects you from challenges to your ownership of the property. You may also want to purchase a life insurance policy that is dedicated to paying the mortgage if anything happens to you. You usually get the best deal if you buy this on your own, not from your mortgage lender or broker.

You'll need to understand not only which property is covered by your policy but what types of losses will be covered. Read it carefully to determine what causes of damage are insurable. Most general business property insurance policies will provide *basic, broad,* or *special* coverage—with special offering the broadest coverage and basic the narrowest.

A basic form policy will normally cover fire, explosions, storms, smoke, riots, vandalism, and sprinkler leaks. A broad form policy typically covers damage from broken windows and other structural glass, falling objects, and water damage. With both basic and broad form policies, certain risks may be listed as excluded—that is, not covered. Note that theft isn't typically covered under either a basic or broad form policy, a fact that surprises many business owners. (See Section 3e, below.)

Special form coverage offers the widest range of protection, as it typically covers all risks—including theft—except for those risks that are specifically excluded. While premiums for special form policies are more expensive, it may be worth the added expense if your business faces unusual risks—or simply to make sure you're covered against theft.

A basic policy may not cover the other property that you have at your business premises—for instance, if you rent a laptop or other equipment, or if customers leave their goods with you as happens at a jeweler, dry cleaner, or repair shop. If you expect to regularly have property that belongs to others at your business, get a policy that covers it.

If the policy you're considering excludes one or more items that you want covered, find out whether it can be included and at what cost. You may have to purchase what's commonly called a "rider" or an "endorsement" to add special coverage to the policy. For example, accounting records, cash, and deeds are often excluded from standard property insurance policies but can usually be covered with some extra paperwork—and an additional premium.

You may find other ways to bring the property you want covered under the scope of the policy. For example, if you want the policy to cover your personal stereo that you keep at the office, but the policy only covers business property, one option is to transfer title of the stereo to the business.

⚠️ **Possible policy adjustments for home-based businesses.** Owners of home-based businesses should figure out whether their homeowner's or renter's policies forbid business use of the home or exclude coverage of business-related claims. Make sure that your policy won't be limited or voided entirely by running a business out of your home. It's better to come clean with your insurance company about your home business and maybe spend some extra premium dollars than to find out after a catastrophe that you had no insurance after all.

Be sure that you clearly understand the dollar limits on your policy and any deductibles or co-payments you'll have to make. Also, make sure the policy covers the replacement cost of the property, not merely its depreciated value. Computer equipment, for example, loses value incredibly fast. If you lose your two-year-old computer to theft, you'd definitely want your insurance to pay for a new computer rather than the value of the stolen one, which might be barely enough to cover the shipping costs of a new machine.

2. Liability Insurance

Find out what an available "commercial general liability" (CGL) insurance policy will cover. Ask, for instance, whether it covers negligence—that is, carelessness or recklessness. Most CGL policies do not cover certain employment law claims such as harassment, discrimination, and wrongful termination. And all insurance companies will refuse to insure you against bad business decisions, criminal acts, or intentional acts of harm.

a. Personal Injury Liability Insurance

Say, for instance, that someone—a customer or supplier—puts a foot through a floorboard weakened by dry rot, trips on an electric cord, or is hit by a shelving unit that falls over. One accident like that could result in a verdict against your business for tens of thousands or even millions of dollars, even if you were only marginally at fault. For this reason, liability insurance is probably a wise investment for any business that has even minimal contact with the public.

Liability coverage insures you against the notorious slip-and-fall situation, when someone gets injured on your premises and sues you for the ranch. A general liability policy (versus a product liability or vehicle liability policy, discussed below) will cover damages that your business is ordered to pay to an individual such as a customer, supplier, or a business associate who was injured on your property.

b. Product Liability Insurance

A related, though technically different, type of insurance is product liability insurance, which protects you from lawsuits by customers claiming to be hurt by a product you made, sold, or provided. If your business has a product that has a risk of harming anyone, no matter how far fetched, you might consider this type of insurance. Plaintiffs have won product liability lawsuits even when they were ignoring warnings or misusing the product. An insurance premium will be less expensive than a big award to a tragically injured plaintiff.

c. Auto Insurance

Auto liability coverage will not be provided by a general business liability policy, but it is legally required in California. Even if it weren't required by law, it's foolish not to protect yourself against this potentially devastating risk. Insurance coverage for employees' personal cars that are used for business is known as "nonowned auto" liability insurance. This protects your business if an employee hurts someone or damages property while driving his or her car on the job. If your employees will use their own cars for business activities, it's important that you get this type of coverage. Many nonowned auto liability insurance policies do not protect employees themselves, just the business; employees usually need to get their own coverage

In California, as in most other states, you must by law purchase a minimum level of insurance. California's liability minimums are 15/30/5, which means $15,000 per person for injuries you cause to another person, up to $30,000 for all injuries you cause, and $5,000 for damage you cause to another party's property. Keep in mind that these minimums are quite low, and car accidents can easily cause damages that far exceed these amounts. The extra premium cost for a policy with higher protection levels may be well worth it.

3. Specialized Insurance

Property and liability insurance are the two most important types of coverage for small businesses, but there are many other kinds of policies. Below we list some of the more common ones. Keep in mind that a broad property or liability policy might already cover one or more risks listed here. For instance, if you have special form property insurance (discussed above), you'll probably be insured against theft.

a. Employment Practices Liability Insurance

This is a relatively new kind of insurance. It can protect you against a number of employee claims including harassment, discrimination, and wrongful termination. It can be a very useful supplement to commercial general liability insurance.

b. Business Interruption Insurance

This type of insurance will cover you if your business is forced to close for a period of time for a reason covered under the policy, such as damage from a fire or earthquake. In that case, your policy will pay approximately what you would have earned if you had been open as normal.

c. "Key Man" Insurance

This is a life insurance policy that the business owns, pays for, and collects on. It protects the business when a crucial person dies unexpectedly and the business grinds to a halt. The "key" person whose life is insured can be the founder, the owner, or an employee—the person who knows everything and holds things together, especially in a small business. This insurance gives the business some extra cash that buys time to decide what to do: whether to hire a replacement, sell the business as a going concern, or wind down gracefully. It is similar in effect to business interruption insurance.

d. Malpractice Insurance

Often expensive, this type of insurance protects you from lawsuits arising from professional mistakes. Doctors, lawyers, real estate agents, accountants, and a number of other professionals typically need malpractice insurance. It is also known as "errors and omissions" (E & O) insurance.

e. Theft Insurance

Since many basic policies do not cover losses due to theft, you may want to purchase specific insurance to cover you in case office equipment is stolen. Be sure to find out whether the policy covers employee theft as well as ordinary burglary and robbery. If not, you can usually purchase that type of coverage separately.

f. Special Coverage

Other types of insurance include credit insurance for accounts receivable, insurance for intellectual property such as trade secrets or patents, and disability insurance for owners of the business. Some businesses need insurance for issues that arise out of advertising, while others might need to guard against a big bill for environmental cleanup of purchased real estate. If you are an importer and travel frequently to dangerous foreign locations, you might want kidnap and ransom insurance. Talk with an insurance agent or broker about whether your specific business activities might warrant one or more of these special types of coverage.

Many corporations have special liability insurance called "directors and officers" (D & O) insurance, because there are occasions when directors and officers are sued individually for making employment and other decisions. This comes up, for example, in sexual harassment cases. An insurance agent can tell you when a small corporation needs this type of coverage.

4. Investigating and Purchasing a Policy

You have to do your homework to make an intelligent and cost-effective insurance purchase. And you must understand both the large and fine print so you can compare policies and purchase the best one for your business. For example, when pricing out different insurance companies, it's useless to compare two policies unless they cover the same types of property, the same risks, and the same payouts and deductibles. You can't make an informed decision until you understand all these details.

Insurance brokers who gather information from different insurance companies can help you decipher policies and figure out your best deal. Make sure any broker you consult understands all the nooks and crannies of your specific business activities and the risks that may be involved. Try to find one who specializes in policies for your type of business. You may be surprised to learn that specially tailored policies already exist that cover your particular needs. For instance, a "producer's package policy" for filmmakers covers several risks unique to the film business, such as the costs of production—often in the tens or hundreds of thousands of dollars—in case your negatives are destroyed. An insurance broker who knows your type of business will be able to direct you to these specialized policies, while a run-of-the-mill broker may not. Check trade magazines for the ads of specialized brokers, and ask other business owners who they use and what they buy.

You'll probably encounter insurance companies that offer package deals that are cheaper than buying several individual policies separately. As long as all your needs are met—and not exceeded—these deals can be a good way to go. As always, be sure you understand the extent of coverage in each area rather than relying on any general promises that the package covers "all your business needs."

Finding help on the Internet. Some websites that may be helpful are Business Insurance Quotes at www.quotefetcher.com; Business Insurance Oracle Home Page at www.insuranceoracle.com; and the Insurance Information Institute at www.iii.org.

Chapter 8 Checklist

☐ Have active risk management strategies. Start by evaluating your risks and identifying specific ways to reduce them.

☐ If your business has employees, establish personnel policies including hiring and firing guidelines, policies prohibiting sexual harassment and other discrimination, and effective enforcement mechanisms.

☐ Research and purchase appropriate insurance for your business. Contact an insurance agent or broker familiar with your business to answer your questions and to price out various policies.

☐ Get a property insurance policy that covers against all the types of losses that your business may face, such as theft, fire, and water damage.

☐ Get a liability insurance policy if your business will have any contact with the general public, or if you determine there's a significant risk that someone could sue your business for injuries or other damage.

☐ Get auto liability coverage for any vehicles used for business, including the personal cars of employees that are used for business.

☐ Consider other, specialized insurance coverage.

Paying Your Taxes

It's no fun for any profitable business to share its hard-won earnings with the government. But like it or not, as soon as your business is in the black, everyone, from your city and county to the State of California and, of course, the IRS, will demand a piece of the action. Although it's not necessary to become a tax expert before going into business, you do need to know what taxes you'll have to pay and how to pay them. Understanding your tax liability will help you be better able to:

- plan your finances, including whether you'll have enough cash to stay in business.
- avoid reporting and deposit errors, which can result in hefty—sometimes even business-threatening—penalties, and
- make good business decisions that will reduce your tax burden.

Even if your business won't make a fast profit, you may owe taxes. Lots of new businesspeople believe that if there is no profit, there is no tax. Sadly, this is not the case—local taxes on gross receipts and taxes on sales of retail goods (sales taxes) are but two examples of taxes that need to be paid regardless of whether a business is turning a profit. So even if your business may not be profitable for a year or two, you need to prepare to pay some taxes.

This chapter will give you simple, straightforward information on the taxes that owners of sole proprietorships, partnerships, and LLCs will face. It will also provide basic instructions for filing the necessary forms and paying correctly and on time. After covering the basics, we discuss the specific tax rules that apply to each business type—there's a separate section for sole proprietorships, partnerships, and LLCs. Simply read the section that's appropriate for your business form and skip the others. Then, in the last three sections, we cover estimated taxes, local taxes, and sales taxes—all of which apply more or less evenly to all business types. If your business has employees, refer to Chapter 12, for information on the special taxes faced by employers.

⚠ Help with corporate taxation issues.
This chapter offers only some broad outlines of corporate taxation. The full maze of corporate tax rules is far too complicated for us to cover in detail. If you're thinking about incorporating, keep in mind that doing so will subject you to more complicated (and occasionally unpleasant) tax rules. We present an overview of the potential tax advantages and disadvantages of corporations in Chapter 2, Section D. If you need more detailed information, take a look at *Tax Savvy for Small Business,* by Frederick Daily, or *How to Form Your Own California Corporation*, by Anthony Mancuso (both published by Nolo).

⚠ Get professional help. Tax rules and filing procedures can be quite complex, even for a relatively simple business. This chapter is meant to give you the big picture. Especially if your business is large, is incorporated, or has a number of employees, you will likely need to do additional reading and possibly hire an experienced accountant or even a tax lawyer. (Chapter 13 discusses other resources and publications for small business people, as well as how to work with experts.)

A. Tax Basics

One of the first things you should understand is that there's little rhyme or reason to the world of taxes. Don't drive yourself nuts by trying to figure out the logic of a system that has virtually none. The bottom line is that in the U.S.—and especially in California—everything that breathes or moves (and lots of things that don't) are taxed. And this includes virtually every aspect of a business that can be quantified. For example, depending on the type of business and its location, a business might have to pay taxes based on its gross income, net profit, gross retail sales, number of employees, how much employees are paid, how much property the business owns or leases, the seating ca-

Talking About Income—Key Terms Defined

A lot of different jargon is used to describe the money that comes into and flows out of your business. These financial terms are discussed in more detail elsewhere in the book, where we discuss financial projections and accounting (Chapters 5 and 11). But since these concepts are also important in understanding your taxes, here are some brief definitions.

- **Gross vs. net.** It's crucial to understand this distinction. "Gross" generally refers to total revenue, before deducting expenses such as salaries, rent, product costs, or office supplies. "Net" means what's left over after subtracting costs and expenses. (As you can see, a "gross" figure will be higher than a "net" figure, since deductions come out of the "gross" and result in the "net.") Thus "gross income" (sometimes called "gross receipts" or "gross sales") refers to the total money your business brings in, before you've begun to cover any of your costs. "Net profit" refers to your income after deducting costs and expenses. In some contexts, "net" may refer to your after-tax profit—in other words, it may reflect not only your costs and expenses, but also any taxes you owe on your income. Be aware that the terms "gross" and "net" are often bandied about loosely. It's important to understand which deductions are included when using these terms.

- **Fixed vs. variable expenses.** Fixed expenses are the ones that will be more or less the same regardless of how well your business is doing. They include rent, utility bills, insurance premiums, and loan payments. Variable expenses are the costs of the products or services themselves and anything that goes along with your product, such as packaging or shipping. Variable expenses increase or decrease depending on how much business you're doing.

- **Gross profit.** Gross profit refers to how much money you make on each sale above the cost of the item itself (its variable cost). Unlike the term "gross income," which refers to all the money your business brings in before expenses are accounted for, the term "gross profit" does take into account the cost of the product or service you're selling. For example, if a widget costs you $3 and you sell it for $5, your gross profit is $2. The term "profit margin," or "gross margin" is sometimes used to mean the same thing. The key thing to remember about gross profit is that fixed expenses such as rent or utility bills are not deducted—only the cost of the product or service itself.

- **Net profit** is what's left over after subtracting fixed expenses from gross profit. Put another way, net profit means the amount of money you have left over after subtracting all expenses—fixed and variable—from your gross income. Sometimes the term "net income" is used to mean the same thing as net profit.

- **Current vs. capital expenses.** Current expenses include ordinary, day-to-day business expenses such as office supplies and salaries. For tax purposes, you can deduct them from your business income in the year that you pay for them. Capital expenses, on the other hand, include payments for business assets (also called "capital," "fixed," or "depreciable" assets) that have a useful life of one year or more, such as computers or office furniture. Capital expenses generally can't be fully deducted in the year they are incurred, but must be deducted over a number of years—a process known as depreciation, capitalization, or amortization.

pacity of the business, or how many vehicles the business owns—and the list goes on and on.

To complicate matters further, the many different taxes are administered by different government agencies, each with its own rules, forms, and filing procedures. It's little wonder that the mere mention of taxes often induces nausea and sometimes even panic in otherwise well-adjusted business-people.

1. The Agencies Behind the Taxes

The first step in understanding small business taxes is to recognize who levies which taxes. Here's a quick breakdown.

- **Federal taxes.** The United States Internal Revenue Service, the top dog of tax agencies, collects the following taxes from small businesses and their owners: taxes on individual or corporate income, self-employment taxes (which go to the Social Security and Medicare systems), and payroll taxes. (See Chapter 12 for information on payroll taxes.)
- **California taxes.** The State of California collects the following taxes: taxes on personal or corporate income, franchise taxes on corporations, LLC taxes on LLCs, limited partnership taxes on limited partnerships, sales taxes on sales of retail goods (after the business has collected the sales tax from its customers), and payroll taxes. (See Chapter 12 for information on payroll taxes.) California also collects special taxes (called "excise taxes") on certain types of business activities, such as distributing alcohol, cigarettes, or gasoline.
- **County and city taxes.** Cities, counties, or both typically impose taxes on businesses based upon several factors. Most cities assign businesses to categories (for example, retail businesses, wholesalers, or services) then tax each category based on certain criteria, such as gross receipts, gross payroll, or number of employees. Counties in California assess and

collect property taxes on real and personal property owned by businesses within the county. Cities and counties also impose a sales tax. This tax may be collected by the state along with the state sales tax.

⚠️ **A tax by any other name is...a fee.** In addition to the taxes listed above, your business may have to pay additional fees for business licenses and tax registration. For instance, many California cities and counties require all businesses in the area to register with the local tax collector and pay a registration fee. And if your business requires a special license, such as a permit to handle food or a cosmetology license, you'll usually have to pay for it. While these fees arguably could be called taxes, we don't deal with them as such in this chapter. The various registration, permit, and license requirements—including their associated fees—for California small businesses are covered in Chapter 7.

Forms and Schedules and Returns, Oh My!

We talk a lot in this chapter about tax forms, tax schedules, and tax returns. Basically, these are simply different names for the papers you have to fill out and submit to your federal, state, or local tax agency.

Technically, a "tax form" is the principal document that businesses and their owners must use to report all the basic information about the business's or individual's income. For instance, every individual who earns income must fill out Form 1040, *Individual Income Tax Return*, and all partnerships and LLCs must file Form 1065, *Partnership Return of Income*.

A "schedule" is an additional sheet of information that the IRS requires businesses and business owners to attach to their tax forms. For instance, sole proprietors must submit Schedule C with their Form 1040 to report their income from their business, and partners and LLC owners usually need to report their business income on Schedule E. Partnerships and LLCs also have to include various schedules with their Form 1065s.

Finally, a "tax return" is simply a general term for the whole package you send off to the IRS and the state: your tax form and any attached schedules and other documents.

2. Understanding Deductions

Maximizing profits while keeping taxes as low as possible is the name of the game in any business. The main way to do this is by claiming business deductions. When you deduct an expense, you subtract it from your taxable income—which means you'll have less income to report and pay taxes on. Of course you can't deduct just any old expense you want. To stay out of trouble with the IRS, California's Franchise Tax Board (FTB), and your local tax collector, you need to understand which deductions are allowed and which are not.

a. What Expenses Are Deductible?

Allowable deductions are outlined in great length (to put it mildly) in the Internal Revenue Code; we'll summarize the basic guidelines below. You'll need to follow these rules when filling out your federal tax return, which you use to report your business income and deductions. When you file your state income tax return, you'll fill out a form (Schedule CA) that uses the information from your federal return, with a few adjustments to reflect California's different rules on deducting business expenses. As far as local taxes go, they're often based on gross income (also called "gross receipts") without taking any deductions into account. In short, your main concern should be the federal rules on deductions.

The Internal Revenue Code (IRC) states that any "ordinary and necessary" business expenses can be subtracted from your business income for federal tax purposes (IRC § 162). Figuring out whether most expenses qualify is a no-brainer. Product costs, office rent, equipment and machinery, office supplies, your business computer system, business insurance, and office utility bills are just a few examples of costs that easily count as deductible expenses. As long as an expenditure is, in fact, made for business—not personal—purposes, the general rule is that you can deduct it from your business's gross income.

It gets a little more complicated when expenditures aren't clearly made for business reasons. The IRS has special rules for expenses that border on the personal, such as travel, entertainment, and vehicle expenses. These costs are deductible, but only according to special IRS rules.

⚠️ **Resources for the details on expenses.** The rules on allowable travel and entertainment expenses are fully explained in Nolo's *Tax Savvy for Small Business,* by Fred Daily, and in IRS Publication 535, *Business Expenses*, available online at www.irs.gov.

b. How Are Expenses Deducted?

In addition to figuring out whether an expense is deductible, you need to understand how particular expenses may be deducted. First, you need to know that there's a major distinction between current and capital expenses. Current expenses can best be described as your everyday costs of doing business, such as rent, supplies, utility bills, and the like. These expenses are fully deductible in the year they occur. Capital expenses, on the other hand, are not. You incur a capital expense when you purchase an item with a useful life of at least one year—called a "business asset." Business assets include items such as vehicles, furniture, heavy equipment (like a forklift or printing press), and real estate.

Rather than fully deducting a capital expense in the year it was made, you must spread out the deduction over a number of years. This process is variously called "depreciation," "amortization," or "capitalization." Different types of assets have different depreciation rules, and the number of years over which the cost of an item must be depreciated varies. Depreciation rules are explained in IRS Publication 534, *Depreciation*, as well as in other IRS publications that cover specific types of assets.

The Section 179 Deduction

The IRS allows every business to treat a certain amount of capital expenditures as current expenses—and fully deduct them in the year they were made. This major exception is known as a "179 deduction," because it's established by Internal Revenue Code §179.

In 2003, the 179 deduction got even sweeter as a result of the Jobs and Growth Tax Relief Reconciliation Act of 2003. Now, for tax years 2003, 2004, and 2005, businesses can write off up to $100,000 in expenditures that would normally qualify as capital expenses. (In 2002, the limit was just $25,000.) Unless Congress votes to extend the higher Section 179 limit, it will go back to $25,000 for the tax years 2006 and beyond.

Whether and to what extent you should take advantage of a 179 deduction depends on your circumstances. Generally, you should take this deduction only when your taxable income is high enough that the deduction will give you a decent tax benefit right away. Businesses with low incomes might want to depreciate assets instead—taking their deductions slowly—so that they'll have more deductions available in future years when income is likely to be higher.

Start-up expenses must be depreciated over time—you can't deduct their full cost in the year you incur them. For lots of businesses, this rule doesn't matter much because their profits in the first year of operation are small (or, as is often the case, nonexistent), so a big tax deduction wouldn't result in a lot of savings anyway.

This introduction to tax deductions only begins to scratch the surface of a huge and complex body of information. *Tax Savvy for Small Business,* by Frederick W. Daily (Nolo), does an excellent job of leading you through the maze. Especially as your business grows and its finances become more complicated, you may well want to hire a tax advisor to help you use the tax rules to your best advantage. (See Chapter 13 for information on hiring and working with tax professionals.)

Where to Get Tax Forms and Schedules

Although we provide several tax forms in Appendix C and on the CD-ROM (a list is included at the beginning of Appendix C), we've left out many federal and state tax forms because they change from year to year and are readily available from other sources. Besides the flood of tax forms that are available at post offices and libraries as April 15 draws near, you can always obtain the most current forms, schedules, and publications by ordering them over the phone or downloading them off the Web.

- Order federal tax forms and other publications from the IRS by calling 800-829-3676. Or download them from the Web at www.irs.gov.
- California Franchise Tax Board (FTB) forms can be ordered by phone at 800-338-0505, or downloaded from the Web at www.ftb.ca.gov.
- Order forms from the California Board of Equalization (BOE) by calling 800-400-7115, or download them from the Web at www.boe.ca.gov.
- Local tax forms and instructions are generally sent to businesses automatically once they've registered with their city or county. Otherwise, contact the agency in charge of business taxes in your city or county (depending on where your business is located) for more information on how to obtain local tax forms. To find your local tax agency, look in the city government section of your white pages under "Tax Collector," "Business Tax Division," or "City Clerk."

3. Hobby Businesses: A Possible Source of Tax Deductions

For many small business owners, their "business" is more a labor of love than a reliable source of income. This is most often the case when an owner has other means of financial support—such as a regular job or a spouse who brings home wages or other income—that allow a microbusiness to continue even though it makes little or no money. These types of tiny businesses are usually operated from the home (renting an office would be too expensive) and are often based on activities near and dear to the owner, earning them the nickname "hobby businesses."

There is no one type of hobby business. Examples might include a basement jewelry studio, a jazz band for hire, or an antique-refinishing business. The owners would probably keep on making jewelry, playing jazz, or restoring antiques even if they never made a penny, but are making a go of turning their hobbies into profitable businesses.

Often, profits fail to materialize. For most regular businesses, spending more than a year or so losing money is a cue to close up shop. But if you love what you're doing, it might make sense for you to stick with your losing business rather than fold it up. Why? Because if you have another source of income (as many owners of hobby businesses do), the losses from your hobby business can be used to offset that income. Deducting business losses—including everyday expenses and depreciation on assets such as computer equipment—not only lowers the amount of income upon which taxes are calculated, but also may drop you into a lower tax bracket. This is what is commonly referred to as a tax shelter: an unprofitable business whose losses offset the owner's taxable income from other sources.

Of course, most entrepreneurs would much rather earn a healthy profit than lose money with their business. And the savings made possible by a tax shelter do not always justify continuing a mar-

ginal or losing business. But they definitely can make a difference in deciding whether it's worth it to keep your unprofitable—but enjoyable!—business going.

> **EXAMPLE:** Kay and Reza are married and file joint tax returns. Reza earns a salary as a chef in a local restaurant, and Kay is a magazine editor. Kay has a passion for plants, and decides to try to make a business of selling some of the hundreds of plants she grows and propagates in her backyard greenhouse. After she's spent thousands of dollars on exotic plants and better lighting equipment, the greenhouse heater goes on the fritz and over 300 of Kay's expensive, exotic plants die. Her expenses for the year total nearly $10,000, and she has not yet sold any plants. The silver lining for Kay and Reza comes at tax time, when they deduct the $10,000 loss from their joint taxable income of $105,000. This not only reduces their taxable income, but—depending on their income level and any other deductions they take—might drop them into a lower tax bracket as well.

On the down side, if you consistently use your unprofitable business as a tax shelter, deducting your losses from your other income year after year, you'll likely attract the attention of the IRS. One issue that often arises with hobby businesses is whether the venture is really a business at all. In order to deduct expenses from your taxable income, those expenses must have been incurred by a legitimate profit-motivated business—not merely a personal hobby. As you might expect, not every hobby counts as a business. If you claim a loss from your hobby business and you're audited, you'll have to prove to the IRS that your hobby is in fact a legitimate business.

a.   Proving Your Hobby Is a Business

Before you start claiming deductions for the costs of your favorite art projects or toy car collections, make sure your venture will pass IRS scrutiny and qualify as a real business. Thankfully, the IRS's definition is fairly broad. Basically, any activity that you undertake to make a profit counts as a business. In other words, you need only prove to the IRS that you're trying—not necessarily succeeding—to make a profit with your venture. The IRS uses a few different criteria to decide whether your business truly has a profit motive.

The main test for profit motive is called the "3-of-5" test. If your business makes a profit in three out of five consecutive years, it is legally presumed to have a profit motive.

While the IRS gives a lot of weight to the 3-of-5 test, it is not conclusive. In other words, if you flunk the 3-of-5 test, you still may be able to prove that your business is motivated by profit. You can use virtually any kind of evidence to prove this. Business cards, a well-maintained set of books, a separate business bank account, current business licenses and permits, and proof of advertising will all help to persuade an IRS auditor that your activity really is a business.

b.   Watch Out for Local Tax Rules

When planning your hobby business, don't forget that local requirements and taxes will increase your costs of doing business, both in time and money. Owners of lots of small businesses are surprised to find out that state and local tax regulations for small businesses can be more of a bear than IRS rules. For example, if you sell tangible products, you may be subject to state sales taxes. Plus, many cities impose taxes or fees on small businesses and require them to go through some sort of registration process, and counties often have similar requirements for businesses in rural areas. Generally speaking, these rules apply to any money-making activity within the locality—even if the hobby business doesn't intend to claim any federal or state tax deductions. (Local taxes and fees are discussed later in this chapter, in Section F, as well as in Chapter 7, Section D.)

In practice, many tiny hobby businesses—so tiny that the word "business" even seems excessive—might be able to get away unnoticed, assuming you don't deduct business losses on your tax return. Even so, you should be aware that, depending on your local rules, you may be penalized if you're caught doing business without the permits or licenses required by the state or your local government. These penalties may include fines and back taxes.

B. Income Taxes for Sole Proprietors

As mentioned throughout this book, a sole proprietorship is one and the same as its owner (the sole proprietor) for most legal and tax purposes. It follows that the sole proprietor must report and pay federal and state income taxes on all business profits, including any profits the sole proprietor leaves in the business for expansion. In other words, the business itself does not file tax returns or pay income taxes.

1. Federal Income Taxes

You're probably already familiar with the process of filing IRS Form 1040, based on income you earned at a job. Good—this means much of the process of filing federal income taxes as a sole proprietor will already be familiar to you. That's because income from your business will be treated as personal income, which you report on Form 1040 much as you report wages or returns on investments. But there are two additional steps you'll have to take: You'll have to use a separate sheet (called Schedule C) to report your business profit, and you'll also have to pay self-employment taxes based on your income, reported on Schedule SE.

a. Income Tax

You report business profits or losses on Schedule C, Profit or Loss from Business, which you submit once a year with your 1040 return, usually by April 15. (See "Defining Your Business Year" in Section E3 for information on using a business year other than the calendar year for tax-reporting purposes.) A sole proprietor who owns more than one business must file a separate Schedule C for each business. (See "Where to Get Tax Forms and Schedules" in Section A2, above, for information on obtaining the most current forms.)

You're not required to file Schedule C if your sole proprietorship doesn't make at least $400 profit in the business year, though it's a good idea to file one anyway. If your business loses money in any year, filing Schedule C allows the loss to be deducted from any other income you make for that year, reducing your total taxable income. Or you can carry over the loss into a future profitable year to offset those profits and thereby reduce your taxes. Another reason to report losses or profits under $400 on Schedule C is that doing so triggers the beginning of the time window during which the IRS can audit you. Otherwise, the IRS can audit you virtually forever.

Simplified Tax Schedule for Super-Small Sole Proprietorships

Extra-small sole proprietorships may be able to use a simplified schedule to report their incomes, Schedule C-EZ. (This schedule may only be used by sole proprietors.) To use this simplified form, which works just like Schedule C, you must:

- claim less than $2,500 in business expenses
- have had no inventory during the year
- have had no employees during the year
- use the cash method of accounting (see Chapter 11, Section B, for an explanation of the difference between the cash and accrual methods of accounting)
- own and operate only one sole proprietorship during the year
- not deduct expenses for business use of your home, and
- not report a net business loss.

If you depreciate assets or have unallowed passive activity losses from previous years, you may not be able to use this schedule. See the IRS instructions for details on who may use Schedule C-EZ.

Though Schedule C-EZ is easier to fill out than Schedule C, you won't save enough time or trouble to warrant trying to squeeze a too-large business into its parameters. Don't, for example, neglect to claim more than $2,500 in business expenses or to claim depreciation expenses just so you qualify to use the schedule. The marginal convenience of the simplified schedule just isn't worth it.

There's also an important procedural difference between reporting and paying taxes on income from a job and income from a sole proprietorship: Regular employees are subject to tax withholding by their employers, but sole proprietors usually have to estimate their taxes for the year and pay it in quarterly installments. The IRS is a stickler when it comes to making these quarterly payments and won't hesitate to fine you for doing it incorrectly or late, and especially for not doing it at all. Even if you pay your taxes in full by April 15 (or whenever your business year ends), failure to make quarterly payments means you'll be charged a penalty ranging from 6% to 9%. (Be sure to read Section E, below, on who needs to make estimated quarterly tax payments and how to do it.)

b. Self-Employment Taxes

Sole proprietors must also make contributions to the Social Security and Medicare systems, called "self-employment taxes." Regular employees contribute to these two programs through deductions from their paychecks. Sole proprietors must make their contributions when paying their other income taxes. And they have to pay more than employees do—employees only have to pay half as much into these programs because their contributions are matched by their employers. Sole proprietors must pay the entire amount themselves.

For the year 2004, self-employment taxes include:

- Social Security tax of 12.4% on profits up to $87,900, and
- Medicare tax of 2.9% on all profits.

In other words, profits of $87,900 and less will be taxed at 15.3% (both Social Security and Medicare), and profits above that will be taxed at 2.9% (Medicare only). (In comparison, regular employees only pay a 7.65% tax on wages of $87,900 or less, and a 1.45% tax on wages above that.)

Fortunately, there is a small silver lining to this dark tax cloud: Half of the total self-employment tax you'll pay can be deducted from your taxable income at year-end. And if your sole proprietor-

ship makes less than $400 profit in the business year, you don't have to pay self-employment taxes.

Reporting and Paying Are Not the Same

As we discuss the often complex rules of taxes, having to report income does not necessarily mean that you'll have to pay tax on that income. Sometimes, a tax agency such as the IRS or the California Franchise Tax Board requires you to submit a tax return even if you don't owe any taxes. Generally, a "filing" or "reporting" requirement means simply that you need to provide income and expense information, which may or may not create an actual tax obligation.

Self-employment taxes are reported on Schedule SE, which, like Schedule C (Profit or Loss from a Business), is submitted yearly with your 1040 income tax return. (See "Where to Get Tax Forms and Schedules" in Section A2, above, for information on obtaining the latest forms.) Once you determine the amount of self-employment taxes you owe on Schedule SE, you enter the result on your 1040 form in the "Other Taxes" section and add it to your personal income tax obligation. Remember, however, that most sole proprietors must estimate their total taxes for the year and pay them in quarterly installments. (Read Section E, below, for details on estimated tax payments.)

2. California Income Taxes

You must report and pay California income tax in much the same way as federal income tax. Any profit generated by a sole proprietorship is treated as personal income of the sole proprietor and reported on Schedule CA, which is submitted with Form 540, California Resident Income Tax Return. (See "Where to Get Tax Forms and Schedules" in Section A2, above, to find out how to get current

California tax forms.) Unlike the federal system, you must file Schedule CA even if your business loses money or makes less than $400 profit. Obviously you won't owe any taxes unless you've made a profit, but you must file the form in any case.

California law, like federal law, requires many businesses to estimate and pay their income taxes in quarterly installments. (Estimating your taxes and making quarterly payments is covered in Section E, below.)

C. Income Taxes for Partnerships

Although a partnership itself does not pay taxes (its owners do), it does need to submit an annual informational return to the IRS and to the California Franchise Tax Board to report its income. As is true for sole proprietorships, taxes are paid only by the partners (business owners), not the business itself, and the partners have to pay taxes on all business profits, whether or not they take any money out of the business. This section will explain what partnerships need to do to comply with the rules of the IRS and California's FTB.

1. Federal Income Taxes

Partnerships are called "pass-through tax entities," which means that profits pass right through the business to the owners, who report them on their individual income tax returns. The partnership itself is not taxed, though it must report its income and losses each year. (Although few do, a partnership can also elect to be taxed as a corporation, by submitting Form 8832 and electing corporate tax status.) In addition to income taxes, partners must also file and pay self-employment taxes.

a. Income Tax

Even though the partnership itself does not pay taxes on profits, it must report profits and losses on an informational return, Form 1065, U.S. Partnership Return of Income. No tax is due with this return, which is generally due by April 15. (See "Defining Your Business Year" in Section E2 for information on using a business year other than the calendar year.)

Along with Form 1065, the partnership must also submit a Schedule K-1, Partner's Share of Income, Credit and Deductions, for each partner, reporting each partner's share of profits or losses. The K-1 schedule is used to inform the IRS of the partners' chosen profit division. Often, partners own equal shares of the business, which normally means they will choose to share profits and pay taxes equally —such as four partners each getting ¼ of a business's profits and paying ¼ of its taxes. But if they choose, partners can divide profits and losses unequally. (See Chapter 2, Section B, for more on partnerships.) A copy of the completed K-1 must also be given to each partner on or before the date that the partnership return is due to the IRS. (Section A2, above, includes information on obtaining current tax forms.)

As we mentioned above, profits earned by a partnership are taxed as personal income of the individual partners. Each partner reports an allocated share of business income or losses on his or her individual federal income tax return (Form 1040) using Schedule E, Supplemental Income and Loss. Schedule E repeats the income information reported on Schedule K-1 (which each partner should have received from the partnership). Since the partnership already filed Schedule K-1 with the IRS, partners do not need to submit this schedule with their individual tax returns.

Partners who earn income from a profitable partnership often must estimate their taxes and pay the total in quarterly installments. (Section E, below, covers estimated tax payments, an important aspect of taxes for all small businesses.)

b. Self-Employment Taxes

Partners and other self-employed individuals who earn more than $400 profit during the business year must contribute to Social Security and Medicare through federal self-employment taxes. In 2004, self-employment taxes include:

- Social Security tax of 12.4% on profits up to $87,900, and
- Medicare tax of 2.9% on all profits.

Put another way, profits of $87,900 and less will be taxed at 15.3% (both Social Security and Medicare), and profits above that will be taxed at 2.9% (Medicare only).

On a brighter note, you can deduct half of the total self-employment tax from your taxable income at year-end. And if your partnership makes less than $400 in profit, no self-employment taxes need be filed or paid. (See "Reporting and Paying Are Not the Same" in Section B, above, if you're confused about the difference between filing taxes and paying them.)

Self-employment taxes are reported on Schedule SE, which, like Schedule E, Supplemental Income and Loss, is submitted yearly with a partner's 1040 return. Once you determine your self-employment tax with Schedule SE, enter the result on your 1040 form in the "Other Taxes" section, which you must add to your personal income tax obligation. But don't forget about estimating and paying taxes quarterly—most partners of profitable businesses must do so, or face the IRS's penalties. Ouch. (See Section E, below, on how to estimate and pay your taxes.)

2. California Income Taxes

Like the federal government, the state of California requires partnerships to file informational returns reporting business income and losses. Fortunately, California Form 565—which is filed with the state Franchise Tax Board (FTB)—is almost identical to the federal Form 1065. Also like the federal system, a partnership must submit to the FTB a Schedule K-1 for each partner, indicating the partner's share of the business profit or loss. The partnership must give each partner a copy. The California version of this form, Schedule K-1 (565), is similar to the federal version, but accounts for differences between California and federal tax laws. No tax is due with the partnership return or schedules.

Any partnership profit is taxed as personal income of the partners, who report their shares on Schedule CA, which should reflect the information from California Schedule K-1 (565). Schedule CA is submitted with Form 540, California Resident Income Tax Return. Partners do not submit the state Schedule K-1 (565) with their state returns. Unlike the federal rule for partners, a partner must file Schedule CA with the FTB even if the partnership loses money and no taxes are due.

Finally, like federal taxes, California income taxes must often be paid in quarterly installments. (Estimating your taxes and making quarterly payments are covered in Section E, below.)

D. Income Taxes for LLCs

The limited liability company (LLC), explained in greater detail in Chapter 2, Section C, is a relatively new business ownership structure. LLCs combine several key attributes that distinguish the traditional partnership and corporation, allowing LLC owners (usually called "members") to enjoy the protection from personal liability that a corporation offers, yet avoid the complicated and often expensive corporate tax system. LLC profits are taxed to the owners as individuals (like a sole proprietor or owners of a partnership). Although LLC members can instead choose to be taxed like a corporation, this choice is somewhat unusual. (But see Chapter 2, Section C, for reasons why some LLCs may want to be taxed like a corporation.) In this section we will assume your LLC will stick with pass-through tax status.

1. Federal Income Taxes

Like owners of partnerships, most LLC owners will report business profits on their individual federal income tax returns. Although this means the LLC it-self is not taxed, it must still report its income and losses to the IRS each year if it has two or more members. In addition to regular income taxes, members may be obligated to pay self-employment taxes, which are also based on business income.

a. Income Tax

LLCs with only one member are treated as sole proprietorships for tax purposes, so that business profits and losses are reported on Schedule C, to be submitted with the member's regular individual income tax return. If the LLC has two or more members, it must file an annual informational re-turn with the IRS, similar to the requirement faced by partnerships. Since the IRS hasn't yet come up with tax forms specifically for LLCs, LLC profits and losses are reported on Form 1065, U.S. Partnership Return of Income. No tax is paid with this return, which is generally due by April 15. (See "Defining Your Business Year" in Section E for information on using a business year other than the calendar year.)

Along with Form 1065, an LLC must also submit a Schedule K-1 (again, the same schedule used by partnerships) to the IRS for each member, report-ing that member's share of profits or losses. The K-1 schedule is used to inform the IRS of the mem-bers' chosen profit division. A copy of the com-pleted K-1 must also be given to each member on or before the date that the LLC return is due to the IRS.

Often, members own equal shares of the busi-ness, which normally means they will choose to share profits and pay taxes equally—such as four members each getting ¼ of a business's profits and paying ¼ of its taxes. But if they choose, LLC members can divide profits and losses unequally. (See Chapter 2, Section C, for more on LLCs and profit allocations.)

Profits earned by an LLC are taxed as personal income of the individual members. Members use the information from Schedule K-1 to report busi-ness income or losses on their individual federal income tax returns (Form 1040) using Schedule E, Supplemental Income and Loss. Since the LLC al-ready filed Schedule K-1s with the IRS, members do not need to submit this form with their returns. (Section A2, above, provides information on get-ting current tax forms.)

Like sole proprietors and partners, LLC members will have to estimate their taxes for the year and pay them in quarterly installments. (Read Section E, below, for information on estimated tax pay-ments.)

b. Self-Employment Taxes

The current rule is that LLC members who are ac-tively involved in the business must pay self-employment taxes, which include payments into the Social Security and Medicare systems. An LLC member who is not active and merely invests in the company may be exempt from the self-employment tax obligation.

The rules are far from settled. Due to the somewhat contradictory nature of LLCs—partnership-like in some respects, corporation-esque in others—it's not clear to what extent LLC owners are subject to self-employment tax. If the issue affects you, it may be wise to do some re-search or consult a business attorney to find out the latest word on how these taxes apply to LLC members. (Chapter 13 gives information on legal resources beyond this book.)

For tax year 2004, self-employment taxes include:

- Social Security tax of 12.4% on profits up to $87,900, and
- Medicare tax of 2.9% on all profits.

This translates into a 15.3% tax on profits up to $87,900 (both Social Security and Medicare), and a 2.9% tax on profits above that amount (Medicare only). (In comparison, regular employees only pay a 7.65% tax on wages of $87,900 or less, and a 1.45% tax on wages above that.)

Fortunately, if self-employment taxes are due, you can deduct half of your total self-employment taxes from your taxable income at year-end. And if your LLC made less than $400 profit in the business year or lost money, you're totally exempt from having to pay self-employment taxes. (See "Reporting and Paying Are Not the Same" in Section B, above, on the distinction between filing taxes and paying them.)

Self-employment taxes are reported on Schedule SE, which, like Schedule E, Supplemental Income and Loss, is submitted yearly with an LLC member's 1040 return. Once you determine the self-employment taxes you owe on Schedule SE, enter the result on your 1040 form in the "Other Taxes" section, which is added to your individual income tax obligation. If the LLC member is required to pay advance quarterly tax installments, however, any self-employment taxes will be included in those payments. (See Section E, below, for information on estimating taxes and paying them quarterly.)

2. California Taxes: Special LLC Tax and Fee

While the federal government treats LLCs with pass-through tax status almost exactly like partnerships, the State of California's tax treatment is annoyingly schizophrenic. Like an owner of a partnership, an LLC member is subject to California income taxes on any share of business profits. However, California also imposes special taxes on LLCs themselves, despite treating them as pass-through tax entities in most other respects.

a. LLC Tax and Fee

LLCs need to make two payments to the Franchise Tax Board (FTB): one is called an LLC tax, the other, an LLC fee. To make matters more confusing, the LLC tax is really more like a fee, and the LLC fee seems much more like a tax. Here's how this screwy system works.

The LLC tax is an $800 annual payment (it may help you to think of it as a prepaid minimum tax) that the FTB collects, in its words, "for the privilege of doing business in California." It applies to all LLCs even if they're losing money. For newly formed LLCs, the tax is due within three months and 15 days after the LLC is formed. For ongoing LLCs, this tax is due each year within three months and 15 days after the *beginning* of the business year. On the plus side, the $800 can be credited toward the other tax the LLC may owe at year-end. The LLC tax is paid with Form 3522, Limited Liability Tax Voucher. A blank copy of Form 3522 appears on the next page.

The other tax that California imposes on LLCs is the LLC fee. The LLC fee is due three months and 15 days after the *end* of the business year (usually a calendar year, making the deadline the familiar April 15). It's reported and paid with Form 568, Limited Liability Company Return of Income. The LLC fee varies according to the LLC's total income,

Instructions for Form FTB 3522
Limited Liability Company Tax Voucher

General Information

Form FTB 3522 is used to pay the annual limited liability company (LLC) tax of $800 for taxable year 2004. An LLC should use this form if it:

- Has articles of organization accepted by the California Secretary of State (SOS);
- Has a certificate of registration issued by the SOS; or
- Is doing business in California.

You can download, view, and print California tax forms and publications from our Website at **www.ftb.ca.gov**

Access other state agencies' websites through the State Agency Index on California's Website at **www.ca.gov**

Who Must Pay the Annual LLC Tax

Every LLC that is doing business in California or that has articles of organization accepted or a certificate of registration issued by the SOS **is subject to the annual LLC tax of $800**. The tax must be paid for each taxable year until a certificate of cancellation of registration or of articles of organization is filed with the SOS.

How to Complete Form FTB 3522

Enter all the information requested on this form. To ensure the timely and proper application of the payment to the LLC's account, enter the SOS file number (assigned upon registration with the SOS), and the federal employer identification number (FEIN).

Note: If the LLC leases a private mailbox (PMB) from a private business rather than a PO box from the United States Postal Service, include the box number in the field labeled "PMB no." in the address area.

Where to Mail

Detach and mail the voucher portion with the payment to:

FRANCHISE TAX BOARD
PO BOX 942857
SACRAMENTO CA 94257-0631

When to Pay the Annual LLC Tax

The annual LLC tax is due and payable **on or before the 15th day of the 4th month** after the **beginning** of the LLC's taxable year (fiscal year) or April 15, 2004 (calendar year).

Note: The first taxable year of an LLC that was not previously in existence begins when the LLC is organized.

If the 15th day of the 4th month of an existing foreign LLC's taxable year has passed before the foreign LLC commences business in California or registers with the SOS, the annual LLC tax should be paid immediately after commencing business or registering with the SOS.

Example: LLC1, a newly-formed calendar year taxpayer, organizes as an LLC in Delaware on June 1, 2004. LLC1 registers with the SOS on August 16, 2004, and begins doing business in California on August 17, 2004. Because LLC1's initial taxable year began on June 1, 2004, the annual LLC tax is due September 15, 2004 (the 15th day of the 4th month of the short period taxable year). LLC1's short period (June 1, 2004-December 31, 2004) tax return is due April 15, 2005. The annual tax payment for tax year 2005, with form FTB 3522 also is due April 15, 2005.

Penalties and Interest

If the LLC fails to pay its annual tax by the 15th day of the 4th month after the beginning of the taxable year, a late payment penalty plus interest will be assessed for failure to pay the annual LLC tax by the return due date. The penalty and interest will be computed from the due date of the tax to the date of payment.

Late Payment of Prior Year Annual LLC Tax

If a prior year LLC tax of $800 was not paid on or before the 15th day of the 4th month after the beginning of the taxable year, the tax should be remitted as soon as possible, using the appropriate taxable year form FTB 3522. **Do not** use any other form for payment of the tax. This will assure proper application of the payment to the LLC's account.

✄— DETACH HERE — — — — — — **IF NO PAYMENT IS DUE, DO NOT MAIL THIS FORM** — — — — — DETACH HERE —✄

DUE 15TH DAY OF 4TH MONTH OF TAXABLE YEAR (fiscal year) OR APRIL 15, 2004 (calendar year).

TAXABLE YEAR
2004 | Limited Liability Company Tax Voucher

CALIFORNIA FORM
3522

For calendar year 2004 or fiscal year beginning month_____ day_____ year 2004, and ending month_____ day_____ year_____ .

Limited liability company name

Secretary of State (SOS) file number

DBA

Federal employer identification number (FEIN)

Address

STE. no.   PMB no.

City

State   ZIP Code

Make your check or money order payable to "Franchise Tax Board." Write the SOS file number, FEIN, and "FTB 3522 2004" on the check or money order. Mail this voucher and the check or money order to:

FRANCHISE TAX BOARD
PO BOX 942857
SACRAMENTO CA 94257-0631

If amount of payment is zero, do not mail form } ▶

Amount of payment

352204103

FTB 3522 2003

which is calculated on Schedule Q—a form you attach to Form 568. The annual fee for taxable years beginning on or after January 1, 2001, is as follows:

Total Income:	LLC Fee:
0 to $249,999	$0
$250,000 to $499,999	$900
$500,000 to $999,999	$2,500
$1,000,000 to $4,999,999	$6,000
$5,000,000 and over	$11,790

The LLC annual fee changes. To find out the current fee schedule, go to the Franchise Tax Board's website, at www.ftb.ca.gov.

All LLCs doing business in California (and classified as partnerships) must file Form 568 regardless of how much or little income they have made. On that return, you'll subtract the $800 tax that you prepaid for the year, but since you'll also need to prepay for the next year, you'll always be $800 behind (until you dissolve your LLC).

Because the LLC tax is due 3½ months after the start of the business year, and the LLC fee is due 3½ months after the end of the year, once your LLC is up and running you'll have to simultaneously pay two taxes (assuming you bring in a gross income of more than $250,000 per year). For instance, assuming that you use a calendar year, your $800 LLC tax for the year of 2004 and your LLC fee for 2003 will both be due April 15, 2004.

EXAMPLE: Chad plans to open his restaurant, Kitty B's Catfish Shack, as a limited liability company. He files his Articles of Organization on May 31, 2004, which means his $800 minimum tax for the year is due September 15, 2004. When Chad reports taxes for the Catfish Shack the following April in the year 2005, he can count the $800 he prepaid toward any LLC taxes the restaurant owes. However, he'll have to pay another $800 minimum tax by April 15, 2005, as prepayment for that year of business.

You are not required to make advance estimated payments for the LLC tax and the LLC fee.

b. Regular State Income Taxes for Members

Aside from these special rules for the LLC tax and fee, LLCs file state income taxes much like federal income taxes. An LLC must file Form 568, Limited Liability Company Return of Income, accompanied by Schedule K-1 (565) for each LLC member, reporting that member's share of profit or losses. The LLC also needs to supply each member with a copy of the Schedule K-1 (565) submitted to the FTB.

All profits or losses that pass through the LLC to its owners must be reported on their personal California income tax returns, Form 540, using Schedule CA. Schedule CA should reflect the profit or losses reported on the state K-1 (565) return that the LLC provided to each member. Unlike the federal government, California requires an LLC member to file Schedule CA with Form 540 even if the LLC loses money. The member won't owe any taxes unless the LLC made a profit, but the form must be filed in any case.

Like federal taxes, California income taxes for members must generally be paid in quarterly installments. (Estimating your taxes and making quarterly payments is covered in Section E, just below.)

E. Estimating and Paying Your Taxes Quarterly

Anyone who earns income from a business must generally pay income taxes in quarterly installments over the course of the business year. (Some businesspeople who expect to owe little or no tax are exempt from these estimated payment requirements. See Section 1, below.) At year-end, if you've paid more than what you owe, you'll get a refund. On the other hand, if you didn't pay enough in your quarterly installments, you will owe more.

While it might not seem so at first, this system isn't all that different from the way taxes on employment wages are handled. From each paycheck, the state and federal governments require an employer to withhold income taxes based on the employee's expected annual salary or hourly pay. At year-end, the employee calculates and reports the individual tax obligation based on how much money was actually earned during the year. Depending on the dollar amount of the tax obligation, the employee will either owe more money (if the employer didn't withhold enough) or be due a refund (if the employer withheld too much).

The IRS and California's FTB require tax withholding or advance payment of estimated taxes for a simple, practical reason: They know that a sudden multi-thousand dollar bill on April 15 can be difficult for anyone. Spreading out payments by wage withholding or estimated payments is the tax agencies' way of making your life a little easier—and making sure they get their money.

Unfortunately, it's much easier for an employer to figure out an employee's estimated tax burden based on yearly salary or hourly wage than it is for a small business owner to estimate taxes based on future income from a new and unproven business. If you're wondering how you can estimate taxes on business income that hasn't come in yet, you're not alone. Projecting future income in order to estimate your tax obligation can be a dicey task, especially for brand-new business owners whose income hasn't yet evened out into any predictable rhythm. To make matters worse, you'll be socked with a penalty if your estimates are off and you don't pay enough each quarter.

But here's the good news: You don't need to start making estimated tax payments until you earn enough income to subject you to a threshold quarterly payment requirement. This should give you enough time to get a pretty good feel for how much and how quickly money—and, by extension, taxable profits—are coming into your business. And even if you do underestimate your taxes and face a penalty of a few hundred dollars, you can at least take heart that you owe extra only because your business has become profitable sooner than you anticipated.

1. Who Must Pay Estimated Taxes?

In a nutshell, business owners have to pay federal estimated taxes if they expect to owe at least $1,000 in federal taxes for any particular year (including income taxes and self-employment taxes). We'll go into the details later, but generally, this means you'll have to make estimated payments if your adjusted gross income (taxable net profits minus tax exemptions, deductions, and credits) will be between $3,000 and $6,000, depending on your tax bracket. If your business is at all profitable, count on estimating and paying your taxes quarterly. On the other hand, if you're operating at a net business loss or making next to nothing, you may not have to make estimated payments.

> **EXAMPLE:** On December 31, 2004, as part of a New Year's resolution Jason quits his job as computer salesman and opens a river-rafting outfit called the Rapids Transit Company. For the first few months of 2005, every dollar he takes in pays for equipment, insurance, and marketing. At the rate he's going, he doesn't know if he'll make a profit at all that year, so he doesn't worry about estimated taxes. However, starting in June with the heavy tourist season, he starts clearing about $1,300 per month, after all deductions. He thinks he may have at least four more months like that before winter slows business down. If so, his annual profit will be about $6,500 ($1,300 x five months). Depending on his tax status, he'll probably owe between $1,000 and $2,000 in taxes at the end of the year. He realizes he'd better start making estimated quarterly payments—or risk a penalty.

Your Day Job May Help You Avoid Estimated Taxes

If, in addition to the business you own, you work at a job that withholds taxes from your income, you might not have to pay estimated taxes if your income from your business is not a significant part of your total income Why? Because the taxes withheld from your job may cover any estimated taxes owed on your business income. In other words, the IRS wants to make sure that a certain portion of the total taxes you'll owe are paid in installments over the year, but it doesn't care whether those taxes are withheld from your paycheck or paid as estimated taxes. It's possible that the taxes withheld from your paycheck will be enough to meet your entire tax obligation. On the other hand, if your business is bringing in significant income, your wage withholding probably won't cover your tax bill.

Now for the nitty-gritty. The IRS has a relatively straightforward formula (okay, we may be stretching this just a bit) for determining whether you need to estimate and pay your taxes in installments. You'll have to pay estimated taxes if you expect:

- to owe at least $1,000 in federal taxes (including income taxes and self-employment taxes) for the current year, after subtracting any withheld taxes, and
- your withheld taxes are likely to be less than the smaller of:
  - 90% of your total tax obligation for the current tax year, or
  - 100% of your total tax owed for the previous tax year.

This formula sounds complicated, but it's not. First, it requires you to make estimated payments only if you expect to owe at least $1,000 to the IRS at year-end, above and beyond any taxes withheld from wages. This translates to about $3,000 to $6,000 in adjusted gross income from your business, depending on your tax bracket. So if your business is barely breaking even, you probably won't have to make estimated payments.

Second, if you do expect to make at least that amount from your business, you may not have to pay estimated taxes on your business income if enough taxes are withheld from any paycheck you receive. If the taxes that are withheld from your paycheck in the current year will come out to be more than 90% of what you'll owe in taxes, you won't have to make estimated payments. Or, if that's not true, there's one more way you can escape paying estimated tax payments. If the taxes withheld in the current year will add up to more than your entire tax bill for the previous year, you're free of the estimated tax requirement.

EXAMPLE: Nels works as a manager of an auto parts store, which pays him a salary and deducts federal and state taxes from each paycheck. He starts a sole proprietorship called Falcon's Auto Tow. In the first few months of his auto-towing business, Nels operates at a loss. Since his only taxable income during those months is from his paychecks, on which taxes are withheld, he doesn't have to worry about estimated payments. In the fifth month he starts to turn a profit, at which point Nels starts to pay attention to whether he must pay estimated taxes. If he thinks his wage withholding will account for at least 90% of his total tax bill at the end of the year, he doesn't need to file and pay estimated taxes. In other words, if he thinks that taxes on his small business income will account for less than 10% of his total tax bill, he'll just file his taxes at year-end like most people whose entire income is subject to wage withholding.

If you're not sure whether you have to pay federal estimated taxes, help is available. IRS Form 1040-ES contains a worksheet to use to calculate your estimated taxes, and Publication 505, *Tax Withholding and Estimated Tax*, explains in detail whether you have to pay estimated taxes. You can obtain these by calling 800-829-3676, or at www.irs.gov. Or, even better, if you have a computerized accounting program, it can help you with the calculations.

2. California Estimated Taxes: Who Must Pay?

The state follows the same general rule as the federal government. You must pay estimated state taxes if you expect:

- to owe at least $200 in state taxes after any wage withholding is taken into account, and
- your withholding and credits to be less than the smaller of:
  - 90% of your total tax obligation for the current year, or
  - 100% of your total tax owed the previous year.

 **Estimated tax rules vary.** At the federal level, if your 2003 adjusted gross income is more than $150,000 ($75,000 if married filing a separate return), you will have to pay as estimated taxes 90% of your expected tax for 2004 or 110% of the tax shown on your 2003 return, whichever is less, to avoid an estimated tax penalty. In California, an individual whose 2003 adjusted gross income is more than $150,000 (or $75,000 if married filing separate) must pay as estimated taxes a minimum of 90% of his or her tax for 2002 or 110% of that tax for 2003, whichever is less. Note that these figures vary slightly from the general federal and state rules for estimated taxes. (Be sure to consult the federal and state instructions, included in Appendix C and on the CD-ROM that comes with this book, for help calculating your estimated taxes.)

3. When to Make Estimated Tax Payments

As just discussed, you become subject to estimated tax payment requirements when you expect to earn enough profit during a business year to trigger the payment requirement. Once you expect to earn that much income, you need to do your best to estimate your income for the year and pay a quarterly installment based on the taxes due. (See Section 4, below, for more.) Each quarterly payment must be filed a half-month after the end of the quarter. For both federal and state estimated taxes, the quarterly due dates are as follows:

Income made during:	Tax installment due:
Jan. 1 through Mar. 31	April 15
Apr. 1 through May 31	June 15
June 1 through Aug. 31	September 15
Sept. 1 through Dec. 31	January 15 of the next year

If your business uses a fiscal rather than a calendar year, your payments will be due on the 15th day of the 4th, 6th, and 9th months of your fiscal year and the 1st month of the following fiscal year.

Defining Your Business Year

Except for C corporations, a business must use the calendar year as its business year unless it gets permission from the IRS to choose a different starting and ending point. It's important to understand a bit of tax jargon. Any one-year period other than the calendar year (ending on December 31) that a business uses for tax purposes, is called a "fiscal year," a "tax year," or an "accounting period." The IRS allows sole proprietorships, partnerships, LLCs, and S corporations to use a fiscal year only if there is a valid business reason for it, such as significant seasonal fluctuations in business. Fiscal years must begin on the first day of a month and end on the last day of the previous month one year later. An unincorporated business that wants to use a fiscal year must submit Form 8716, Election To Have a Tax Year Other Than a Required Tax Year, to the IRS and have it approved. (This form is included in Appendix C and on the CD-ROM.)

4. Calculating and Paying Your Estimated Taxes

There are three ways to estimate your taxes properly. You can:

- base the estimate on how much tax you owed last year
- estimate your current year's income and deductions, then calculate the taxes you'd owe for those figures, or
- calculate your tax liability after each quarter (called the "annualized income installment method"), prorating your deductions and personal exemptions. (You must also file Form 2210 if you use this method.)

With the exception of the first method, you'll need help making these calculations. Instructions and worksheets that can help you calculate your estimated tax payments are included with the fed-eral Form 1040-ES and the California Form 540-ES (the forms you'll send to the IRS and to the California FTB), which are included in Appendix C and the CD-ROM that accompanies this book. These forms also include vouchers to submit with each periodic payment. For more information on federal estimated tax payments, refer to IRS Publication 505, *Tax Withholding and Estimated Tax*. For more state estimated tax information, call the Franchise Tax Board at 800-852-5711.

Don't overlook your self-employment taxes. Self-employment taxes (see Section B1, C1, or D1, above), like income taxes, are subject to the estimated tax payment requirement. Be sure to include them when figuring your estimated tax burden for the year.

F. City and County Taxes

Unlike the federal or state governments, most cities and counties in California impose taxes directly on your business, even if your business is a pass-through entity such as a sole proprietorship, partnership, or limited liability company. Of course, you, as the owner of the business, are personally liable for these financial obligations, but the difference is that your business itself—not merely the profits that flow through to you and any other owners—incurs taxes by local governments. Often, these taxes can be more of a burden than federal or state ones because many of them are based on your business income before you deduct business costs and expenses. Some areas, for instance, impose a gross receipts tax, which calculates the tax based simply on how much total income your business brings in, without regard for your expenses.

Local taxes vary a lot from one area to the next, but your business can always expect to face some sort of "business taxes" from your city or county, as well as property taxes imposed by your county.

1. Business Taxes

This vague term simply refers to the tax your local government imposes on all businesses within the city or county limits. Businesses in rural areas will probably only deal with the county tax authority. Whether the tax is imposed by a city or a county tax authority, the information about business taxes provided in this section generally applies.

Unlike the IRS and the California FTB, which simply collect taxes after they're incurred, most local tax collectors require you to go through a tax registration process before you start your business. (Information on this process is provided in Chapter 7, Section D). Once you've registered, you'll obtain what's commonly called a "tax registration certificate" (or sometimes a "business license"). Registration gives notice to your local tax authorities that your business exists and allows them to tax it, based on whatever method your locality has adopted for your type of business.

The schemes used to tax your business in various California cities and counties are usually based on certain attributes of your business. Most localities divide businesses into a number of different categories or types, such as retail sales, wholesale sales, hotels/apartments, and service businesses. Each category uses a certain criterion to calculate taxes on, also called a tax base. A common tax base, for example, is "gross receipts" (total income, before expenses). Each category also has a certain tax rate for each tax base. Other criteria used as tax bases include total payroll, number of employees, or number of company vehicles.

In Oakland, for example, limousine companies pay a tax rate of $75 per vehicle. And San Jose charges all businesses a basic rate of $150 for up to eight employees and adds $18 for each additional employee. Other tax bases exist as well. In Sacramento, for instance, certain professionals such as accountants, attorneys, and podiatrists are taxed based on the number of years they have been licensed in the state of California.

In many cities and counties, you start paying your local taxes when you purchase your business license or registration certificate. Often, a locality will base its registration fee on your expected local tax for the year. In some localities, your registration fee is like a prepaid tax that can be applied toward your total year-end tax. In other places, the registration cost is purely an administrative fee and cannot be applied to your tax bill. And in still other areas, part of the registration cost is a prepaid tax that can be credited toward your tax bill, and part is an administrative fee.

Since rules vary widely from city to city and county to county, you'll need to check with your local tax agency to find out how it will tax your business. When searching for the appropriate tax agency, look in the government section of your white pages under City Government (or County Government if you live in an unincorporated area) for names such as "Tax Collector," "Business Licenses and Permits," or "Business Tax Division." And since local taxation of businesses is usually closely tied to start-up registration requirements, most businesses will automatically receive tax information either when they register or soon thereafter by mail. (For more information on start-up registration requirements, see Chapter 7.)

2. Property Taxes

Under state law, each county is responsible for assessing and collecting tax on certain kinds of property within the county. For businesses, this includes real estate and business equipment (sometimes called "business personal property"). An important exception is that business inventory (or items that will go into making a product or providing a service) is *not* subject to property tax.

Real estate is appraised by the county assessor only when it changes ownership or when construction is completed. Business personal property, on the other hand, is assessed every year. Some businesses must send the assessor a property statement each year, with information on the cost of all supplies, equipment, and fixtures at each business location.

The tax rate is 1% on the assessed value of the property, plus any additional tax that may have been approved by voters in your county. For specific information on your county's property tax system, call your county assessor's office, which is often part of the county clerk's office.

G. Sales Taxes

In California, retail sales are subject to state, county, and local district sales taxes. We often just refer to them as state sales taxes, since they're filed and paid to the California Board of Equalization (BOE) on one return. It's up to the BOE to distribute the collected taxes to the counties and districts across the state.

! **Sales tax and seller's permits are related.**
Recall that all businesses that sell tangible goods must apply for a seller's permit. All businesses that have a seller's permit must file a sales tax return, even if the business ultimately makes no taxable sales—for instance, if all sales fall into a tax-exempt category, such as groceries. Refer to Chapter 7, Section E, for help figuring out whether your business needs a seller's permit.

1. Taxable vs. Nontaxable Sales

For a sale to be taxable, it must:
- involve the sale of a tangible item, and
- be made to the final user of the item.

Tangible items are things you can touch, such as books, toys, or furniture. Nontangible items might include services, downloadable books, software, or intellectual property items such as patents or copyrights. (See Chapter 7, Section E, for more information about what constitutes a tangible item.)

A final user is a consumer—either an individual or a business—rather than a reseller (a wholesaler or distributor). Sales that are made directly to end users (consumers) are retail sales (taxable). Sales to resellers are wholesale sales (nontaxable). If you operate as a wholesaler and sell tangible goods to resellers, who will in turn sell them to consumers, you probably won't have to pay sales tax. (See Section 4, below, for rules on sales to resellers.)

Sales Tax Exemptions

The rules on sales taxes are clouded by swarms of exceptions and exemptions. Here are several examples of common exemptions from sales tax—that is, sales transactions that are generally not taxed:
- most groceries (but not restaurant or take-out food)
- sales to out-of-state customers
- sales to the U.S. government, and
- some sales related to the entertainment industry.

⚠️ **You may need a seller's permit.** As discussed in Chapter 7, businesses that sell tangible goods must obtain a seller's permit from the California BOE before sales begin, even if the sales aren't taxable. Selling tangible goods without a seller's permit is technically a misdemeanor crime, but typically the BOE will give you the opportunity to comply by getting a permit before it files any criminal charges. If you made any sales that were taxable before you got your seller's permit, the BOE will require you not only to get a permit, but also to pay all back taxes that are due.

2. The Nexus Requirement

Not all sales of tangible goods to end-users are subject to sales tax. One additional requirement applies: A sale is taxable only if it is made to a customer who is a resident of the state in which you're doing business. In other words, sales to out-of-state customers (such as by mail order) are not subject to sales tax.

The general rule—established by the U.S. Supreme Court in *Quill v. North Dakota,* 504 U.S. 298 (1992)—is that your business has to collect sales taxes only on sales conducted within the states in which your business is physically located. In legal terms, this is known as having a "nexus," which essentially means a physical presence. For instance, if your business has a store in California and warehouses in Texas and Illinois, then your business would have a nexus in those states and would need to collect sales taxes from customers there. On the other hand, orders shipped to customers in Wisconsin, where your business has no physical presence, would not be taxed. This explains why mail-order forms often contain language such as "California residents add 8.5% sales tax." When you see such language, you can infer that the business is located in California and must collect sales tax from customers in the state, but not from residents of other states.

Your business is likely to be deemed to have a nexus with a state if:

- you operate a retail store in the state
- your company's salespeople conduct business within the state, or
- you own or lease a warehouse or office in the state, even if it's not open to the public.

Generally, simply shipping a product or a catalog to a customer in a certain state isn't enough to establish a nexus there (assuming that you use a third-party shipper such as UPS or the U.S. Post Office).

Once a nexus exists with a given state, your business will be subject to all of that state's sales tax laws, including any seller's permit and sales tax collecting and reporting requirements. For this reason, many businesses limit their physical presence to one or two states and conduct nationwide business by mail-order or e-commerce. This approach is sound in theory, but the explosion of e-commerce has created a number of wrinkles you should know about. We cover these in the next section.

3. Sales Taxes Online

While the Web can help you leap geographical boundaries and bring the world into your living room, it also makes a quagmire out of state and local laws that are supposed to apply only to specific areas on the map. Sales tax laws have had a particularly hard time adapting to the new world of e-commerce. As more and more companies have started selling products online, there's been increasing confusion over which of these sales are subject to sales tax and which state's rules apply. Online businesses charge sales tax in a seemingly random manner, causing many lawmakers and businesspeople to call for the reform of sales tax laws. In particular, brick-and-mortar businesses are bitter that many online businesses unfairly escape paying sales taxes, giving them a competitive advantage over the real-world stores. Before we go into any details, simply keep in mind that online

sales tax rules are still emerging and highly controversial. Expect a good deal of development and change over the next few years.

Currently, the rules that apply to businesses that sell products online are no different than those for non-Web retailers. Businesses that sell products over the Web are subject to the sales tax laws in the states in which the business has a physical presence. And even for online businesses, only a traditional physical presence counts with regard to sales taxes; the fact that customers can access your website from a particular state currently isn't enough to create a nexus with that state. So online retailers don't need to pay sales taxes for transactions in every state where the website appears (which, of course, is everywhere). E-tailers need only to pay sales taxes on sales in states where the business has an office, salespeople, or other type of physical presence. Of course, if the business has a nexus with a state that doesn't charge sales taxes, then transactions there are tax free.

EXAMPLE: Killer Computers sells computers and related accessories from its website, killercomputers.com. Killer Computers has a main office in California, a phone bank in Nebraska, and warehouses in Oregon, Texas, and New Hampshire. Because of its physical presence in these five states, Killer Computers will need to comply with those states' sales tax laws. This means that when killercomputers.com sells computers to customers in California, Nebraska, Oregon, Texas, and New Hampshire, the sales tax laws of those states will apply to transactions within their borders. Since Oregon and New Hampshire don't charge sales taxes, Killer Computers doesn't have to worry about paying sales taxes when it sells computers to customers in those two states. California, Nebraska, and Texas, on the other hand, do charge sales taxes on retail sales, so when killercomputers.com sells to California, Nebraska, or Texas residents, those sales will be subject to sales taxes.

If you think that the rules for online retailers sound pretty much like the rules for other businesses, you're right. Things get a little kooky, however, when it comes to certain large e-tailers. Major chains such as Barnes & Noble and WalMart have found a way to sell their goods online free of sales tax, even to customers who live in states teeming with Barnes & Noble and WalMart retail stores. How can they get away with paying no sales tax on their online sales, even in states where they have a physical presence? By doing what big corporations do best: being crafty. The website called barnesandnoble.com is a different legal entity from the Barnes & Noble company, so the fact that Barnes & Noble has a physical presence in virtually every state doesn't matter. The barnesandnoble.com website only needs to charge sales taxes for sales to residents in states in which the website is headquartered or has some other physical presence. And the website has a nexus only with states that don't charge sales tax (Alaska, Delaware, Montana, New Hampshire, and Oregon).

It's tough to say what the future holds. The questionable practice of creating legally separate, tax-free websites is under attack. And the e-business boom in general is being blamed for billions of dollars in lost sales tax revenues each year. State revenue departments as well as brick-and-mortar companies are lobbying heavily for sales tax reform to make the system more fair for everyone.

It may be a while before any significant reform takes place. There is a great deal of legislative activity on the issue, much of it focused on streamlining the state sales tax systems so that multistate sellers could reasonably comply with more than one state's rules and regulations. Under an initiative known as the Streamlined Sales and Use Tax Agreement (SSUTA), states are working together to simplify their sales tax systems with the ultimate goal of compelling out-of-state sellers to comply with their sales tax laws.

The states' plan is to meet certain measures of streamlining (for instance, with coordinated automatic tax collection systems), then to appeal to the U.S. Congress for expanded powers to collect sales taxes from out-of-state sellers. As of early 2004, approximately 20 states have passed SSUTA legislation and are working through the details of streamlining their complex sales tax codes. The sheer immensity of the task makes progress slow going, however, so it's hard to say what the long-term future holds.

 Help with taxes. For information on the ever-changing world of e-commerce taxes, check out the Vertix Tax Cybrary at www.vertex.inc.com/taxcybrary. Another resource is EcommerceTax.com.

4. Sales to Final Users vs. Sales to Resellers

As mentioned above, states generally tax only sales to the final user. The idea behind this rule is to make sure that items are taxed only once. Rather than taxing the sale of a lamp, for instance, each time it is sold—from its manufacturer, to the wholesaler, to the final customer—it is taxed only when it is sold to the final consumer. (Some transactions that are exempt from sales tax, however, may be subject to a nearly identical tax, a "use tax." See Section 6, below.)

How can you be sure that a customer is a final user? Customers who intend to resell your product should present you with a "resale certificate," which states that the product is being purchased for resale. The certificate must contain certain information, including:

- the purchaser's name and address
- the number of the purchaser's seller's permit
- a description of the property to be purchased
- a statement that the property is being used for resale, in terms such as "will be resold" or "for resale" (language such as "nontaxable" or "exempt" is not enough)
- the date of the sale, and
- the signature of the purchaser or an authorized agent.

If you are not presented with such a certificate, you should assume the customer is the final user and treat the sale as taxable. If you sell to the same customer repeatedly, you need only collect one resale certificate, which you should keep on file at your office. From then on, whenever you sell items to that company, there is no need to collect another resale certificate.

5. Using Resale Certificates

Just as your customers can escape paying you sales taxes by presenting a resale certificate, you can use one to purchase goods and supplies free of sales tax, as long as the goods and supplies are for legitimate resale. This applies whether you'll resell purchased goods as is, or whether you'll incorporate purchased supplies into your products. (But see the discussion of "use tax" in Section 6, below.) If you buy regularly from the same supplier, you should only have to present your resale certificate once.

Appendix C and the CD-ROM that comes with it contain blank resale certificates approved by the BOE. Simply give a completed resale certificate, with your valid seller's permit number and the other information listed above, to any company from which you buy goods in order to be exempt from sales tax. There is no need to file a copy of the form with the state.

This exception doesn't apply to goods and supplies that you don't plan to resell or use in manufacturing products. You must pay sales taxes on all items that you'll use in your business and not pass on to a customer. In other words, when you are actually the final user, you have to pay sales tax like anyone else. This includes sales tax on goods and supplies you use to perform services or operate your business. For example, a hairdresser must pay sales tax on the shampoo used to wash people's hair, but not on shampoo offered for sale to salon customers. Similarly, if you purchase a computer to keep track of your sales, you should pay the sales tax on that purchase. When purchasing a combination of goods, only some of which you intend to resell, you must clearly indicate which items are for resale and pay sales taxes on the rest.

6. Use Taxes

Before you get too excited about sales tax exemptions and exceptions, you should know that California usually finds a way to get a piece of the action, even on sales that aren't subject to sales tax. While it's true that some sales of tangible goods are exempt from sales tax, many of these transactions are actually subject to a use tax. In keeping with its name, a use tax is due when you use a tangible good in the state of California, but didn't pay sales tax for it. The use tax rate is the same as the sales tax rate in that county.

Use taxes commonly apply to purchases of tangible goods from out of state that are used in California. For instance, if you order 20 computers, 20 chairs, and 20 desks for your office from an out-of-state mail order catalog, you probably didn't pay sales taxes on those items, because most states don't require businesses to collect sales tax from out-of-state purchasers. But under California's use tax law, the state can collect use taxes from you, the buyer, to make up for the revenue it would have gotten if you had bought the equipment within the state. In that way, California collects taxes from the purchaser that it can't collect from the out-of-state seller.

Other transactions subject to use tax include purchases of items you originally intended to resell (and bought tax-free because you used your resale certificate), but used for another purpose. Also, items used in manufacturing are subject to use tax (unless they become a physical part of the final product sold), as are items you lease, if the items were bought or leased tax free with a resale certificate. Inventory that you store for future resale is not subject to use tax. (See BOE Publication 110, *California Use Tax Basics* for more info.)

You report the use taxes you owe at the same time you report sales taxes, on Form BT-401, California State, Local and District Sales and Use Tax Return. You must list the total use tax you owe on Line 2 of the return. (But if you paid another state's sales or use tax for some purchases, do not include the tax you paid in your total on line 2. Put the tax you paid on line 20 instead—you may get a credit for this amount.) If you are confused about how the sales and use tax laws apply to your specific activity or transaction, call the State Board of Equalization office at 800-400-7115.

There's a high blow-off factor when it comes to use taxes. Use taxes have largely been ignored by individuals and businesses, and the inherent difficulty of enforcing this tax allows virtually everyone to get away with it. However, many states that have traditionally been lax in enforcing and collecting use taxes are now stepping up their efforts to collect them. Particularly in today's environment of thriving e-commerce, sales taxes on out-of-state purchases are becoming a burning issue. Keep an eye out for developments in this area, and don't get caught with your use taxes down.

7. Keeping Track of Your Sales

When you obtain a seller's permit, you obligate yourself to file a sales (and use) tax return. This means that you'll need to keep careful records of both your sales and purchases. The BOE requires that you keep:

- books or computer files recording your sales and purchases
- bills, receipts, invoices, contracts, or other documents (called "documents of original entry") that support your books, and
- schedules and working papers used in preparing your tax returns.

In addition, if you conduct business in more than one county, you'll need to keep separate records of sales made in each county.

Finally, your records should show all sales your business makes, even sales that aren't taxable.

8. Calculating, Paying, and Filing Sales Taxes

The standard statewide sales tax rate is 7.25%, which is the total of a 6% state tax, a .25% county tax, and a 1% local tax. However, if you conduct business in an area that has imposed an additional tax (there are a number of them, listed in "Special Tax Districts"), your sales in those areas will be subject to the higher rate.

Special Tax Districts	
(Counties unless otherwise noted)	
Alameda	8.25%
City of Avalon	8.75%
City of Calexico	8.25%
City of Clearlake	7.75%
City of Clovis	8.175%
Contra Costa	8.25%
Fresno	7.875%
Imperial	7.75%
Inyo	7.75%
Los Angeles	8.25%
Madera	7.75%
Mariposa	7.75%
Napa	7.75%
Nevada	7.375%
Orange	7.75%
City of Placerville	7.50%
Riverside	7.75%
Sacramento	7.75%
San Bernardino	7.75%
San Diego	7.75%
San Francisco	8.50%
San Joaquin	7.75%
San Mateo	8.25%
Santa Barbara	7.75%
Santa Clara	8.25%
Santa Cruz	8%
City of Sebastopol	7.625%
Solano	7.375%
Sonoma	7.50%
Stanislaus	7.375%
Town of Truckee	7.875%
City of Woodland	7.75%

Source: California State Board of Equalization, 10/1/03.

Fortunately, you can report and pay all of your sales taxes on one form: BT-401, California State, Local and District Sales and Use Tax Return. (Many small businesses can fill out a shortened version of that form, BT-401EZ. See "Simplified Sales Tax Return" below.) All types of businesses, including sole proprietorships, partnerships, LLCs, and corporations (for-profit as well as nonprofit), use the same form and are subject to the same sales tax rules.

Businesses that have been issued a seller's permit will automatically receive Form BT-401 in the mail, along with an account number, due date, and filing instructions. Depending on your sales volume, you'll need to submit your sales tax return yearly, quarterly, or monthly.

Sellers may be required to file sales tax returns. If you applied for and received a seller's permit because you anticipated selling goods, you'll need to submit Form BT-401 even if you never made a sale. If you didn't make any taxable sales, you won't owe any taxes, but you still need to submit the form. If you don't, you risk losing your seller's permit, which means you couldn't legally make any retail sales at all.

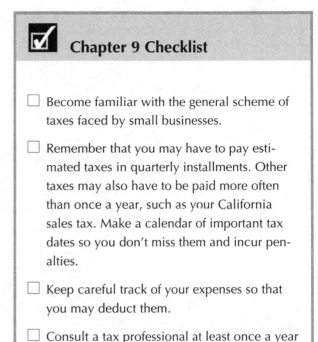

Chapter 9 Checklist

☐ Become familiar with the general scheme of taxes faced by small businesses.

☐ Remember that you may have to pay estimated taxes in quarterly installments. Other taxes may also have to be paid more often than once a year, such as your California sales tax. Make a calendar of important tax dates so you don't miss them and incur penalties.

☐ Keep careful track of your expenses so that you may deduct them.

☐ Consult a tax professional at least once a year to help you organize your books and reduce your taxes.

☐ File and pay your annual taxes each year, and other taxes as they become due.

Simplified Sales Tax Return

Some businesses can fill out a simplified sales tax return, Form BT-401EZ. Your business can use the simplified form if you:

- sell in only one county
- do not sell fixed-price contracts or leases
- do not sell fuel, cars, boats, or aircraft, or sell to aircraft common carriers
- do not claim sales tax exemptions for discounts, returned items, or bad debts, and
- do not claim a credit for sales tax paid to another state.

Entering Into Contracts and Agreements

As a business owner, you'll often have to enter into contracts—legal agreements—with other businesses and people: suppliers, customers, creditors, and landlords, for example. While a few of these transactions will be simple enough to complete with a handshake, most will be sufficiently complicated, long-term, or financially important to require a written contract.

Thankfully—and contrary to what many people believe—a contract is often a fairly simple legal document. A contract usually consists of mutual promises to do specific acts: "A promises to pay B $1,000 if B delivers 50,000 twist-ties to A's warehouse on or before March 1, 2005." A written contract usually includes the main terms of the agreement: the price of goods, important dates, and the time and place of delivery. For most contractual agreements, standard forms are readily available. Except in the relatively few instances in which lots of money or cutting legal issues are involved, you probably won't need a lawyer to complete your contract.

Simple as some types of contracts may be, you must remember that they are legally enforceable. If you fail to keep your end of the bargain, you can be sued and forced to pay monetary damages to the other party or, in some circumstances, to do the things you promised in the contract.

This chapter will explain some contract basics, including what makes a contract enforceable and which contracts are legally required to be in writing.

Kimberly Torgerson, owner of Your Word's Worth, a freelance editing and writing service in Berkeley:

Several years ago, I took on a short-term project managing the last-minute editing for a medical software program. The timeline was extremely tight, and I needed to locate and manage about ten additional freelance editors, who got paid directly from the company that hired me. Because I had not worked with the company before, or many of the editors I had located, I drafted an agreement that spelled out delivery,

completion, and payment terms for everyone involved. To draft this agreement, I looked at my previous professional service agreements and a Nolo book, and ran it by a friend who is a lawyer. A seat-of-the-pants approach, but it worked.

A. Contract Basics

Although lots of contracts are filled with mind-bending legal gibberish, there's no reason why this has to be true. For most contracts, legalese is not essential or even helpful. On the contrary, the agreements you should put into a written contract are best expressed in simple, everyday English.

 Don't be afraid to redraft. When reading a contract that has been presented to you, your first task is to make sure you understand all of its terms. It is just plain foolish to sign a contract if you're unclear on the meaning of any of its language. If a clause is poorly written, hard to understand, or doesn't accomplish your key goals, rewrite it in clearer language. By refusing to sign at the "X" unless your goals are clearly met, you'll be less likely to find yourself in a breach-of-contract lawsuit later on. A breach of contract occurs when one party fails to live up to the terms or promises in the contract. (For more on changing contract language, see Section D, below.)

1. Elements of a Valid Contract

A contract will be valid if:
- all parties are in agreement (after an offer has been made by one party and accepted by the other), and
- something of value has been exchanged, such as cash, services, or goods, for something else of value (or there is a promise to make such an exchange).

In a few situations, such as the sale of real estate, the agreement must also be in writing. (See Section 2, below.) Of course, because oral contracts can be difficult or impossible to prove, it is wise to write out most agreements.

Now let's look at each of these elements in more detail.

a. Agreement Between Parties

Although it may seem like stating the obvious, an essential element of a valid contract is that all parties really do agree on all major issues. In real life there are plenty of situations that blur the line between a full agreement and a preliminary discussion about the possibility of making an agreement. To help clarify these borderline cases, legal rules have developed to define when an agreement legally exists.

The most basic rule of contract law is the "offer and acceptance rule." that a legal contract exists when one party makes an offer and the other party accepts it. For most types of contracts, this can be done either orally or in writing. (For a few, discussed in Section 2, below, the offer and acceptance must be made in writing.)

Let's say, for instance, you're shopping around for a print shop to produce brochures for your business. One printer confirms, either orally or in writing, that he'll print 5,000 two-color flyers for $200. This constitutes his offer. If you tell him to go ahead with the job, you've accepted his offer. In the eyes of the law, when you tell the printer to go ahead, you create a contract, which means you're liable for your side of the bargain (in this case, payment of $200). But if you tell the printer you're not sure and want to continue shopping around (or don't even respond, for that matter), you clearly haven't accepted his offer and no agreement has been reached. Or if you say his offer sounds great, except that you want three colors instead of two, no contract has been made, since you have not accepted all of the important terms of the offer—you've changed one. (Depending on

your wording, you may have made a "counteroffer," which is discussed below.)

Advertisements as Offers

Generally, an advertisement to the public does not count as an offer in the legal sense. In other words, if you advertised your catering services in your local weekly newspaper, and included a price quote of $300 for your standard menu serving 20 people, you would not be legally bound to live up to that service if someone called you and said, "I accept!" If, for instance, you were too busy with other catering jobs and unable to do the job for the eager caller, you could decline. Since your ad wasn't, legally speaking, an offer, the caller couldn't claim a legal acceptance to create a binding contract.

Despite this rule, however, you do need to watch what you say in your advertisements. Generally, you must stock enough of an advertised item to meet reasonably expected demand, or else your ad must state that stock is limited.

Of course, false or misleading advertising is always a bad idea. Federal laws regulating trade and state consumer protection laws prohibit deceptive advertising, even if no one was actually misled. And check your ad's facts—false advertising is illegal, even if you believed the ad to be truthful when you ran it.

In real, day-to-day business, the seemingly simple steps of offer and acceptance can become quite convoluted. For instance, sometimes when you make an offer, it isn't quickly and unequivocally accepted; the other party may want to think about it for a while or try to get a better deal. And before your offer is accepted by anyone, you might change your mind and want to withdraw or amend it. Delaying acceptance of an offer, revoking an offer, and making a counteroffer are common situations in business transactions that often lead to confusion and conflict. To cut down on the potential for dispute, make sure you understand the following issues and rules.

- **How long an offer stays open.** Unless an offer includes a stated expiration date, it remains open for a "reasonable" period of time. What's reasonable, of course, is open to interpretation and will depend on the type of business and the particular situation. Because the law in this area is so vague, if you want to accept someone else's offer, the best approach is to do it as soon as possible, while there's little doubt that the offer is still open. Keep in mind that until you accept, the person or company who made the offer—called the offeror—may revoke it.

   If you are the offeror, be very clear about how long your offer will remain open. The best way to do this is to include an expiration date in the offer. But to leave yourself room to revoke the offer, don't promise that an offer will remain open until a certain date. Instead, state that the offer will expire on that date.

Include an expiration date clause in all bids. In many types of businesses, from replacing roofs to redesigning websites, it is common to bid (in other words, to make an offer to create a contract) on lots more jobs than you really need or want. But sometimes this strategy can backfire. With lots of offers floating around, there is always the chance that too many will be accepted, raising the embarrassing possibility that you won't be able to deliver on all the work. One easy way to minimize this problem is to print right on your bid or offer form that all offers are good for only ten days (or some other relatively short period) unless extended in writing.

- **Revoking an offer.** Anyone who makes an offer can revoke it as long as it hasn't yet been accepted. This means if you make an offer and the other party needs some time to think it through, you can revoke your original offer. If your offer is accepted while it is still open, however, you'll have a binding agreement. In other words, revocation must happen before acceptance.

- **Options.** Sometimes the offeror promises that an offer will remain open for a stated period of time—and that it cannot and will not be revoked during that time. This type of agreement is called an option, and options don't usually come free. Say someone offers to sell you a forklift for $10,000, and you want to think the offer over without having to worry that the seller will revoke the offer or sell the forklift to someone else. You and the seller could agree that the offer will stay open for a certain period of time, say 30 days. Often, however, the offeror will ask you to pay for this 30-day option—which is understandable, since during the 30-day option period the offeror can't sell to anyone else. But payment or no payment, when an option agreement exists, the offeror cannot revoke the offer until the time period ends.

- **Counteroffers.** Often when an offer is made, the other party's response will not be to accept the terms of the offer right off, but to start bargaining. Of course, haggling over price is the most common type of negotiating that occurs in business situations. When one party responds to an offer by proposing something different, this proposal is called a "counteroffer." When a counteroffer is made, the legal responsibility to accept or decline the offer or make another counteroffer shifts to the original offeror. For instance, if your printer (here, the original offeror) offers to print 5,000 brochures for you for $300, and you respond by saying you'll pay $250 for the job, you have not accepted his offer (no contract has been formed), but instead have made a counteroffer. It is then up to your printer to accept, decline, or counteroffer. If your printer agrees to do the job exactly as you have specified for $250, he's accepted your counteroffer and a legal contract has been formed.

b. Exchange of Things of Value

Even if both parties agree to the terms, a contract isn't valid unless the parties exchange something of value in anticipation of the completion of the contract. The "thing of value" being exchanged— which every law student who ever lived has been taught to call "consideration"—is most often a promise to do something in the future, such as a promise to perform a certain job or a promise to pay a fee for that job. Let's return to the example of the print job. Once you and the printer agree on terms, there is an exchange of things of value (consideration): the printer has promised to print the 5,000 brochures and you have promised to pay $250 for them.

This requirement helps differentiate a contract from generous statements and one-sided promises, neither of which are enforceable by law. If a friend offers to do you a favor, for instance, such as helping you move a pile of rocks, without asking anything in return, that arrangement wouldn't count as a contract because you didn't give or promise him anything of value. If your friend never followed through with the favor, you would not be able to force him or her to keep the promise. However, if in exchange for helping you move rocks on Saturday, you promise to help your friend weed a vegetable garden on Sunday, the two of you have a contract.

Although the exchange of value requirement is met in most business transactions by an exchange of promises ("I'll promise to pay money if you promise to paint my building next month"), actually doing the work or paying the money can also satisfy the rule. If, for instance, you leave your printer a voice mail message that you'll pay an extra $100 if your brochures are cut and stapled when you pick them up, the printer doesn't have to respond—he can create a binding contract by actually doing the cutting and stapling. And once he does so, you can't weasel out of the deal by claiming you changed your mind.

2. Oral vs. Written Contracts

Before we tell you which contracts have to be in writing to be legally enforceable, here's some advice: Put all of your contracts in writing, regardless. For compelling practical reasons, all contracts of more than a trivial nature should be written out and signed by both parties. Here is why:

- Writing down terms tends to make both parties review them more carefully, eliminating misunderstandings and incorrect assumptions right from the start.
- An oral agreement—no matter how honestly made—is hard to remember accurately.
- Oral agreements are subject to willful misinterpretation by a not-so-innocent party who wants to get out of the deal.

- Oral contracts are sometimes difficult, and often impossible, to prove, making them hard to enforce in court.

EXAMPLE: Kay opens a plant shop called The Green Scene. Because she needs specialized grow-lights for her extensive line of tropical plants, she checks with several contractors who install lighting systems. One company, Got a Light, says it will install a system for $3,000, which would include the cost of the lights themselves and installation charges. That quote is the lowest among the companies Kay has checked, so she tells Got a Light she'll accept the offer—but only with a written contract.

When Got a Light sends Kay a contract, she notices that it doesn't address rewiring her shop. She calls Got a Light and talks with Dan, who tells her that she needs to have an electrician add several new circuits and provide six specialized outlets before Got a Light can install the lighting system. Based on this discovery, Kay and Dan discuss exactly what needs to be done before Got a Light's work begins, and they include this new agreement in an additional contract clause. Dan recommends an electrician, whom Kay hires to do the rewiring. She also manages to negotiate a lower price with Got a Light, based on the fact that the rewiring will be done according to Got a Light's specifications, making the installation much easier.

That's our good advice. Now here's what the law says: California has a law called the Statute of Frauds that requires certain contracts to be in writing. (California Civil Code § 1624.) The Statute of Frauds typically requires the following types of contracts to be in writing:

- An agreement that by its terms can't be completed in a year or less. For example, a contract for a bakery to provide fresh bread to a restaurant for two years must be in writing. On the other hand, if the contract might take longer than a year to complete but could be completed within a year, it doesn't need to be in writing. For example, a contract for a gardener to landscape five big properties would not need to be written, because it is quite possible that the gardener would finish the work within one year. Similarly, a contract for a bakery to bake bread for a restaurant with no time period stated would not need to be in writing.

- A lease with a term longer than one year, or an agreement authorizing an agent to execute such a lease on your behalf.

- Any sale of real estate (or of an interest in real estate), or an agreement authorizing an agent to purchase or sell it on your behalf.

- An agreement that by its terms will not be completed during the lifetime of one of the parties. This includes a promise to leave someone your business when you die.

- A promise to pay someone else's debt, such as a business partner's promise to pay your car payments or an agreement that the person who prints your brochure will also pay the cost of photographic work done at another shop.

In addition to the Statute of Frauds law, California has a special body of law on commercial issues called the Uniform Commercial Code (UCC). (California Commercial Code §§ 1101 et seq.) Under the UCC, a sale of goods for $500 or more requires at least a brief written note or memo indicating the agreement between buyer and seller. The note can be much less detailed than a normal contract; it only has to show an agreement between the parties and the quantity of goods being sold. Other terms that are typically covered in contracts, such as the price of goods or the time and place of delivery, aren't required. This written memo usually has to be signed, although if one party doesn't object to the memo within ten days of receiving it, then his or her signature isn't required.

Special Requirements for Certain Contracts

Other state laws impose additional requirements for contracts involving particular businesses or certain kinds of transactions. For instance, contracts for weight-loss services, dating services, and fitness services must be in writing, regardless of the dollar value or length of time covered by the contract. Plus, these contracts must include the following special language in at least ten-point boldface type:

> **"You, the buyer, may cancel this agreement, without any penalty or obligation, at any time prior to midnight of the original contract seller's third business day following the date of this contract, excluding Sundays and holidays. To cancel this agreement, mail or deliver a signed and dated notice, or send a telegram which states that you, the buyer, are canceling this agreement, or words of similar effect." (California Civil Code §§ 1694 & 1812.)**

Unfortunately, there's no centralized place where a business owner can learn about any special contract laws that apply to a particular type of business.

You can always search through California's business statutes for any mention of your type of business. However, if doing legal research is too time-consuming or overwhelming for you, a good alternative is to use the limited help of a lawyer who's generally familiar with small business issues and, if possible, already works with businesses in your field (other plant nurseries, website designers, or restaurants, for example). Many small business lawyers are now more flexible in offering just as much or as little help as clients need, and offer coaching services to those who want to handle their simple legal affairs themselves. Using a legal coach is especially useful for small businesspeople who often need answers to simple legal questions, rather than full-blown attorney services. (Chapter 13 discusses working with lawyers and finding one who's willing to coach you through simple legal matters.)

B. Using Standard Contracts

By now you should understand that your contracts should be written, but you may still have no idea how to write the ones you'll need. Luckily for you and most other businesspeople, virtually every type of business transaction is covered by a readily available standard contract. Service contracts, rental agreements, independent contractor agreements, contracts for sales of goods, and licensing agreements are just a few examples of blank-form contracts you should easily be able to find.

Anyone who has ever picked up a fill-in-the-blank lease or promissory note from an office supply store, torn one out of a self-help law book, or downloaded one from a website is familiar with how this works. Blank rental agreements, for example, are widely available at office supply stores, through landlords' associations, at most public libraries, in Nolo's *LeaseWriter* software and from many other sources. Once you find the blank contract you need, you simply fill it in and, if necessary, modify it before signing.

If you can't easily find a blank-form contract that meets your needs, try these sources:

- Trade associations are excellent resources for fill-in-the-blank contracts.
- Your competitors might be less than willing to share their contracts with you, but similar businesses in faraway locations (which you won't be competing with) might be willing to show you theirs.
- The Web has oceans of information for small businesses, including sample contracts. Try searching for terms particular to your type of business to find specific contracts you need.
- For general business contracts on paper and CD-ROM, a great resource is *Legal Forms for Starting and Running a Small Business*, by Fred S. Steingold (Nolo).

Once you've found a contract that generally fits your needs, you can amend it for your particular situation. It's entirely appropriate and often necessary to change the clauses of a fill-in-the-blank contract to suit your needs. Of course, it's crucial that you understand what you're doing. Don't just strike a clause because you don't understand what it means, or add a clause without fully knowing the consequences of including it. To help you educate yourself about typical contract language, the next section explains some of the clauses that commonly appear in contracts.

C. How to Draft a Contract

If you can't find a form agreement or if you find one that needs a load of revisions, you may need to draft a clause or two—or possibly even a whole contract—from scratch. Don't be intimidated. Either way, your goal is simple: to state clearly what each party is agreeing to do and the specifics of how they'll do it (usually called the terms of the contract). Put another way, your written contract should be the most accurate reflection possible of the understanding you have with the other party.

Contract Writing Basics

- Avoid the use of "he," "she," "they," or other pronouns in your contracts to prevent confusion over whom you're talking about. Use either the actual names of the parties or their roles, such as Landlord and Tenant. It might seem repetitive or clumsy to write this way, but your goal is to be clear—not to write beautiful prose.

- Stay away from legalistic words such as wherefore, herewith, or hereinafter. Far from making your contract sound more impressive, this type of language is simply unnecessary, outdated, and confusing. Stick to modern, clear English. Likewise, don't include legal expressions you think you may have heard elsewhere. Legal-sounding jargon will not make your contract more binding—and if you get it wrong, you may be bound to terms you didn't want, or your contract may be void.

- Make at least a couple of drafts of your contract. After the first draft, let it rest a day or so and then reread it. Does it leave any questions in your mind? If it does, fill in the gaps on your second try.

This section explains the important terms you'll need to include in most contracts, and alerts you to situations that might require more specialized provisions. The information we provide will help you edit or draft amendments to a standard contract, or draft a contract from scratch if necessary. We'll present examples of how to state certain terms—although, as mentioned above, clear English is usually all that's necessary.

Don't get too specific. Although a good contract covers all the important aspects of a deal, don't be too anal specifying every minute detail. For instance, if you hire a cleaning service to scrub your floors, you probably don't need to specify what type of brushes it will use. Better to put your energy into picking the right person or company to do the job and leave some of the specifics of the actual work up to them. How do you know when enough detail is enough? You'll simply have to judge for yourself which nit-picky details are so important that they should be covered in your contract and which ones you can safely ignore. For example, if you need fresh salmon for a party at 6 p.m., the time of delivery and quality of the fish are extremely important points, but the exact weight of each fish or the method of delivery may be a lot less so.

1. What to Include in a Basic Contract

So you've reached an agreement with another party and are ready to put it into writing. Before you start editing a form contract or writing one on your own, step back a moment to consider the goals of all contracts:

- to clearly outline what each party is agreeing to do (including timelines and payment arrangements)

- to anticipate areas of confusion or points of potential conflict, and

- to provide for recourse (remedy) in case the agreement is not followed through to completion.

The more you have at stake, the more carefully you'll have to approach the task of putting together your contract. For example, if you're entering into a contract to buy a truckload of bicycle tires for $1,000, you won't need your agreement to be outlined nearly as meticulously as you would in a contract for the construction of a building.

For complex agreements, you may need an attorney. More complex contracts—especially those in areas unfamiliar to you—are often best handled with the help of a lawyer. Certainly, if a transaction is so huge or elaborate that it makes your head spin, you shouldn't go it alone. First, decide how much help you need. Rather than having an attorney draft your contract from start to finish, you could simply have her look over a contract that you or the other party has written. Ideally, you should hire a lawyer with some experience with small business, preferably your type of business. Even better would be an attorney who knows the ins and outs of your business, based on a long-term working relationship. (See Chapter 13 on getting legal assistance.)

Let's look at the information most contracts include to fulfill these three goals and how to present it. Except where noted, you don't need to use any special language to get this information across.

- **Title.** Generally a contract will have a simple, to-the-point title such as "Contract for Printing Services" or "Agreement for Sale of Ball Bearings."

- **The names and addresses of all the parties.** It should be clear what role each party has in the contract, such as seller or buyer; landlord or tenant; client or service provider.

  The addresses of the parties generally appear at the end of a contract in the section with the signature.

  EXAMPLE: Christopher Johnson ("Client") desires to enter into a contract with Virgil's Printing ("Printer") for printing services for Client's newspaper.

- **A brief description of the background of the agreement (called "recitals").** While not always included, this type of information is often necessary to frame the contents of the agreement. Typically this section includes a brief description of what kinds of businesses the parties run and the nature of the transaction covered in the contract.

  EXAMPLE: Client prints and distributes a free, weekly, 24-page newspaper called *El Norte* with a circulation of 40,000. Printer operates a full-service print shop with three printing presses. The subject of this contract is an agreement that Printer shall print Client's newspaper each week in exchange for payment.

- **A full description of what each party is promising to do as part of the agreement.** This section, sometimes called the "specifications," or just "specs," describes the terms of the deal. If a product is being sold, describe the product and delivery terms. If a service is being performed, describe the job and then state when it will be completed, including any intermediate deadlines that must be met before the final completion date. Indi-

cate whether strict compliance with deadlines is necessary by throwing in the phrase, "Time is of the essence." This is a standard phrase used in contracts—it simply means that deadlines will be enforced strictly.

If specifications are complicated (for example, intricate performance details for a software contract), they should normally be set out in attachments to the contract, which may include scale drawings, formulas, or other detailed information about the transaction.

EXAMPLE: Client promises to deliver materials ("boards") for printing to Printer's shop no later than 10 a.m. each Wednesday morning. Printer promises to print, fold, and bundle 40,000 copies of Client's newspaper and have them ready for Client to pick up from Printer's shop by 8 p.m. that same Wednesday. Time is of the essence regarding this contract. If, however, Client fails to deliver boards to Printer by 10 a.m. Wednesday morning, Printer may take extra time to complete the job. The amount of extra time will depend on how late Client is in delivering the boards and on Printer's schedule of other jobs, but in no case shall be longer than 24 hours after delivery of the boards.

- **The price of the product or service.** This section states how much one party will pay for the other party's goods or services. If the price may vary (say, based on the time or quality of performance) or if it will be established later, a description of how it will be calculated should be included.

EXAMPLE: Client will pay Printer $1,000 for every 10,000 24-page newspapers printed, up to 50,000 newspapers. The price will be renegotiated if Client orders more than 50,000 newspapers, or if the number of pages per newspaper changes.

- **Payment arrangements.** This section should explain when payment is due, whether it will be paid all at once or in installments, and whether interest will be charged if payments are late. Also include any other special requirements such as whether payment must be by certified or cashier's check (otherwise a garden-variety check will normally suffice). Again, if strict compliance with payment deadlines is necessary, use the phrase "Time is of the essence."

EXAMPLE: Client will pay Printer the full amount of each week's printing cost within three days of picking up the completed newspapers.

- **A statement of any warranties made by either party regarding the product or service being provided.** A warranty is essentially a guarantee made by one party to another that a product or service will meet certain standards. If either party gives a warranty, the contract should state what will happen if the guarantee isn't satisfied—for instance, if certain standards aren't met, the party who got the raw end of the deal will be given a refund or may give the other party another chance to do the job right.

EXAMPLE: Printer warrants that the completed newspapers shall be free from printing defects or errors attributable to Printer. In case such errors do occur, Printer and Client may negotiate a discount not to exceed actual damages suffered by Client.

Automatic Warranties

Under California's Uniform Commercial Code (UCC), all sales of products are automatically covered by some warranties whether or not the seller promised anything to the buyer. These warranties are called "implied warranties," and include two guarantees: that the product is fit for its ordinary use and that it is fit for any special purpose for which the seller knows the buyer wants to use it. For example, the sale of a kitchen knife comes with an implied warranty that the knife will work in ordinary kitchen uses. If the buyer asked the retailer to help pick out a knife that would cut through heavy beef bones, then whatever knife the retailer sold would come with a warranty that it would work for cutting heavy beef bones. This is true regardless of whether or not the knife came with an express, written warranty that it could be used for heavy butcher work.

Be aware of the existence of implied warranties when drafting your contracts. Even if you don't make specific promises in your contracts, you will still be legally bound by the two kinds of implied warranties described above: fitness for ordinary use and fitness for a particular purpose. The law regarding warranties can be complex. You may want to consult an attorney for more detailed information about your obligations as a seller.

- **A statement whether either party may transfer the contract to an outside party.** Transferring contract rights is also called assigning. If you have chosen a company to provide products or services because of particular characteristics, such as good personal service or artistic detail, you may not want that company to be able to hand off the job to someone else, who may not do as good a job.

EXAMPLE: Neither Printer nor Client may assign this contract or any part of it to another party.

- **The contract term.** This section, usually only one sentence, establishes how long the contract will be in effect.

EXAMPLE: This contract will remain in effect for a period of one year, or until it is terminated by one of the parties, whichever is first.

- **A description of any conditions under which either party may terminate the agreement.** For some types of contracts (for example, contracts to provide an ongoing service), a termination clause often states that either party must give a written termination notice to end the contract, often 30 or 60 days in advance.

EXAMPLE: Upon written notice of at least 30 days to the other party, either Printer or Client may terminate this agreement.

But you may not want the parties to be able to terminate the contract, even with advance notice, just on a whim. In this case, you can specify a limited number of certain events that might allow a party to end a contract. For instance, say you want to be able to rely on using your website hosting service for at least a year, so you include a clause in your contract that neither party can terminate the contract for the next 12 months except if either party goes bankrupt, in which

case either party would have the right to terminate the contract.

On the other hand, there may be situations in which you want to be able to terminate a contract yourself. For instance, say you own a rock shop that sells lots of agate, so you contract with a supplier to sell you a half-ton of agate each month for a year. To protect yourself, you could include a clause in your contract stating that if you resell less than a quarter-ton of agate in any calendar month, you may terminate the agreement.

- **An outline of how you will deal with a breach.** Though signing a contract may not head off a subsequent dispute, it can channel the dispute in ways that will allow it to be resolved as quickly and cheaply as possible. There are a number of different approaches you can take if someone fails to abide by the contract—or breaches it.

You can decide, in advance, the amount of damages (financial compensation) a breaching party will have to pay. This will help you avoid the often lengthy and contentious process of calculating a party's damages after the other party breaches the contract. When damages are preset in a contract, they are called liquidated damages. In order for a liquidated damages clause to be valid, the dollar amount of damages that you set must be a reasonable estimate of what actual damages would be, not merely a preset penalty for breaking the contract.

Another option is for both parties to agree in the contract to try mediation and, if that fails, arbitration to settle a dispute as an alternative to going to court.

EXAMPLE: If any dispute arises under the terms of this agreement, the parties agree to select a mutually agreeable, neutral third party to help them mediate it. The costs of mediation will be shared equally. If the dispute is not resolved after 30 days in mediation, the parties agree to choose a mutually agreeable arbitrator who will arbitrate the dispute. The costs of arbitration will be assigned to the parties by the arbitrator. The results of any arbitration will be binding and final.

If one or both of you prefers going to court, you can provide in the contract that the losing party in a dispute must pay the other party's legal fees, or you can establish that each party is responsible for their own legal fees regardless of who prevails. Note that, for some commercial transactions, neither party in a lawsuit can collect attorney's fees from the other unless it is provided for in a written contract.

- **For contracts with out-of-state entities, a statement of which state's laws apply.** Although contract law in all states is very similar, using California law will generally be the simplest for you, since you'll have more resources at your disposal, including law libraries and local attorneys.

  EXAMPLE: This contract shall be governed by and interpreted according to the laws of California.

  - **Signatures, dates, and addresses.** Your signature section should always include room for the date the contract was signed, as well as the addresses of the parties.

Jennifer F. Mahoney, owner of an illustration service in Northern California:

My creativity is exercised just as much by drawing up a good agreement with a client as it is by the way I create art for that client.

2. Putting Your Contract Together

In addition to making sure your contract includes all the necessary information, you'll need to present it in an easy-to-follow, professional format. Generally, contract clauses are organized in a series of numbered paragraphs for easy reference to specific terms.

If your agreement includes any hard-to-articulate details, such as the specifications of a software product, drawing a company logo, or originating architectural blueprints, you can include them as attachments to the main contract. If you do include an attachment, be sure to label it and refer to it in the main contract. To officially make it a part of the contract, state somewhere in the main contract that you "include the Attachment in the contract," or that you "incorporate the Attachment into the contract."

EXAMPLE 1: Company agrees to pay artist $100 for use of logo. Logo is attached to this contract as Attachment A and is hereby included in this contract.

EXAMPLE 2: Contractor agrees to complete remodeling within one year. The final plans are attached to this contract as Exhibit B and are incorporated into this contract.

D. Reading and Revising a Contract

If you don't like certain terms of a contract that's presented to you, you can propose changes. By doing this, you are technically making a counteroffer. Contracts are commonly negotiated back and forth (offer and counteroffer) this way until all the terms are accepted by both parties. Remember, if the parties aren't in agreement, there's no contract—oral or otherwise. (See Section A, above, on offers and counteroffers.)

Changes to a contract—whether to a form contract or one drafted from scratch—can be made in a number of ways. You can simply cross out language and fill in new language directly on the contract itself. Both parties should initial any such changes to show that they approve of them, then sign the contract as a whole.

In today's world, however, it's more than likely that there will be an electronic copy of the contract on someone's computer. If so, it makes much more sense to make the necessary changes on the computer and then print out a clean copy for both parties to sign. However, some industries (such as the real estate industry) commonly use a separate document when making a counteroffer that states the desired changes and refers back to the original offer. In that case, the original offer and the counteroffer together form the contract.

A contract can also be amended at a later date with a separate document called an addendum. The addendum should state that its terms prevail over the terms of the original contract, especially if the terms are in direct conflict, as would be the case if the price or completion time for a job is changed. Both parties should sign the addendum.

E. Electronic Contracts

While the basics we've covered generally apply to any contract regardless of form—whether the contract is printed in a formal document, scratched on a cocktail napkin, or just spoken and sealed with a handshake—there are new and emerging rules that apply specifically to contracts created online. Before we give you a very general overview of the special issues involved in electronic contracts, keep in mind that law in this area is rapidly evolving—scrambling, in fact—to catch up with fast-evolving technology.

1. What Is an Electronic Contract?

An electronic contract essentially means any agreement that is created and executed in electronic form—in other words, no paper or other hard copies are used. Typically, electronic agreements are created either via email or on interactive Web pages. For instance, many companies use interactive forms at their websites that users must complete to purchase goods or software, join a membership organization, participate in a mail listserve, or do whatever else the company is offering. Besides asking the user to enter various items of personal information, these forms typically display the terms of the contract between the company and the user, and ask the user to agree to the terms by clicking on a button such as "I Accept."

Here's another example of an electronic contract: a business associate of yours emails you a request to purchase a specified number of items you sell, at a named price, for immediate delivery. If you email back that you agree to all the proposed terms, you've probably just entered into a legally enforceable electronic contract. Why "probably"? Because there is no way for you to sign the contract with pen and ink, and states vary in how they treat digital signatures. Read on.

2. Taking Traditional Contract Principles Online

As mentioned above, contract law is only beginning to grapple with the details of paperless agreements. When electronic contracts have been challenged, courts have had a difficult time determining whether an actual binding contract existed, since it can be unclear whether all the traditional elements of contract formation were met.

Shortcut Contracts for e-Commerce

When it comes to small transactions in which you pay for goods by credit card, most sites get around the issue of whether a valid contract has been formed by noting that if you are dissatisfied for any reason, they will give you your money back. This is another way of saying that if you don't want a contract to exist, it doesn't. Or put another way, the company concedes in advance that it won't try to enforce the contract. This trust-the-customer approach works well for small transactions, but has obvious limitations when it comes to major purchases (a car, for example) or significant business-to-business transactions. In these situations, a real signature on an enforceable contract is needed.

a. Clickwrap Agreements

Businesses have traditionally used standard contracts that aren't open to negotiation; customers have to either accept the contract as is or not complete the transaction. Examples might include a car purchase contract or an agreement to rent a moving truck, in which a consumer who insisted on changing any of the terms of the company's standard contract would not be able to buy the car or rent the truck. Over the years, these types of contracts have been challenged on the grounds that they are not fair to the consumer since they are typically presented in a take-it-or-leave-it manner, giving the consumer little or no power to amend a contract that is often highly favorable to the seller. Whether or not these types of contracts (sometimes called contracts of adhesion, because consumers are forced to "adhere" to the contract) are valid has long been a contentious area of contract law. Generally, adhesion contracts are held to be valid, as long as the terms are clear to the consumer and not grossly unreasonable.

Today, Internet click-to-agree contracts—often called clickwrap, webwrap, or browsewrap agreements—are facing similar challenges. So are other nonnegotiated agreements, such as the software licenses included with packaged software, sometimes called shrinkwrap agreements. While these types of agreements have generally been found valid, courts have refused to enforce certain terms that are deemed too burdensome or unfair to the consumer.

A federal case decided in 2002 sheds some light on the question of when a clickwrap agreement may be deemed invalid. In that case, an Internet user who downloaded software from a website operated by the Netscape company later sued Netscape, claiming that the software license was not binding. To download the software, the user had simply clicked a "Download" button and was not required to view the software license or click any button such as "I Agree" to indicate consent to license terms. To view the license, the user would have had to scroll below the Download button and click on another link to a separate page where the license terms were posted.

The U.S. Court of Appeals for the Second Circuit ruled in favor of the user, based on the principle that for a contract to be binding, both parties must assent to be bound. The court found that the structure of Netscape's software download page "with license terms on a submerged screen" and no button to clearly indicate consent was not sufficient to create a binding contract with the user. (*Specht v. Netscape Communications Corp.*, 306 F.3d 17 (2d Cir. 2002).)

The *Netscape* case establishes that downloading alone does not indicate acceptance of license terms. To make sure a clickwrap agreement is binding, the site must be set up to ensure that a user can clearly indicate consent to the license terms of any downloads. Keep this in mind if you plan to use any clickwrap agreements with your business.

Legislative Attempts to Solve Clickwrap Issues

Over the past few years there have been a number of state legislative efforts to deal with the issues and problems raised by clickwrap agreements. However, state laws governing electronic contracts are not consistent, which has actually done more harm than good. And the state courts that have heard and ruled upon electronic contract cases have come up with different decisions, with the result that checking an "I Accept" box may create a contract in one state, but not in another. No question, this lack of uniformity has been a real thorn in the side of e-commerce, which of course recognizes no state boundaries.

In response, the National Conference of Commissioners on Uniform State Laws (NCCUSL) decided to tackle the problem by drafting model legislation for adoption by the states. One of these proposed laws, the Uniform Computer Information Transactions Act (UCITA), addresses the issue of clickwrap and shrinkwrap agreements, essentially making these types of contracts valid and binding. California has not adopted the UCITA—and doesn't seem likely to do so in the future.

In fact, few states have adopted UCITA in the years since it was drafted. One reason may be that many consumer advocates, as well as over 25 state attorneys general, argue that the UCITA is biased in favor of software vendors and information services providers, leaving consumers with significantly less protection than they have under current law. The Computer Professionals for Social Responsibility offers a UCITA Fact Sheet at the following case-senstive URL: www.cpsr.org/program/UCITA/ucita-fact.html.

b. Electronic and Digital Signatures

One of the stickier issues involving electronic contracts has to do with whether agreements executed in a purely online environment have been "signed" (outside of clickwrap agreements, discussed above). For many centuries, the traditional way to indicate your acceptance of a contract (and most other binding documents) has been to sign it with your unique signature. But electronic contracts can't be signed this way. Instead, people use other means to indicate they accept the terms of a contract, such as simply typing their names into the signature areas of the documents. But increasingly, better technological approaches to the problem of signing contracts online are being developed, such as fingerprint and iris scanning, in addition to a cryptographic technology known as Public Key Infrastructure (PKI). These methods are collectively known as electronic signatures. The term "digital signature" refers specifically to cryptographic signature methods such as the PKI.

What Is PKI?

Security experts currently favor the cryptographic signature method known as Public Key Infrastructure (PKI) as the most secure and reliable method of signing contracts online. Without going too deep into the technical details, PKI involves using an algorithm to encrypt the document so that only the parties will be able to modify it or "sign" it. The process of encrypting the document is known as creating a digital signature. Each party will have a "key" allowing it to read and sign the document, ensuring that no one else will be able to sign it fraudulently. PKI standards are still evolving, but the technology is already widely accepted as the best electronic signature method available. A good (though slightly tech-heavy) source for more information on PKI technology is the Center for Information Technology Standards—Public Key Infrastructure (PKI) Standardization Home Page—at www-pki.itsi.disa.mil.

Until relatively recently, most states didn't have any laws stating which of these ways to "sign" an electronic document was legally acceptable. In response, the NCCUSL drafted another model law, the Uniform Electronic Transactions Act (UETA), which specifically addresses electronic signatures. In a nutshell, the UETA provides that electronic signatures (in all their forms) and contracts are just as valid and legally binding as their paper counterparts. More than 40 states have enacted the UETA, California among them. But the fact that some other states don't recognize digital signatures created a problem for the many California businesses that wanted to enter into electronic contracts with out-of-state customers, clients, and suppliers.

c. Federal Law on Electronic Signatures

Fortunately, as the states were mulling over whether to adopt the UETA, the UCITA, or both, the U.S. Congress forged ahead and passed federal legislation establishing the validity of electronic signatures nationwide. This bill, known as the Electronic Signatures in Global and National Commerce Act, was signed into law in June 2000 and became effective on October 1, 2000. The law applies to all states that had not already adopted the UETA or a similar electronic signature law by mid-2000. In states such as California that already adopted essentially the same legislation, state law will govern electronic signatures; the other states will be bound by the federal law. In this way, the law finally gives some much-needed consistency to the way states treat electronic signatures in online transactions.

This law is similar to the model UETA in that it makes electronic signatures and contracts (including clickwrap agreements) just as valid as paper ones. While certain transactions are exempt from this law and must still be completed on paper (wills, cancellation of utility services, court orders, and other official court documents, among others), the law allows an enormous range of business and consumer transactions to be completed totally online. In essence, it throws the door wide open for all types of e-commerce, allowing businesses and consumers to create (in theory at least) reliable, binding contracts online, without the inconvenience of shuttling paper documents back and forth.

 For more information on electronic contracts. See the Internet Law Center at www.nolo.com.

3. Tips for Creating Contracts Online

While the new federal e-signature law, along with the UETA, creates a solid legal framework for online contracts, electronic signature technology is still evolving, which means the reality of online contracts still falls somewhat short of its promise. Like the UETA, the new e-signature law does not specify any particular technology for electronic signatures, leaving that up to software companies and the free market to establish. As mentioned above, Public Key Infrastructure (PKI) technology is currently favored by security experts, though its standards aren't completely nailed down or ready for common use. As developments in PKI and other electronic signature methods create solid, worldwide standards, e-commerce will only become more efficient and widespread.

While we wait for reliable standards to develop, it will be important to approach online contracts carefully. Of particular concern is the possibility for fraud, especially since there is no set standard for what constitutes a valid electronic signature. Until the technology is airtight, make sure that you trust the other party to an online contract and are comfortable with the type of electronic signature that you're using. If you're not comfortable creating a contract online, you may want to stay low tech and stick with paper contracts, either faxed back and forth or sent by overnight mail.

The nonprofit Consumers Union, which publishes *Consumer Reports* magazine, has issued a set of tips to follow when using electronic signatures and creating online contracts. These include:

- Don't consent to using an online contract if you are uncomfortable using a computer or do not understand how to use email.

- Don't agree to use an online contract or to receive electronic documents until you are sure that your computer's software and hardware will be able to read and use the documents provided by the company.

- Remember that the electronic signatures law allows you to opt to receive documents on paper instead of electronically if you prefer.

- Keep back-up paper copies of the electronic documents you receive, and keep a list of the businesses with which you agree to create electronic documents.

- Notify the businesses of any changes that may affect your ability to receive and read email and attachments, such as changing your email address, your hardware, or your software.

- Close any unused email accounts.

- Don't give out your email address to any business if you don't want to receive email notices from it.

- Notify the business right away if you have any problems receiving its emails or opening its documents.

You can find these tips and other information about online contracts at the Consumers Union website at www.consumersunion.org.

Beware of e-viruses. Never open attachments to email if you aren't expecting the email or don't know who it's from. Nasty viruses are often spread through email attachments, so it's good policy to just throw away suspicious mail as soon as you see it. Even when you know the sender of the email, you need to be cautious. Some viruses use a computer user's email address book to replicate themselves, by sending themselves out to everyone in the book. This means that if you get an email with an attachment from your friend Steve Smith, there's a chance that Steve Smith didn't actually send the email. For this reason, you shouldn't open attachments unless you're expecting them.

✓ Chapter 10 Checklist

☐ Become familiar with the legal basics of contracts.

☐ Put all your contracts into writing whenever possible. (Contracts created online or by email are considered to be "in writing.")

☐ Try to respond to offers promptly, and when making an offer, include an expiration date.

☐ When you need to draft a contract from scratch, try using standard form contracts to get started.

☐ Be thorough in your contracts. Make sure that any points of potential conflict are clearly spelled out.

☐ Use caution when entering into electronic contracts (also called online contracts or digital contracts). If you're uncomfortable creating a contract online or by email, don't do it—opt for a paper contract.

Bookkeeping, Accounting, and Financial Management

Perhaps the hardest part of accounting is getting over the psychological hang-up that most people seem to have about it. Many of us are loath to balance our checkbooks on any regular basis, much less keep detailed accounts of how our money comes and goes. The good news is that you don't need to be a financial wizard to start a small business; you just need a comfortable working knowledge of the basics.

If you read Chapter 5, some of this material may be a review. In that chapter, we explained how to generate financial projections using sales and expense estimates to see if your business was likely to turn a profit. The financial tools used in business planning—particularly profit/loss analysis and cash flow projection—are the same tools used in accounting, just employed slightly differently. In this chapter, we'll focus on how to use these and other tools to keep track of current financial data (as
opposed to projections) for your business.

This chapter will give you an idea of what records your business should keep and will describe simple ways to keep them. We'll also explain how to use the information in your financial records to calculate how much profit your business is making and to ensure that enough cash is regularly flowing through your business to pay your important bills on time.

Fortunately for today's entrepreneurs, inexpensive, powerful, and easy-to-use software is available that will help simplify the accounting process. Programs such as *Quickbooks, Quicken Home & Business,* and *MYOB Accounting* make this once unsavory task much more palatable. Once your income and expenses are entered into the system, you're only a few mouse clicks away from sophisticated financial reports that would have taken many hours and considerable skill to generate just a decade ago. In fact, these programs are so affordable (typically under $200) and user friendly it makes little sense not to use one of them.

Don't expect software to do your accounting. You shouldn't simply rely on the numbers that your software program spits out if you don't fully understand them. The accounting concepts and processes described in this chapter are the same whether done manually or by computer— and you should take the time to learn them. While accounting software makes it much easier to manipulate the numbers you've entered and to generate informative financial reports, you still need to understand what all the numbers mean to make them work for your business.

It often pays to get help. The basic information provided in this chapter will be valuable for all business owners who are unfamiliar with accounting basics. But depending on the size and nature of your business, you may eventually want to do additional reading or hire experienced help. Our approach here is to provide enough information to get a new businessperson sensibly started. But even so, the owner of a small, relatively simple business can almost always benefit from an hour or two with an experienced small-business accountant who can often offer creative strategies for keeping records, selecting and configuring your computerized accounting system, and managing your money.

Accounting Glossary

A big part of understanding the financial side of your business consists of nothing more than learning the language of accounting. Once you're familiar with some common terms, you'll be better able to make sense of basic written reports and to communicate with others about important financial information. And you'll also be well positioned to cope with a common business problem: people who use key financial terms imprecisely or even incorrectly, thus needlessly confusing themselves and others.

- **Accounting** is a general term that refers to the overall process of tracking your business's income and expenses, then using these numbers in various calculations and formulas to answer specific questions about the financial and tax status of the business.

- **Bookkeeping** refers to the task of recording the amount, date, and source of all business revenues and expenses. Bookkeeping is essentially the starting point of the accounting process. Only with accurate bookkeeping can there be meaningful accounting.

- An **invoice** is a written record of a transaction, often submitted to a customer or client when requesting payment. Invoices are sometimes called **bills** or **statements**, though statement has its own technical meaning. (See below.)

- A **statement** is a formal written summary of an account. Unlike an invoice, a statement is not generally used as a formal request for payment, but is more of a reminder to a customer or client that payment is due.

- A **ledger** is a physical collection of related financial information, such as revenues, expenditures, accounts receivable, and accounts payable. Ledgers used to be kept in books preprinted with lined ledger paper (which explains why a business's financial information is often referred to as the "books"), but are now commonly kept in computer files.

- An **account** is a collection of financial information grouped according to customer or purpose. For example, if you have a regular customer, your information regarding that customer's purchases, payments, and debts would be called his or her "account." A written record of an account is called a **statement**.

- A **receipt** is a written record of a transaction. A buyer receives a receipt to show that he or she paid for an item. The seller keeps a copy of the receipt to show that he or she received payment for the item. Receipts are sometimes called **sales slips**.

- **Accounts payable** are amounts that your business owes. For example, unpaid utility bills and purchases your business makes on credit are included in your accounts payable.

- **Accounts receivable** are amounts owed to your business that you expect to receive, including sales your business makes on credit.

A. Accounting Basics

Accounting has two basic goals:

- to keep track of your income and expenses, improving your chances of making a profit, and
- to collect the necessary financial information about your business to file your various tax returns and local tax registration papers.

Sounds pretty simple, doesn't it? And it can be, especially if you remind yourself of these two goals whenever you feel overwhelmed by the details of keeping your financial records. Hopefully you will also be reassured to know that there is no requirement that your records be kept in any specific organizational system. (There is a requirement, however, that some businesses use a certain method of crediting their accounts. See Section B, below, on cash vs. accrual accounting.) In other words, there's no official system or format to organize your books. As long as your records accurately reflect your business's income and expenses, the IRS will find them acceptable.

Organization is everything. One thing that all good bookkeeping systems have in common is organization. A well-organized system with accessible, reasonably neat files will not only be a godsend in the event of an audit, but it will help you keep track of your business as well.

The actual process of accounting can be broken down into three steps.

1. Keep receipts or other acceptable records of every payment to, and every expenditure from, your business.

2. Summarize your income and expense records on some periodic basis (generally daily, weekly, or monthly).

3. Use these summaries to create financial reports that will tell you specific information about your business, such as how much monthly profit you're making or how much your business is worth at a specific time.

And, whether you do your accounting by hand on ledger sheets or with accounting software, these principles are exactly the same.

Are you beginning to believe that you don't need to be afraid of accounting? Good, because it's something you absolutely need to embrace as part of running any business. Failing to keep track of income and expenses is one of the surest ways to run any business off a cliff. Here are a few more ways that a simple set of books will help your business.

- **You'll be able to price your goods and services more competitively.** Only by staying on top of your business's income and expenses will you know how much money you'll need to bring in each week, month, or year to make a profit. And, this knowledge is essential to allow you to price your goods and services appropriately. For instance, if you don't know your break-even point, you will only be able to guess how much you should charge your customers for products or services, with the likely result that you'll charge too little (and make an inadequate profit) or too much (and alienate customers).

- **You'll be able to pace your growth more effectively.** A good set of books will give you the information you need to decide when and how to expand your business. If your numbers tell you that sales and profits have been growing consistently for several months, that may be a signal that it's time to hire additional employees or enter into a new market—or both. Without meaningful financial numbers, making any decisions about growth can be a gamble. For example, just because your business has a lot of money in its checking account doesn't necessarily mean you're making good money. You might have received several big payments from past sales, while current sales are actually slowing down.

- **You may be able to reduce your taxes.** Knowing your company's finances inside and out will help you save money when tax time comes around. For example, if the end of the year is nearing and your up-to-date records clearly show the year to be profitable, you can purchase needed supplies or equipment and write off these expenses, reducing your taxable income. Also, keeping careful track of your expenses will remind you to claim them as deductions at year-end. Businesses that are sloppy about bookkeeping often miss opportunities for saving tax dollars. Don't be one of them.

- **You'll avoid tax penalties.** In addition to helping you legally save tax dollars, responsible bookkeeping will help you avoid errors in your tax returns that can subject you to fines and other penalties. If your business is audited, the IRS can be really nasty if it finds your books in bad shape—in extreme situations, it may even refuse to recognize perfectly legitimate expenses. In short, neglecting your responsibility to maintain basic, accurate records is likely to result in the kind of trouble with the IRS that you would not wish on your worst enemy.

B. Cash vs. Accrual Accounting

Before we discuss several simple systems for keeping your records, you need to understand the two principal methods of keeping track of a business's income and expenses: cash method and accrual method accounting (sometimes called cash basis and accrual basis accounting). In a nutshell, these methods differ only in the timing of when transactions—both sales and purchases—are credited or debited to your accounts.

1. How Each Method Works

If you use the cash method, income is counted when cash (or a check) is actually received, and expenses are counted when they are actually paid.

But under the more common accrual method, transactions are counted when they happen—regardless of when the money is actually received or paid. In other words, with the accrual method, income is counted when the sale occurs, and expenses are counted when you receive goods or services. You don't have to wait until you see the money, or until you actually pay money out of your checking account, to record the transaction.

Say you purchase a new laser printer on credit in May and pay $2,000 for it in July, two months later. Using cash method accounting you would record a $2,000 expense for the month of July, the month when the money was actually paid. But under the accrual method, the $2,000 payment would be recorded in May, when you took the laser printer and became obligated to pay for it. Similarly, if your computer installation business finished a job on November 30, 2004, and didn't get paid until January 10, 2005, you'd record the payment in January 2005 if you used the cash method. Under the accrual method the income would be recorded in your books in November of 2004.

Timing can be tricky. Some sales aren't completed all at once. If you use accrual accounting, you may wonder exactly when you can enter the transaction into your books. For instance, say someone buys two CDs from your record store but also makes a special order for another CD, and pays for all three at once. Or say your landscaping company finishes a large project, save for the last step of applying a final lawn fertilizing treatment two weeks after laying the sod. For those using the accrual accounting method, the key date here is the job completion date. Not until you deliver all of the goods, finish all parts of a service, or otherwise meet all terms of a contract can you put the income down in your books. If a job is mostly completed but will take another few days to add the finishing touches, it doesn't go on your books until it is completely done.

Both methods can produce the same results. As you can see, the results produced by the cash and accrual accounting methods will only be different if you do some transactions on credit. If all your transactions are paid in cash as soon as completed, including your sales and purchases, then your books will look the same, regardless of the method you use.

2. Accounting Methods and Taxes

The most significant way your business is affected by the accounting method you choose involves the tax year in which income and expense items will be counted. (See "Tax Years and Accounting Periods," below.) For instance, if you use the cash method, and you incur expenses in the 2004 tax year but don't pay them until the 2005 tax year, you won't be able to claim them on your 2004 tax return. But you would be able to claim them if you use the accrual method, since that system records transactions when they occur, not when money actually changes hands.

> **EXAMPLE 1:** Zara runs a small flower shop called ZuZu's Petals. On December 22, 2004, Zara buys office supplies for which she will be billed $400. She takes the supplies that day, but according to the terms of the purchase, doesn't pay for them for 30 days. Under her accrual system of accounting, she counts the $400 expense during the December 2004 accounting period, even though she didn't actually write the check until January of the next year. This means that Zara can deduct the $400 from her taxable income of 2004.

> **EXAMPLE 2:** Scott and Lisa operate A Stitch in Hide, a leather repair shop. They're hired to repair an antique leather couch, and they finish their job on December 15, 2004. They bill the customer $750, and receive payment for

the work on January 20, 2005. Since they use the accrual method of accounting, Scott and Lisa count the $750 income in December 2004, because that's when they earned the money by finishing the job. This income must be reported in their 2004 tax return even though they didn't receive the money that year.

Tax Years and Accounting Periods

Income and expenses must be reported to the IRS for a specific period of time, alternately called your "tax year," your "accounting period," or your "fiscal year." Unless you have a valid business reason to use a different period or your business is a corporation, you'll have to use the calendar year, beginning on January 1 and ending on December 31. Most business owners do use the calendar year for the tax year, simply because they find it easy and natural to use. But if you want to use a different period, you must request permission from the IRS by filing Form 8716, Election to Have a Tax Year Other Than a Required Tax Year. Also, your fiscal year can't begin and end on just any day of the month; it must begin on the first day of a month and end on the last day of the previous month one year later.

3. Which Method to Use

Most businesses that have sales of less than $5 million per year are free to adopt either accounting method, with one big exception: If your business stocks an inventory of items that you will sell to the public, the IRS requires you to use the accrual accounting method. Inventory includes any merchandise you sell as well as supplies you will incorporate into products you intend to sell.

Whichever method you use, it's important to realize that either one only gives you a partial picture of the financial status of your business.

While the accrual method shows the ebb and flow of business income and debts more accurately, it may leave you in the dark as to what cash reserves are actually available—and not knowing this information could result in a serious cash flow problem. For instance, your income ledger may show thousands of dollars in sales, while in reality your bank account is empty because your customers haven't paid you yet.

And though the cash method will give you a more accurate idea of how much actual cash your business has, it may offer a misleading picture of longer-term profitability. Under the cash method, for instance, your books may show one month to be spectacularly profitable because many credit customers paid their bills, when actual sales for the month have been slow. To have a firm and true understanding of your business's finances, you need more than just a collection of monthly totals; you need to understand what your numbers mean and how to use them to answer specific financial questions, as discussed in the rest of this chapter.

C. Step One: Keeping Your Receipts

Comprehensive summaries of your business's income and expenses are the heart of the accounting process. But unless you want to flirt with tax fraud, you can't just make up the information in your books. Each of your business's sales and expenditures must be backed up by some type of record containing the amount, the date, and other relevant information about that transaction. This is true whether your accounting is done by computer or on hand-posted ledgers.

From a legal point of view, your method of keeping receipts can range from slips kept in a cigar box to a sophisticated cash register hooked into a computer system. Practically, you'll want to choose a system that fits your business needs. For example, a small service business that handles only relatively few jobs may get by with a bare-bones approach. But the more sales and expenditures your business makes, the better your receipt filing system needs to be. This section discusses common ways of keeping your receipts. The bottom line is to choose or adapt one to suit your needs.

1. Receipts of Income

Every time your business brings in money, you need a record of it. Most of your revenue will come from sales of your products or services. How you keep track of sales will vary a great deal depending on what type of business you run and how many sales you make.

a. Keeping Sales Records

Businesses such as grocery stores that make hundreds or even thousands of sales a day will likely need a cash register to produce a record of each sale. Other businesses with slower sales, such as hair salons or auto shops, can get by simply writing out a receipt for each sale from a receipt book. Hand-written receipts should include the date and a brief description of the goods or services sold. If some of your sales are made on credit, your receipts should indicate whether the customer paid and if not, when payment is due.

Whether you use a cash register tape or hand-written receipts, make sure that you and your employees know the system and use it consistently. If your income records aren't accurate, the ledgers or financial statements you make from them won't be, either.

Receipts are most important for you. While it's good business practice to give receipts to customers who purchase goods or services, it's a legal requirement that you keep a copy for yourself. Therefore, if you write out your own receipts, you'll need to make two copies—one for you, and one for the customer. Cash registers and most receipt books make each record in duplicate.

b. Distinguishing Taxable From Nontaxable Sales

Your income records must reflect whether a sale is taxable for state sales-tax purposes. This distinction will be essential when you compute and file your California sales taxes. (See "Taxable Sales vs. Taxable Income," below.) If you use a cash register, this distinction can be made by the push of a button at the time of each sale. If you write out a receipt of each sale by hand, be sure to show any sales tax separately, not just as part of a total. If the sale is nontaxable, make that clear by writing "no tax," "nontaxable," or the like.

Assuming you follow our advice to keep your receipts of taxable sales separate from receipts of nontaxable sales, posting them to your accounting system (discussed in Section D) should be easy. If you plan to post daily, a simple method involves keeping your receipts for the day in two envelopes or two sections of an accordion folder (one for taxable sales, one for nontaxable) and adding them up at the end of the day. If you use a cash register, the process is simplified—you can run totals at the end of the day for taxable sales and nontaxable sales. Depending on your machine, you may also be able to print out totals for other periods of time, such as one week or a specified number of days.

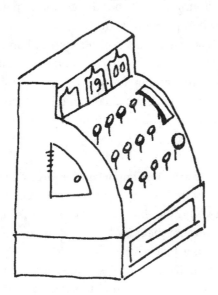

Taxable Sales vs. Taxable Income

As discussed above (and in more detail in Chapter 9, Section G), many sales of goods are subject to California sales tax, which retailers must pay to the state. But other large categories of sales are exempt from sales tax, such as sales of services, sales to out-of-state residents, or sales to resellers. So some sales income is taxable and some is not.

However, whether a sale is taxable for sales-tax purposes is a different issue from whether income is taxable for income-tax purposes. Generally, taxable income—that is, money you take in that is subject to income taxes at the end of the year—includes any money earned by your business, minus certain deductions. All of this income must be reported on your year-end income tax return, whether or not it is subject to state sales tax.

Jennifer F. Mahoney, owner of an illustration service in Northern California:

It's helpful to learn about the accounts payable process for each client and to understand who in the company releases checks. It's often an entirely different person or department from the one who calls you to offer work. You don't necessarily want to strain your relationship with the person who calls offering you work just because a different department of the business doesn't pay on time. Pave the way for timely payments as much as possible by getting to know the correct procedure, and when it's time to press for payment, you'll know the right person to call.

You should also document any income your business receives from sources other than sales and keep these receipts separate from your sales receipts. If you get a loan or contribute your own personal money to the business, record this fact with some sort of receipt or promissory note. Be sure your written records adequately describe the source of income so you'll know whether to count it as taxable income or not. Most sales income, for example, will be taxed at the end of the year, while income that you personally contribute to the business will not.

2. Expenditure Receipts

Ever hear the business wisdom that the key to small-business success is to keep your costs down? While this isn't the only thing a successful business owner needs to do, watching those pennies is always a good idea. The first step in keeping costs down is keeping accurate track of what they are. Just as you keep a record of each individual sale, you need to keep a record each time you spend money for your business. Business expenditures include paychecks to employees, money spent on supplies, and payments on loans, as well as all other costs associated with your business. Legally and practically, each and every one of these expenses must be recorded.

First of all, be sure to get a written receipt for every transaction in which you spend money for the business. Not only is keeping and tallying these receipts an easy way to keep track of your expenses, but receipts also come in handy if there's a problem with any of the goods or services you purchased or a dispute over whether you paid a particular bill.

Many businesspeople like to use their checkbook registers to keep track of expenses. This is fine, but there are two pitfalls to watch. Since you will pay for many of your expenditures by check, you may have two records of the same transaction: the notation in your checkbook and the receipt from the seller. Make sure you don't count that transaction twice! And don't forget to record cash purchases—they won't show up in your checkbook register. There are several easy ways to avoid counting some expenses twice and forgetting others. One is to use your receipts as the sole record of expenditures, and not to count the amounts in

your checkbook. Since most businesspeople don't want to sort through a pile of odd-sized bits of paper, another way is to rely solely on your checkbook for expenditure records, instead of on receipts. Fine, as long as you make sure to include the receipts of cash transactions in your checkbook register.

Don't let multiple receipts muddle you.
Sometimes you'll receive a number of sales slips for just one purchase: a credit card slip, a register receipt, and an itemized statement, for example. If you throw all three receipts into your files to be posted later, you run the risk of counting all three separately. You might think that you'll remember the transaction, or that it will be obvious to you as you're posting your ledger that the three receipts correspond to a single transaction. But when dealing with dozens of receipts at the end of a long day, it's all too easy for mistakes to creep into your paperwork. To avoid counting transactions more than once, either discard multiple copies of receipts immediately after the transaction or staple them all together.

Each record of an expenditure should include the date, the amount, the method of payment, who was paid, and—most important—a description of what type of expense it was, such as rent, supplies, or utilities. The description is important because later, when you post (enter) your expenses to your ledgers, you'll need to assign them into categories such as rent, advertising, supplies, utilities, and taxes. These categories are important for tax purposes because different types of expenses have different rules for deductibility. To make your bookkeeping job easier, be sure your expense receipts contain enough information to allow you to assign the expense to the appropriate category when you post it in your ledger. Also, it's best to keep your expense receipts separated by category during the month prior to posting them. In other words, keep all of your utilities receipts in one box or envelope, your supplies receipts in another, and so on. (We discuss the various expense categories in Section D2, below.)

D. Step Two: Setting Up and Posting to Ledgers

A completed ledger is really nothing more than a summary of revenues and expenditures, as well as whatever else you're tracking, entered from your receipts according to category and date. Later, you'll use these summaries to answer specific financial questions about your business—such as whether you're making a profit and if so, how much.

You'll start with a blank ledger page (a sheet with lines) or, more often these days, a computer file of empty rows and columns. On some regular basis—every day, once a week, or once a month—you should transfer ("post") the amounts from your receipts for sales and expenditures into your ledger. How often you do this depends on how many sales and expenditures your business makes and how detailed you want your books to be.

Generally, the more sales you make, the more often you should post to your ledger. A retail store that does hundreds of sales amounting to thousands or tens of thousands of dollars every day should probably post daily. With that volume of sales, it's important to see what's happening every day and not to fall behind with the paperwork. To do this, the busy retailer should use a cash register that totals and posts the day's sales to a computerized bookkeeping system at the push of a button. A slower business, however, or one with just a few large transactions per month, such as a small website design shop, a dog-sitting service, or a swimming-pool repair company, would probably be fine if it posted weekly or even monthly.

To get started on a hand-entry system, get ledger pads from any office supply store. Or, as is more practical these days, purchase an accounting software program that will generate its own ledgers as you enter your information. All but the tiniest new businesses are well advised to use an accounting software package to help keep their books. Micro-businesses can often get by with personal finance software such as *Quicken*. Once you've entered your daily, weekly, or monthly numbers, accounting software makes preparing monthly and yearly financial reports incredibly easy.

Learn bookkeeping by hand. Even though a computerized accounting system allows you to generate sophisticated financial reports with a few mouse clicks, you should still take the time to understand how the numbers fit together and what they mean. A good way to do this is to learn how financial reports are done by hand, as we explain below, even if you plan to use a computer to generate them. The more you know about your numbers and the relationships between various figures, the better able you'll be to make positive and profitable business decisions.

Every business should have both an income ledger and an expenditure ledger for posting transactions. We'll walk you through each of these ledgers below, and offer samples of each type. In Section 3, below, we'll also introduce you to some other types of ledgers that you may want to use, depending on your business.

1. Income Ledger

Despite its name, an income ledger should include only money earned in the course of business—your sales income—not income from every source. For example, income from a loan or transfer of personal money into the business should not be included with sales income on this ledger.

Check out the following example.

1	**2**	**3**	**4**	**5**		**6**
				Nontaxable Sales		
Date	Sales Period	Taxable Sales	Sales Tax	Sales to Retailers	Nontaxable Services	Other	Total Sales
1		$452.58	$38.47	$96.50	$75.00	$45.00	$707.55
2	closed						
3							
4	(May 3-4)	765.50	65.07	143.50	125.00	65.75	$1,164.82
5		407.88	34.67	76.25	60.00	45.00	$623.80
31		502.45	42.71	105.00	90.00	53.50	$793.66
Totals		**$9,456.82**	**$803.83**	**$1,845.50**	**$1,365.50**	**$854.00**	**$14,325.65**

Income for May 2004

Most income ledgers—whether on paper or part of your accounting software—are set up like the above sample, covering a one-month period and allowing space for daily entries. Your income should be divided into taxable sales, sales tax, and nontaxable sales. Also, the California Board of Equalization requires that you keep records of your nontaxable sales in separate categories, such as food sales, sales to retailers, and sales to the U.S. government. The categories you must use may vary depending on what kind of business you run. Contact the BOE for information on the specific categories your particular business must use. The BOE has a number of published regulations on recordkeeping and tax tip pamphlets that explain the bookkeeping requirements for various businesses. Go to www.boe.ca.gov or call 800-400-7115 for a list of available publications.

When you're ready to post your sales income, however often you decide to do it, go through your receipts for that period and enter the totals into the appropriate columns. Mark each receipt or cash register tape "posted" (stamping is often easiest) once you've recorded it in your ledger. If you post daily, you'll have entries on each line except for days your business is closed, in which case you

should enter "closed" in the Sales Period column. If you don't post daily, indicate in the Sales Period column which days are included for the totals you're entering (for example, "June 3 to June 6").

At the end of each month, total the entries in each column. Voila! You now have an income ledger for one month of business. As you can see, even without the help of a computer, creating one is easy. When you've finished a ledger for one month, start a new income ledger for the next month.

After you've completed an income ledger each month for a year, it's easy to add the monthly totals to arrive at your yearly sales income, broken down into taxable and nontaxable sales and sales tax amounts. Simply use a separate ledger sheet or computer file to post your monthly totals into a year-end income ledger. It will look very similar to your monthly income ledgers.

Remember, however, that businesses using the cash method of accounting can only count transactions actually paid during the year. If your business uses the cash method and did any sales on credit, you may need to do a year-end adjustment. If you never recorded unpaid sales in your monthly ledgers, then you're all set—no adjustment is neces-

Income for 2004						
1	2	3	4			5
			Nontaxable Sales			
Month	Taxable Sales	Sales Tax	Sales to Retailers	Nontaxable Services	Other	Monthly Total
January	$7,873.46	$669.24	$1,595.75	$1,310.75	$749.50	$12,198.70
February	8,567.45	728.23	1,787.25	1,280.75	683.00	$13,046.68
March	8,349.05	709.67	1,640.50	1,150.50	745.50	$12,595.22
April	8,995.65	764.63	1,788.00	1,335.75	823.70	$13,707.73
December	10,483.88	891.13	1,825.25	1,458.50	880.50	$15,539.26
Total for Year	100,468.48	9,108.72	20,364.50	14,076.25	9,539.90	$153,557.85
Accounts Receivable	10,345.15	724.16	1,565.45	986.90	450.55	$14,072.21
Adjusted Year-End Totals	**$90,123.33**	**$8,384.56**	**$18,799.05**	**$13,089.35**	**$9,089.35**	**$139,485.64**

sary. If, however, you included your total sales figures in your monthly ledgers, including unpaid credit sales, then you'll need to account for these in your year-end totals. Simply add an Accounts Receivable row at the bottom of the year-end ledger, with the totals of any unpaid sales, and subtract them from your yearly totals.

Here's a sample year-end ledger (see above).

Keep your completed ledgers in a safe place—whether they're hard copies or computer files. For hard copies, keep them in a well-organized file, preferably in a fireproof file cabinet. For computer files, be sure to make regular printouts and backups. Your ledgers will be essential to create financial reports that will give you a picture of your business's financial health (explained in Section E below), and to complete your local, state, and federal taxes. Losing your ledgers can be an expensive disaster—dealing with an IRS audit without your records is just one nightmare scenario—so be sure to treat them as the important business documents that they are.

2. Expenditure Ledger

The process of creating an expenditure ledger is quite similar to the income ledger process, but there are some key differences. Most importantly, the categories into which you'll divide your expenses are different. Here you won't use the "taxable sales," "sales tax," and "nontaxable sales" categories; instead, you'll divide your expenses into categories such as rent, utilities, computer equipment, employee wages, legal fees, postage, or travel, to name a few. Categorizing your expenses is important because different types of expenses have different rules for deductibility for tax purposes. Some expenditures can be deducted right away in full, others may be deducted only over several years (referred to as "depreciating expenses"), while other costs may not be deductible at all.

The IRS has oceans of rules. For more information on different types of business expenses and their deductibility, read *Tax Savvy for*

Small Business, by Frederick Daily (Nolo). Reading the rules issued by the IRS isn't a bad idea, either. IRS Publication 334, *Tax Guide for Small Businesses,* is a good place to start.

Categorizing your expenses also allows you to separate them into fixed costs vs. variable costs when you use your ledger information to generate financial reports. Variable costs, you may remember from Chapter 5, are the ones tied to your products or services, while fixed costs (overhead) are the ones that more or less stay the same regardless of your production and sales volume. Since the distinction between variable and fixed costs will be important when generating your profit and loss forecast, be sure to keep track of them separately in your expenditure ledger. For instance, if you run a Web development business and give your work to clients on a Zip disk, make sure to keep track of Zip disks for clients (a variable cost) separately from the Zip disks you use within your office (a fixed cost). One way to do this is to create a Zip disk category for client disks, and to simply count your office Zip disks in a general "office supplies" category.

The sample expenditure ledger below is a very simplified one, showing just a few common expense categories. Your business will almost certainly have more categories of expenses. In defining your categories, keep in mind the distinction between variable and fixed expenses, and do your best to keep your categories tightly defined—but not so narrow that you end up with dozens of tiny groups. As a general reference, here's a list of common expense categories:

- advertising
- automobile
- bank charges
- copying
- delivery/freight/shipping
- dues and fees
- education (classes, workshops, etc.)
- employee wages
- equipment/furniture/computers
- equipment rental
- insurance
- interest on business debt
- legal and professional fees
- meals (business related)
- office expenses/supplies
- office rent
- online services
- postage
- publications (books, magazines, etc.)
- software
- tax preparation fees
- taxes
- telephone
- travel, and
- utilities (gas, electric).

Expenditures for February 2004

1	2	3	4	5	6	7	8	9
Date	Payment Method	Transaction	Payee	Office Supplies	Rent	Utilities	Misc.	Monthly Totals
2-1	ck. 1204	Rent	landlord		$1,000.00			
2-5	Visa	Stationery	Office Depot	$78.00				
2-13	cash	Business lunch	Monte Vista Café				$32.00	
2-22	ck. 1206	Electric bill	Electric Co.			$65.00		
Feb. Totals				$78.00	$1,000.00	$65.00	$32.00	$1,175.00

An accountant can help set up ledgers. It's a good idea for every small business to use at least a minimal amount of help from an accountant, particularly in the early days when you're figuring out your accounting system. An accountant can help you figure out which expense categories your business should use. For example, a carpenter will undoubtedly want to use different categories (such as a category for wood and another for hardware like nails and screws) than a Web designer (who might have a category for printing costs and another for storage media like Zip disks). An accountant, particularly one who's familiar with your type of business, has the expertise to know which expenses should be grouped together.

Just as with your income receipts, you must periodically transfer (post) the information from your expenditure receipts to your expense ledger. Ideally you should do this reasonably promptly after you incur the expense. In the Payment Method column, enter "cash" if you paid in cash; the name of the credit card if you paid with plastic; or the check number if you paid by check. Remember, if you use the cash method of accounting, you will only record expenditures when they are paid—not when you incur them—so for credit card purchases, you'll only record them when you pay your bill. (See Section B above for a review of cash vs. accrual accounting.) In the Transaction column, enter a brief description of the purchase, and in the Payee column, enter whom you paid. Then enter the amount of the purchase in the appropriate category column.

Unlike your income ledgers, a new expenditure ledger isn't started each month—you'll have one running expense ledger. At the end of the month, simply add up the expenses for that month in each category, and enter each category's total in the next empty row. Then add up all the totals for each category and enter the result in the Monthly Totals column. Draw a double line under the monthly totals, and then continue entering expenses for the next month on the same sheet. Use a new sheet when you run out of room.

At year-end, you'll summarize your monthly expenditure totals on a separate ledger in much the same way that you summarized your monthly income totals. Remember that if you use the accrual

Year-End Expenditure Summary

1	2	3	4	5	6
Month	Rent	Office Supplies	Utilities	Misc.	Totals
January	$1,100	$120	$254	$154	$1,628
February	1,100	75	236	209	$1,620
March	1,100	56	244	130	$1,530
April	1,100	90	197	104	$1,491
December	1,100	69	233		
Year Totals	13,200	1,082	2,164	1,845	$18,291
Accounts Payable	0	210	62	347	$619
Adjusted Year-End Totals	**13,200**	**$1,292**	**$2,226**	**$2,192**	**$18,910**

accounting method, you'll need to include all expenses for the year, even if you haven't paid them yet. For those using accrual accounting, you'll be all caught up if, every month, you posted all expenses into your expenditure ledger as they became due, even if you didn't pay them. But if you only posted the expenses that you actually paid (as is common for ease of posting), then you'll need to account for your unpaid bills. Do this by including the totals of any unpaid bills in an Accounts Payable row, categorized like your other expenses, and add it to your yearly total.

3. Designing a Ledger System

The two ledgers just described will help you keep track of your most basic business functions—earning and spending money. Depending on how you conduct your business, you may also need to use one or more additional ledgers. If you sell products or services on credit, you'll want to keep track of these sales (the amount you are owed) using an accounts receivable ledger. Similarly, if you make purchases on credit, you can keep track of what you owe with an accounts payable ledger. And if your business has assets such as machinery, computers, or vehicles, you'll need to keep track of their depreciation with an equipment ledger. (Depreciation is explained in Chapter 9, Section A.) You'll find prototypes of various types of ledgers at office supply stores, or as a component of any accounting software product.

E. Step Three: Creating Financial Reports

Financial reports are important because they bring together several key pieces of financial information about your business in one place. Think of it this way: While your income ledger may tell you that your business brought in a lot of money during the year, you have no way of knowing whether you turned a profit without measuring your income

against your expenses. And even comparing your monthly totals of income and expenses won't tell you whether your credit customers are paying fast enough to keep adequate cash flowing through your business to pay your bills on time. That's why you need financial reports: to combine data from your ledgers and sculpt it into a shape that shows you the big picture of your business.

The financial reports we talk about in this section are nothing to freak out about. They're really just the income and expense numbers from your ledgers, tweaked a bit in order to help you answer questions about how your business is doing. For instance, the mysterious-sounding "profit and loss statement" consists of nothing more than your income and expense numbers, combined so that you know how much profit (or loss) you're making over a specified period. As long as you've been consistent and thorough in keeping your ledgers, you'll be able to generate this and other reports easily and quickly.

1. Profit and Loss Statement

If the typical owners of a small business start-up got a nickel for every time they asked themselves, "Will my business make a profit?" they'd probably be rich enough to retire before the doors were even open. A profit and loss statement (also called a P & L, or an income statement) is designed to answer this very question. In Chapter 5, we discussed creating a profit and loss statement with projected numbers. Here we explain how to do it after you've opened your doors and have actual numbers with which to work.

A P & L is made by totaling your revenues and then subtracting your expenses from that total for a specific period of time, usually each month. If you use accounting software, it will generate a P & L automatically with the data you enter from your sales and expense records. For each month, you'll be able to see whether your revenues are higher or lower than your expenses and by how much. At year-end you can total the monthly results to obtain your annual profit or loss.

To create a profit and loss statement, you'll need to subtract your "fixed costs" and your "variable costs" from your sales revenue, but first you'll need to understand the difference between the two. Fixed costs (also called overhead) are the costs associated with running your business in general, not with individual products or services themselves. Variable costs (also called costs of sale, or product or labor costs) are the expenses that are directly tied to the product or service that you're selling.

For example, say your business produces and sells greeting cards. Your variable costs would include the cost of the paper and printing the cards and the labor cost for the workers that make, package, and distribute the cards. As the name implies, these costs will vary depending on the amount and type of product you make and sell or service you perform. For example, if you produce more or less of a particular greeting card or if you emboss or use a heavier grade of card stock, your variable expenses will be affected.

Labor costs: sometimes variable, sometimes fixed. If you ask a group of accountants whether the labor costs associated with making a product are fixed or variable, you're likely to get conflicting answers. Some argue that as long as the workers will get paid regardless of whether they're working on that product, their salaries should be considered fixed, like rent or utilities. Others say that to have accurate financial records you need to reflect the cost of the labor that goes into a product. You or your accountant can decide how your business will categorize labor costs for making a product. Labor costs for providing services, on the other hand, are almost always treated as variable costs.

But other costs—your fixed costs—will not go up or down depending on the products you make or the services you perform. These costs, such as rent, office utility bills, and the insurance you purchase for your company vehicles will be more or less the same, regardless of the amount or type of greeting cards you make. This is exactly why age-old business wisdom cautions keeping overhead costs as low as you can. In times of slow sales you want to be saddled with as few fixed costs as possible.

Now that you know the distinction between variable and fixed costs, you need to understand how they're each subtracted from your revenue on a typical profit and loss statement. Hang in there—we're almost done.

- A profit and loss statement starts with your total sales revenues (remember, you enter that information on your income ledger), then subtracts your variable costs (recorded in one or more columns of your expenditure ledger). The result is called your gross profit—how much money you've earned from sales of your products or services over and above their cost to you.

- Next you subtract your fixed costs (again, from your expenditure ledger) from your gross profit. Any money you're left with is your real profit—also called net income, net profit, or pretax profit. Other than the various taxes you'll need to pay on this income, this is your (and any other business owners') money.

To sum up, the formula used in a profit and loss statement is basically as follows:

sales revenue
– variable costs (costs of sale)
= gross profit (gross margin)
– fixed costs
= net profit

Here's a typical P & L:

2004 Profit/Loss Statement							
	January	**February**	**March**	**April**	**May**	**December**	**Year Total**
Sales Revenues	$1,900	$1,950	$2,000	$1,850	$2,000	$2,100	$23,550
Variable Costs	300	310	350	300	325	350	3,840
Gross Profit	**1,600**	**1,640**	**1,650**	**1,550**	**1,675**	**1,750**	**19,710**
Fixed Expenses							
Rent	700	700	700	700	700	700	8,400
Supplies	150	100	75	90	125	100	1,220
Utilities	200	200	200	200	200	200	2,400
Advertising	150	150	150	150	150	150	1,800
Misc.	75	80	65	70	75	85	830
Total Fixed Expenses	**1,275**	**1,230**	**1,190**	**1,210**	**1,250**	**1,235**	**14,650**
Net Income (Loss)	**$325**	**$410**	**$460**	**$340**	**$425**	**$515**	**$5,060**

The P & L will not only tell you whether you're making or losing money, but will also help you identify which aspects of your business need adjusting in order to boost profits. Often, a profitability problem can be found in your expenses. Being able to see the totals of each of your various expense categories over the course of several months, all on one sheet, can help you pinpoint areas in which you're spending too much money (and hopefully help give you the courage to do something about it). And, of course, accurately tracking income totals month by month will help you quickly spot a downturn in revenue and prompt you to take action to boost sales.

2. Cash Flow Projection

We discussed cash flow projections in Chapter 5, as a way to find out if your business would be able to pay its bills once it got started. A cash flow projection is also a crucial tool to use in your on-going business. It's essential for your business to have enough cash available at any given time to pay its operating costs. Having lots of customers and thriving sales isn't enough, especially if you sell on credit. If your customers pay you in 90 days, but you must pay your expenses in 30 days, or even immediately, you may face a situation where, even though your financial statement says you are making a profit, you can't pay your rent, utilities, delivery services, or other key bills. Unless you make some changes, you may have to take out a line of credit or even close up shop.

Helping you understand why you may not be able to pay your bills despite being profitable—and how to take steps to avoid this—is the role of a cash flow projection. A cash flow projection focuses on the actual cash payments made to and by your business. We call these payments cash-ins and cash-outs (or inflows and outflows) to differentiate them from sales and expenses, which may not be paid right away. Estimating your cash-ins and cash-outs for upcoming months can help you predict when you might run short, allowing you to take action early by tightening up on your credit terms, raising more capital, getting a loan or line of credit, or putting more effort into collecting accounts receivable. If you don't know when a cash shortage might happen, it may be too late to do anything about it once it happens—except lock your doors and close your business.

Your cash flow projection will use most of the same numbers as your profit and loss statement, along with a few new ones. The big difference is that your cash flow projection will include all of your sources of income—not just sales income—and only income that's paid in cash (not credit). In other words, while your profit and loss statement is concerned with how much revenue your business is earning through sales of its products or services, your cash flow projection is designed to show you how much cash you will have on hand from all sources, including paid sales, loans, interest from investments, transfers from your personal accounts, lottery winnings, or whatever else might bring in some money. That's because when it comes to paying bills, the bottom line is whether you have enough money, period. Similarly, your cash flow projection will include all money you pay out of the business, whether for supplies, taxes (including any estimated taxes you owe; see Chapter 9, Section E), loan repayments, or any other expenditure.

The basic formula for cash flow analysis is:

> cash in bank at beginning of month
> + cash receipts for the month
> − cash disbursements for the month
> = cash in bank at end of month

In a cash flow projection, each month starts with the amount of money you have in the bank. (This will generally be the same amount that's left over from the previous month.) Next, you'll add any cash that came in during the month in all relevant categories, such as sales income, loans, interest earned, and any personal money you put into the business—your total cash-ins for the month. Next,

subtract the money you spent during the month, your cash-outs. The result is the cash left at the end of the month. Enter that figure into the beginning of the next month's column, and do the same process for the next month. If you use accounting software, a cash flow spreadsheet can be generated automatically once you've entered figures for income and expenses.

Now that you see the basic formula behind cash flow analysis, you need to understand that the real power of this tool is not in tracking actual cash-ins and cash-outs, but in predicting future cash flows. Periodically, say once a month or every couple months, you should use your actual figures to help make estimates for upcoming months and complete a cash flow projection for the future, generally up to one year. Hopefully you'll see that you will have enough cash to cover your expenses each month. If not, don't panic. First, pat yourself on the back for doing a cash flow analysis and figuring out ahead of time that you won't be able to cover all your expenses. Then come up with a plan—either put off some expenses that can wait, get more money (perhaps through collecting accounts receivable or getting a short-term loan or line of credit), or sell, sell, sell more product.

Especially when you're in the early stages of a business and don't have much of a business history, predicting cash-ins and cash-outs for future months isn't easy. (Cash-outs, however, are often easier to predict than cash-ins because you have more control over them and many costs recur each month.) You'll need to make estimates of how much income will come in and what expenses must be covered—a task that may seem only slightly easier than reading tea leaves.

The key is to do your best—with an emphasis on "do." Accept the fact that your estimates won't be close to 100% accurate, but make them anyway. As the months tick by and the flow of cash into and out from your business settles into daily, weekly, and monthly patterns, making estimates will inevitably become easier and you'll find them increasingly more accurate.

An example of a cash flow projection you can do on a simple spreadsheet is shown on the following pages.

As you can see, arranging income and expense information into a cash flow projection reveals a lot about the financial workings of a business. For example, our sample cash flow forecast shows that cash is tight each and every month (look at the "Cash at End of Month" row), so the business owner might consider ways to cut costs or tighten credit terms.

Of more pressing importance is the projected cash shortfall starting in June. Knowing a few months in advance that a shortage is likely will help the business owner figure out what to do while there's still time to take action. The owner could contribute some personal money to the business (note that the cash flow didn't include any loans or personal transfers to the business), or could try to cut some nonessential expenses, at least until later in the year when there will be a bit (but only a small bit) more cash available.

Credit lines provide flexibility and cash flow. One good strategy for the owner of a small business who expects seasonal fluctuations in cash flow is to apply for a revolving line of credit from the bank. A line of credit works on the same principle as a credit card. The business can borrow funds up to the credit line limit on an as-needed basis and has to pay interest only on the outstanding balance (not the entire credit line). The business can choose to pay funds back and reborrow them as necessary during the time the credit line is open. Credit lines can be open for a specified period, such as five or ten years, or can be open-ended (like a credit card).

Compare your projection to reality. Each month, replace your projections with actual results from your accounting system. It's a great way to see how accurate your projections are.

Who Needs to Do a Cash Flow Analysis?

David Rothenberg, a CPA and chief financial officer at Nolo, gives the following advice: "If your business is wildly profitable, you have little or no debt, you are not planning on expanding your business anytime soon, and you don't grant your customers a long time to pay, you probably don't need to do a cash flow analysis. You already know you'll have plenty of cash to meet your needs. But if this doesn't sound like your business, then you probably will benefit from keeping a close eye on your cash flow. Remember, the cash flow statement isn't for the IRS and it isn't for the bank; it's for you. You're the one who won't sleep at night if your bank account is empty. So what are you waiting for? Get out there and start projecting!"

Chapter 11 Checklist

☐ Decide whether to use the cash or accrual system of accounting.

☐ Keep records of all payments to and from your business. Create an organized system for keeping your receipts.

☐ Summarize your income and expense records into ledgers on a regular basis. Businesses with high volumes of sales or expenses should do this frequently—daily or weekly.

☐ Use your income and expense ledgers to create financial reports such as a profit/loss statement and a cash flow analysis.

☐ Consult with an accountant or tax professional at least once a year to keep your system on track.

Cash Flow Projection, Completed April 2004

	Jan	Feb	Mar	April	May
Cash at Beginning of Month	$2,000	$1,250	$600	$700	$350
Cash-ins					
Sales Paid	15,000	14,750	15,500	14,750	15,500
Loans and Transfers	0	0	0	0	0
Total Cash-ins	**15,000**	**14,750**	**15,500**	**14,750**	**15,500**
Cash-outs					
Variable Costs	3,000	3,100	3,500	3,000	3,250
Rent	7,000	7,000	7,000	7,000	7,000
Supplies	1,500	1,000	750	900	1,250
Utilities	2,000	2,000	2,000	2,000	2,000
Loan Payments	1,500	1,500	1,500	1,500	1,500
Misc.	750	800	650	700	750
Total Cash-outs	**15,750**	**15,400**	**15,400**	**15,100**	**15,750**
Cash at End of Month	**$1,250**	**$600**	**$700**	**$350**	**$100**

June	July	Aug	Sept	Oct	Nov	Dec
$100	($300)	$150	$0	$0	($550)	$300
15,000	16,100	16,250	15,500	15,250	16,750	16,900
0	0	0	0	0	0	0
15,000	**16,100**	**16,250**	**15,500**	**15,250**	**16,750**	**16,900**
3,150	3,450	3,500	3,250	3,300	3,400	3,550
7,000	7,000	7,000	7,000	7,000	7,000	7,000
900	1,100	850	1,000	1,100	950	900
2,000	2,000	2,000	2,000	2,000	2,000	2,000
1,500	1,500	1,500	1,500	1,500	1,500	1,500
850	600	1,550	750	900	1,050	850
15,400	**15,650**	**16,400**	**15,500**	**15,800**	**15,900**	**15,800**
($300)	**$150**	**$0**	**$0**	**($550)**	**$300**	**$1,400**

Building Your Business and Hiring Workers

If all your careful planning, hard work, and good karma pay off, you may soon find yourself needing help to handle your thriving business (if you haven't already). While part of you will surely be happy that your business is taking off, another, more practical side of you may worry about what's involved in hiring help. This chapter offers a broad overview of the many legal requirements that apply to businesses that have one or more employees. If you're thinking about hiring an employee but aren't sure, the information we give here should help you understand what you might be getting into—and help you figure out if there's a better way to go.

Besides the practical and financial concerns involved in hiring one or more people to work for your business, you need to be aware of several legal rules that apply to businesses with outside workers. First of all, you'll need to understand the difference between two types of workers: employees and independent contractors. This distinction is crucial, because different rules will apply to your business depending on what kind of workers you hire. If the government considers your workers to be employees, you'll have to follow a number of state and federal laws and pay employment-related taxes. If, on the other hand, your workers can be characterized as independent contractors, you'll be spared many—but not all—of these financial and legal requirements.

A. Employees vs. Independent Contractors

Anyone who works for your business—other than a business owner—is either an employee or an independent contractor. In a nutshell, an employee is someone who works for you, on your site, with your tools and equipment, and according to your rules and procedures. Independent contractors, on the other hand, are in business for themselves; they work on their own time and with their own tools, and perform services for a number of different clients.

This is not a distinction to be taken lightly. Businesspeople who hire employees owe a number of employment taxes, such as payroll tax and unemployment tax, while those who hire only independent contractors do not owe these taxes. If you treat an employee as an independent contractor and fail to pay employment taxes, you risk subjecting yourself to a huge back-tax bill, plus interest and other state and federal penalties. More than a few businesses have been torpedoed and sunk into bankruptcy after making this mistake.

With that warning in mind, here's the lowdown on classifying your workers.

1. Controlling Government Agencies

Since paying taxes is the main drawback to classifying workers as employees, it shouldn't surprise you to learn that the IRS takes a great interest in whether your workers are classified properly. At the federal level, the IRS will take swift and severe action if it finds out that you're treating a worker as an independent contractor, when in fact the worker meets the criteria of an employee.

At the state level, the California Employment Development Department (EDD) (the agency that collects employment taxes) will also punish a business that avoids paying taxes by misclassifying workers. Don't make the mistake of ignoring state rules and requirements—state penalties can be at least as harsh as those imposed by the IRS.

2. Determining a Worker's Classification

The IRS's Publication 15A, *Employer's Supplemental Tax Guide*, offers information and examples to help you determine whether a worker is, in fact, an independent contractor or an employee. The EDD also has a brochure that gives some guidance on the issue, though for the most part the EDD uses the same standards as the IRS. (See Appendix A for contact information for the EDD.)

A worker should normally be considered an employee, not an independent contractor, when he or she:

- works only for you and not for any other business
- works on your premises
- uses your tools and equipment
- follows work hours you set
- follows your instructions on how to complete a job
- receives reimbursement for expenses incurred in doing a job
- supervises any of your other workers, or
- receives any employee benefits, such as holiday pay, paid vacation, or health insurance.

On the flip side, a worker should probably be considered an independent contractor if he or she:

- works for a number of different businesses or clients
- has a personal office, studio, garage, or other permanent place to work
- owns the equipment and tools used for the work
- sets his or her own hours
- uses independent judgment as to how best to complete a job
- doesn't get reimbursed for expenses incurred in doing a job, or
- advertises services to the public.

Of course, a worker you hire might display some characteristics of both categories, which makes it harder to say for sure how that worker should be classified. Ultimately, you'll need to consider all these factors and weigh them against each other to decide whether a worker should be classified as an employee or as an independent contractor.

EXAMPLE 1: Bob does a lot of freelance proofreading for a publisher of books on alternative health, Wholeness Press. He often works for Wholeness Press (about ten projects per year), but he also does four or five jobs per year for other publishers. He always works at home, receives minimal instructions as to how to do his work, and does his proofreading whenever he feels like it. Bob can probably be categorized as an independent contractor.

EXAMPLE 2: Susan programs almost exclusively for one software developer, Fizz Games, but she also does approximately one outside project per year. She sometimes works from home, but often uses a computer at Fizz Games' office. She works closely with the software development team at Fizz Games, following instructions from some of the developers while training some of the newer workers in programming techniques. The government is likely to see Susan as an employee. It would be risky to try to treat her as an independent contractor.

In borderline situations, it's safer to treat a worker as an employee than risk the penalties that may result if the IRS or the EDD decides you've misclassified an employee as an independent contractor. Keep in mind that the IRS and the EDD tend to disfavor independent contractor status—they'd much rather see borderline workers classified as employees, so that they can collect taxes on them.

If you can't decide how one of your workers should be classified, there are a few ways you can proceed. One is to consult a lawyer or an accountant who understands business tax laws. Another option is to go straight to the horse's mouth and ask the IRS or the EDD to tell you how they would classify a certain worker. You can file Form SS-8, Determination of Employee Work Status, to request a formal ruling from the IRS on a worker's status. You can get this form from an IRS office or from the agency's website at www.irs.gov. Don't be surprised if the IRS classifies your worker as an employee! For an EDD determination, file Form DE 1870, Determination of Employment Taxes and Personal Income Tax Withholding, which is also available online or from an EDD office. (See Appendix A for contact

Classifying Workers: Don't Make the Same Mistake Microsoft Did

Who would think that lowly temporary workers would be able to beat Microsoft, one of the world's mightiest economic juggernauts? But that's just what they did, which should be a lesson to all businesses that hire independent contractors. Like many software companies, Microsoft supplemented its regular core of employees with a pool of workers it classified as "freelancers," paying them cash compensation (sometimes more than its employees) but none of the fringe benefits available to regular employees. Microsoft had the workers sign agreements providing that they were independent contractors, which meant Microsoft wouldn't give them fringe benefits or withhold or pay any taxes for them.

The problem with Microsoft's designation of these workers as independent contractors (ICs) was that it failed to treat them like ICs—that is, people running their own independent businesses. Instead, Microsoft integrated the workers into its workforce: they often worked on teams along with regular employees, sharing the same supervisors, performing identical functions, and working the same core hours. And because Microsoft required that they work onsite, they received admittance card keys, office equipment, and supplies from the company. Microsoft's treatment of the workers clearly spelled out "employee," not independent contractor.

When the IRS audited the company's payroll tax accounts in 1989 and 1990, it determined that Microsoft treated the workers as employees—not independent contractors who control the manner and means of how their services are performed—and therefore, owed employment taxes for them. Microsoft agreed with the IRS and admitted that the workers should have been classified as employees for tax purposes. The company paid back-payroll taxes and overtime for the workers and moved some of them to permanent employee status.

Upon learning of the IRS's decision, eight of the formerly misclassified workers sued Microsoft for full employee benefits for the time they worked as independent contractors. The workers finally won their lawsuit, and Microsoft had to pay a small fortune to its misclassified workers. (Vizcaino v. Microsoft Corp., 120 F.3d 1006 (9th Cir. 1997).)

This case demonstrates that merely having a worker sign an agreement that he or she is an IC will not make him or her one in the eyes of the law. Rather, the worker must be treated like an IC on the job. Since the penalties for misclassification can be severe, make sure that everyone who deals with ICs in your company understands that they can't be supervised or otherwise controlled in the same way as employees.

information.) Like the IRS, the EDD commonly classifies workers as employees rather than independent contractors. You'll have to decide for yourself whether it makes sense to leave the determination up to these agencies, or whether you feel confident enough to classify your workers on your own. If you decide that all of your workers will be independent contractors, the rest of the rules in this chapter won't apply to you. You may still want to read on, however, if you'd like to get an overview of the regulations that apply to businesses with employees.

Hiring ICs triggers some requirements. If you pay any independent contractor over $600 in a year, you need to report those payments on Form 1099-MISC, then send it to the worker and to the IRS. In addition, if you are required to file a federal 1099-MISC, you must also report certain information about that contractor to the EDD. More information about this requirement is available from the EDD at 916-657-0529 or at www.edd.cahwnet.gov. For in-depth information about hiring independent contractors, see *Hiring Independent Contractors: The Employer's Legal Guide*, by Stephen Fishman (Nolo).

B. Special Hurdles for Employers

As soon as you hire your first employee, you unleash a swarm of legal requirements that apply specifically to employers. Not only will you have to pay a number of employment taxes, but you'll also need to register with certain government agencies, pay for certain types of insurance, and comply with various laws, such as those requiring you to keep a smoke-free workplace and to post certain notices at your business premises.

While the many laws that apply to employers are beyond the scope of this book, here's an overview of the major requirements that apply to businesses with employees. If you can't meet your needs by hiring an independent contractor and you must hire an employee, you'll need to consult additional resources to make sure you comply with the many state and federal laws governing employers. (We list some additional resources at the end of this chapter.)

In general, owners of businesses with one or more employees are required to do the following:

- Report all new hires to the EDD within 20 days of the employee's first day of work, as part of the New-Employee Registration Program—a government system designed to help states track down parents who owe child support. (See www.edd.cahwnet.gov/taxrep/txner.htm.)
- Obtain workers' compensation insurance and follow rules on notifying employees of their rights to workers' compensation benefits. You may purchase this insurance from the State Compensation Insurance Fund (call 415-565-1234 or visit online at www.scif.com) or from a private insurance company.
- Comply with state and federal job safety laws, administered by the federal Occupational Safety and Health Administration (OSHA) and California's Department of Industrial Relations, Division of Occupational Safety and Health (DOSH). This includes filing an illness and injury prevention plan, reporting work-related injuries and illnesses that result in lost work time and keeping a log of all work-related injuries and illnesses. For more information about OSHA regulations, visit the OSHA website at www.osha.gov, or the California OSHA Consultation Services's website at www.dir.ca.gov/DOSH/consultation.html. Or, call the Cal/OSHA assistance line at 800-963-9424.
- Withhold federal income taxes and FICA taxes (which basically consist of Social Security and Medicare taxes) from employees' paychecks and periodically report and send these withheld taxes to the IRS.
- Report wages and withholding to each employee and to the IRS with Form W-2.
- Pay the employer's portion of Social Security and Medicare tax for each employee, based on the employee's wages. The employer's portion is the same amount as the employee's share: 7.65% of the employee's wages up to $87,900 in 2004, and 1.45% of wages in excess of that amount.
- Withhold state income taxes from employees' paychecks and periodically deposit them with the Franchise Tax Board.
- Withhold employees' contributions to the State Disability Insurance (SDI) program from their paychecks and periodically deposit them with the state. The SDI rate for 2004 is 0.9% of an employee's wages, with a wage cap of $56,916 per year. (See www.edd.ca.gov/direp/diind.htm.)
- Register and pay for California Unemployment Insurance (UI) tax. The UI tax rate for new employers is 3.4% of each employee's first $7,000 in wages. This rate lasts for three years, then changes depending on how many claims your former employees have filed. The more they've filed, the higher your tax will be. The range in 2004 is between 1.5% and 6.2% of the first $7,000 of wages per employee. Unlike disability insurance, the employer is solely responsible for paying unemployment insurance tax and may not deduct it from employees' paychecks.

- Pay federal unemployment taxes. It's the sole responsibility of the employer to pay the Federal Unemployment Tax (FUTA) directly to the IRS; you may not deduct it from employees' paychecks. The general rule is that you must pay FUTA taxes if you paid a total of $1,500 or more in wages in any calendar quarter or if you had one or more employees for at least some part of a day in each of 20 or more calendar weeks (not necessarily consecutive) during the year. If you have to pay FUTA taxes, you must pay a 6.2% tax on the first $7,000 of wages that you pay each employee during the year. However, if you paid the state unemployment tax on the same wages on time, you are allowed a state credit of up to 5.4%. The federal tax rate becomes a mere 0.8% after

this credit. The FUTA tax is reported annually on IRS Form 940, Employer's Annual Federal Unemployment Tax Return.

Thinking twice about becoming an employer? There's no way around it: Adding employees to your business will greatly complicate your life. (And we haven't even discussed providing optional benefits, such as health insurance and 401(k) plans.) (See the following sidebar on the Health Insurance Act of 2003 that will require some California businesses to provide health benefits for their employees beginning in 2006.)

If there's a way to meet your needs with independent contractors rather than employees, it may be a much more practical road to take. At the very least, you shouldn't jump into hiring employees without having a clear reason to do so.

New Health Plan Requirements for California Employers

On October 5, 2003, the Health Insurance Act of 2003, or Senate Bill 2 (SB 2), was signed into law. This law will require California employers to pay a fee into a state fund that will be used to provide health benefits to eligible employees at firms that do not offer coverage. As an alternative, if an employer offers its employees health benefits that meet SB 2's minimum requirements, the fee will be waived. In other words, if the employer offers the required health coverage to its employees, it will not have to pay into the state fund.

Certain SB 2 requirements and effective dates depend on how many employees you have, as follows:

Firms with 200 or more California employees will be required to offer coverage for both employees and their dependents, and to pay 80% of the premium for both employees and dependents, or pay into the state fund. The law will go into effect January 1, 2006.

Firms with 50 to 199 California employees will be required to offer coverage for employees only—not dependents—and to pay 80% of the employee

premium, or pay into the state fund. The law will go into effect January 1, 2007.

Firms with 20 to 49 employees may be required to offer coverage for employees only, not dependents, and to pay 80% of the employee premium, or pay into the state fund. SB 2 will not apply to firms in this size category unless the state of California provides a tax credit to those firms equal to 20 percent of the employer's net cost of the fee. The law will go into effect January 1, 2007, but only if the tax credit is implemented.

Firms with fewer than 20 employees are exempt from SB 2.

There are many more details in SB 2 than we can cover here, and still more details will be included in regulations that have not yet been issued for implementing the new law. Also keep in mind that SB 2 may be challenged by opponents in court, or with a referendum to repeal the law. Depending on the results of any such challenges, SB 2 may be only partially implemented, or not implemented at all. (For current information, see the SB 2 Resource Page at the California HealthCare Foundation's website at www.chcf.org/sb2.)

For more information on being an employer.
The Employer's Legal Handbook, by Fred S. Steingold, is an indispensable, comprehensive reference for employers that covers the legal rules on hiring, firing, taxes, workplace safety, and much more. For practical information and guidance on handling workplace issues—including performance evaluations, investigations, discipline, and firing—see *Dealing With Problem Employees,* by Amy Delpo and Lisa Guerin. Or, if you're strapped for time, but want a quick guide to steering clear of legal problems with your employees, check out *Everyday Employment Law: The Basics,* by Lisa Guerin and Amy Delpo. For information on hiring independent contractors, be sure to read *Hiring Independent Contractors: The Employer's Legal Guide,* by Stephen Fishman. (All are published by Nolo).

Chapter 12 Checklist

☐ Become familiar with the legal differences between employees and independent contractors.

☐ Before hiring help, determine whether you need to hire employees or whether you could hire independent contractors instead.

☐ Don't avoid your obligations by misclassifying your workers as independent contractors. If the IRS or the EDD decides that your workers are really employees, you can face serious penalties including payment of back payroll taxes.

☐ Make sure you're ready to take care of all the legal, bureaucratic, and tax requirements that apply to businesses with employees before hiring your first employee.

Getting Professional Help

Most business owners, especially sole proprietors and partners in general partnerships, won't need to rely on professional help for the vast majority of their day-to-day business affairs. As the chapters in this book have shown, the legal tasks required to start a business, as well as many of those relating to its ongoing operation, involve nothing more than complying with simple bureaucratic requirements, filling out standard forms, and paying fees.

But life's not always so simple, of course. From time to time, you may find yourself feeling like you're in over your head. Maybe you're struggling to decide whether it's a good time, financially speaking, to expand your business. Or perhaps there's a dispute brewing between you and a business partner. These are just a couple of examples of the types of situations in which an expert can come in handy.

Even when things are running smoothly, virtually every business should at least occasionally consult an accountant or other tax expert for help in preparing tax returns. A tax professional can also help you manage your business's finances to keep down your business taxes. Contacting both a lawyer and a tax person early in your business life is often a sensible step. As your business grows, you'll be able to consult these pros for help with ongoing questions.

Once you decide you want to hire a professional, your next question very likely will be, "How do I find someone I can trust?" This chapter will offer strategies that will help you find and hire a professional such as a lawyer or an accountant who's competent and aboveboard. We'll also talk about an increasingly popular type of service called "legal coaching," which is starting to replace traditional lawyering in many cases.

A. Working With Lawyers

Despite the fact that the attorney section of the Yellow Pages is often the biggest section of the phone book, a good lawyer can be hard to find. This section explains how to find a lawyer who meets your needs and how to make sure you're getting the most for your hard-earned money.

1. What to Look for in a Lawyer

Here are some of the qualities to look for in a lawyer. First, make sure to find an attorney who has some experience with small business issues, preferably for your specific type of small business. Plus, you want someone who's intelligent and competent—two qualities that don't necessarily go hand in hand with having a law degree. And, of course, you want a lawyer whom you can trust.

In today's world of ever-increasing specialization, lawyers often focus their areas of expertise rather narrowly. For example, an expert negotiator may not be an effective courtroom lawyer, and vice versa. Make sure that your lawyer can handle the particular type of problem you're facing, in terms of both its subject matter and the type of work involved.

In addition to finding a lawyer with the skills and experience relevant to your situation, it's important that you and the lawyer get along on a personal level. If an otherwise perfect lawyer—smart, experienced, and trustworthy—is condescending or rude, you should keep looking for someone with better personal skills. This general rule is especially true for small business owners, who will ideally develop a long-term relationship with a lawyer. An attorney who knows you and your business, will be better equipped to provide the best advice and assistance for your specific situation.

Finally, you may want to make a special effort to find a lawyer who is willing to work with you collaboratively on certain matters that you can handle at least partially on your own. Handling some routine legal issues, such as amending your partnership agreement or executing a contract for services, may be well within your abilities, though you may be more comfortable having a lawyer review your work or give you limited advice. While lawyers traditionally offered their services on an all-or-nothing basis (and charged fees accordingly), a trend has recently emerged where lawyers act as coaches for their clients, giving only as much service as the clients want. (Legal coaching is discussed in more detail in Section 3, below.)

For more on hiring and working with a lawyer. See *The Lawsuit Survival Guide*, by Joseph Matthews (Nolo).

2. How to Find a Lawyer

Unfortunately, the easiest and quickest ways to find a lawyer are usually the least effective. Sure, you'll find hundreds of lawyers' names in the Yellow Pages, but how will you choose among them? You'll have the same problem if you look in legal newspapers for attorney ads. By the way, flashy, aggressive advertising is definitely not a good indicator of quality legal services. Also, watch out for commercial referral services that collect fees from lawyers who are in their referral database. To filter out the lawyers who are wrong for you, you'll need to do more research.

The best way to find a good lawyer is to get a personal referral, preferably from another person who runs a small business. Even better is a referral from an owner of a business that's similar to yours. Book publishers, for instance, face different types of legal issues than do auto repair shops, and would be best served by a lawyer familiar with legal areas such as copyright and freedom of speech. Ask other businesspeople for lawyer recommendations.

If you just can't find anyone who can give you a personal referral, try investigating lawyers who work in your industry. One good way to do this is to keep your eyes and ears open for names of attorneys who have worked on cases in your field.

For example, a trade magazine might have an article about a current lawsuit involving a business similar to yours that mentions the names of the attorneys working on it. You can also contact organizations and visit websites that focus on your type of business. They can often direct you to lawyers who have worked in your industry. Once you get some names, try calling those lawyers and asking if they're available. If not, there's a good chance they will know someone else who might be able to help you.

Speak with the lawyer personally. You can probably get a good idea of how the attorney operates by paying close attention to the way your initial call is handled. Is the lawyer available right away, and, if not, is your call promptly returned? Is the lawyer willing to spend at least a few minutes talking with you to determine whether the two of you are good fits? Do you get a good personal feeling from your conversation? The way you're treated during your initial call can be a good indicator of how the lawyer treats clients in general.

3. Using a Lawyer as a Coach

In a traditional attorney/client relationship, a client hires an attorney to take care of a legal problem and then hands over all responsibility for—and control over—the matter to the lawyer. While some clients like it this way, many would rather be more involved in their cases, both to maintain some control and to save money on legal fees. But until recently, limited legal help from a lawyer wasn't much of an option. Most lawyers wouldn't take cases unless they could handle them fully on their own.

A new model of legal services is finally emerging. In this approach, sometimes called "legal coaching" or "unbundled legal services," a lawyer provides only the services that a client wants, and nothing more. For example, a client who wants legal help in drafting a contract can arrange a short consultation with a lawyer to get answers to general questions, go home and draft the contract, then fax it to the lawyer, who will review it and suggest changes. Or a client who wants to represent himself or herself in small claims court can use a lawyer to help draft motions and prepare for hearings, but otherwise pursue the case alone.

For the owner of a small business, using a lawyer as a coach can be especially useful. More often than not, the legal issues that arise in the course of business are relatively simple, and—with a bit of good legal advice—most businesspeople can handle them fairly easily. Many times, a business owner needs nothing more than some guidance through the bureaucratic maze that small businesses need to navigate. For instance, a businessperson facing a zoning conflict may be perfectly served by a five-minute explanation from a legal coach on the process of appealing a planning commission's decision. Rather than hiring an attorney for upwards of $1,000 to deal with the problem, using a coach might cost $50 and enable the business owner to proceed alone.

Despite the good sense to this approach, it still can take some effort to find a lawyer who is willing to be just a coach. To find a legal coach, use the same strategies discussed above (personal referrals, for example) but take the extra step of asking the lawyer directly whether he or she is willing to help you in your efforts to solve your own legal problems. If you don't find one right away, be persistent.

4. Dealing With Bills and Payments

No matter what their field or practice, most lawyers share one area of expertise: billing for their services. Before you hire any lawyer, be sure you fully understand how your fees will be calculated. All too often, clients are unpleasantly surprised by their bills because they didn't pay enough attention to the billing terms when they hired the lawyer. For instance, make sure you understand who's responsible for items such as court fees, copy fees, transcription costs, and phone bills. These costs aren't trivial, and can quickly send your otherwise affordable bill into the keep-you-awake-at-night range.

Lawyers generally use one of the following methods of calculating fees for their services.

- **Hourly fees.** This arrangement works just like it sounds: You pay an hourly rate for the number of hours the attorney spends working on your case. Simple as this system is, there are some details to consider. First, find out what hourly increments the lawyer uses for billing. For instance, if an attorney bills in half-hour increments, you'll be charged for a full half-hour even if you talk for just five minutes. That can easily total $100 or more for a five-minute phone call—a rate that would make even AT&T blush. You'd be better off if your lawyer uses ten- or 15-minute periods, though not all attorneys break down their time into such small increments.

  Another issue to ask about is whether all time spent on the case—even if the attorney isn't doing the work—is billed at the attorney's regular rate. For example, it's reasonable to expect a discounted rate for time spent by the attorney's administrative staff on making copies or organizing paperwork. Make sure that the hourly fee for the attorney applies only to the work of the actual attorney.

  Hourly fees for attorneys range from $100 or so to over $400 per hour. High rates may reflect a lawyer's extensive experience—or they might simply reflect a need to pay for a swank office. Don't pay the highest rates unless you feel the lawyer's expertise—not that Armani suit—is worth it.

- **Flat fees.** For some types of cases, attorneys will charge a flat fee for a specific task, such as negotiating a contract or filing articles of incorporation. As long as the job goes as expected, you'll pay only the agreed-upon price, regardless of how many hours the lawyer spent on the job. If the lawyer hits a snag, however, or if the case becomes convoluted for some reason, the price can go up. Be sure you and the lawyer are on the same page regarding the situations that may result in a higher fee. Also, find out if any expenses, such as court costs or copy fees, are charged in addition to the flat fee.

- **Contingency fees.** In a contingency fee arrangement, you pay an attorney's fee only if the lawyer wins money for you through a court judgment or a negotiated settlement. In that case, the fee you'd pay would be a percentage of the monetary award, usually one-third to one-half. In contingency fee arrangements, you need to be especially careful of costs such as travel expenses, transcription fees, and phone bills. If you lose your case, you won't owe attorneys' fees (because your lawyer didn't recover any money), but you will often be responsible for the lawyer's out-of-pocket expenses while working on your case.

  Small business matters don't typically require contingency fee arrangements. This payment method is usually used in personal injury cases and others in which a plaintiff sues someone in hopes of winning a large money award.

- **Retainers.** Sometimes you can hire a lawyer to be more or less "on call" by paying a regular fee (usually monthly) called a retainer. This type of arrangement is useful when you have regular, ongoing legal needs such as contract review or negotiation. Based upon your expected needs, you and the lawyer settle on a mutually acceptable monthly fee. Then, you simply have the lawyer take care of any routine legal matters that arise. If you run into a sudden, complex legal dispute, or if your problems escalate greatly, you'll likely have to make additional payments. For this type of arrangement to work, it's important that you and the lawyer have a clear understanding of the routine services that you expect. Unless your legal needs are regular and predictable, a retainer arrangement is probably not your best option.

By California law, your fee agreement must be in writing if your lawyer estimates the total cost of legal services to be more than $1,000, or if you have a contingency fee arrangement. Even if it's not legally required, it's always a good idea to get your fee agreement in writing. A written agreement will help prevent disputes over billing, and is the best way to avoid getting gouged.

B. Working With Accountants and Others

Many of the issues that small businesses face can be solved by professionals other than lawyers. In particular, tax professionals are often indispensable in helping you deal with tax laws, which have a huge impact on your business both financially and legally. In fact, tax advice is so essential to a successful small business that we recommend that every small business owner consult with a tax expert at least occasionally—say, once a year.

Obviously, you want to manage your business and the money flowing through it so as to minimize your tax bill. But you also need to be extremely careful not to violate any tax laws—which are insanely complex—and to avoid making simple mistakes that can result in costly penalties. While complicated tax troubles may indeed call for a tax attorney, many other more common questions can usually be answered by an accountant.

1. Matching People to Your Needs

For routine maintenance of your books, you probably don't need the experience—or expense—of an accountant (certified or otherwise). An experienced bookkeeper will be able to implement an effective system of tracking your income and expenses and staying on top of your important bills, including the various taxes your business will owe. Depending on the complexity of your business, you may even decide to do your own bookkeeping—a job that's undoubtedly easier these days with the availability of accounting software. As your business grows, however, an experienced bookkeeper will become an invaluable investment.

If you find yourself seeking specific tax advice or encountering a tricky financial problem, you may need to go up a step on the professional ladder and hire an accountant who's intimate with tax laws. The top dogs of accountants are called certified public accountants (CPAs), who are licensed and regulated by the state. California also licenses uncertified accountants called public accountants. Since the licensing requirements for CPAs are more stringent, they are considered to be the most experienced and knowledgeable type of accountants, and accordingly will be the most expensive.

In addition to bookkeepers and accountants, there are other professionals out there who specialize in tax preparation. The main thing to keep in mind is that some are licensed and some are not. An enrolled agent (EA) is a tax professional, licensed by the IRS, who can answer tax questions and help you prepare your returns. Others who simply use the title "tax preparer" or "tax return preparer" may not be licensed at all. If a tax professional doesn't have a license as an enrolled agent or as a public or certified public accountant, it may mean that the "professional" has no official qualifications whatsoever.

The bottom line is that you should use a professional who is best equipped to meet your particular needs. Obviously, you shouldn't pay a CPA to do simple bookkeeping, nor should you use a bookkeeper for preparing complex tax returns.

2. Finding Good Professional Help

Finding a tax professional is a lot like finding a lawyer: Your goal is to find someone both competent and trustworthy. The strategies discussed above for finding a lawyer are equally useful in finding other professionals. Getting a personal referral is the best way to find someone you can trust. Referrals from businesspeople in your field are particularly valuable. Since virtually every business has consulted a tax pro at one point or another, it shouldn't be too hard to get a decent list of names.

As with attorneys, choose your tax professional carefully, with an eye to developing a long-term relationship. Don't be shy about asking questions. Find out about the person's experience with small businesses similar to yours, and about his or her knowledge of bookkeeping methods, the tax code, the IRS, or anything else that's relevant to the work you want the professional to do for you.

Also be sure you understand the professional's fee structure up front, before he or she does any work. Most charge hourly fees, which vary a great deal depending on what kind of qualifications the professional has. Like your attorney fee agreement, your fee agreement with a tax professional should be in writing; written fee agreements reduce the possibility of disputes over the bill.

C. Internet Legal Research

Some of the legal questions you may run into won't warrant an expensive consultation with an attorney, but may be beyond the scope of a self-help book. For instance, you may need to look up specific consumer protection regulations on warranties and advertising, or find out what California's rules are on hiring and firing practices. If you don't want to call your lawyer every time you have a question, you might consider doing a little legal research yourself.

Finding basic small business law is usually not difficult—much of the information you'll need can be found on the Internet. Start by visiting Nolo's Small Business Law Center at www.nolo.com to see if your question has already been answered, or to get some background information in the area of the law in which you're interested. If you still need to go to the horse's mouth for the answer, you can try looking up the text of the actual law by going to Nolo's legal research center at www.nolo.com/lawcenter/statute. From there you can access the California Code, where you'll be able to find corporation and LLC statutes, laws on contracts and products liability, regulations on health and safety, and much more. You can also easily research federal law at Nolo's legal research center, including laws on copyrights, environmental regulations, bankruptcy, and IRS rules, to mention a few areas that might be of interest to small business owners.

Here are some other websites that offer helpful information on small business and tax law:

- National Federation of Independent Business at www.nfib.com. Here you can find small business news and practical information.
- Internal Revenue Service at www.irs.gov. You can download forms and instructions as well as a wide range of publications that do a fairly good job of explaining the tax laws.
- U.S. Small Business Administration at www.sba.gov. This site has a lot of good information on starting and financing your own business. The SBA also offers links to state websites related to business issues.
- SCORE (Service Corps of Retired Executives) at www.score.org. SCORE's association of retired executives and business owners offers email counseling and mentoring and an excellent directory of small business resources on the Web.
- A great resource for information on California law is the Official California Legislative Information website at www.leginfo.ca.gov. It offers searchable databases of existing California law, as well as pending legislation.
- The Thomas Legislative Information site at http://thomas.loc.gov. Here you can read small business bills pending in Congress as well as laws that have recently been adopted.

Help with legalese. If, during your legal meandering, you come across strange phrases like "blue sky," "naked option," or "commercial frustration," and you just know there's got to be a legal meaning behind them, try looking them up in Nolo's online Legal Dictionary at www.nolo.com.

More help with legal research. We've given you a few helpful hints on getting answers to your small business questions, but there may be times when you'll need more guidance. An excellent resource that teaches you how to find answers to your legal questions is Nolo's book *Legal Research: How to Find and Understand the Law,* by Stephen R. Elias and Susan Levinkind. Learning how to use legal resources online or at the law library will empower you to take care of a wide range of simple, everyday matters yourself rather than paying someone else to handle them.

☑ Chapter 13 Checklist

☐ Ask business associates and friends for recommendations for lawyers as well as accountants or other tax professionals. Also check trade magazines and other industry sources.

☐ Try to find a lawyer who will work as a legal coach, if that approach appeals to you.

☐ Get your fee agreements in writing.

☐ Become familiar with online sources of legal information such as nolo.com, the IRS website (www.irs.gov) and the legislative information site of the State of California (www.leginfo.ca.gov).

Resources and Contact Information

A note on the organization of this Appendix: If a resource can be located on the Web, its website address, along with information about what's available online, is included here. There's also a separate category for interactive websites—those that offer more than merely another way to contact a particular office. For instance, the searchable federal trademark database gets its own listing in the website category, even though it's also listed in the Government Agencies category under the U.S. Patent and Trademark Office.

A. Government Agencies

Government agencies are a lot like Russian dolls: One office often contains another office, which often contains yet another office, in a long, confusing chain of government subbranches. Getting the right phone number and the right government clerk can be incredibly frustrating. Be patient, and be persistent. Don't be afraid to ask questions. Do your best to explain what or who you need as clearly as you can; the clerk on the other end of the line is often your best source of accurate contact information.

Find the **Internal Revenue Service (IRS)** before it finds you. In addition to collecting income taxes, the IRS is also in charge of issuing federal employer identification numbers (FEINs, sometimes called EINs) to new businesses. For general questions on taxes, forms, or FEINs, call 800-829-1040. You can also visit the IRS on the Web at www.irs.gov. If you have a computer, a printer, and Internet access, getting forms and instructions online is convenient—and much more pleasant than spending an eternity on hold.

The **Small Business Administration (SBA)** specializes in assisting small businesses with financing, often by guaranteeing loans. If your small business is having trouble securing a loan through a bank, the SBA may guarantee all or part of it, which will make the bank much more likely to approve the loan. There are many different SBA loan programs that you can learn about at a local SBA office; contact information for District Offices appears below. Or visit the SBA online at www.sba.gov.

San Francisco SBA District Office

455 Market Street, 6th Floor
San Francisco, CA 94105
415-744-6820
Fax: 415-744-6812

Sacramento SBA District Office

650 Capitol Mall, Suite 7-500
Sacramento, CA 95814
916-930-3700
Fax: 916-930-3737

San Diego SBA District Office

550 W. C Street, Suite 550
San Diego, CA 92101
619-557-7250
Fax: 619-557-5894

Santa Ana SBA District Office

200 W. Santa Ana Boulevard, #700
Santa Ana, CA 92701
714-550-7420
Fax: 714-550-0191

Fresno SBA District Office

2719 N. Air Fresno Drive, Suite 200
Fresno, CA 93727
559-487-5791
Fax: 559-487-5636

Los Angeles SBA District Office

330 N. Brand Boulevard, Suite 1200
Glendale, CA 91203
818-552-3210
Fax: 818-552-3260

The **U.S. Patent and Trademark Office (PTO)** offers federal trademark information and forms. You can call the general information line at 800-PTO-9199 or 703-308-HELP. Better yet is to visit the trademark area of the PTO's website, at www.uspto.gov. In addition to the extensive information on trademark law and procedure available online, you can search the PTO's trademark database free, and fill out and submit your trademark application electronically.

For information on payroll taxes and other rules for employers, contact the **California Employment Development Department (EDD)** at 888-745-3886. Or visit the EDD's website, which offers contact details for the EDD offices in your area and substantive information on the laws that apply to employers. The Web address is www.edd.cahwnet.gov.

For sales tax and seller's permit information and forms, contact the **California Board of Equalization (BOE)** at 800-400-7115. Or visit the BOE's website at www.boe.ca.gov. Many forms and informational pamphlets are available for downloading. You'll also find useful information about property taxes, which are assessed and collected by counties but regulated by the BOE. You can download the free publication, *California Property Tax: An Overview*, which contains lots of valuable information, including calendars of important tax deadlines and contact details for each county assessor.

The **California Secretary of State** handles a number of different business-related issues, including corporate and LLC filings and trademark and service mark registrations. The phone number for general information is 916-653-6814. Or visit the Secretary of State online at www.ss.ca.gov, where you'll find a wide range of information and downloadable forms.

Contact information for local offices follows.

Sacramento Headquarters

1500 11th Street

Sacramento, CA 95814

919-657-5448

Fresno Branch

1315 Van Ness Avenue, Suite 203

Fresno, CA 93721

559-445-6900

Los Angeles Branch

300 S. Spring Street, Room 12513

Los Angeles, CA 90013

213-897-3062

San Diego Branch

1350 Front Street, Suite 2060

San Diego, CA 92101

619-525-4113

San Francisco Branch

2 Rincon Center

121 Spear Street, Suite 420

San Francisco, CA 94105

415-904-2344

The **California Franchise Tax Board (FTB)** is California's version of the IRS. This is the agency that collects state income taxes from individuals, corporations, and LLCs. For general information, call 800-852-5711. Most California tax forms and instructions are also available online. The FTB's Web address is www.ftb.ca.gov.

B. Associations

As every new entrepreneur quickly learns, city and state laws and regulations—from zoning issues to sales tax laws—have a significant impact on small businesses each and every day. **The California Small Business Association (CSBA)** is a nonprofit grassroots organization dedicated to advocating the interests of small businesses to government officials. In addition to political activism, this group offers member benefits such as discounted health insurance and Internet access. Contact CSBA at 800-350-CSBA or 310-642-0838; Fax: 310-642-0849. Or visit its website at www.csba.com.

The **California Chamber of Commerce** tracks business-related legislation in California and lobbies for business interests. The Chamber also publishes a number of business guides. To find your local chamber, contact the central office at 916-444-6670; Fax: 916-444-6685. Or visit its website at www.calchamber.com.

The **Graphic Artists Guild (GAG)** is an excellent resource for anyone in the business of visual art. In advocating for the rights and interests of working artists, GAG has been a leader in the effort to reform California sales tax laws as well as laws regulating home businesses. The Guild is also a good source of information about copyright and contract issues for professional artists. You can contact the Northern California chapter of GAG online at http://norcal.gag.org.

C. Books and Publications

A number of books and guides published by Nolo and other presses and organizations offer invaluable information to small business owners on a plethora of topics.

Business Plans

Business Plan Pro 2004
by Palo Alto Software
> A fast, easy way to generate the plan you need to launch or expand your business.

How to Write a Business Plan
by Mike McKeever
> Explains how to write a business plan, whether for your own purposes or to attract money from lenders or investors—including how to evaluate the profitability of your business idea; estimate operating expenses; determine assets, liabilities, and net worth; and find potential sources of financing. (Published by Nolo.)

Business Operations, Generally

Drive a Modest Car & 16 Other Keys to Small Business Success
by Ralph Warner
> Ideas, strategies, and lessons for successful entrepreneurs. (Published by Nolo.)

Legal Forms for Starting & Running a Small Business
by Fred S. Steingold
> Dozens of legal forms and documents crucial for the success of a small business. (Published by Nolo.)

Legal Guide for Starting & Running a Small Business
by Fred S. Steingold
> All the legal information you need to get your business off the ground and running—including how to raise start-up money, attract the best help, buy or sell a business or franchise, negotiate a favorable lease, insure your business, and resolve legal disputes. (Published by Nolo.)

Quicken Legal Business Pro 2004

A software package containing more than 140 legal forms and the complete text of six of Nolo's bestselling business titles—including *Legal Guide for Starting & Running a Small Business*, *Tax Savvy for Small Business*, *Everyday Employment Law: The Basics*, *Everybody's Guide to Small Claims Court*, *Marketing Without Advertising*, and *Leasing Space for Your Small Business*.

Small Time Operator

by Bernard Kamoroff

An accessible, useful guide geared towards the special needs of small business owners. This book, written by a CPA, is especially helpful in explaining basic bookkeeping systems and small business taxes. (Published by Bell Springs Publishing.)

Working From Home: Everything You Need to Know About Living and Working Under the Same Roof

by Paul and Sarah Edwards

This book offers extensive information on how to manage home businesses. (Published by Jeremy P. Tarcher/Putnam Publishing Group.)

Forms of Ownership

Buy-Sell Agreement Handbook: Plan Ahead for Changes in the Ownership of Your Business

by Anthony Mancuso and Bethany K. Laurence

Explains how to protect your business interests by drawing up an agreement (akin to a prenuptial agreement in a marriage) among you and the other business owners that sets out a plan for what happens if you or a co-owner leaves the company. A must for any new business with more than one owner. (Published by Nolo.)

The Corporate Minutes Book: A Legal Guide to Taking Care of Corporate Business

by Anthony Mancuso

All the plain-English information, step-by-step instructions, and easy to use forms you need to handle meeting minutes. (Published by Nolo.)

Form Your Own Limited Liability Company

by Anthony Mancuso

Offers instructions and forms to create an LLC in your state, as well as a full explanation of LLCs and how they work. (Published by Nolo.)

How to Form Your Own California Corporation and How to Form a California Professional Corporation

by Anthony Mancuso

These two titles explain in detail the legal and practical implications of incorporating—and walk you through the incorporation process. (Published by Nolo.)

LLC Maker

by Anthony Mancuso

Windows software that assembles LLC articles of organization according to state legal requirements, plus an operating agreement and other LLC formation paperwork. (Published by Nolo.)

Nolo's Quick LLC: All You Need to Know About Limited Liability Companies

by Anthony Mancuso

Explains the basics of limited liability companies, and helps you figure out whether structuring your business as an LLC is the right way to go. (Published by Nolo.)

The Partnership Book: How to Write a Partnership Agreement

by Denis Clifford and Ralph Warner

Describes the legal and practical issues of creating a partnership—including financial and tax liabilities, contributions and distributions, and changes in ownership. (Published by Nolo.)

Leases

Leasing Space for Your Small Business

by Janet Portman and Fred S. Steingold

A guide to the ins and outs of finding a space for your business, negotiating a lease, and solving problems that arise from it. (Published by Nolo.)

Marketing

How to Get Your Business on the Web
by Fred S. Steingold

> The legal forms you need to get your business on the Internet—and make it a success. (Published by Nolo.)

Marketing Without Advertising: Inspire Customers to Rave About Your Business & Create Lasting Success
by Michael Phillips and Salli Rasberry

> Explains the secret of attracting customers without pricey ads—including how to build trust with potential customers, encourage customer recommendations, improve customer service, list products and services widely and inexpensively, and use the Internet to market services and products. (Published by Nolo.)

Permits and Licenses

> The **California Permit Handbook** is a useful guide to California's environmental regulatory process. It's only available on the Web, not in hard copy, so noncomputer users may be out of luck (unless they have a computer-using friend print it out for them). To read the guide, go to http://commerce.ca.gov and click on "Permits & Licenses."

> **The License Handbook** is a helpful, free resource that will help you get familiar with all the state agencies, departments, and offices and their divisions and branches that administer the swarms of licenses, permits, and other business regulations in California. To read it online, go to http://commerce.ca.gov/handbook/index.html and click on "Permits and Licenses."

Protecting Business Assets

Nondisclosure Agreements: Protect Your Trade Secrets & More
by Richard Stim and Stephen Fishman

> This book, with forms on CD-ROM, explains how to protect your trade secrets with a nondisclosure agreement (or "confidentiality agreement") before sharing them with potential partners and employees, and includes 19 different legal forms. (Published by Nolo.)

Tax

Tax Savvy for Small Business
by Frederick W. Daily

> Offers plain-English tax laws and rules on business deductions, plus tax information on LLCs, partnerships, corporations, and more. (Published by Nolo.)

Workplace Laws

The Employer's Legal Handbook
by Fred S. Steingold

> All the basics of employment law in one place. It covers safe hiring and firing practices, wages, hours, employee benefits, taxes and liability, discrimination, and sexual harassment. (Published by Nolo.)

Hiring Independent Contractors: The Employer's Legal Guide
by Stephen Fishman

> This book explains all the tricky IRS rules and provides forms and instructions for hiring ICs. (Published by Nolo.)

D. Websites

CalGOLD is a website sponsored by the California Environmental Protection Agency, but the help it offers isn't limited to environmental matters. After prompting you to enter a bit of information about the business you're starting, this interactive site directs you to the government agencies whose registration requirements may apply to you. CalGOLD is located at www.calgold.ca.gov.

The California Department of Finance sponsors a website by the **California Demographic Research Unit**, which offers a range of state demographic data. At this site you can obtain a number of different free reports and research papers on California's population, such as the annual percentage growth in each city and county. For small business owners, this information can be really useful—not to mention fascinating. The Web address is www.dof.ca.gov/html/Demograp/druhpar.htm.

Download the latest California tax forms from the **Franchise Tax Board** at www.ftb.ca.gov.

Download a seller's permit application and other **Board of Equalization (BOE)** publications from www.boe.ca.gov.

Download the latest federal tax forms from the **Internal Revenue Service (IRS)** at www.irs.gov.

You can now search the online database of federal trademarks and apply for a trademark online at the website run by the **U.S. Patent and Trademark Office**. Go to www.uspto.gov.

For a list of approved domain name registrars, go to **InterNic** at www.internic.com. This site allows you to look up who owns a particular domain name (known as a "whois" search) and offers general information about domain names and the registration process.

E. Patent and Trademark Depository Libraries

Los Angeles
Los Angeles Public Library
213-228-7220
www.lapl.org/central/science.html

Sacramento
California State Library
Courts Building
916-654-0069
www.library.ca.gov/html/gps.cfm

San Diego
San Diego Public Library
619-236-5813
www.san-diego.gov/public-library

San Francisco
San Francisco Public Library
415-557-4500
http://sfpl.4.sfpl.org

Sunnyvale
SCI^3, Sunnyvale Public Library
408-730-7300
www.sci3.com

F. County Clerk/Recorders' Offices

Alameda County Clerk
1106 Madison Street
Oakland, CA 94607
510-272-6363
www.co.alameda.ca.us

Alpine County Clerk
P.O. Box 158
Markleeville, CA 96120
530-694-2281
www.alpinecountyca.com

Amador County Recorder
500 Argonaut Lane
Jackson, CA 95642
209-223-6468

Butte County Clerk-Recorder
25 County Center Drive
Oroville, CA 95965
530-538-7691
http://Sclerk-recorder.buttecounty.net

Calaveras County Clerk
891 Mountain Ranch Road
San Andreas, CA 95249
209-754-6371
www.co.calaveras.ca.us

Colusa County Clerk-Recorder
546 Jay Street
Colusa, CA 95932
530-458-0500
www.colusacountyclerk.com

Contra Costa County Clerk-Recorder
822 Main Street
P.O. Box 350
Martinez, CA 94553
925-646-2360
www.co.contra-costa.ca.us/depart/elect/clerk

Del Norte County Clerk-Recorder
981 H Street, Suite 160
Crescent City, CA 95531
707-464-7216

El Dorado County Recorder-Clerk
360 Fair Lane, Building B
Placerville, CA 95667
530-621-5490
www.co.el-dorado.ca.us/countyclerk

Fresno County Clerk
2221 Kern Street
Fresno, CA 93721-2600
559-488-3428

Glenn County Clerk-Recorder
526 W. Sycamore Street
Willows, CA 95988
530-934-6412

Humboldt County Clerk-Recorder
825 5th Street, 5th Floor
Eureka, CA 95501
707-445-7593

Imperial County Clerk-Recorder
940 W. Main Street, Suite 202
El Centro, CA 92243
760-482-4427

Inyo County Clerk
P.O. Box F
Independence, CA 93526
760-878-0223

Kern County Clerk
1115 Truxtun Avenue
Bakersfield, CA 93301
661-868-3588
www.auditor.co.kern.ca.us

Kings County Clerk-Recorder
Government Center
1400 West Lacey Boulevard
Hanford, CA 93230
559-582-3211, ext. 2470
www.countyofkings.com

Lake County Clerk-Auditor
255 North Forbes Street, 2nd Floor
Lakeport, CA 95453
707-263-2311
www.co.lake.ca.us

Lassen County Clerk
Courthouse, Suite 5
220 South Lassen Street
Susanville, CA 96130
530-251-8217
http://clerk.lassencounty.org

Los Angeles Register-Recorder/County Clerk

Business Filing and Registration

P.O. Box 1024

Norwalk, CA 90651

800-815-2666

http://regrec.co.la.ca.us

Madera County Clerk

209 West Yosemite Avenue

Madera, CA 93637

559-675-7720

www.madera-county.com

Marin County Clerk-Recorder

3501 Civic Center Drive, Room 247

P.O. Box E

San Rafael, CA 94913

415-499-6152

www.co.marin.ca.us/depts/CC/main

Mariposa County Clerk

P.O. Box 247

4982 10th Street

Mariposa, CA 95338

209-966-2007

www.mariposacounty.org

Mendocino County Clerk

501 Low Gap Road, Room 1020

Ukiah, CA 95482

707-463-4370

www.co.mendocino.ca.us/acr/index.html

Merced County Clerk

2222 M Street, Room 14

Merced, CA 95340

209-385-7501

Modoc County Clerk

P.O. Box 130

Alturas, CA 96101

530-233-6200

Mono County Clerk

74 School Street N, Annex 1

P.O. Box 237

Bridgeport, CA 93517

760-932-5530

Monterey County Clerk's Office

P.O. Box 29

Salinas, CA 93902

831-755-5450

www.co.monterey.ca.us/Recorder

Napa County Clerk-Recorder

900 Coombs, Room 116

P.O. Box 298

Napa, CA 94559

707-253-4246

www.co.napa.ca.us/departments/recorder

Nevada County Recorder

950 Maidu Avenue

Nevada City, CA 95959

530-265-1221

www.recorder.co.nevada.ca.us

Orange County Clerk-Recorder's Office

Hall of Records

12 Civic Center Plaza, Rooms 101 & 106

Santa Ana, CA 92702

714-834-2500

Placer County Recorder's Office

2954 Richardson Drive

Auburn, CA 95603

530-886-5600

www.placer.ca.gov/clerk/fbn.htm

Plumas County Clerk

520 W. Main Street, Room 102

Quincy, CA 95971

530-283-6218

http://countyofplumas.com

Riverside County Clerk and Recorder's Office
2724 Gateway Drive
Riverside, CA 92502
909-486-7000

Sacramento County Business License Section
600 8th Street
P.O. Box 839
Sacramento, CA 95814
916-874-6334
www.co.sacramento.ca.us

San Benito County Clerk
440 5th Street, Room 206
Hollister, CA 95023
831-636-4029

San Bernardino Fictitious Businesses
222 W. Hospitality Lane
San Bernardino, CA 92415
909-386-8970
www.sbcounty.gov/acr/FBNinfo.htm

San Diego Recorder-County Clerk
1600 Pacific Highway, Room 260
San Diego, CA 92101
619-237-0502
www.sdarcc.com

San Francisco County Clerk
1 Dr. Carlton B. Goodlett Place
City Hall, Room 168
San Francisco, CA 94102
415-554-4955
www.sfgov.org/countyclerk

San Joaquin County Recorder
P.O. Box 1968
Stockton, CA 95201
209-468-3939

San Luis Obispo County Clerk-Recorder
1144 Monterey Street, Suite A
San Luis Obispo, CA 93408
805-781-5080
www.sloclerkrecorder.org

San Mateo Special Services
555 County Center, 1st Floor
Attn: Special Services
Redwood City, CA 94063
650-363-4500
www.care.co.sanmateo.ca.us/index.htm

Santa Barbara County Clerk-Recorder
1100 Anacapa Street
Santa Barbara, CA 93101
805-568-2250

Santa Clara County Clerk-Recorder
70 W. Hedding Street
1st Floor, East Wing
San Jose, CA 95110
408-299-2160

Santa Cruz County Clerk
701 Ocean Street, Room 230
Santa Cruz, CA 95060
831-454-2470

Shasta County Clerk
P.O. Box 990880
Redding, CA 96099-0880
530-225-5730
www.co.shasta.ca.us

Sierra County Clerk-Recorder
100 Courthouse Square
Downieville, CA 95936
530-289-3295

Siskiyou County Clerk
P.O. Box 338
311 4th Street, Room 201
Yreka, CA 96097
530-842-8084
www.co.siskiyou.ca.us/clerk

Solano Tax Collector-County Clerk
600 Texas Street, Suite 105
Fairfield, CA 94533
707-421-7485
www.solanocounty.com

Sonoma County Clerk

2300 County Center Drive, Suite B177

Santa Rosa, CA 95403

707-565-3800

www.sonoma-county.org/clerk/business.htm

Stanislaus County Clerk

1021 I Street, Suite 101

Modesto, CA 95354

209-525-5250

www.criis.com

Sutter County Recorder

P.O. Box 1555

Yuba City, CA 95992

530-822-7120

Tehama County Clerk-Recorder

P.O. Box 250

Red Bluff, CA 96080

530-527-3350

Trinity Recorder

P.O. Box 1215

Weaverville, CA 96093

530-623-1215

www.trinitycounty.org

Tulare County Clerk-Recorder

221 S. Mooney Boulevard, Room 105

Visalia, CA 93291-4593

559-733-6518

Tuolumne County, Elections Department

2 S. Green Street

Sonora, CA 95370

209-533-5570

Ventura County Clerk

Hall of Administration, L 1210

800 S. Victoria Avenue

Ventura, CA 93009-1210

805-654-2263

www.ventura.org/recorder/clerk.htm

Yolo County Clerk-Recorder

P.O. Box 1130

Woodland, CA 95776

530-666-8130

www.yolorecorder.org

Yuba County Clerk-Recorder

935 14th Street

Marysville, CA 95901

530-741-6341

How to Use the Forms CD-ROM

The tear-out forms in Appendix C are included on a CD-ROM disk in the back of the book. This CD-ROM, which can be used with Windows computers, installs files that can be opened, printed, and edited using a word processor or other software. It is not a stand-alone software program. Please read this Appendix and the README.TXT file included on the CD-ROM for instructions on using the Forms CD.

Note to Mac users: This CD-ROM and its files should also work on Macintosh computers. Please note, however, that Nolo cannot provide technical support for non-Windows users.

How to View the README File

If you do not know how to view the file README.TXT, insert the Forms CD-ROM into your computer's CD-ROM drive and follow these instructions:

- Windows 9x, 2000, Me, and XP: (1) On your PC's desktop, double click the My Computer icon; (2) double click the icon for the CD-ROM drive into which the Forms CD-ROM was inserted; (3) double click the file README.TXT.
- Macintosh: (1) On your Mac desktop, double click the icon for the CD-ROM that you inserted; (2) double click on the file README.TXT.

While the README file is open, print it out by using the Print command in the File menu.

Two different kinds of forms are contained on the CD-ROM:

- Word processing (RTF) forms that you can open, complete, print, and save with your word processing program (see Section B, below), and
- Forms from the IRS and various California state agencies (PDF) that can be viewed only with Adobe Acrobat Reader 4.0 or higher.

You can install Acrobat Reader from the Forms CD (see Section C below). Some of these forms have "fill-in" text fields and can be completed using your computer. You will not, however, be able to save the completed forms with the filled-in data. PDF forms without fill-in text fields must be printed out and filled in by hand or with a typewriter.

See Appendix C for a list of forms, their file names, and file formats.

A. Installing the Form Files Onto Your Computer

Before you can do anything with the files on the CD-ROM, you need to install them onto your hard disk. In accordance with U.S. copyright laws, remember that copies of the CD-ROM and its files are for your personal use only.

Insert the Forms CD and do the following:

1. Windows 9x, 2000, Me, and XP Users

Follow the instructions that appear on the screen. (If nothing happens when you insert the Forms CD-ROM, then (1) double click the My Computer icon; (2) double click the icon for the CD-ROM drive into which the Forms CD-ROM was inserted; and (3) double click the file WELCOME.EXE.)

By default, all the files are installed to the \CA Business Start-Up Forms folder in the \Program Files folder of your computer. A folder called "CA Business Start-Up Forms" is added to the "Programs" folder of the Start menu.

2. Macintosh Users

Step 1:   If the "CA Business Start-Up CD" window is not open, open it by double clicking the "CA Business Start-Up CD" icon.

Step 2:   Select the "CA Business Start-Up Forms" folder icon.

Step 3:   Drag and drop the folder icon onto the icon of your hard disk.

B. Using the Word Processing Files to Create Documents

This section concerns the Partnership Agreement form that can be opened and edited with your word processing program. (Files in PDF format are discussed in Section C, below.)

A Partnership Agreement can be created using the file PARTAGRE.RTF. RTF files can be read by most recent word processing programs, including all versions of MS Word for Windows and Macintosh, WordPad for Windows, and recent versions of WordPerfect for Windows and Macintosh.

To use an RTF to create your documents you must: (1) open the file in your word processor or text editor; (2) edit the form by filling in the required information; (3) print it out; (4) rename and save your revised file.

The following are general instructions on how to do this. However, each word processor uses different commands to open, format, save, and print documents. Please read your word processor's manual for specific instructions on performing these tasks.

Do not call Nolo's technical support if you have questions on how to use your word processor.

Step 1: Opening a File

There are three ways to open the word processing files included on the CD-ROM after you have installed them onto your computer.

Windows users can open a file by selecting its "shortcut" as follows: (1) Click the Windows "Start" button; (2) open the "Programs" folder; (3) open the "CA Business Start-Up Forms" subfolder; and (4) click on the shortcut to the form you want to work with.

Both Windows and Macintosh users can open a file directly by double clicking on it. Use My Com-

puter or Windows Explorer (Windows 9x, 2000, Me, or XP) or the Finder (Macintosh) to go to the folder you installed or copied the CD-ROM's files to. Then, double click on the specific file you want to open.

You can also open a file from within your word processor. To do this, you must first start your word processor. Then, go to the File menu and choose the Open command. This opens a dialog box where you will tell the program (1) the type of file you want to open (*.RTF); and (2) the location and name of the file (you will need to navigate through the directory tree to get to the folder on your hard disk where the CD's files have been installed). If these directions are unclear you will need to look through the manual for your word processing program—Nolo's technical support department will not be able to help you with the use of your word processing program.

Where Are the Files Installed?

Windows Users
- RTF files are installed by default to a folder named \CA Business Start-Up Forms in the \Program Files folder of your computer.

Macintosh Users
- RTF files are located in the "CA Business Start-Up Forms" folder.

Step 2: Editing Your Document

Fill in the appropriate information according to the instructions and sample agreements in the book. Underlines are used to indicate where you need to enter your information, frequently followed by instructions in brackets. *Be sure to delete the underlines and instructions from your edited document.* If you do not know how to use your word processor to edit a document, you will need to look through the manual for your word processing program—Nolo's technical support department will not be able to help you with the use of your word processing program.

Editing Forms That Have Optional or Alternative Text

The Partneship Agreement form has check boxes before text. The check boxes indicate:

- Optional text, where you choose whether to include or exclude the given text.
- Alternative text, where you select one alternative to include and exclude the other alternatives.

If you are using the tear-out form in Appendix C, you simply mark the appropriate box to make your choice.

If you are using the Forms CD, however, we recommend that instead of marking the check boxes, you do the following:

Optional text

If you don't want to include optional text, just delete it from your document.

If you do want to include optional text, just leave it in your document.

In either case, delete the check box itself, as well as the italicized instructions that the text is optional.

Alternative text

First delete all the alternatives that you do not want to include.

Then delete the remaining check boxes, as well as the italicized instructions that you need to select one of the alternatives provided.

Step 3: Printing Out the Document

Use your word processor's or text editor's "Print" command to print out your document. If you do not know how to use your word processor to print

a document, you will need to look through the manual for your word processing program—Nolo's technical support department will not be able to help you with the use of your word processing program.

Step 4: Saving Your Document

After filling in the form, use the "Save As" command to save and rename the file. Because all the files are "read-only," you will not be able to use the "Save" command. This is for your protection. If you save the file without renaming it, the underlines that indicate where you need to enter your information will be lost, and you will not be able to create a new document with this file without recopying the original file from the CD-ROM.

If you do not know how to use your word processor to save a document, you will need to look through the manual for your word processing program—Nolo's technical support department will not be able to help you with the use of your word processing program.

C. Using PDF Forms

Electronic copies of useful government forms are included on the CD-ROM in Adobe Acrobat PDF format. You must have the Adobe Acrobat Reader installed on your computer (see below) to use these forms. All forms, their file names, and file formats are listed in Appendix C. These form files were created by by the IRS and various California state agencies, not by Nolo.

Some of these forms have fill-in text fields. To create your document using these files, you must: (1) open a file; (2) fill-in the text fields using either your mouse or the tab key on your keyboard to navigate from field to field; and (3) print it out.

NOTE: While you can print out your completed form, you will NOT be able to save your completed form to disk.

Forms without fill-in text fields cannot be filled out using your computer. To create your document using these files, you must: (1) open the file; (2) print it out; and (3) complete it by hand or type-writer.

Installing Acrobat Reader

To install the Adobe Acrobat Reader, insert the CD into your computer's CD-ROM drive and follow these instructions:

- **Windows 9x, 2000, Me, and XP:** Follow the instructions that appear on screen. (If nothing happens when you insert the Forms CD-ROM, then (1) double click the My Computer icon; (2) double click the icon for the CD-ROM drive into which the Forms CD-ROM was inserted; and (3) double click the file WELCOME.EXE.)
- **Macintosh:** (1) If the "CA Business Start-Up CD" window is not open, open it by double clicking the "CA Business Start-Up CD" icon; and (2) double click on the "Acrobat Reader Installer" icon.

If you do not know how to use Adobe Acrobat to view and print the files, you will need to consult the online documentation that comes with the Acrobat Reader program.

Do *not* call Nolo technical support if you have questions on how to use Acrobat Reader.

Step 1: Opening PDF Files

PDF files, like the word processing files, can be opened one of three ways.

Windows users can open a file by selecting its "shortcut" as follows: (1) Click the Windows "Start" button; (2) open the "Programs" folder; (3) open the "CA Business Start-Up Forms" subfolder; and (4) click on the shortcut to the form you want to work with.

Both Windows and Macintosh users can open a file directly by double clicking on it. Use My Computer or Windows Explorer (Windows 9x, 2000, Me, or XP) or the Finder (Macintosh) to go to the folder you created and copied the CD-ROM's files to. Then, double click on the specific file you want to open.

You can also open a PDF file from within Acrobat Reader. To do this, you must first start Reader. Then, go to the File menu and choose the Open command. This opens a dialog box where you will tell the program the location and name of the file (you will need to navigate through the directory tree to get to the folder on your hard disk where the CD's files have been installed). If these directions are unclear you will need to look through Acrobat Reader's help—Nolo's technical support department will not be able to help you with the use of Acrobat Reader.

Step 2: Filling in PDF Files

Use your mouse or the Tab key on your keyboard to navigate from field to field within these forms. Be sure to have all the information you will need to complete a form on hand, because you will not be able to save a copy of the filled-in form to disk. You can, however, print out a completed version.

NOTE: This step is only applicable to forms that have been created with fill-in text fields. Forms without fill-in fields must be completed by hand or typewriter after you have printed them out.

Where Are the PDF Files Installed?

- **Windows Users:** PDF files are installed by default to a folder named \CA Business Start-Up Forms in the \Program Files folder of your computer.
- **Macintosh Users:** PDF files are located in the "CA Business Start-Up Forms" folder.

Step 3: Printing PDF Files

Choose Print from the Acrobat Reader File menu.
This will open the Print dialog box. In the "Print
Range" section of the Print dialog box, select the
appropriate print range, then click OK. ■

Tear-Out Forms

Form Name	File Name
Partnership Agreement	Partnership.rtf
LLC Articles of Organization	llc-1.pdf*
Sample Articles of Incorporation	corp_artsclose.pdf
Certificate of Limited Partnership	lp-1.pdf*
Limited Liability Partnership Registration	llp-1.pdf
Application for Employer Identification Number (IRS Form SS-4)	fss4.pdf*
Instructions for Form SS-4	iss4.pdf
California Fictitious Business Name Statement	fictbus.pdf
California Seller's Permit Application and Instructions (Individuals and Partnerships)	boe400mip.pdf*
California Seller's Permit Application and Instructions (Corporations, LLCs and Organizations)	boe400mco.pdf*
California Resale Certificate	boe230.pdf*
Swap Meets, Flea Markets, or Special Events Certification	boe410d.pdf*
California Board of Equalization Publications Order Form	boe663.pdf
Estimated Tax Form and Instructions (IRS Form 1040ES)	f1040es.pdf*
California Estimated Tax Form (FTB form 540ES)	04_540es.pdf*
Instructions for Form 540-ES	04_540esins.pdf*
Limited Liability Company Tax Voucher (FTB Form 3522)	04_3522.pdf*
Entity Classification Election (IRS Form 8832)	F8832.PDF*

Tear-Out Forms (continued)

Election To Have a Tax Year Other Than a   f8716.pdf*
Required Tax Year (IRS Form 8716)

Determination of Employee Work Status for   fss8.pdf*
Purposes of Federal Employment Taxes and
Income Tax Withholding (IRS Form SS-8)

*These PDF forms have fill-in text fields (See Appendix B, Section C)

Partnership Agreement

1. Partners

_____ (Partners) make

the following Partnership Agreement.

2. Creation of Partnership

As of _____, the Partners agree to enter into a Partnership for

the purpose of operating a business known as: _____

_____ (Partnership Business).

The name of the Partnership (if different from name of Partnership Business) shall be: _____

_____ (Partnership Name).

3. Nature of Partnership Business

The Partnership Business will consist of the following business activities: _____

_____.

4. Contributions to the Partnership

The Partners will make the following contributions to the Partnership:

Partner Name	Cash Contribution	Other Contribution (describe property and/or work; give cash value)	Total Contribution Value
	$	Total cash value:	$
	$	Total cash value:	$
	$	Total cash value:	$
	$	Total cash value:	$

5. Profit and Loss Allocation

The Partners will share business profits and losses as follows:

☐ in the same proportions as their contributions to the business.

☐ as follows:_____.

6. Management of Partnership Business

The Partners will have the following management powers and responsibilities:

☐ The Partners will have equal management powers and responsibilities.

☐ The Partners will share management powers and responsibilities as follows: _____

7. Addition of a Partner

A new Partner may be added to the Partnership under the following conditions:

☐ unanimous vote of all Partners

☐ majority vote of Partners

☐ other conditions: _____

8. Departure of a Partner

A Partner can be expelled by:

☐ unanimous vote of the other Partners.

☐ majority vote of the other Partners.

Any Partner who leaves voluntarily will give at least 30 days' written notice.

If any Partner leaves the Partnership for any reason, including voluntary withdrawal, expulsion, or death, the Partnership will ☐ survive ☐ dissolve.

If the Partnership survives, the remaining Partner(s) will pay, within a reasonable time, the departing Partner, or the deceased Partner's estate, the fair market value of the departing Partner's share of the business as of the date of his or her departure. The Partnership's accountant will determine the fair market value of the departing Partner's share of the business according to the following method: _____

_____

9. Dispute Resolution

If a dispute arises under this Agreement, the Partners agree to first try to resolve the dispute with the help of a mutually agreed-on mediator. Any costs and fees other than attorney fees will be shared equally by the Partners. If it is impossible to arrive at a mutually satisfactory solution, the Partners agree to submit the dispute to binding arbitration in the same city or region, conducted on a confidential basis pursuant to the Commercial Arbitration Rules of the American Arbitration Association.

10. Amendment of Agreement

This agreement cannot be amended without the written consent of all Partners.

11. Partner Signatures

Name: _____ Date: _____

Address: _____

Signature: _____ SSN: _____

Name: _____ Date: _____

Address: _____

Signature: _____ SSN: _____

State of California
Kevin Shelley
Secretary of State

File # _____

LIMITED LIABILITY COMPANY
ARTICLES OF ORGANIZATION

A $70.00 filing fee must accompany this form.

IMPORTANT – Read instructions before completing this form.

This Space For Filing Use Only

1. **NAME OF THE LIMITED LIABILITY COMPANY** (END THE NAME WITH THE WORDS "LIMITED LIABILITY COMPANY," "LTD. LIABILITY CO.,"OR THE ABBREVIATIONS "LLC" OR "L.L.C.")

2. **THE PURPOSE OF THE LIMITED LIABILITY COMPANY IS TO ENGAGE IN ANY LAWFUL ACT OR ACTIVITY FOR WHICH A LIMITED LIABILITY COMPANY MAY BE ORGANIZED UNDER THE BEVERLY-KILLEA LIMITED LIABILITY COMPANY ACT.**

3. **CHECK THE APPROPRIATE PROVISION BELOW AND NAME THE AGENT FOR SERVICE OF PROCESS.**

   [   ] AN INDIVIDUAL RESIDING IN CALIFORNIA. PROCEED TO ITEM 4.

   [   ] A CORPORATION WHICH HAS FILED A CERTIFICATE PURSUANT TO SECTION 1505. PROCEED TO ITEM 5.

   AGENT'S NAME: _____

   _____

4. **ADDRESS OF THE AGENT FOR SERVICE OF PROCESS IN CALIFORNIA, IF AN INDIVIDUAL:**

   ADDRESS

   CITY   STATE **CA**   ZIP CODE

5. **THE LIMITED LIABILITY COMPANY WILL BE MANAGED BY: (CHECK ONE)**

   [   ] ONE MANAGER
   [   ] MORE THAN ONE MANAGER
   [   ] ALL LIMITED LIABILITY COMPANY MEMBER(S)

6. **OTHER MATTERS TO BE INCLUDED IN THIS CERTIFICATE MAY BE SET FORTH ON SEPARATE ATTACHED PAGES AND ARE MADE A PART OF THIS CERTIFICATE. OTHER MATTERS MAY INCLUDE THE LATEST DATE ON WHICH THE LIMITED LIABILITY COMPANY IS TO DISSOLVE.**

7. **NUMBER OF PAGES ATTACHED, IF ANY:**

8. **TYPE OF BUSINESS OF THE LIMITED LIABILITY COMPANY. (FOR INFORMATIONAL PURPOSES ONLY)**

9. **IT IS HEREBY DECLARED THAT I AM THE PERSON WHO EXECUTED THIS INSTRUMENT, WHICH EXECUTION IS MY ACT AND DEED.**

   _____   _____
   SIGNATURE OF ORGANIZER   DATE

   _____
   TYPE OR PRINT NAME OF ORGANIZER

10. **RETURN TO:**

    NAME
    FIRM
    ADDRESS
    CITY/STATE
    ZIP CODE

APPROVED BY SECRETARY OF STATE

INSTRUCTIONS FOR COMPLETING THE ARTICLES OF ORGANIZATION (LLC-1)

For easier completion, this form is available in a "fillable" version online at the Secretary of State's website at http://www.ss.ca.gov/business/business.htm. The form can be filled in on your computer, printed and mailed to the Secretary of State, Document Filing Support Unit, P O Box 944228, Sacramento, CA 94244-2280 or can be delivered in person to the Sacramento office, 1500 11th Street, 3rd Floor, Sacramento, CA 95814. If you are not completing this form online, please type or legibly print in black or blue ink.

FILING FEE: The filing fee is $70.00. Make the check(s) payable to the Secretary of State and send the executed document and filing fee to the address stated above.

Statutory filing provisions can be found in California Corporations Code section **17051**. All statutory references are to the California Corporations Code, unless otherwise stated.

Pursuant to California Corporation Code section **17375**, nothing in this title shall be construed to permit a domestic or foreign limited liability company to render professional services, as defined in subdivision (a) of Section **13401**, in this state.

Complete the Articles of Organization (Form LLC-1) as follows:

Item 1. Enter the name of the limited liability company. The name shall contain the words "Limited Liability Company," or the abbreviations "LLC" or "L.L.C." The words "Limited" and "Company" may be abbreviated to "Ltd." and "Co." The name of the limited liability company may not contain the words "bank," "trust," "trustee," incorporated," "inc.," "corporation," or "corp.," and shall not contain the words "insurer" or "insurance company" or any other words suggesting that it is in the business of issuing policies of insurance and assuming insurance risks. (Section **17052**.)

Item 2. Execution of this document confirms the following statement which has been preprinted on the form and may not be altered: "The purpose of the limited liability company is to engage in any lawful act or activity for which a limited liability company may be organized under the Beverly-Killea Limited Liability Company Act." Provisions limiting or restricting the business of the limited liability company may be included as an attachment.

Item 3. Enter the name of the agent for service of process. Check the appropriate provision indicating whether the agent is an individual residing in California or a corporation which has filed a certificate pursuant to Section **1505** of the California Corporations Code. If an individual is designated as agent, proceed to item 4. If a corporation is designated, proceed to item 5.

Item 4. If an individual is designated as the initial agent for service of process, enter an address in California. Do not enter "in care of" (c/o) or abbreviate the name of the city. DO NOT enter an address if a corporation is designated as the agent for service of process.

Item 5. Check the appropriate provision indicating whether the limited liability company is to be managed by one manager, more than one manager or all limited liability company member(s). (Section **17051(a)(5)**.)

Item 6. The Articles of Organization (LLC-1) may include other matters that the person filing the Articles of Organization determines to include. Other matters may include the latest date on which the limited liability company is to dissolve. If other matters are to be included, attach one or more pages setting forth the other matters.

Item 7. Enter the number of pages attached, if any. All attachments should be 8½" x 11", one-sided and legible.

Item 8. Briefly describe the type of business that constitutes the principal business activity of the limited liability company. Note restrictions in the rendering of professional services by Limited Liability Companies. Professional services are defined in California Corporations Code, Section **13401(a)** as: "Any type of professional services that may be lawfully rendered only pursuant to a license, certification, or registration authorized by the Business and Professions Code or the Chiropractic Act."

Item 9. The Articles of Organization (LLC-1) shall be executed with an original signature of the organizer.

The person executing the Articles of Organization (LLC-1) need not be a member or manager of the limited liability company.

If an entity is signing the Articles of Organization (LLC-1), the person who signs for the entity must note the exact entity name, his/her name, and his/her position/title.

If an attorney-in-fact is signing the Articles of Organization (LLC-1), the signature must be followed by the words "Attorney-in-fact for (name of person)."

If a trust is signing the Articles of Organization (LLC-1), the articles must be signed by a trustee as follows: _____, trustee for _____ trust (including the date of the trust, if applicable). Example: Mary Todd, trustee of the Lincoln Family Trust (U/T/A 5-1-94).

Item 10. Enter the name and the address of the person or firm to whom a copy of the filing should be returned.

- For further information contact the Business Filings Section at (916) 657-5448.

ORGANIZATION OF CALIFORNIA CLOSE CORPORATIONS

Business corporations authorized to issue stock, excluding such special organizations as cooperatives, credit unions, etc., are organized under the General Corporation Law, and particularly Title 1, Division 1, Chapter 2, California Corporations Code.

California Corporations Code **Sections 200-202** outline the minimum content requirements of Articles of Incorporation for stock corporations. **Section 158** of the Code specifically deals with statutory close corporations. The attached sample has been drafted to meet those **minimum** statutory requirements. The sample may be used as a guide in preparing documents to be filed with the Secretary of State to incorporate. It is, however, suggested that you seek private counsel for advice regarding the proposed corporation's specific business needs, which may require the inclusion of special permissive provisions or the formation of the corporation as a general stock corporation rather than formation as a close corporation.

The fee for filing Articles of Incorporation on behalf of a stock corporation is $100.00. Check(s) should be made payable to the Secretary of State.

PLEASE NOTE: Businesses incorporating in California are subject to California corporation franchise tax requirements until such time as they formally dissolve. Information regarding franchise tax requirements can be obtained from the **Franchise Tax Board's Internet Web site** or by calling the Franchise Tax Board at 1-800-852-5711.

The original and at least two copies of the Articles of Incorporation should be included with your submittal. The Secretary of State will certify two copies of the filed document without charge, **provided that the copies are submitted to the Secretary of State with the original to be filed**. Any additional copies submitted with the original will be certified upon request and payment of the $8.00 per copy certification fee.

Documents can be mailed or hand delivered for over-the-counter processing to the Sacramento office at:

Business Programs Division   (916) 657-5448
1500 11th Street
Sacramento, CA 95814
Attention: Document Filing Support Unit

OR

can be hand delivered for over-the-counter processing to any of the regional offices located in:

- Fresno   (559) 445-6900
  1315 Van Ness Avenue, Suite 203
  Fresno, CA 93721-1729

- Los Angeles   (213) 897-3062
  The Ronald Reagan Building
  12th Floor South Tower, Room 12513
  300 South Spring Street
  Los Angeles, CA 90013-1233

- San Diego   (619) 525-4113
  1350 Front Street, Suite 2060
  San Diego, CA 92101-3609

- San Francisco   (415) 004-2344
  121 Spear Street, Suite 420
  San Francisco, CA 94105-1584

NOTE: • Cash is not accepted in the Fresno, Los Angeles or San Diego regional offices.

• Duplicate original documents must be submitted when filing in any of the regional offices.

• Regional offices do not process mailed in documents.

A $15.00 **special handling fee** is applicable for processing documents delivered in person at the public counter in the Sacramento office or in any of the regional offices located in Fresno, Los Angeles, San Diego and San Francisco. The $15.00 special handling fee must be remitted by separate check and will be retained whether the documents are filed or rejected. The special handling fee does not apply to documents submitted by mail.

Preclearance or expedited filing of *eligible corporate documents* can be requested in a specified time frame, for an additional fee (in lieu of the $15.00 special handling fee), as described in the **Preclearance/Expedited Filing Service Information**. The preclearance/expedited filing service is not available in the regional offices.

When forming a new corporation you may need to contact one or more of the following agencies for additional information:

♦ The **Franchise Tax Board** - for information regarding **franchise tax requirements**.

♦ The **Board of Equalization** - for information regarding **sales tax** and/or **use tax** liability.

♦ The **Department of Corporations** - for information regarding **issuance** and **sale** of securities in California; Franchise Investment Law; Personal Property Brokers Law and/or Escrow Law requirements.

♦ The **Department of Consumer Affairs** - for information regarding **licensing** requirements.

♦ The **Employment Development Department** - for information regarding **disability unemployment insurance tax**.

♦ The **Department of Industrial Relations**, Division of Worker's Compensation - for information regarding **worker's compensation** requirements.

♦ The **city and/or county clerk and/or recorder** where the principal place of business is located - for information regarding business licenses, fictitious business names (if doing business under a name other than the corporate name), and for specific requirements regarding zoning, building permits, etc. based on the business activities of the corporation.

♦ The **Internal Revenue Service** (IRS) - for information regarding **federal employer identification numbers**.

The Secretary of State <u>does not</u> license corporations or business entities. For licensing requirements, please contact the city and/or county where the principal place of business is located and/or the state agency with jurisdiction over the business, e.g. Contractors' State License Board.

CLOSE CORPORATIONS

The statutory concept of a "close" corporation is often confused with two other concepts having some elements in common. The three differing concepts are as follows:

    a) Statutory close corporation, as defined in **Section 158**, California Corporations Code.

    b) Issuance of shares under a notice filing procedure with the Commissioner of Corporations pursuant to **Section 25102(f)** or **25102(h)**, California Corporations Code.

    c) "S" corporation election pursuant to **Section 1372**, Internal Revenue Code.

Adding to the confusion, the terms "close" corporation, "closed" corporation or "closely held" corporation are often used in a nontechnical sense simply to describe a corporation having a relatively small number of shareholders.

Each of the three concepts: statutory close corporation, notice filing procedure, and "S" election, is independent of the other two. It is not a condition to the use of the notice filing procedure or to the making of an "S" corporation election that the Articles of Incorporation state that the corporation is a close corporation or limit the number of shareholders of record. Experienced corporate counsel advises that the appropriate use of the statutory close corporation, even among corporations having 35 or fewer shareholders, is infrequent.

The three differences in the mandatory provisions of Articles of Incorporation forming a statutory close corporation and the Articles of Incorporation forming a general stock corporation are the name style requirement, the inclusion of wording denoting close corporation status and the reference to the number of persons entitled to hold issued shares.

INSTRUCTIONS:

Using the attached sample as a guide, Articles of Incorporation must be drafted to include all required provisions and may include other provisions, such as the names and addresses of the initial directors, if those provisions are permitted under California law. The Secretary of State's office, however, does not provide samples that include permissive provisions. The document **must** be typed with letters in dark contrast to the paper. Documents that would produce poor quality microfilm will be returned unfiled.

Article I – The Articles must include a statement of the name of the corporation, which name must be exactly as you want it to appear on the records of the Secretary of State. The name of a close corporation must include the word "corporation", "incorporated" or "limited" or an abbreviation of one of these three words.

Article II – This **exact** statement is required by the California Corporations Code and cannot be modified.

Article III – The Articles must include a statement as to the name and California address of the initial agent for service of process. The designated agent, whether an individual or a corporation, **must** agree to accept service of process on behalf of the corporation prior to designation. A corporation cannot designate itself as its own agent for service of process. When designating another corporation as agent, that other corporation **must have previously filed** a **Certificate Pursuant to Section 1505, California Corporations Code**, with the Secretary of State. When a corporate agent is used, the address of the designated corporation must be omitted.

Article IV – The Articles must include a statement of the total number of shares that the corporation will be authorized to issue.

NOTE: Before shares of stock are sold or issued the corporation must comply with the Corporate Securities Law administered by the **Department of Corporations**. For information regarding permits to issue shares please contact that agency.

Article V – This provision must be included as stated with the number of persons completed. Please note that the number of persons cannot exceed 35.

The Articles of Incorporation must be originally signed by an incorporator, or by directors, if initial directors have been named in the document. If directors are named, each director must both sign and acknowledge the articles. The names of incorporators or directors must be typed beneath their signatures.

The original and at least two copies of the Articles of Incorporation, together with the applicable fee, must be mailed or hand delivered to the Secretary of State's office in Sacramento or hand delivered to the one of the regional offices located in Fresno, Los Angeles, San Diego or San Francisco. Regional offices do not process mailed in documents. If documents are submitted to a regional office, a duplicate original is also required.

To facilitate the processing of documents mailed to the Sacramento office, a self-addressed envelope and a letter referencing the corporate name as well as your own name, return address and telephone number should also be submitted.

SAMPLE

ARTICLES OF INCORPORATION

I

The name of this corporation is _____ *(NAME OF CORPORATION)* _____ .

II

The purpose of the corporation is to engage in any lawful act or activity for which a corporation may be organized under the **GENERAL CORPORATION LAW** of California other than the banking business, the trust company business or the practice of a profession permitted to be incorporated by the California Corporations Code.

III

The name and address in the State of California of this corporation's initial agent for service of process is:

Name _____

Address _____

City _____ State **CALIFORNIA** Zip _____

IV

This corporation is authorized to issue only one class of shares of stock; and the total number of shares which this corporation is authorized to issue is _____ .

V

This corporation is a **CLOSE CORPORATION**. All of the corporation's issued shares of stock, of all classes, shall be held of record by not more than _____ persons.

_____ *(Signature of Incorporator)* _____
(Typed Name of Incorporator), Incorporator

State of California
Secretary of State
Kevin Shelley

CERTIFICATE OF LIMITED PARTNERSHIP

A $70.00 filing fee must accompany this form.
IMPORTANT – Read instructions before completing this form

This Space For Filing Use Only

1. Name of the limited partnership (end the name with the words "Limited Partnership" or the abbreviation "L.P.")

2. Street address of principal executive office   City and state   Zip code

3. Street address of California office where records are kept   City   State   Zip code
   CA

4. Complete if limited partnership was formed prior to July 1, 1984 and is in existence on the date this certificate is executed.

   The original limited partnership certificate was recorded on _____ with the recorder

   of _____ county.   File or recordation number _____

5. Name the agent for service of process and check the appropriate provision below:

   _____ , which is

   [ ] an individual residing in California. Proceed to item 6.
   [ ] a corporation which has filed a certificate pursuant to section 1505. Proceed to item 7.

6. If an individual, complete the California address of the agent for service of process:

   Address:

   City: State: **CA**   Zip code:

7. Names and addresses of all general partners: (Attach additional pages, if necessary)
   A. Name:

   Address:

   City: State: Zip code:
   B. Name:

   Address:

   City: State: Zip code:

8. Indicate the <u>number</u> of general partners' signatures required for filing certificates of amendment, restatement, merger, dissolution, continuation and cancellation.

9. Other matters to be included in this certificate may be set forth on separate attached pages and are made a part of this certificate. Other matters may include the purpose of business of the limited partnership (e.g., "Gambling Enterprise").

10. I declare that I am the person who executed this instrument, which execution is my act and deed.

   _____   _____
   Signature of Authorized Person   Position or Title of Authorized Person

   _____   _____
   Type or Print Name of Authorized Person   Date

   _____   _____
   Signature of Authorized Person   Position or Title of Authorized Person

   _____   _____
   Type or Print Name of Authorized Person   Date

LP-1 (REV. 12/2003)   Approved by Secretary of State

INSTRUCTIONS FOR COMPLETING CERTIFICATE OF LIMITED PARTNERSHIP (FORM LP-1)

For easier completion, this form is available in a "fillable" version online at the Secretary of State's website at http://www.ss.ca.gov/business/business.htm. The form can be filled in on your computer, printed and mailed to the Secretary of State, Document Filing Support Unit, P O Box 944225, Sacramento, CA 94244-2250 or can be delivered in person to the Sacramento office, 1500 11th Street, 3rd Floor, Sacramento, CA 95814. If you are not completing this form online, please type or legibly print in black or blue ink.

FILING FEE: The filing fee is $70.00. Make the check(s) payable to the Secretary of State and send the executed document and filing fee to the address stated above.

Statutory filing provisions can be found in California Corporations Code **section 15621.** All statutory references are to the California Corporations Code, unless otherwise stated.

Complete the Certificate of Limited Partnership (Form LP-1) as follows:

Item 1. Enter the name of the limited partnership as it appears in the partnership agreement. The name shall contain the words "limited partnership" or the abbreviation "L.P." at the end. The name of the limited partnership may not contain the words "bank," "insurance," "trust," "trustee," "incorporated," "inc.," "corporation," or "corp.". (**Section 15612.**)

Item 2. Enter the complete street address, including the zip code, of the principal executive office. DO NOT show a P.O. Box or abbreviate the name of the city.

Item 3. Enter the complete street address, including the zip code, of the California address where the records are kept. DO NOT show a P.O. Box or abbreviate the name of the city. (**Section 15614.**)

Item 4. This item is to be completed only by those limited partnerships formed prior to July 1, 1984. (**Section 15712(b)(2).**)

Item 5. Enter the name of the agent for service of process in this state. The agent for service of process must be an individual residing in California or a corporation that has filed a certificate pursuant to **Section 1505.** Check the appropriate provision.

Item 6. If an individual is designated as the agent for service of process, enter a business or residential address in California. **DO NOT** enter "in care of" (c/o) or abbreviate the name of the city. **DO NOT** enter an address if a corporation is designated as the agent for service of process.

Item 7. Enter the names and addresses, including the zip code, of all general partners. DO NOT abbreviate names of the cities. Attach additional pages, if necessary.

If a general partner is a trust, both the names of the trust (including the date of the trust, if applicable) and the trustee must be listed. Example: Mary Todd, trustee of the Lincoln Family Trust U/T/A 5-1-94.

Item 8. Indicate the number of general partners' signatures required for filing certificates of amendment, restatement, merger, dissolution, continuation, and cancellation.

Item 9. The Certificate of Limited Partnership (LP-1) may include other matters that the person filing the Certificate of Limited Partnership determines to include. Other matters may include the purpose of business of the limited partnership (e.g., "gambling enterprise"). If other matters are to be included, attach one or more pages setting forth the other matters. All attachments should be 8½" x 11", one-sided and legible.

Item 10. The Certificate of Limited Partnership (LP-1) shall be executed and acknowledged with the original signatures of all general partners, unless it is filed pursuant to the provisions of Sections **15625** or **15633.**

If the Certificate is filed by any person other than the general partner(s), the signature must be followed by the words "signature pursuant to Section _____," identifying the appropriate code section (**Section 15625(c).**)

If the Certificate is signed by an attorney-in-fact the signature must be followed by the words "Attorney-in-fact for (name of the partner)."

If an association is designated as a general partner, the person who signs for the association must state the **exact** name of the association, his/her name, and his/her position/title.

If a trust is designated as a general partner, the certificate must be signed by a trustee as follows: _____ trustee for _____ trust (including the date of the trust, if applicable). Example: Mary Todd, trustee of the Lincoln Family Trust (U/T/A 5-1-94).

- For further information contact the Business Filings Section at (916) 657-5448.

State of California
Kevin Shelley
Secretary of State

File #_____

REGISTERED LIMITED LIABILITY PARTNERSHIP REGISTRATION

A $70.00 filing fee must accompany this form.
IMPORTANT – Read instructions before completing this form.

This Space For Filing Use Only

1. Name of the registered limited liability partnership or foreign limited liability partnership:
   (End the name with the word "Registered Limited Liability Partnership" or "Limited Liability Partnership" or one of the abbreviations "L.L.P.", "LLP", "R.L.L.P.", or "RLLP.")

2. ☐ Domestic (California) **OR** ☐ Foreign (Not in California) | 3. Jurisdiction

4. Address of the principal office: City   State   Zip Code

5. Name the agent for service of process in this state and check the appropriate provision below:

   _____ which is

   [ ] an individual residing in California. Proceed to item 6.
   [ ] a corporation which has filed a certificate pursuant to California Corporations Code Section 1505. Proceed to item 7.

6. If an individual, California address of the agent for service of process:
   Address
   City   State **CA**   Zip Code

7. Indicate the business in which the limited liability partnership shall engage: (check one)
   ☐ Practice of Architecture   ☐ Practice of Public Accountancy
   ☐ Practice of Law   ☐ Related:_____

8. Indicate whether the limited liability partnership is complying with the alternative security provisions (California Corporations Code 16956[c]):   ☐ Yes. Attach Alternative Security Provision (LLP-3)   ☐ No

9. Future Effective Date, if any   Month   Day   Year

10. Other matters to be included in this registration may be set forth on separate attached pages and are made a part of this registration. Total number of pages attached, if any:

11. **Declaration:** By filing this Registered Limited Liability Partnership (LLP-1) with the Secretary of State, the partnership named above is registering as a domestic registered limited liability partnership or foreign limited liability partnership. **(DO NOT ALTER THIS STATEMENT)** Further, I declare that I am the person who executed this instrument, which execution is my act and deed.

   _____   _____
   Signature of Authorized Partner/Person   Type or Print Name of Authorized Partner/Person   Date

12. **RETURN TO:**

   NAME
   FIRM
   ADDRESS
   CITY/STATE
   ZIP CODE

SEC/STATE (REV. 01/03)   FORM LLP-1 – FILING FEE $70
                                                Approved by Secretary of State

INSTRUCTIONS FOR COMPLETING THE REGISTERED LIMITED LIABILITY PARTNERSHIP REGISTRATION (LLP-1)

DO NOT ALTER THIS FORM
Type or legibly print in black ink.

Statutory filing provisions are found in California Corporations Code Sections 16953 and 16959, unless otherwise indicated.

FILING FEE: The fee for filing the Registered Limited Liability Partnership Registration (LLP-1) is $70 (Government Code Section12189).

For further information contact the Limited Liability Partnership Unit at (916) 651-7142.

- **Make check(s) payable to the Secretary of State.** Send the executed document and filing fee to:
  California Secretary of State, Limited Liability Partnership Unit, P.O. Box 944228, Sacramento, CA 94244-2280

- The original and at least two copies of the document should be included with your submittal. The Secretary of State will certify two copies of the filed document without charge, **provided that the copies are submitted to this office along with the original to be filed.** Any additional copies submitted with the original will be certified upon request and the payment of the $8.00 (per copy) certification fee.

Fill in the items as follows:

Item 1. Enter the name of the registered limited liability partnership or foreign limited liability partnership. The name of the limited liability partnership shall contain the words "Limited Liability Partnership," "Registered Limited Liability Partnership," or one of the abbreviations "L.L.P.," "LLP," "R.L.L.P.," or "RLLP" (California Corporations Code Section 16952).

Item 2. Check if the registering limited liability partnership is Domestic (California) or Foreign (not in California). If it is a foreign limited liability partnership, attach an original certificate of good standing from an authorized public official of the jurisdiction under which the foreign limited liability partnership was formed. If issuance of such a certificate is not permissible in that jurisdiction, then attach a statement by the foreign limited liability partnership indicating such.

Item 3. Enter the jurisdiction of formation of the foreign limited liability partnership.

Item 4. Enter the complete address, including the zip code, of the principal office. Do not abbreviate the name of the city.

Item 5. Enter the name and address of agent for service of process in this state. The agent for service of process must be an individual residing in California or a corporation which has filed a certificate pursuant to California Corporations Code Section 1505. Check the appropriate provision.

Item 6. If an individual is designated as the agent for service of process, enter an address in California. Do not enter "in care of" (c/o) or abbreviate the name of the city. DO NOT enter an address if a corporation is designated as the agent for service of process.

Item 7. Check the appropriate provision indicating whether the limited liability partnership shall engage in the practice of architecture, the practice of public accountancy, the practice of law, or a related activity as provided in Section 16101(6)(A).

The inclusion of the practice of architecture as a professional limited liability partnership service permitted by Section 16101 commenced January 1, 1999 and shall extend only until January 1, 2007.

Item 8. Upon registering as a registered limited liability partnership or foreign limited liability partnership, and while transacting intrastate business, the limited liability partnership shall provide security for claims against it. Check the appropriate provision indicating whether the limited liability partnership is complying with the alternative security provisions. If the limited liability partnership is complying with such alternative security provisions, attach the Alternative Security Provision using form LLP-3 (California Corporations Code Section 16956[c]).

If the limited liability partnership is not utilizing the Alternative Security Provisions, information regarding the security for claims against the limited liability partnership or foreign limited liability partnership is not required to be filed with the Secretary of State.

Item 9. Enter the future effective date of the Registered Limited Liability Partnership Registration (LLP-1), if any. If none is indicated, the Registration shall be effective upon filing with the California Secretary of State.

Item 10. The Registered Limited Liability Partnership Registration (LLP-1) may include other matters that the person filing the Registration determines to include. If other matters are to be included, attach one or more pages setting forth the other matters. Enter the number of pages attached, if any. All attachments should be 8½" x 11", one-sided and legible.

Item 11. The Registered Limited Liability Partnership Registration (LLP-1) must be executed with the original signatures of one or more partners authorized to execute a registration, if a domestic limited liability partnership, or by an authorized person if a foreign limited liability partnership. A facsimile or photocopy of the signature is not acceptable for the purpose of filing with the California Secretary of State.

Execution of this document confirms the following statement, which has been preprinted on this form and may not be altered. "BY FILING THIS REGISTERED LIMITED LIABILITY PARTNERSHIP REGISTRATION (LLP-1) WITH THE SECRETARY OF STATE, THE PARTNERSHIP NAMED ABOVE IS REGISTERING AS A DOMESTIC REGISTERED LIMITED LIABILITY PARTNERSHIP OR FOREIGN LIMITED LIABILITY PARTNERSHIP."

Item 12. Enter the name and address of the individual or firm to whom a copy of the filing is to be returned.

Form **SS-4**
(Rev. December 2001)
Department of the Treasury
Internal Revenue Service

Application for Employer Identification Number

(For use by employers, corporations, partnerships, trusts, estates, churches,
government agencies, Indian tribal entities, certain individuals, and others.)

▶ See separate instructions for each line.   ▶ Keep a copy for your records.

EIN

OMB No. 1545-0003

Type or print clearly.

1 Legal name of entity (or individual) for whom the EIN is being requested

2 Trade name of business (if different from name on line 1)

3 Executor, trustee, "care of" name

4a Mailing address (room, apt., suite no. and street, or P.O. box)

5a Street address (if different) (Do not enter a P.O. box.)

4b City, state, and ZIP code

5b City, state, and ZIP code

6 County and state where principal business is located

7a Name of principal officer, general partner, grantor, owner, or trustor

7b SSN, ITIN, or EIN

8a **Type of entity** (check only one box)

☐ Sole proprietor (SSN) _____
☐ Partnership
☐ Corporation (enter form number to be filed) ▶ _____
☐ Personal service corp.
☐ Church or church-controlled organization
☐ Other nonprofit organization (specify) ▶ _____
☐ Other (specify) ▶ _____

☐ Estate (SSN of decedent) _____
☐ Plan administrator (SSN) _____
☐ Trust (SSN of grantor) _____
☐ National Guard   ☐ State/local government
☐ Farmers cooperative   ☐ Federal government/military
☐ REMIC   ☐ Indian tribal governments/enterprises
Group Exemption Number (GEN) ▶ _____

8b If a corporation, name the state or foreign country (if applicable) where incorporated

State

Foreign country

9 **Reason for applying** (check only one box)

☐ Started new business (specify type) ▶ _____
_____
☐ Hired employees (Check the box and see line 12.)
☐ Compliance with IRS withholding regulations
☐ Other (specify) ▶

☐ Banking purpose (specify purpose) ▶ _____
☐ Changed type of organization (specify new type) ▶ _____
☐ Purchased going business
☐ Created a trust (specify type) ▶ _____
☐ Created a pension plan (specify type) ▶ _____

10 Date business started or acquired (month, day, year)

11 Closing month of accounting year

12 First date wages or annuities were paid or will be paid (month, day, year). **Note:** *If applicant is a withholding agent, enter date income will first be paid to nonresident alien. (month, day, year)* . . . . ▶

13 Highest number of employees expected in the next 12 months. **Note:** *If the applicant does not expect to have any employees during the period, enter "-0-."* . . . . ▶

Agricultural	Household	Other

14 Check **one** box that best describes the principal activity of your business.

☐ Construction ☐ Rental & leasing ☐ Transportation & warehousing
☐ Real estate   ☐ Manufacturing   ☐ Finance & insurance

☐ Health care & social assistance   ☐ Wholesale–agent/broker
☐ Accommodation & food service   ☐ Wholesale–other   ☐ Retail
☐ Other (specify)

15 Indicate principal line of merchandise sold; specific construction work done; products produced; or services provided.

16a Has the applicant ever applied for an employer identification number for this or any other business? . . . . . ☐ Yes   ☐ No
Note: *If "Yes," please complete lines 16b and 16c.*

16b If you checked "Yes" on line 16a, give applicants legal name and trade name shown on prior application if different from line 1 or 2 above.
Legal name ▶   Trade name ▶

16c Approximate date when, and city and state where, the application was filed. Enter previous employer identification number if known.
Approximate date when filed (mo., day, year) | City and state where filed | Previous EIN

Third Party Designee	Complete this section **only** if you want to authorize the named individual to receive the entity's EIN and answer questions about the completion of this form.	
	Designees name	Designees telephone number (include area code) ( )
	Address and ZIP code	Designees fax number (include area code) ( )

Under penalties of perjury, I declare that I have examined this application, and to the best of my knowledge and belief, it is true, correct, and complete.

Applicants telephone number (include area code) ( )

Name and title (type or print clearly) ▶

Signature ▶   Date ▶

Applicants fax number (include area code) ( )

For Privacy Act and Paperwork Reduction Act Notice, see separate instructions.   Cat. No. 16055N   Form **SS-4** (Rev. 12-2001)

Do I Need an EIN?

File Form SS-4 if the applicant entity does not already have an EIN but is required to show an EIN on any return, statement, or other document.[1] **See also the separate instructions for each line on Form SS-4.**

IF the applicant...	AND...	THEN...
Started a new business	Does not currently have (nor expect to have) employees	Complete lines 1, 2, 4a- 6, 8a, and 9- 16c.
Hired (or will hire) employees, including household employees	Does not already have an EIN	Complete lines 1, 2, 4a- 6, 7a- b (if applicable), 8a, 8b (if applicable), and 9- 16c.
Opened a bank account	Needs an EIN for banking purposes only	Complete lines 1- 5b, 7a- b (if applicable), 8a, 9, and 16a- c.
Changed type of organization	Either the legal character of the organization or its ownership changed (e.g., you incorporate a sole proprietorship or form a partnership)[2]	Complete lines 1- 16c (as applicable).
Purchased a going business[3]	Does not already have an EIN	Complete lines 1- 16c (as applicable).
Created a trust	The trust is other than a grantor trust or an IRA trust[4]	Complete lines 1- 16c (as applicable).
Created a pension plan as a plan administrator[5]	Needs an EIN for reporting purposes	Complete lines 1, 2, 4a- 6, 8a, 9, and 16a- c.
Is a foreign person needing an EIN to comply with IRS withholding regulations	Needs an EIN to complete a Form W-8 (other than Form W-8ECI), avoid withholding on portfolio assets, or claim tax treaty benefits[6]	Complete lines 1- 5b, 7a- b (SSN or ITIN optional), 8a- 9, and 16a- c.
Is administering an estate	Needs an EIN to report estate income on Form 1041	Complete lines 1, 3, 4a- b, 8a, 9, and 16a- c.
Is a withholding agent for taxes on non-wage income paid to an alien (i.e., individual, corporation, or partnership, etc.)	Is an agent, broker, fiduciary, manager, tenant, or spouse who is required to file **Form 1042,** Annual Withholding Tax Return for U.S. Source Income of Foreign Persons	Complete lines 1, 2, 3 (if applicable), 4a- 5b, 7a- b (if applicable), 8a, 9, and 16a- c.
Is a state or local agency	Serves as a tax reporting agent for public assistance recipients under Rev. Proc. 80-4, 1980-1 C.B. 581[7]	Complete lines 1, 2, 4a- 5b, 8a, 9, and 16a- c.
Is a single-member LLC	Needs an EIN to file **Form 8832,** Classification Election, for filing employment tax returns, **or** for state reporting purposes[8]	Complete lines 1- 16c (as applicable).
Is an S corporation	Needs an EIN to file **Form 2553,** Election by a Small Business Corporation[9]	Complete lines 1- 16c (as applicable).

[1] For example, a sole proprietorship or self-employed farmer who establishes a qualified retirement plan, or is required to file excise, employment, alcohol, tobacco, or firearms returns, must have an EIN. **A partnership, corporation, REMIC (real estate mortgage investment conduit), nonprofit organization (church, club, etc.), or farmers' cooperative must use an EIN for any tax-related purpose even if the entity does not have employees.**

[2] However, **do not** apply for a new EIN if the existing entity only **(a)** changed its business name, **(b)** elected on Form 8832 to change the way it is taxed (or is covered by the default rules), or **(c)** terminated its partnership status because at least 50% of the total interests in partnership capital and profits were sold or exchanged within a 12-month period. (The EIN of the terminated partnership should continue to be used. See Regulations section 301.6109-1(d)(2)(iii).)

[3] Do not use the EIN of the prior business unless you became the "owner" of a corporation by acquiring its stock.

[4] However, IRA trusts that are required to file **Form 990-T,** Exempt Organization Business Income Tax Return, must have an EIN.

[5] A plan administrator is the person or group of persons specified as the administrator by the instrument under which the plan is operated.

[6] Entities applying to be a Qualified Intermediary (QI) need a QI-EIN even if they already have an EIN. **See Rev. Proc. 2000-12.**

[7] See also *Household employer* on page 4. (**Note:** State or local agencies may need an EIN for other reasons, e.g., hired employees.)

[8] Most LLCs **do not** need to file Form 8832. See **Limited liability company (LLC)** on page 4 for details on completing Form SS-4 for an LLC.

[9] An existing corporation that is electing or revoking S corporation status should use its previously-assigned EIN.

Instructions for Form SS-4

(Rev. September 2003)

Department of the Treasury
Internal Revenue Service

For use with Form SS-4 (Rev. December 2001)
Application for Employer Identification Number.

Section references are to the Internal Revenue Code unless otherwise noted.

General Instructions

Use these instructions to complete **Form SS-4,** Application for Employer Identification Number. Also see **Do I Need an EIN?** on page 2 of Form SS-4.

Purpose of Form

Use Form SS-4 to apply for an employer identification number (EIN). An EIN is a nine-digit number (for example, 12-3456789) assigned to sole proprietors, corporations, partnerships, estates, trusts, and other entities for tax filing and reporting purposes. The information you provide on this form will establish your business tax account.

 *An EIN is for use in connection with your business activities only. Do **not** use your EIN in place of your social security number (SSN).*

Items To Note

Apply online. You can now apply for and receive an EIN online using the internet. See **How To Apply** below.

File only one Form SS-4. Generally, a sole proprietor should file only one Form SS-4 and needs only one EIN, regardless of the number of businesses operated as a sole proprietorship or trade names under which a business operates. However, if the proprietorship incorporates or enters into a partnership, a new EIN is required. Also, each corporation in an affiliated group must have its own EIN.

EIN applied for, but not received. If you do not have an EIN by the time a return is due, write "Applied For" and the date you applied in the space shown for the number. **Do not** show your SSN as an EIN on returns.

If you do not have an EIN by the time a tax deposit is due, send your payment to the Internal Revenue Service Center for your filing area as shown in the instructions for the form that you are filing. Make your check or money order payable to the "United States Treasury" and show your name (as shown on Form SS-4), address, type of tax, period covered, and date you applied for an EIN.

How To Apply

You can apply for an EIN online, by telephone, by fax, or by mail depending on how soon you need to use the EIN. Use only one method for each entity so you do not receive more than one EIN for an entity.

Online. You can receive your EIN by internet and use it immediately to file a return or make a payment. Go to the IRS website at **www.irs.gov/businesses** and click on **Employer ID Numbers** under **topics.**

Telephone. You can receive your EIN by telephone and use it immediately to file a return or make a payment. Call the IRS at **1-800-829-4933.** (International applicants must call 215-516-6999.) The hours of operation are 7:00 a.m. to 10:00 p.m. The person making the call must be authorized to sign the form or be an authorized designee. See **Signature** and **Third Party Designee** on page 6. Also see the **TIP** below.

If you are applying by telephone, it will be helpful to complete Form SS-4 before contacting the IRS. An IRS representative will use the information from the Form SS-4 to establish your account and assign you an EIN. Write the number you are given on the upper right corner of the form and sign and date it. Keep this copy for your records.

If requested by an IRS representative, mail or fax (facsimile) the signed Form SS-4 (including any Third Party Designee authorization) within 24 hours to the IRS address provided by the IRS representative.

 *Taxpayer representatives can apply for an EIN on behalf of their client and request that the EIN be faxed to their **client** on the same day. **Note:** By using this procedure, you are authorizing the IRS to fax the EIN without a cover sheet.*

Fax. Under the Fax-TIN program, you can receive your EIN by fax within 4 business days. Complete and fax Form SS-4 to the IRS using the Fax-TIN number listed on page 2 for your state. A long-distance charge to callers outside of the local calling area will apply. Fax-TIN numbers can only be used to apply for an EIN. **The numbers may change without notice.** Fax-TIN is available 24 hours a day, 7 days a week.

Be sure to provide your fax number so the IRS can fax the EIN back to you. **Note:** By using this procedure, you are authorizing the IRS to fax the EIN without a cover sheet.

Mail. Complete Form SS-4 at least 4 to 5 weeks before you will need an EIN. Sign and date the application and mail it to the service center address for your state. You will receive your EIN in the mail in approximately 4 weeks. See also **Third Party Designee** on page 6.

Call 1-800-829-4933 to verify a number or to ask about the status of an application by mail.

Where To Fax or File

If your principal business, office or agency, or legal residence in the case of an individual, is located in:	Call the Fax-TIN number shown or file with the "Internal Revenue Service Center" at:
Connecticut, Delaware, District of Columbia, Florida, Georgia, Maine, Maryland, Massachusetts, New Hampshire, New Jersey, New York, North Carolina, Ohio, Pennsylvania, Rhode Island, South Carolina, Vermont, Virginia, West Virginia	Attn: EIN Operation P. O. Box 9003 Holtsville, NY 11742-9003 Fax-TIN 631-447-8960
Illinois, Indiana, Kentucky, Michigan	Attn: EIN Operation Cincinnati, OH 45999 Fax-TIN 859-669-5760
Alabama, Alaska, Arizona, Arkansas, California, Colorado, Hawaii, Idaho, Iowa, Kansas, Louisiana, Minnesota, Mississippi, Missouri, Montana, Nebraska, Nevada, New Mexico, North Dakota, Oklahoma, Oregon, Puerto Rico, South Dakota, Tennessee, Texas, Utah, Washington, Wisconsin, Wyoming	Attn: EIN Operation Philadelphia, PA 19255 Fax-TIN 215-516-3990
If you have no legal residence, principal place of business, or principal office or agency in any state:	Attn: EIN Operation Philadelphia, PA 19255 Telephone 215-516-6999 Fax-TIN 215-516-3990

How To Get Forms and Publications

Phone. You can order forms, instructions, and publications by phone 24 hours a day, 7 days a week. Call 1-800-TAX-FORM (1-800-829-3676). You should receive your order or notification of its status within 10 workdays.

Personal computer. With your personal computer and modem, you can get the forms and information you need using the IRS website at **www.irs.gov** or File Transfer Protocol at **ftp.irs.gov**.

CD-ROM. For small businesses, return preparers, or others who may frequently need tax forms or publications, a CD-ROM containing over 2,000 tax products (including many prior year forms) can be purchased from the National Technical Information Service (NTIS).

To order **Pub. 1796,** Federal Tax Products on CD-ROM, call **1-877-CDFORMS** (1-877-233-6767) toll free or connect to **www.irs.gov/cdorders.**

Tax Help for Your Business

IRS-sponsored Small Business Workshops provide information about your Federal and state tax obligations.

For information about workshops in your area, call 1-800-829-4933.

Related Forms and Publications

The following **forms** and **instructions** may be useful to filers of Form SS-4:
* **Form 990-T,** Exempt Organization Business Income Tax Return
* **Instructions for Form 990-T**
* **Schedule C (Form 1040),** Profit or Loss From Business
* **Schedule F (Form 1040),** Profit or Loss From Farming
* **Instructions for Form 1041 and Schedules A, B, D, G, I, J, and K-1,** U.S. Income Tax Return for Estates and Trusts
* **Form 1042,** Annual Withholding Tax Return for U.S. Source Income of Foreign Persons
* **Instructions for Form 1065,** U.S. Return of Partnership Income
* **Instructions for Form 1066,** U.S. Real Estate Mortgage Investment Conduit (REMIC) Income Tax Return
* **Instructions for Forms 1120 and 1120-A**
* **Form 2553,** Election by a Small Business Corporation
* **Form 2848,** Power of Attorney and Declaration of Representative
* **Form 8821,** Tax Information Authorization
* **Form 8832,** Entity Classification Election
    For more **information** about filing Form SS-4 and related issues, see:
* **Circular A,** Agricultural Employer's Tax Guide (Pub. 51)
* **Circular E,** Employer's Tax Guide (Pub. 15)
* **Pub. 538,** Accounting Periods and Methods
* **Pub. 542,** Corporations
* **Pub. 557,** Exempt Status for Your Organization
* **Pub. 583,** Starting a Business and Keeping Records
* **Pub. 966,** Electronic Choices for Paying ALL Your Federal Taxes
* **Pub. 1635,** Understanding Your EIN
* **Package 1023,** Application for Recognition of Exemption Under Section 501(c)(3) of the Internal Revenue Code
* **Package 1024,** Application for Recognition of Exemption Under Section 501(a)

Specific Instructions

Print or type all entries on Form SS-4. Follow the instructions for each line to expedite processing and to avoid unnecessary IRS requests for additional information. Enter "N/A" (nonapplicable) on the lines that do not apply.

Line 1—Legal name of entity (or individual) for whom the EIN is being requested. Enter the legal name of the entity (or individual) applying for the EIN exactly as it appears on the social security card, charter, or other applicable legal document.

Individuals. Enter your first name, middle initial, and last name. If you are a sole proprietor, enter your individual name, not your business name. Enter your business name on line 2. Do not use abbreviations or nicknames on line 1.

Trusts. Enter the name of the trust.

Estate of a decedent. Enter the name of the estate.

Partnerships. Enter the legal name of the partnership as it appears in the partnership agreement.

Corporations. Enter the corporate name as it appears in the corporation charter or other legal document creating it.

Plan administrators. Enter the name of the plan administrator. A plan administrator who already has an EIN should use that number.

Line 2—Trade name of business. Enter the trade name of the business if different from the legal name. The trade name is the "doing business as " (DBA) name.

 *Use the full legal name shown on line 1 on all tax returns filed for the entity. (However, if you enter a trade name on line 2 and choose to use the trade name instead of the legal name, enter the trade name on **all returns** you file.) To prevent processing delays and errors, **always** use the legal name only (or the trade name only) on **all** tax returns.*

Line 3—Executor, trustee, "care of" name. Trusts enter the name of the trustee. Estates enter the name of the executor, administrator, or other fiduciary. If the entity applying has a designated person to receive tax information, enter that person's name as the "care of" person. Enter the individual's first name, middle initial, and last name.

Lines 4a-b—Mailing address. Enter the mailing address for the entity's correspondence. If line 3 is completed, enter the address for the executor, trustee or "care of" person. Generally, this address will be used on all tax returns.

 *File **Form 8822**, Change of Address, to report any subsequent changes to the entity's mailing address.*

Lines 5a-b—Street address. Provide the entity's physical address **only** if different from its mailing address shown in lines 4a-b. **Do not** enter a P.O. box number here.

Line 6—County and state where principal business is located. Enter the entity's primary **physical** location.

Lines 7a-b—Name of principal officer, general partner, grantor, owner, or trustor. Enter the first name, middle initial, last name, and SSN of **(a)** the principal officer if the business is a corporation, **(b)** a general partner if a partnership, **(c)** the owner of an entity that is disregarded as separate from its owner (disregarded entities owned by a corporation enter the corporation's name and EIN), or **(d)** a grantor, owner, or trustor if a trust.

If the person in question is an **alien individual** with a previously assigned individual taxpayer identification number (ITIN), enter the ITIN in the space provided and submit a copy of an official identifying document. If

necessary, complete **Form W-7,** Application for IRS Individual Taxpayer Identification Number, to obtain an ITIN.

You are **required** to enter an SSN, ITIN, or EIN unless the only reason you are applying for an EIN is to make an entity classification election (see Regulations sections 301.7701-1 through 301.7701-3) and you are a nonresident alien with no effectively connected income from sources within the United States.

Line 8a—Type of entity. Check the box that best describes the type of entity applying for the EIN. If you are an alien individual with an ITIN previously assigned to you, enter the ITIN in place of a requested SSN.

 *This is not an election for a tax classification of an entity. See **Limited liability company (LLC)** on page 4.*

Other. If not specifically listed, check the "Other" box, enter the type of entity and the type of return, if any, that will be filed (for example, "Common Trust Fund, Form 1065" or "Created a Pension Plan"). Do not enter "N/A." If you are an alien individual applying for an EIN, see the **Lines 7a-b** instructions above.

• **Household employer.** If you are an individual, check the "Other" box and enter "Household Employer" and your SSN. If you are a state or local agency serving as a tax reporting agent for public assistance recipients who become household employers, check the "Other" box and enter "Household Employer Agent." If you are a trust that qualifies as a household employer, you do not need a separate EIN for reporting tax information relating to household employees; use the EIN of the trust.

• **QSub.** For a qualified subchapter S subsidiary (QSub) check the "Other" box and specify "QSub."

• **Withholding agent.** If you are a withholding agent required to file Form 1042, check the "Other" box and enter "Withholding Agent."

Sole proprietor. Check this box if you file Schedule C, C-EZ, or F (Form 1040) and have a qualified plan, or are required to file excise, employment, alcohol, tobacco, or firearms returns, or are a payer of gambling winnings. Enter your SSN (or ITIN) in the space provided. If you are a nonresident alien with no effectively connected income from sources within the United States, you do not need to enter an SSN or ITIN.

Corporation. This box is for any corporation **other than a personal service corporation.** If you check this box, enter the income tax form number to be filed by the entity in the space provided.

 *If you entered "1120S" after the "Corporation" checkbox, the corporation **must** file Form 2553 **no later than the 15th day of the 3rd month of the tax year the election is to take effect.** Until Form 2553 has been received and approved, you will be considered a Form 1120 filer. See the Instructions for Form 2553.*

Personal service corp. Check this box if the entity is a personal service corporation. An entity is a personal service corporation for a tax year only if:

• The principal activity of the entity during the testing period (prior tax year) for the tax year is the performance of personal services substantially by employee-owners, and

• The employee-owners own at least 10% of the fair market value of the outstanding stock in the entity on the last day of the testing period.

Personal services include performance of services in such fields as health, law, accounting, or consulting. For more information about personal service corporations, see the Instructions for Forms 1120 and 1120-A and Pub. 542.

Other nonprofit organization. Check this box if the nonprofit organization is other than a church or church-controlled organization and specify the type of nonprofit organization (for example, an educational organization).

 *If the organization also seeks tax-exempt status, you **must** file either Package 1023 or Package 1024. See Pub. 557 for more information.*

If the organization is covered by a group exemption letter, enter the four-digit **group exemption number (GEN).** (Do not confuse the GEN with the nine-digit EIN.) If you do not know the GEN, contact the parent organization. Get Pub. 557 for more information about group exemption numbers.

Plan administrator. If the plan administrator is an individual, enter the plan administrator's SSN in the space provided.

REMIC. Check this box if the entity has elected to be treated as a real estate mortgage investment conduit (REMIC). See the Instructions for Form 1066 for more information.

Limited liability company (LLC). An LLC is an entity organized under the laws of a state or foreign country as a limited liability company. For Federal tax purposes, an LLC may be treated as a partnership or corporation or be disregarded as an entity separate from its owner.

By **default,** a domestic LLC with only one member is **disregarded** as an entity separate from its owner and must include all of its income and expenses on the owner's tax return (e.g., **Schedule C (Form 1040)**). Also by default, a domestic LLC with two or more members is treated as a partnership. A domestic LLC may file Form 8832 to avoid either default classification and elect to be classified as an association taxable as a corporation. For more information on entity classifications (including the rules for foreign entities), see the instructions for Form 8832.

 *Do not file Form 8832 if the LLC accepts the default classifications above. **However, if the LLC will be electing S Corporation status, it must timely file both Form 8832 and Form 2553.***

Complete Form SS-4 for LLCs as follows:
• A single-member domestic LLC that accepts the default classification (above) does not need an EIN and generally should not file Form SS-4. Generally, the LLC

should use the name and EIN of its **owner** for all Federal tax purposes. However, the reporting and payment of employment taxes for employees of the LLC may be made using the name and EIN of **either** the owner or the LLC as explained in Notice 99-6. You can find Notice 99-6 on page 12 of Internal Revenue Bulletin 1999-3 at **www.irs.gov/pub/irs-irbs/irb99-03.pdf. (Note:** If the LLC applicant indicates in box 13 that it has employees or expects to have employees, the owner (whether an individual or other entity) of a single-member domestic LLC will also be assigned its own EIN (if it does not already have one) even if the LLC will be filing the employment tax returns.)

• A single-member, domestic LLC that accepts the default classification (above) and wants an EIN for filing employment tax returns (see above) or non-Federal purposes, such as a state requirement, must check the "Other" box and write "Disregarded Entity" or, when applicable, "Disregarded Entity—Sole Proprietorship" in the space provided.

• A multi-member, domestic LLC that accepts the default classification (above) must check the "Partnership" box.

• A domestic LLC that will be filing Form 8832 to elect corporate status must check the "Corporation" box and write in "Single-Member" or "Multi-Member" immediately below the "form number" entry line.

Line 9—Reason for applying. Check only **one** box. Do not enter "N/A."

Started new business. Check this box if you are starting a new business that requires an EIN. If you check this box, enter the type of business being started. **Do not** apply if you already have an EIN and are only adding another place of business.

Hired employees. Check this box if the existing business is requesting an EIN because it has hired or is hiring employees and is therefore required to file employment tax returns. **Do not** apply if you already have an EIN and are only hiring employees. For information on employment taxes (e.g., for family members), see Circular E.

 You may be required to make electronic deposits of all depository taxes (such as employment tax, excise tax, and corporate income tax) using the Electronic Federal Tax Payment System (EFTPS). See section 11, Depositing Taxes, of Circular E and Pub. 966.

Created a pension plan. Check this box if you have created a pension plan and need an EIN for reporting purposes. Also, enter the type of plan in the space provided.

 Check this box if you are applying for a trust EIN when a new pension plan is established. In addition, check the "Other" box in line 8a and write "Created a Pension Plan" in the space provided.

Banking purpose. Check this box if you are requesting an EIN for banking purposes only, and enter the banking purpose (for example, a bowling league for depositing dues or an investment club for dividend and interest reporting).

Changed type of organization. Check this box if the business is changing its type of organization. For example, the business was a sole proprietorship and has been incorporated or has become a partnership. If you check this box, specify in the space provided (including available space immediately below) the type of change made. For example, "From Sole Proprietorship to Partnership."

Purchased going business. Check this box if you purchased an existing business. **Do not** use the former owner's EIN unless you became the "owner" of a corporation by acquiring its stock.

Created a trust. Check this box if you created a trust, and enter the type of trust created. For example, indicate if the trust is a nonexempt charitable trust or a split-interest trust.

Exception. Do **not** file this form for certain grantor-type trusts. The trustee does not need an EIN for the trust if the trustee furnishes the name and TIN of the grantor/owner and the address of the trust to all payors. See the Instructions for Form 1041 for more information.

 Do not check this box if you are applying for a trust EIN when a new pension plan is established. Check "Created a pension plan."

Other. Check this box if you are requesting an EIN for any other reason; and enter the reason. For example, a newly-formed state government entity should enter "Newly-Formed State Government Entity" in the space provided.

Line 10—Date business started or acquired. If you are starting a new business, enter the starting date of the business. If the business you acquired is already operating, enter the date you acquired the business. If you are changing the form of ownership of your business, enter the date the new ownership entity began. Trusts should enter the date the trust was legally created. Estates should enter the date of death of the decedent whose name appears on line 1 or the date when the estate was legally funded.

Line 11—Closing month of accounting year. Enter the last month of your accounting year or tax year. An accounting or tax year is usually 12 consecutive months, either a calendar year or a fiscal year (including a period of 52 or 53 weeks). A calendar year is 12 consecutive months ending on December 31. A fiscal year is either 12 consecutive months ending on the last day of any month other than December or a 52-53 week year. For more information on accounting periods, see Pub. 538.

Individuals. Your tax year generally will be a calendar year.

Partnerships. Partnerships must adopt one of the following tax years:
• The tax year of the majority of its partners,
• The tax year common to all of its principal partners,
• The tax year that results in the least aggregate deferral of income, or
• In certain cases, some other tax year.

See the Instructions for Form 1065 for more information.

REMICs. REMICs must have a calendar year as their tax year.

Personal service corporations. A personal service corporation generally must adopt a calendar year unless:
• It can establish a business purpose for having a different tax year, or
• It elects under section 444 to have a tax year other than a calendar year.

Trusts. Generally, a trust must adopt a calendar year except for the following:
• Tax-exempt trusts,
• Charitable trusts, and
• Grantor-owned trusts.

Line 12—First date wages or annuities were paid or will be paid. If the business has or will have employees, enter the date on which the business began or will begin to pay wages. If the business does not plan to have employees, enter "N/A."

Withholding agent. Enter the date you began or will begin to pay income (including annuities) to a nonresident alien. This also applies to individuals who are required to file Form 1042 to report alimony paid to a nonresident alien.

Line 13—Highest number of employees expected in the next 12 months. Complete each box by entering the number (including zero ("-0-")) of "Agricultural," "Household," or "Other" employees expected by the applicant in the next 12 months. For a definition of agricultural labor (farmwork), see Circular A.

Lines 14 and 15. Check the **one** box in line 14 that best describes the principal activity of the applicant's business. Check the "Other" box (and specify the applicant's principal activity) if none of the listed boxes applies.

Use line 15 to describe the applicant's principal line of business in more detail. For example, if you checked the "Construction" box in line 14, enter additional detail such as "General contractor for residential buildings" in line 15.

Construction. Check this box if the applicant is engaged in erecting buildings or other structures, (e.g., streets, highways, bridges, tunnels). The term "Construction" also includes special trade contractors, (e.g., plumbing, HVAC, electrical, carpentry, concrete, excavation, etc. contractors).

Real estate. Check this box if the applicant is engaged in renting or leasing real estate to others; managing, selling, buying or renting real estate for others; or providing related real estate services (e.g., appraisal services).

Rental and leasing. Check this box if the applicant is engaged in providing tangible goods such as autos, computers, consumer goods, or industrial machinery and equipment to customers in return for a periodic rental or lease payment.

Manufacturing. Check this box if the applicant is engaged in the mechanical, physical, or chemical transformation of materials, substances, or components into new products. The assembling of component parts of manufactured products is also considered to be manufacturing.

Transportation & warehousing. Check this box if the applicant provides transportation of passengers or cargo; warehousing or storage of goods; scenic or sight-seeing transportation; or support activities related to these modes of transportation.

Finance & insurance. Check this box if the applicant is engaged in transactions involving the creation, liquidation, or change of ownership of financial assets and/or facilitating such financial transactions; underwriting annuities/insurance policies; facilitating such underwriting by selling insurance policies; or by providing other insurance or employee-benefit related services.

Health care and social assistance. Check this box if the applicant is engaged in providing physical, medical, or psychiatric care using licensed health care professionals or providing social assistance activities such as youth centers, adoption agencies, individual/family services, temporary shelters, etc.

Accommodation & food services. Check this box if the applicant is engaged in providing customers with lodging, meal preparation, snacks, or beverages for immediate consumption.

Wholesale—agent/broker. Check this box if the applicant is engaged in arranging for the purchase or sale of goods owned by others or purchasing goods on a commission basis for goods traded in the wholesale market, usually between businesses.

Wholesale—other. Check this box if the applicant is engaged in selling goods in the wholesale market generally to other businesses for resale on their own account.

Retail. Check this box if the applicant is engaged in selling merchandise to the general public from a fixed store; by direct, mail-order, or electronic sales; or by using vending machines.

Other. Check this box if the applicant is engaged in an activity not described above. Describe the applicant's principal business activity in the space provided.

Lines 16a-c. Check the applicable box in line 16a to indicate whether or not the entity (or individual) applying for an EIN was issued one previously. Complete lines 16b and 16c **only** if the "Yes" box in line 16a is checked. If the applicant previously applied for **more than one** EIN, write "See Attached" in the empty space in line 16a and attach a separate sheet providing the line 16b and 16c information for each EIN previously requested.

Third Party Designee. Complete this section **only** if you want to authorize the named individual to receive the entity's EIN and answer questions about the completion of Form SS-4. The designee's authority terminates at the time the EIN is assigned and released to the designee. **You must complete the signature area for the authorization to be valid.**

Signature. When required, the application must be signed by **(a)** the individual, if the applicant is an individual, **(b)** the president, vice president, or other

principal officer, if the applicant is a corporation, **(c)** a responsible and duly authorized member or officer having knowledge of its affairs, if the applicant is a partnership, government entity, or other unincorporated organization, or **(d)** the fiduciary, if the applicant is a trust or an estate. Foreign applicants may have any duly-authorized person, (e.g., division manager), sign Form SS-4.

Privacy Act and Paperwork Reduction Act Notice. We ask for the information on this form to carry out the Internal Revenue laws of the United States. We need it to comply with section 6109 and the regulations thereunder which generally require the inclusion of an employer identification number (EIN) on certain returns, statements, or other documents filed with the Internal Revenue Service. If your entity is required to obtain an EIN, you are required to provide all of the information requested on this form. Information on this form may be used to determine which Federal tax returns you are required to file and to provide you with related forms and publications.

We disclose this form to the Social Security Administration for their use in determining compliance with applicable laws. We may give this information to the Department of Justice for use in civil and criminal litigation, and to the cities, states, and the District of Columbia for use in administering their tax laws. We may also disclose this information to Federal and state agencies to enforce Federal nontax criminal laws and to combat terrorism.

We will be unable to issue an EIN to you unless you provide all of the requested information which applies to your entity. Providing false information could subject you to penalties.

You are not required to provide the information requested on a form that is subject to the Paperwork Reduction Act unless the form displays a valid OMB control number. Books or records relating to a form or its instructions must be retained as long as their contents may become material in the administration of any Internal Revenue law. Generally, tax returns and return information are confidential, as required by section 6103.

The time needed to complete and file this form will vary depending on individual circumstances. The estimated average time is:

Recordkeeping . . . . 6 min.
Learning about the law or the form . . . . 22 min.
Preparing the form . . . . 46 min.
Copying, assembling, and sending the form to the IRS . . . . 20 min.

If you have comments concerning the accuracy of these time estimates or suggestions for making this form simpler, we would be happy to hear from you. You can write to the Tax Products Coordinating Committee, Western Area Distribution Center, Rancho Cordova, CA 95743-0001. **Do not** send the form to this address. Instead, see **How To Apply** on page 1.

Printed on recycled paper

<table>
<tr><td colspan="2">Office of the County Clerk</td><td>Fees</td><td>FILING STAMP ONLY</td></tr>
<tr><td colspan="2">Address _____

City _____</td><td>$ _____ for 1 FBN
and registrant
$ _____ for each additional
FBN filed on same
statement and doing
business at same location
$ _____ for each additional
registrant</td><td></td></tr>
<tr><td>☐ First Filing</td><td>☐ Renewal Filing</td><td></td><td>File Number: _____</td></tr>
</table>

FICTITIOUS BUSINESS NAME STATEMENT

THE FOLLOWING PERSON(S) IS (ARE)

1

Fictitious Business Name(s)

1

2

3.

Articles of Incorporation Number (if applicable)

AL#

2 Street Address & City of Principal Place of Business in California (P.O. Box alone not acceptable)   Zip Code

3 Full Name of Registrant   if corporation—incorporated in what state

Residence Street Address   City   State   Zip Code

3a Full Name of Registrant   if corporation—incorporated in what state

Residence Street Address   City   State   Zip Code

3b Full Name of Registrant   if corporation—incorporated in what state

Residence Street Address   City   State   Zip Code

4 This Business is conducted by:

( ) an individual   ( ) a general partnership   ( ) joint venture   ( ) a business trust
( ) co-partners   ( ) husband and wife   ( ) a corporation   ( ) a limited partnership
( ) an unincorporated association other than a partnership   ( ) other—please specify _____

5 ( ) The registrant commenced to transact business under name or names listed on (date): _____
( ) Registrant has not yet begun to transact business under the fictitious business name or names listed herein.

6 If registrant is not a corporation or a limited liability company sign below:

_____ SIGNATURE   _____ TYPE OR PRINT NAME

_____ SIGNATURE   _____ TYPE OR PRINT NAME

_____ SIGNATURE   _____ TYPE OR PRINT NAME

6a If registrant is a corporation or a limited liability company sign below:

_____ COMPANY NAME

_____ SIGNATURE & TITLE

_____ TYPE OR PRINT NAME AND TITLE

This statement was filed with the County Clerk of _____ County on date indicated by file stamp above.

NOTICE—THIS FICTITIOUS NAME STATEMENT EXPIRES FIVE YEARS FROM DATE IT WAS FILED IN THE OFFICE OF THE COUNTY CLERK.

A NEW FICTITIOUS BUSINESS NAME STATEMENT MUST BE FILED PRIOR TO THAT DATE. The filing of this statement does not of itself authorize the use in this state of a fictitious business name in violation of the rights of another under federal, state, or common law (SEE SECTION 14400 et seq., Business and Professional Code).

This form should be **typed** *or* **printed** *legibly in* **black ink.**

BOE-400-MIP REV 18 (1-03)

California Seller's Permit Application

Individuals/Partnerships

 STATE BOARD OF EQUALIZATION

SELLER'S PERMIT APPLICATION • SELLER'S PERMIT APPLICATION • SELLER'S PERMIT APPLICATION • SELLER'S PERMIT

APPLICATION • SELLER'S PERMIT APPLICATION • SELLER'S PERMIT APPLICATION • SELLER'S PERMIT APPLICATION •

SELLER'S PERMIT APPLICATION • SELLER'S PERMIT APPLICATION • SELLER'S PERMIT APPLICATION • SELLER'S PERMIT

APPLICATION • SELLER'S PERMIT APPLICATION • SELLER'S PERMIT APPLICATION • SELLER'S PERMIT APPLICATION •

Frequently Asked Questions

Who must have a permit?

You are generally required to obtain a California seller's permit if you sell or lease merchandise, vehicles, or other tangible personal property in California. A seller's permit allows you to sell items at the wholesale or retail level. You cannot legally sell taxable items in California until you have been issued a seller's permit.

Do I need more than one permit?

If you sell taxable items from more than one location, you must display a permit at each location. If this applies to you, please attach to your application a list that includes the address for each location, and we will issue the permits you need. This requirement applies to retailers as well as wholesalers.

Is there a charge for a permit?

No. However, we may require a security deposit. Security deposits are used to cover any unpaid taxes that may be owed at the time a business closes.

Is information regarding my account subject to public disclosure?

Your records are generally covered by state laws that protect your privacy. However, some records are subject to public disclosure, such as the information on your seller's permit, names of owners or partners, your business address, and your permit status. See also the disclosure information on the back page.

Why do you need to verify my driver license number?

This is required to ensure the accuracy of the information provided and to protect you against fraudulent use of your identification.

What are my rights and responsibilities as a seller?

When you obtain a seller's permit, you acquire certain rights and responsibilities. For example,

- **You may purchase property for resale without paying tax to your supplier**. By providing the vendor with a completed resale certificate, you are not required to pay sales tax on tangible personal property you purchase for resale. You cannot use a resale certificate to purchase property for your own use (even if you plan to sell the property after you have used it).

- **You must keep records** to substantiate your sales, deductions reported on your returns, and any purchases you have made for your business. You must keep your records for four years.

- **You must file returns** on or before the last day of the month following the close of your reporting period. You must file your tax returns even if you have no tax to report.

- **You must pay the sales tax due** on your retail sales in California. However, you may be reimbursed by collecting the amount of tax from your customers.

- **You must notify the Board if you move, change ownership of, or sell your business.** Your permit is valid only at the address and for the type of ownership specified on the permit. You must notify the Board of any change in ownership. If you do not, you could be held liable for the continuing business's taxes. In addition, you must immediately notify us in writing if you discontinue your business. Your notification will help us to close your account and return any security you may have on deposit.

- **You must notify us immediately if you drop or add a partner.** This may protect former partners from tax liabilities incurred by the business after the partnership change.

How Do I Apply for My Seller's Permit?

Step 1: Complete Your Application

Fill out and return the application provided on page 5. The application is perforated to make it easy to remove. Be sure to refer to the "Tips" on page 4 as you complete your application. If you need assistance, please call our Information Center, 800-400-7115.

Be sure to provide all the information required for your permit. If you don't, this will delay the issuance of your permit.

Note: If your business is located outside California, you should also complete form BOE-403-B, *Registration Information for Out-of-State Account*. Call 800-400-7115 to request a copy by mail or by fax (select the automated fax-back option). Or visit our Internet site, www.boe.ca.gov.

Step 2: Send It in for Processing

If you have not been instructed to return your application to our Information Center in Sacramento, you should send or take it to the district office nearest your place of business. If you need a district office address, call our Information Center, 800-400-7115, or visit our Internet site at www.boe.ca.gov. If you plan to travel to a district office, you should call ahead to find out when they are open.

Make a copy of your application for your files.

Reminder: You must have a seller's permit before you begin making sales that are subject to Calfornia sales and use tax. Consequently, you should let us know if you have an urgent need for a permit.

Step 3: After Your Application Has Been Approved

You should receive your permit approximately two weeks after we have received your application, assuming your application is complete. There is no charge for the permit.

Based on the information on your application, you will be given regulations, forms, and other publications that may apply to your business. You will also be notified whether you must file returns on a monthly, quarterly, or annual basis.

When you receive your permit, you must post it at your place of business in a location that is easily seen by your customers.

You will also start receiving tax returns for reporting and paying the taxes due on your sales and purchases.

Message from the Executive Director

We appreciate the fact that, as a business owner, you have many responsibilities. You may be responsible for income and sales and use tax payments and for a variety of other obligations, such as payroll taxes, insurance, and employee benefits.

For that reason, we want to make it as easy as possible for you to work with us. As you can see on page 7, we provide many services to help you with your questions.

If you are unable to find the answers you need, please call our Information Center. Our trained representatives will be glad to help.

James E. Speed

James E. Speed

4

Tips for Filling Out Your Application

FIELD OFFICES

CALL FOR ADDRESSES

City	Area Code	Number
Bakersfield	661	395-2880
Culver City	310	342-1000
El Centro	760	352-3431
Eureka	707	445-6500
Fresno	559	248-4219
Laguna Hills	949	461-5711
Norwalk	562	466-1694
Oakland	510	622-4100
Rancho Mirage	760	346-8096
Redding	530	224-4729
Riverside	909	680-6400
Sacramento	916	227-6700
Salinas	831	443-3003
San Diego	619	525-4526
San Francisco	415	356-6600
San Jose	408	277-1231
San Marcos	760	510-5850
Santa Ana	714	558-4059
Santa Rosa	707	576-2100
Stockton	209	948-7720
Suisun City	707	428-2041
Torrance	310	516-4300
Van Nuys	818	904-2300
Ventura	805	677-2700
West Covina	626	480-7200

**Businesses Located
Out-of-State**

916-227-6600

Section I: Ownership Information

Items 1-15:

All applicants. You must provide the information requested for each owner or partner (attach additional sheets if necessary).

All partnerships. Partnerships should provide a copy of their written partnership agreement, if one exists. If you file your agreement with us *at the time you apply for a permit* and your agreement specifies that all business assets are held *in the name of the partnership,* the law requires the Board to attempt to collect any delinquent tax liability from the partnership assets before it attempts to collect from the partners' personal assets.

You should notify us immediately if you add or drop partners (see pg. 2).

Items 5,6,11,12: Driver License/Social Security Number

You must provide your social security number and driver license or California Identification Card number. You must also provide a photocopy of your driver license or California Identification Card. This information is kept in the strictest confidence.

Section II: Business Information

Item 22: Types of Items Sold

Be specific. For example, for a beauty supply business, you would write "beauty supplies," rather than "general merchandise." If you use a broad description, such as "market-driven products," you should list examples of the types of products sold — for example, sports equipment, household appliances, or garden supplies.

Item 25: Ownership Changes

If you are purchasing an existing business, we need to know the previous owner's name and seller's permit number. To make sure you won't have to pay any unpaid taxes owed by the previous owner, you should write to us and request a tax clearance before you buy.

If you are changing from one type of business organization to another (for example, from a sole owner to a general partnership or from a general partnership to a limited partnership), provide the previous owner's name and seller's permit number.

Section III: Sales and Employer Information

Be realistic in you projection. When starting a business, you should have an idea of how much (in dollars and cents) you will be selling a month. Your estimates help us determine how often you need to file a return. If your actual monthly sales vary, we may adjust your filing requirements.

✒ Certification

This section *must* be signed by the owner or, in the case of a partnership or co-ownership, by each partner or co-owner.

APPLICATION FOR SELLER'S PERMIT AND REGISTRATION
AS A RETAILER (INDIVIDUALS/PARTNERSHIPS)

Use additional sheet(s) to include information for more than two partners

SECTION I: OWNERSHIP INFORMATION

FOR BOARD USE ONLY

TAX	IND	OFFICE	NUMBER
SR			

1. PLEASE CHECK TYPE OF OWNERSHIP

☐ Sole Owner ☐ Husband/Wife Co-ownership

☐ General Partnership ☐ Limited Partnership
Provide documents if filed with Secretary of State.

☐ Limited Liability Partnership *(registered to practice law, accounting or architecture) Provide documents filed with Secretary of State.*

Enter Federal Employer Identification Number (FEIN), if any

BUSINESS CODE

AREA CODE

APPLICATION PROCESSED BY

VERIFICATION:
☐ DL ☐ Other

OWNER OR PARTNER

2. PARTNERSHIP NAME *(if applicable)*

3. Did you include a copy of your partnership agreement? ☐ Yes ☐ No

4. FULL NAME *(first, middle, last)*

5. SOCIAL SECURITY NUMBER

6. DRIVER LICENSE NUMBER *(attach verification)*

7. RESIDENCE ADDRESS *(street, city, state, zip code)*

8. RESIDENCE TELEPHONE NUMBER
(   )

9. NAME, ADDRESS & TELEPHONE NUMBER OF A PERSONAL REFERENCE WHO DOES NOT LIVE WITH YOU

CO-OWNER OR PARTNER

10. FULL NAME *(first, middle, last)*

11. SOCIAL SECURITY NUMBER

12. DRIVER LICENSE NUMBER *(attach verification)*

13. RESIDENCE ADDRESS *(street, city, state, zip code)*

14. RESIDENCE TELEPHONE NUMBER
(   )

15. NAME, ADDRESS & TELEPHONE NUMBER OF A PERSONAL REFERENCE WHO DOES NOT LIVE WITH YOU

SECTION II: BUSINESS INFORMATION

16. BUSINESS NAME [DBA] *(complete if different than entity name)*

17. BUSINESS ADDRESS *(street, city, state, zip code) [do not list P.O. Box or mailing service]*

18. BUSINESS TELEPHONE NUMBER
(   )

19. MAILING ADDRESS *(street, city, state, zip code) [if different from business address]*

20. BUSINESS FAX NUMBER
(   )

21. DATE YOU WILL BEGIN BUSINESS ACTIVITIES *(month, day & year)*   22. TYPE OF ITEMS SOLD

23. NUMBER OF SELLING LOCATIONS *(if 2 or more, attach list of all locations)*

24. TYPE OF BUSINESS *(check one that best describes your business)*

☐ Retail ☐ Wholesale ☐ Mfg. ☐ Repair ☐ Service ☐ Construction Contractor

CHECK ONE
☐ Full Time ☐ Part Time

25. OWNERSHIP CHANGES

Are you buying an existing business? ☐ Yes ☐ No If yes, complete items 26 through 30 below.

Are you changing from one type of business organization to another (for example, from a sole owner to a general partnership or from a general partnership to a limited liability company, etc.)? ☐ Yes ☐ No If yes, complete items 28 and 29 below.

Other: _____

26. PURCHASE PRICE
$

27. VALUE OF FIXTURES & EQUIPMENT
$

28. FORMER OWNER'S NAME

29. SELLER'S PERMIT ACCOUNT NUMBER

30. IF AN ESCROW COMPANY IS REQUESTING A TAX CLEARANCE ON YOUR BEHALF, PLEASE LIST THEIR NAME, ADDRESS, TELEPHONE NUMBER AND THE ESCROW NUMBER

31. DO YOU MAKE INTERNET SALES?
☐ Yes ☐ No If yes, answer 32.

32. WEBSITE ADDRESS

Continued on Reverse

— tear at dotted line —

33. IF ALCOHOLIC BEVERAGES ARE SOLD, PLEASE LIST YOUR ALCOHOLIC BEVERAGE CONTROL LICENSE NO. AND TYPE

34. NAME, ADDRESS & TELEPHONE NUMBER OF BUSINESS LANDLORD

35. NAME, ADDRESS & TELEPHONE NUMBER OF PERSON MAINTAINING YOUR RECORDS

36. NAME & LOCATION OF BANK OR OTHER FINANCIAL INSTITUTION *(note whether business or personal)*	CHECKING ACCOUNT NUMBER(S)
	SAVINGS ACCOUNT NUMBER(S)
37. NAMES & ADDRESSES OF MAJOR SUPPLIERS	PRODUCTS PURCHASED

SECTION III: SALES AND EMPLOYER INFORMATION

38. PROJECTED MONTHLY SALES *(if unknown, enter an estimated amount)*

Total gross sales $ Taxable sales $

39. INFORMATION CONCERNING EMPLOYMENT DEVELOPMENT DEPARTMENT *(EDD)*

Are you registered with EDD? .... ☐ Yes ☐ No

If no, will your payroll exceed $100 per quarter? .... ☐ Yes ☐ No

If yes, you must apply with EDD.

Number of employees   (See pamphlet DE 44, *California Employer's Guide*)

I received pamphlet DE 44, *California Employer's Guide*. .... ☐ Yes ☐ No

CERTIFICATION

All owners and partners must sign below.

I am duly authorized to sign the application and certify that the statements made are correct to the best of my knowledge and belief.
I also represent and acknowledge that the applicant will be engaged in or conduct businesses as a seller of tangible personal property.

NAME *(typed or printed)*	SIGNATURE	DATE
NAME *(typed or printed)*	SIGNATURE	DATE
NAME *(typed or printed)*	SIGNATURE	DATE
NAME *(typed or printed)*	SIGNATURE	DATE

Where Can I Get Help?

No doubt you will have questions about how the Sales and Use Tax Law applies to your business operations. For assistance, you may take advantage of the resources listed below.

INFORMATION CENTER

1-800-400-7115

FOR TDD ASSISTANCE

From TDD phones: 1-800-735-2929

From voice phones: 1-800-735-2922

Customer service representatives are available from 8 a.m. through 5 p.m., Monday-Friday, excluding State holidays.

Fax-Back Service. To order fax copies of selected forms and notices, call 1-800-400-7115 and choose the fax-back option. You can call at any time for this service.

Translator Services. We can provide bilingual services for persons who need assistance in a language other than English.

WRITTEN TAX ADVICE

It is best to get tax advice from the Board in writing. You may be relieved of tax, penalty, or interest charges if we determine you did not correctly report tax because you reasonably relied on our written advice regarding a transaction.

For this relief to apply, your request for advice must be in writing, identify the taxpayer to whom the advice applies, and fully describe the facts and circumstances of the transaction.

Send your request for written advice to: State Board of Equalization; Public Information and Administration Section, MIC:44; P.O. Box 942879, Sacramento, CA 94279-0044.

CLASSES

You may enroll in a basic sales and use tax class offered by some local Board offices. You should call ahead to find out when your local office conducts classes for beginning sellers.

INTERNET

www.boe.ca.gov

You can log onto our website for additional information. For example, you can find out what the tax rate is in a particular county, or you can download numerous publications — such as laws, regulations, pamphlets, and policy manuals — that will help you understand how the law applies to your business. You can also verify sellers' permit numbers online, read about upcoming Taxpayers' Bill of Rights hearings, and obtain information on Board field office addresses and telephone numbers.

Another good resource — especially for starting businesses — is the California Tax Information Center at www.taxes.ca.gov.

TAXPAYERS' RIGHTS
ADVOCATE OFFICE

If you would like to know more about your rights as a taxpayer or if you are unable to resolve an issue with the Board, please contact the Taxpayers' Rights Advocate office for help. Call 916-324-2798 (or toll-free, 1-888-324-2798). Their fax number is 916-323-3319.

If you prefer, you can write to: State Board of Equalization; Taxpayers' Rights Advocate, MIC:70; PO Box 942879; Sacramento, CA 94279-0070.

To request a copy of publication 70, *The California Taxpayers' Bill of Rights*, call the Information Center or visit our Internet site.

FIELD OFFICES

See page 4.

Sales and Use Tax Privacy Notice

Information Provided to the Board of Equalization

We ask you for information so that we can administer the state's sales and use tax laws (Revenue and Taxation Code sections 6001-7176, 7200-7226, 7251-7279.6, 7285-7288.6). We will use the information to determine whether you are paying the correct amount of tax and to collect any amounts you owe. You must provide all of the information we request, including your social security number (used for identification purposes [see Title 42 U.S. Code sec.405(c)(2)(C)(i)]).

What happens if I don't provide the information?

If your application is incomplete, we may not issue your seller's permit or use tax certificate. If you do not file complete returns, you may have to pay penalties and interest. Penalties may also apply if you don't provide other information we request or that is required by law, or if you give us fraudulent information. In some cases, you may be subject to criminal prosecution.

In addition, if you don't provide information we request to support your exemptions, credits, exclusions, or adjustments, we may not allow them. You may end up owing more tax or receiving a smaller refund.

Can anyone else see my information?

Your records are covered by state laws that protect your privacy. However, we may share information regarding your account with certain government agencies. We may also share certain information with companies authorized to represent local governments.

Under some circumstances we may release to the public the information printed on your permit, account start and closeout dates, and names of business owners or partners. When you sell a business, we can give the buyer or other involved parties information regarding your outstanding tax liability.

With your written permission, we can release information regarding your account to anyone you designate.

We may disclose information to the proper officials of the following agencies, among others:

- United States government agencies: U.S. Attorney's Office; Bureau of Alcohol, Tobacco and Firearms; Depts. of Agriculture, Defense, and Justice; Federal Bureau of Investigation; General Accounting Office; Internal Revenue Service; Interstate Commerce Commission

- State of California government agencies and officials: Air Resources Board; Dept. of Alcoholic Beverage Control; Auctioneer Commission; Dept. of Motor Vehicles, Employment Development Department; Energy Commission; Exposition and Fairs; Dept. of Food and Agriculture; Board of Forestry; Forest Products Commission; Franchise Tax Board; Dept. of Health Services; Highway Patrol; Dept. of Housing and Community Development; California Parent Locator Service

- State agencies outside of California for tax enforcement purposes

- City attorneys and city prosecutors; county district attorneys, police and sheriff departments.

Can I review my records?

Yes. Please contact your closest Board office (see the white pages of your phone book). If you need more information, you may contact our Disclosure Officer in Sacramento by calling 916-445-2918. You may also want to obtain publication 58-A, *Inspecting and Correcting Your Records.* You may order a copy from our Information Center: 800-400-7115 or download it from the Internet: *www.boe.ca.gov* (look under "Forms and Publications").

Who is responsible for maintaining my records?

The deputy director of the Sales and Use Tax Department, whom you may contact by calling 916-445-6464 or writing at the address shown.

Deputy Director, Sales and Use Tax Department MIC:43
450 N Street
Sacramento, CA 95814

BOE-400-MCO REV 12 (1-03)

California Seller's Permit Application

Corporations / Limited Liability Companies / Organizations

 STATE BOARD OF EQUALIZATION

Frequently Asked Questions

Who must have a permit?

You are generally required to obtain a California seller's permit if you sell or lease merchandise, vehicles, or other tangible personal property in California. A seller's permit allows you to sell items at the wholesale or retail level. You cannot legally sell taxable items in California until you have been issued a seller's permit.

Do I need more than one permit?

If you sell taxable items from more than one location, you must display a permit at each location. If this applies to you, please attach to your application a list that includes the address for each location, and we will issue the permits you need. This requirement applies to retailers as well as wholesalers.

Is there a charge for a permit?

No. However, we may require a security deposit. Security deposits are used to cover any unpaid taxes that may be owed at the time a business closes.

Is information regarding my account subject to public disclosure?

Your records are generally covered by state laws that protect your privacy. However, some records are subject to public disclosure, such as the information on your seller's permit, names of owners, your business address, and your permit status. See also the disclosure information on the back page.

Why do you need to verify my driver license number?

This is required to ensure the accuracy of the information provided and to protect you against fraudulent use of your identification.

What are my rights and responsibilities as a seller?

When you obtain a seller's permit, you acquire certain rights and responsibilities. For example,

- **You may purchase property for resale without paying tax to your supplier**. By providing the vendor with a completed resale certificate, you are not required to pay sales tax on tangible personal property you purchase for resale. You cannot use a resale certificate to purchase property for your own use (even if you plan to sell the property after you have used it).

- **You must keep records** to substantiate your sales, deductions reported on your returns, and any purchases you have made for your business. You must keep your records for four years.

- **You must file returns** on or before the last day of the month following the close of your reporting period. You must file your tax returns even if you have no tax to report.

- **You must pay the sales tax** due on your retail sales in California. However, you may be reimbursed by collecting the amount of tax from your customers.

- **You must notify the Board if you move, change ownership of, or sell your business**. Your permit is valid only at the address and for the type of ownership specified on the permit. You must notify the Board of any change in ownership, including a business reorganization or change of officers. If you do not, you could be held liable for the continuing business's taxes. In addition, you must immediately notify us in writing if you discontinue your business. Your notification will help us to close your account and return any security you may have on deposit.

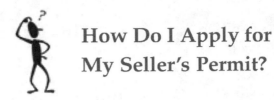

How Do I Apply for My Seller's Permit?

Message from the Executive Director

We appreciate the fact that as a business owner, you have many responsibilities. You may be responsible for income and sales and use tax payments and for a variety of other obligations, such as payroll taxes, insurance, and employee benefits.

For that reason, we want to make it as easy as possible for you to work with us. As you can see on page 7, we provide many services to help you with your questions.

If you are unable to find the answers you need, please call our Information Center. Our trained representatives will be glad to help.

James E. Speed

James E. Speed

Step 1: Complete Your Application

Fill out and return the application provided on page 5. The application is perforated to make it easy to remove. Be sure to refer to the "Tips" on page 4 as you complete your application. If you need assistance, please call our Information Center, 1-800-400-7115.

Be sure to provide all the information required for your permit. If you don't, the issuance of your permit may be delayed.

Note: If your business is located outside California, you should also complete form BOE-403-B, *Registration Information for Out-of-State Account*. Call 1-800-400-7115 to request a copy by mail or by fax (select the automated fax-back option). Or visit our Internet site, www.boe.ca.gov.

Step 2: Send It in for Processing

If you have not been instructed to return your application to our Information Center in Sacramento, you should send or take it to the district office nearest your place of business. If you need a district office address, call our Information Center, 1-800-400-7115, or visit our Internet site at www.boe.ca.gov. If you plan to travel to a district office, you should call ahead to find out when they are open.

Make a copy of your application for your files.

Reminder: You must have a seller's permit before you begin making sales that are subject to California sales and use tax. Consequently, you should let us know if you have an urgent need for a permit.

Step 3: After Your Application Has Been Approved

You should receive your permit approximately two weeks after we have received your application, assuming your application is complete. There is no charge for the permit.

Based on the information on your application, you will be given regulations, forms, and other publications that may apply to your business. You will also be notified whether you must file returns on a monthly, quarterly, or annual basis.

When you receive your permit, you must post it at your place of business in a location that is easily seen by your customers.

You will also start receiving tax returns for reporting and paying the taxes due on your sales and purchases.

Tips for Filling Out Your Application

Section I: Ownership Information

Check your type of ownership and provide the names and personal information for the officers, managers, etc. If there are more than three officers, please provide additional officer information on a separate sheet of paper.

Please include a copy of the articles or charter with your application. If you have incorporated/organized in another state, attach the authorization from California's Secretary of State. Remember to send the necessary documents to avoid a delay in the issuance of your permit.

Items 6,7,12,13,18,19: Driver License/Social Security Number

You must provide your social security number and driver license or California Identification Card number. You must also provide a photocopy of your driver license or California Identification Card. This information is kept in the strictest confidence.

Section II: Business Information

Item 27: Types of Items Sold

Be specific. For example, for a beauty supply business, you would write "beauty supplies," rather than "general supplies." If you use a broad description, such as "market-driven products," you should list examples of the types of products sold — for example, sports equipment, household appliances, or garden supplies.

Item 32: Ownership Changes

If you are purchasing an existing business, we need to know the previous owner's name and seller's permit number. To make sure you won't have to pay any unpaid taxes owed by the previous owner, you should write to us and request a tax clearance before you buy.

If you are changing from one type of business organization to another (for example, from a corporation to a partnership or a limited liability company), provide the previous owner's name and seller's permit number.

Section III: Sales and Employer Information

Line 45: Projected Monthly Sales

Be realistic in your projection. When starting a business, you should have an idea of how much (in dollars and cents) you will be selling a month. Your estimates help us determine how often you need to file a return. If your actual monthly sales vary, we may adjust your filing requirements.

Certification

This section *must* be signed by a corporate officer or officer of the organization.

APPLICATION FOR SELLER'S PERMIT AND REGISTRATION
AS A RETAILER (CORPORATIONS/LIMITED LIABILITY COMPANY/ORGANIZATIONS)

STATE OF CALIFORNIA
BOARD OF EQUALIZATION

Use additional sheets to include information for more than three individuals.

SECTION I: OWNERSHIP INFORMATION	FOR BOARD USE ONLY			

1. PLEASE CHECK TYPE OF OWNERSHIP

☐ Corporation   ☐ Limited Liability Company (LLC)

☐ Unincorporated Business Trust

☐ Other _____
(describe)

Enter Federal Employer Identification Number (FEIN), if any
_____

TAX	IND	OFFICE	NUMBER
S			

BUSINESS CODE | AREA CODE

APPLICATION PROCESSED BY | VERIFICATION:
☐ DL   ☐ Other

2. ENTER FULL NAME OF CORPORATION, LIMITED LIABILITY CO. (LLC), OR UNINCORPORATED BUSINESS TRUST

3. CORPORATE, OR LLC NUMBER/STATE OF INCORPORATION OR ORGANIZATION | **4. STATE OF INCORPORATION OR ORGANIZATION**

CHECK ONE ☐ LLC or Corporate Officer ☐ LLC Manager ☐ LLC Member ☐ Trustee ☐ Beneficiary

5. FULL NAME *(first, middle, last)* | **6. TITLE**

7. SOCIAL SECURITY NUMBER *(corporate officers excluded)* | **8. DRIVER LICENSE NUMBER** *(attach verification)*

9. RESIDENCE ADDRESS *(street, city, state, zip code)* | **10. RESIDENCE TELEPHONE NUMBER** ( )

CHECK ONE ☐ LLC or Corporate Officer ☐ LLC Manager ☐ LLC Member ☐ Trustee ☐ Beneficiary

11. FULL NAME *(first, middle, last)* | **12. TITLE**

13. SOCIAL SECURITY NUMBER *(corporate officers excluded)* | **14. DRIVER LICENSE NUMBER** *(attach verification)*

15. RESIDENCE ADDRESS *(street, city, state, zip code)* | **16. RESIDENCE TELEPHONE NUMBER** ( )

CHECK ONE ☐ LLC or Corporate Officer ☐ LLC Manager ☐ LLC Member ☐ Trustee ☐ Beneficiary

17. FULL NAME *(first, middle, last)* | **18. TITLE**

19. SOCIAL SECURITY NUMBER *(corporate officers excluded)* | **20. DRIVER LICENSE NUMBER** *(attach verification)*

21. RESIDENCE ADDRESS *(street, city, state, zip code)* | **22. RESIDENCE TELEPHONE NUMBER** ( )

SECTION II: BUSINESS INFORMATION

23. BUSINESS NAME [DBA] *(if any)*

24. BUSINESS ADDRESS *(street, city, state, zip code) [do not list P.O. Box or mailing service]* | **25. BUSINESS TELEPHONE NUMBER** ( )

26. MAILING ADDRESS *(street, city, state, zip code) [if different from business address]* | **27. BUSINESS FAX NUMBER** ( )

28. DATE YOU WILL BEGIN BUSINESS ACTIVITIES *(month, day and year)* | **29. TYPE OF ITEMS SOLD** | **30. NUMBER OF SELLING LOCATIONS** *(if 2 or more, attach list of all locations)*

31. TYPE OF BUSINESS *(check one that best describes your business)* | *check one*

☐ Retail   Wholesale ☐ Mfg. ☐ Repair ☐ Service ☐ Construction Contractor   ☐ Full Time ☐ Part Time

32. OWNERSHIP CHANGES

Are you buying an existing business?   ☐ Yes ☐ No   If yes, complete items 33 through 37.

Are you changing from one type of business organization to another (for example, from a sole owner to a corporation or from a partnership to a limited liability company, etc.)? ☐ Yes ☐ No   If yes, complete items 35 and 36 on the back of this form.

Other: _____

33. PURCHASE PRICE

$

34. VALUE OF FIXTURES & EQUIPMENT

$

Continued on Reverse

35. FORMER OWNER'S NAME	36. SELLER'S PERMIT ACCOUNT NUMBER

37. IF AN ESCROW COMPANY IS REQUESTING A TAX CLEARANCE ON YOUR BEHALF, PLEASE LIST THEIR NAME, ADDRESS, TELEPHONE NUMBER AND THE ESCROW NUMBER

38. DO YOU MAKE INTERNET SALES? ☐ Yes ☐ No If yes, answer 39.	39. WEBSITE ADDRESS

40. IF ALCOHOLIC BEVERAGES ARE SOLD, PLEASE LIST YOUR ALCOHOLIC BEVERAGE CONTROL LICENSE NO. AND TYPE

41. NAME, ADDRESS & TELEPHONE NUMBER OF PERSON MAINTAINING YOUR RECORDS

42. NAME, ADDRESS & TELEPHONE NUMBER OF BUSINESS LANDLORD

43. NAME & LOCATION OF BANK OR OTHER FINANCIAL INSTITUTION *(note whether business or personal)*	CHECKING ACCOUNT NUMBER(S)
	SAVINGS ACCOUNT NUMBER(S)

44. NAMES & ADDRESSES OF MAJOR SUPPLIERS	PRODUCTS PURCHASED

SECTION III: SALES AND EMPLOYER INFORMATION

45. PROJECTED MONTHLY SALES *(if unknown, enter an estimated amount)*

Total gross sales $ _____   Taxable sales $ _____

46. INFORMATION CONCERNING EMPLOYMENT DEVELOPMENT DEPARTMENT *(EDD)*

Are you registered with EDD? .... ☐ Yes ☐ No
If no, will your payroll exceed $100 per quarter? .... ☐ Yes ☐ No
If yes, you must apply with EDD.
Number of employees _____ (See pamphlet DE 44, *California Employer's Guide*)
I received pamphlet DE 44, *California Employer's Guide*. .... ☐ Yes ☐ No

CERTIFICATION

The corporate officer or officer of the organization must sign below.

I am duly authorized to sign the application and certify that the statements made are correct to the best of my knowledge and belief.
I also represent and acknowledge that the applicant will be engaged in or conduct businesses as a seller of tangible personal property.

NAME *(typed or printed)*	SIGNATURE	DATE
NAME *(typed or printed)*	SIGNATURE	DATE
NAME *(typed or printed)*	SIGNATURE	DATE
NAME *(typed or printed)*	SIGNATURE	DATE

FOR BOARD USE ONLY
Furnished to Taxpayer

REPORTING BASIS

SECURITY REVIEW

☐ BOE-598 $ _____
☐ BOE-1009

BY

APPROVED BY

REMOTE INPUT DATE

BY

☐ Permit Issued   Date _____

FORMS

☐ BOE-8   ☐ BOE-400-Y
☐ BOE-162   ☐ BOE-519
☐ BOE-467
☐ BOE-1241-D

REGULATIONS

☐ REG. 1668   ☐ REG. 1698
☐ REG. 1700

PUBLICATIONS

☐ PUB 73   ☐ PUB DE 44

_____
_____
_____

RETURNS

_____
_____
_____
_____

Where Can I Get Help?

No doubt you will have questions about how the Sales and Use Tax Law applies to your business operations. For assistance, you may take advantage of the resources listed below.

INFORMATION CENTER
1-800-400-7115

FOR TDD ASSISTANCE

From TDD phones: 1-800-735-2929

From voice phones: 1-800-735-2922

Customer service representatives are available from 8 a.m. through 5 p.m., Monday-Friday, excluding State holidays.

Fax-Back Service. To order fax copies of selected forms and notices, call 1-800-400-7115 and choose the fax-back option. You can call at any time for this service.

Translator Services. We can provide bilingual services for persons who need assistance in a language other than English.

WRITTEN TAX ADVICE

It is best to get tax advice from the Board in writing. You may be relieved of tax, penalty, or interest charges if we determine you did not correctly report tax because you reasonably relied on our written advice regarding a transaction.

For this relief to apply, your request for advice must be in writing, identify the taxpayer to whom the advice applies, and fully describe the facts and circumstances of the transaction.

Send your request for written advice to: State Board of Equalization; Public Information and Administration Section, MIC:44; P.O. Box 942879, Sacramento, CA 94279-0044.

CLASSES

You may enroll in a basic sales and use tax class offered by some local Board offices. You should call ahead to find out when your local office conducts classes for beginning sellers.

INTERNET
www.boe.ca.gov

You can log onto our website for additional information. For example, you can find out what the tax rate is in a particular county, or you can download numerous publications – such as laws, regulations, pamphlets, and policy manuals – that will help you understand how the law applies to your business. You can also verify sellers' permit numbers online, read about upcoming Taxpayers' Bill of Rights hearings, and obtain information on Board field office addresses and telephone numbers.

Another good resource — especially for starting businesses — is the California Tax Information Center at www.taxes.ca.gov.

TAXPAYERS' RIGHTS
ADVOCATE OFFICE

If you would like to know more about your rights as a taxpayer or if you are unable to resolve an issue with the Board, please contact the Taxpayers' Rights Advocate office for help. Call 916-324-2798 (or toll-free, 1-888-324-2798). Their fax number is 916-323-3319.

If you prefer, you can write to State Board of Equalization; Taxpayers' Rights Advocate, MIC:70; PO Box 942879; Sacramento, CA 94279-0070.

To request a copy of publication 70, *The California Taxpayers' Bill of Rights*, call the Information Center or visit our Internet site.

FIELD OFFICES

See page 4.

Sales and Use Tax Privacy Notice

Information Provided to the Board of Equalization

We ask you for information so that we can administer the state's sales and use tax laws (Revenue and Taxation Code sections 6001-7176, 7200-7226, 7251-7279.6, 7285-7288.6). We will use the information to determine whether you are paying the correct amount of tax and to collect any amounts you owe. You must provide all of the information we request, including your social security number (used for identification purposes [see Title 42 U.S. Code sec.405(c)(2)(C)(i)]).

What happens if I don't provide the information?

If your application is incomplete, we may not issue your seller's permit or use tax certificate. If you do not file complete returns, you may have to pay penalties and interest. Penalties may also apply if you don't provide other information we request or that is required by law, or if you give us fraudulent information. In some cases, you may be subject to criminal prosecution.

In addition, if you don't provide information we request to support your exemptions, credits, exclusions, or adjustments, we may not allow them. You may end up owing more tax or receiving a smaller refund.

Can anyone else see my information?

Your records are covered by state laws that protect your privacy. However, we may share information regarding your account with certain government agencies. We may also share certain information with companies authorized to represent local governments.

Under some circumstances we may release to the public the information printed on your permit, account start and closeout dates, and names of business owners or partners. When you sell a business, we can give the buyer or other involved parties information regarding your outstanding tax liability.

With your written permission, we can release information regarding your account to anyone you designate.

We may disclose information to the proper officials of the following agencies, among others:

- United States government agencies: U.S. Attorney's Office; Bureau of Alcohol, Tobacco and Firearms; Depts. of Agriculture, Defense, and Justice; Federal Bureau of Investigation; General Accounting Office; Internal Revenue Service; Interstate Commerce Commission

- State of California government agencies and officials: Air Resources Board; Dept. of Alcoholic Beverage Control; Auctioneer Commission; Dept. of Motor Vehicles, Employment Development Department; Energy Commission; Exposition and Fairs; Dept. of Food and Agriculture; Board of Forestry; Forest Products Commission; Franchise Tax Board; Dept. of Health Services; Highway Patrol; Dept. of Housing and Community Development; California Parent Locator Service

- State agencies outside of California for tax enforcement purposes

- City attorneys and city prosecutors; county district attorneys, police and sheriff departments.

Can I review my records?

Yes. Please contact your closest Board office (see the white pages of your phone book). If you need more information, you may contact our Disclosure Officer in Sacramento by calling 916-445-2918. You may also want to obtain publication 58-A, *Inspecting and Correcting Your Records*. You may order a copy from our Information Center: 800-400-7115 or download it from the Internet: *www.boe.ca.gov* (look under "Forms and Publications").

Who is responsible for maintaining my records?

The deputy director of the Sales and Use Tax Department, whom you may contact by calling 916-445-6464 or writing at the address shown.

Deputy Director, Sales and Use Tax Department MIC:43
450 N Street
Sacramento, CA 95814

California Resale Certificate

I HEREBY CERTIFY:

1. I hold valid seller's permit number:

2. I am engaged in the business of selling the following type of tangible personal property:

_____

3. This certificate is for the purchase from _____ of the item(s) I have listed in paragraph 5 below.
   [Vendor's name]

4. I will resell the item(s) listed in paragraph 5, which I am purchasing under this resale certificate in the form of tangible personal property in the regular course of my business operations, and I will do so prior to making any use of the item(s) other than demonstration and display while holding the item(s) for sale in the regular course of my business. I understand that if I use the item(s) purchased under this certificate in any manner other than as just described, I will owe use tax based on each item's purchase price or as otherwise provided by law.

5. Description of property to be purchased for resale:

6. I have read and understand the following:

   For Your Information: A person may be guilty of a misdemeanor under Revenue and Taxation Code section 6094.5 if the purchaser knows at the time of purchase that he or she will not resell the purchased item prior to any use (other than retention, demonstration, or display while holding it for resale) and he or she furnishes a resale certificate to avoid payment to the seller of an amount as tax. Additionally, a person misusing a resale certificate for personal gain or to evade the payment of tax is liable, for each purchase, for the tax that would have been due, plus a penalty of 10 percent of the tax or $500, whichever is more.

NAME OF PURCHASER

SIGNATURE OF PURCHASER, PURCHASER'S EMPLOYEE OR AUTHORIZED REPRESENTATIVE

PRINTED NAME OF PERSON SIGNING | TITLE

ADDRESS OF PURCHASER

TELEPHONE NUMBER | DATE
(   )

**SWAP MEETS, FLEA MARKETS, OR
SPECIAL EVENTS CERTIFICATION**

People who sell merchandise in California are generally required to hold a seller's permit.

You **may not** sell at this event unless you have a seller's permit or are not required to hold a permit. You are required to have a permit if you are selling, even temporarily, new or handcrafted items or used items you purchased for the purpose of reselling to others. You are not required to hold a permit if you are only making "occasional" sales, selling products that are not taxable when sold at retail, or selling on behalf of a section 6015 retailer.

Seller's permits can be obtained at any local Board of Equalization office at no cost to you. To find a Board office near you, call our Information Center at 800-400-7115 or check our website at *www.boe.ca.gov.* Permit applications can also be found online at *www.boe.ca.gov/sutax/ sutprograms.htm.* If you obtain a temporary seller's permit, the business address on your temporary permit should be the address of the temporary selling location and the mailing address should be your permanent place of business or residence.

Occasional and Nontaxable Sales - Occasional sellers are usually people who are not required to hold a seller's permit because they will not be making a series of qualifying sales. A person who has cleared their garage of used items *accumulated for their own use* and who sells *only* those items would usually qualify as an occasional seller, provided they make sales no more than twice in a 12-month period. Some sellers who make only nontaxable sales are also not required to hold seller's permits. Examples include sellers of fresh produce or other cold food products sold "to go." Please note, however, some food sales are taxable, including sales of food for consumption in places where admission is charged.

Section 6015 Retailers - Revenue and Taxation Code section 6015 relieves certain individuals of the requirement to obtain a seller's permit when: (1) the product supplier is a Board approved section 6015 retailer, (2) the product supplier reports and pays tax on the actual "retail selling price," (3) the individual is selling only those items purchased from the section 6015 retailer, and (4) the individual provides the name of the product supplier. Typical section 6015 retailers include multi-level marketing retailers that solicit sales through a network of individual salespeople/representatives (e.g., Avon, Tupperware).

Verification of a seller's status is required by law. Please complete all four sections of this form. Please print.

1. EVENT INFORMATION

EVENT NAME AND PLACE

EVENT DATE(S)   TABLE/BOOTH/LOCATION ID#

2. VENDOR/EXHIBITOR INFORMATION

OWNER'S NAME

MAILING ADDRESS *(street number or P.O. box)*

(city, state and zip code)   TELEPHONE NUMBER
                                                        (   )

DRIVER LICENSE NUMBER OR STATE ID NUMBER AND STATE

TYPE OF BUSINESS, DESCRIPTION OF ITEMS TO BE SOLD/DISPLAYED

3. STATUS — *Check appropriate boxes, and provide requested information*

☐ I hold a valid seller's permit. My number is: **S**

☐ No sales of tangible personal property are being made or solicited at this event.

☐ I am not required to hold a seller's permit because:
    ☐ My retail product sales are not subject to tax   ☐ My sales are exempt occasional sales
    ☐ I sell on behalf of a section 6015 retailer _____

4. CERTIFICATION — *Partners/additional sellers, complete a separate copy of this form*

The above statements are certified to be correct to the best knowledge and belief of the undersigned.

NAME *(typed or printed)*   TITLE

SIGNATURE   DATE

See reverse for disclosure information.

Sales and Use Tax Privacy Notice
Information Provided
to the Board of Equalization

We ask you for information so that we can administer the state's sales and use tax laws (Revenue and Taxation Code sections 6001-7176, 7200-7226, 7251-7279.6, 7285-7288.6). We will use the information to determine whether you are paying the correct amount of tax and to collect any amounts you owe. You must provide all of the information we request, including your social security number (used for identification purposes [see Title 42 U.S. Code sec.405(c)(2)(C)(i)]).

What happens if I don't provide the information?

If your application is incomplete, we may not issue your seller's permit or use tax certificate. If you do not file complete returns, you may have to pay penalties and interest. Penalties may also apply if you don't provide other information we request or that is required by law, or if you give us fraudulent information. In some cases, you may be subject to criminal prosecution.

In addition, if you don't provide information we request to support your exemptions, credits, exclusions, or adjustments, we may not allow them. You may end up owing more tax or receiving a smaller refund.

Can anyone else see my information?

Your records are covered by state laws that protect your privacy. However, we may share information regarding your account with certain government agencies. We may also share certain information with companies authorized to represent local governments.

Under some circumstances we may release to the public the information printed on your permit, account start and closeout dates, and names of business owners or partners. When you sell a business, we can give the buyer or other involved parties information regarding your outstanding tax liability.

With your written permission, we can release information regarding your account to anyone you designate.

We may disclose information to the proper officials of the following agencies, among others:

- United States government agencies: U.S. Attorney's Office; Bureau of Alcohol, Tobacco and Firearms; Depts. of Agriculture, Defense, and Justice; Federal Bureau of Investigation; General Accounting Office; Internal Revenue Service; Interstate Commerce Commission

- State of California government agencies and officials: Air Resources Board; Dept. of Alcoholic Beverage Control; Auctioneer Commission; Dept. of Motor Vehicles, Employment Development Department; Energy Commission; Exposition and Fairs; Dept. of Food and Agriculture; Board of Forestry; Forest Products Commission; Franchise Tax Board; Dept. of Health Services; Highway Patrol; Dept. of Housing and Community Development; California Parent Locator Service

- State agencies outside of California for tax enforcement purposes

- City attorneys and city prosecutors; county district attorneys, police and sheriff departments.

Can I review my records?

Yes. Please contact your closest Board office (see the white pages of your phone book). If you need more information, you may contact our Disclosure Officer in Sacramento by calling 916- 445-2918. You may also want to obtain publication 58-A, *Inspecting and Correcting Your Records*. You may order a copy from our Information Center: 800-400-7115 or download it from the Internet: *www.boe.ca.gov* (look under "Forms and Publications").

Who is responsible for maintaining my records?

The deputy director of the Sales and Use Tax Department, whom you may contact by calling 916-445-6464 or writing at the address shown.

Deputy Director, Sales and Use Tax Department MIC:43
450 N Street
Sacramento, CA 95814

PUBLICATIONS ORDER

Please enter the quantity of each publication you wish to order and send your completed order form to the State Board of Equalization, Supply Unit, 3920 West Capitol Avenue, West Sacramento, CA 95691 or FAX your order to (916) 372-6078.

NAME OF BUSINESS	FOR OFFICE USE ONLY	REQUEST ☐ New ☐ One Time ☐ Replacement
ATTENTION	RECEIVED BY	IS FOR ☐ Distribution Change
MAILING ADDRESS	DATE REQUEST RECEIVED	
CITY STATE ZIP	SHIPPED BY	
TELEPHONE NUMBER ( )	DATE MATERIAL SHIPPED	

PAMPHLETS *(No Charge)*

QTY.	NO.	TITLE	QTY.	NO.	TITLE
	1	Sales and Use Tax Law		31K	Tax Tips for Grocery Stores (Korean)
	2	Uniform Local Sales & Use Tax Law and Transactions & Use Tax Law		31S	Tax Tips for Grocery Stores (Spanish)
	3	Use Fuel Tax Law		31V	Tax Tips for Grocery Stores (Vietnamese)
	4	California Cigarette and Tobacco Products Tax Law		32	Tax Tips for Sales to Purchasers from Mexico
	5	Alcoholic Beverage Tax Law		32S	Tax Tips for Sales to Purchasers from Mexico (Spanish)
	6	Motor Vehicle Fuel License Tax Law		33AC	Making Sales in California (Arabic)
	6A	Motor Vehicle Tax Law		33AN	Making Sales in California (Armenian)
	7	Tax on Insurers Law		33CN	Making Sales in California (Cambodian)
	8	Private Railroad Car Tax Law		33GN	Making Sales in California (German)
	9	Tax Tips for Construction and Building Contractors		33HG	Making Sales in California (Hmong)
	10	Energy Resources Surcharge Law		33HI	Making Sales in California (Hindi)
	11	Energy Resources Surcharge Regulations		33JE	Making Sales in California (Japanese)
	12	California Use Fuel Tax: A Guide for Vendors and Users		33PE	Making Sales in California (Portuguese)
	14	Motor Vehicle Fuel License Tax Regulations		33PI	Making Sales in California (Pilipino)
	15	Cigarette Tax Regulations		33PO	Making Sales in California (Punjabi)
	16	Alcoholic Beverage Tax Regulations and Instructions		34	Tax Tips for Motor Vehicle Dealers (New & Used)
	17	Appeals Procedures: Sales & Use Taxes and Special Taxes		35	Tax Tips for Interior Designers and Decorators
	18	Tax Tips for Nonprofit Organizations		36	Tax Tips for Veterinarians
	19	Diesel Fuel Tax Law		39	Emergency Telephone Users Surcharge Regulations
	20	California Emergency Telephone Users Surcharge Law		40	Tax Tips for the Watercraft Industry
	21	State Board of Equalization		41	Taxes and Fees Administered by the Board of Equalization
	22	Tax Tips for the Dining and Beverage Industry		42	Resale Certificate Tips
	22K	Tax Tips for the Dining and Beverage Industry (Korean)		42S	Resale Certificate Tips (Spanish)
	22S	Tax Tips for the Dining and Beverage Industry (Spanish)		43	Timber Yield Tax Law
	24	Tax Tips for Liquor Stores		44	Tax Tips for District Taxes
	25	Tax Tips for Auto Repair Garages and Service Stations		45	Tax Tips for Hospitals
	25S	Tax Tips for Auto Repair Garages and Service Stations (Spanish)		46	Tax Tips for Leasing of Tangible Personal Property in California
	26	Tax Information Bulletin Index		47	Tax Tips for Mobilehomes and Factory-Built Housing
	27	Tax Tips for Drug Stores		48	Property Tax Exemptions for Religious Organizations
	28	Tax Information for City and County Officials Sales and Use Tax		49	California Underground Storage Tank Maintenance Fee Law
	29	California Property Tax: An Overview		50	Guide to the International Fuel Tax Agreement
	30	Residential Property Assessment Appeals		50S	Guide to the International Fuel Tax Agreement (Spanish)
	31	Tax Tips for Grocery Stores		50-A	Introduction to the International Fuel Tax Agreement
	31C	Tax Tips for Grocery Stores (Chinese)		50-A-S	Introduction to the International Fuel Tax Agreement (Spanish)

QTY.	NO.	TITLE		QTY.	NO.	TITLE
_____	51	Guide to Board of Equalization Services		_____	86	Timber Yield Tax (brochure)
_____	51C	Guide to Board of Equalization Services (Chinese)		_____	87	Guide to the Timber Yield Tax
_____	51K	Guide to Board of Equalization Services (Korean)		_____	88	Underground Storage Tank Fee
_____	51S	Guide to Board of Equalization Services (Spanish)		_____	90	Environmental Fee
_____	51V	Guide to Board of Equalization Services (Vietnamese)		_____	91	Tire Recycling Fee
_____	52	Vehicles and Vessels: How to Request a Use Tax Clearance for DMV Registration		_____	92	Alcoholic Beverage Tax
				_____	93	Cigarette & Tobacco Products Tax
_____	54	Tax Collection Procedures		_____	94	Occupational Lead Poisoning Prevention Fee
_____	55	Homeowners & Renters Assistance Appeals		_____	100	Shipping and Delivery Charges
_____	56	Offers In Compromise		_____	100S	Shipping and Delivery Charges (Spanish)
_____	58-A	How to Inspect & Correct Your Records		_____	101	Sales Delivered Outside California
_____	59	Local Motor Vehicle Fuel Taxation Law		_____	101S	Sales Delivered Outside California (Spanish)
_____	60	Hazardous Substances Tax Law		_____	102	Sales to the U.S. Government
_____	61	Sales and Use Taxes: Exemptions and Exclusions		_____	102S	Sales to the U.S. Government (Spanish)
_____	62	Tax Tips for Locksmiths		_____	103	Sales for Resale
_____	64	Tax Tips for Jewelry Stores		_____	103S	Sales for Resale (Spanish)
_____	66	Tax Tips for Retail Feed and Farm Supply Stores		_____	104	Sales to Residents of Other Countries
_____	68	Tax Tips for Photographers, Photo Finishers and Film Processing Laboratories		_____	104S	Sales to Residents of Other Countries (Spanish)
				_____	105	District Taxes and Delivered Sales
_____	69	California Integrated Waste Management Fee Law		_____	105S	District Taxes and Delivered Sales (Spanish)
_____	70	The California Taxpayers' Bill of Rights		_____	106	Gift Wrapping Charges
_____	70C	The California Taxpayers' Bill of Rights (Chinese)		_____	107	Do You Need a California Sellers Permit?
_____	70K	The California Taxpayers' Bill of Rights (Korean)		_____	107S	Do You Need a California Sellers Permit? (Spanish)
_____	70S	The California Taxpayers' Bill of Rights (Spanish)		_____	108	When Is Labor Taxable?
_____	70V	The California Taxpayers' Bill of Rights (Vietnamese)		_____	108S	When Is Labor Taxable? (Spanish)
				_____	109	Are Your Internet Sales Taxable?
_____	71	California City and County Sales and Use Tax Rates		_____	109S	Are Your Internet Sales Taxable? (Spanish)
_____	71C	California City and County Sales and Use Tax Rates (Chinese)		_____	110	California Use Tax Basics
				_____	110S	California Use Tax Basics (Spanish)
_____	71S	California City and County Sales and Use Tax Rates (Spanish)		_____	111	Operators of Swap Meets, Flea Markets and Special Events
_____	72	Summary of Constitutional & Statutory Authorities		_____	111S	Operators of Swap Meets, Flea Markets and Special Events (Spanish)
_____	73	Your California Seller's Permit		_____	112	Purchases From Out-of-State Vendors
_____	73C	Your California Seller's Permit (Chinese)		_____	112S	Purchases From Out-of-State Vendors (Spanish)
_____	73F	Your California Seller's Permit (Farsi)		_____	113	Coupons and Sales Tax
_____	73K	Your California Seller's Permit (Korean)		_____	113S	Coupons and Sales Tax (Spanish)
_____	73S	Your California Seller's Permit (Spanish)		_____	114	Consignment Sales
_____	73V	Your California Seller's Permit (Vietnamese)		_____	115	Applying Sales Tax to Tips
_____	74	Closing Out Your Seller's Permit		_____	115S	Applying Sales Tax to Tips (Spanish)
_____	74C	Closing Out Your Seller's Permit (Chinese)		_____	116	Sales and Use Tax Records
_____	74S	Closing Out Your Seller's Permit (Spanish)		_____	Other	_____
_____	75	Interest and Penalty Payments				_____
_____	76	Audits				_____
_____	76F	Audits (Farsi)				_____
_____	76K	Audits (Korean)				_____
_____	76S	Audits (Spanish)				_____
_____	77	Out-of-State Sellers: Do You Need to Register with California				

MISCELLANEOUS *(No Charge)*

QTY.	NO.	TITLE
_____	79	Documented Vessels & California Tax
_____	79A	Aircraft and California Tax
_____	79B	California Individual Use Tax
_____	80	Electronic Funds Transfer Program
_____	81	Franchise and Personal Income Tax Appeals
_____	82	Prepaid Sales Tax on Sales of Fuel
_____	83	Tire Recycling Fee Law
_____	84	Use Fuel Permit Requirements

QTY.	
_____	Annual Calendar of Board Meetings
_____	Annual Report of the State Board of Equalization
_____	State of California Sales Tax Reimbursement Schedules
_____	Tax Information Bulletin (published quarterly) Issue (mo./year) _____
_____	Other _____

Form **1040-ES**

Department of the Treasury
Internal Revenue Service

Estimated Tax for Individuals

This package is primarily for first-time filers of estimated tax.

OMB No. 1545-0087

2004

Purpose of This Package

Use this package to figure and pay your estimated tax. Estimated tax is the method used to pay tax on income that is not subject to withholding (for example, earnings from self-employment, interest, dividends, rents, alimony, etc.). In addition, if you do not elect voluntary withholding, you should make estimated tax payments on unemployment compensation and the taxable part of your social security benefits. See the 2003 instructions for your tax return for details on income that is taxable.

This package is primarily for first-time filers who are or may be subject to paying estimated tax. This package can also be used if you did not receive or have lost your preprinted 1040-ES package. The estimated tax worksheet on page 4 will help you figure the correct amount to pay. The payment vouchers in this package are for crediting your estimated tax payments to your account correctly if you are paying by check or money order. You may also be able to pay by Electronic Federal Tax Payment System (EFTPS), electronic funds withdrawal, or credit card. See page 3 for details. Use the **Record of Estimated Tax Payments** on page 6 to keep track of the payments you have made and the number and amount of your remaining payments.

After we receive your first payment voucher from this package (or if you make your first payment by EFTPS, electronic funds withdrawal, or credit card), we will mail you a 1040-ES package with your name, address, and social security number (SSN) preprinted on each payment voucher. Use the preprinted vouchers to make your **remaining** estimated tax payments for the year if you are paying by check or money order. This will speed processing, reduce processing costs, and reduce the chance of errors.

Do not use the vouchers in this package to notify the IRS of a **change of address.** If you have a new address, file **Form 8822,** Change of Address. The IRS will update your record and send you new preprinted payment vouchers.

Who Must Make Estimated Tax Payments

In most cases, you must make estimated tax payments if you expect to owe at least $1,000 in tax for 2004 (after subtracting your withholding and credits) and you expect your withholding and credits to be less than the **smaller** of:

1. 90% of the tax shown on your 2004 tax return or

2. The tax shown on your 2003 tax return (110% of that amount if you are not a farmer or fisherman and the adjusted gross income shown on that return is more than $150,000 or, if married filing separately for 2004, more than $75,000).

However, if you did not file a 2003 tax return or that return did not cover 12 months, item **2** above does not apply.

For this purpose, include household employment taxes (before subtracting advance EIC payments made to your employee(s)) when figuring the tax shown on your tax return if:

● You will have Federal income tax withheld from wages, pensions, annuities, gambling winnings, or other income or

● You would be required to make estimated tax payments to avoid a penalty even if you did not include household employment taxes when figuring your estimated tax.

Exception. You do not have to pay estimated tax if you were a U.S. citizen or resident alien for all of 2003 and you had no tax liability for the full 12-month 2003 tax year.

The estimated tax rules apply to:

● U.S. citizens and residents,

● Residents of Puerto Rico, the Virgin Islands, Guam, the Commonwealth of the Northern Mariana Islands, and American Samoa, and

● Nonresident aliens (use Form 1040-ES (NR)).

If you also receive salaries and wages, you may be able to avoid having to make estimated tax payments on your other income by asking your employer to take more tax out of your earnings. To do this, file a new **Form W-4,** Employee's Withholding Allowance Certificate, with your employer.

You can also choose to have Federal income tax withheld from certain government payments. For details, see **Form W-4V,** Voluntary Withholding Request.

 You may not make joint estimated tax payments if you or your spouse is a nonresident alien, you are separated under a decree of divorce or separate maintenance, or you and your spouse have different tax years.

Additional Information You May Need

Most of the information you will need can be found in **Pub. 505,** Tax Withholding and Estimated Tax.

Other available information:

● **Pub. 553,** Highlights of 2003 Tax Changes.

● Instructions for the 2003 Form 1040 or 1040A.

● **What's Hot** at www.irs.gov.

For details on how to get forms and publications, see page 7 of the instructions for Form 1040 or 1040A.

If you have tax questions, call 1-800-829-1040 for assistance. For TTY/TDD help, call 1-800-829-4059.

Changes Effective for 2004

Use your 2003 tax return as a guide in figuring your 2004 estimated tax, but be sure to consider the following changes. For more information on these changes and other changes that may affect your 2004 estimated tax, see Pub. 553.

IRA deduction allowed to more people covered by retirement plans. You may be able to take an IRA deduction if you were covered by a retirement plan and your 2004 modified adjusted gross income (AGI) is less than $55,000 ($75,000 if married filing jointly or qualifying widow(er)).

Tuition and fees deduction expanded. You may be able to take a deduction of up to $4,000 if your 2004 AGI is not more than $65,000 ($130,000 if married filing jointly) or a deduction of up to $2,000 if your 2004 AGI is not more than $80,000 ($160,000 if married filing jointly).

Standard mileage rates. The 2004 rate for business use of your vehicle is 37½ cents a mile. The 2004 rate for use of your vehicle to get medical care or to move is 14 cents a mile.

Deduction for clean-fuel vehicles. If you place a qualified clean-fuel vehicle in service in 2004, the maximum amount you can deduct is:

● $1,500.

● $3,750 for a truck or van with a gross vehicle weight rating over 10,000 pounds but not more than 26,000 pounds.

● $37,500 for a truck or van with a gross vehicle weight rating over 26,000 pounds or a bus with a seating capacity of at least 20 adults (not including the driver).

Certain credits no longer allowed against alternative minimum tax (AMT). The credit for child and dependent care expenses, credit for the elderly or the disabled, education credits, and mortgage interest credit will no longer be allowed against AMT. However, the child tax credit, adoption credit, and credit for qualified retirement savings contributions will still be allowed against your AMT.

Health savings accounts. Beginning in 2004, eligible individuals covered by a high-deductible health insurance plan may be able to open a health savings account (HSA). Within limits, contributions to an HSA are deductible and are excludable if made by the employer of an eligible individual. Earnings from an HSA are tax deferred. Distributions from an HSA for medical expenses are not taxable.

Cat. No. 11340T

Expired tax benefits. At the time this form went to print, the following benefits were scheduled to expire.

- Deduction for educator expenses paid or incurred after 2003.
- District of Columbia first-time homebuyer credit for homes purchased after 2003.
- Credit for increasing research activities (applies to amounts paid or incurred after June 30, 2004).

Standard deduction. If you do not itemize your deductions, you may take the 2004 standard deduction listed below for your filing status.

2004 Filing Status	Standard Deduction
Married filing jointly or Qualifying widow(er)	$9,700
Head of household	$7,150
Single or Married filing separately	$4,850

However, if you can be claimed as a dependent on another person's 2004 return, your standard deduction is the **greater** of:

- $800 or
- Your earned income plus $250 (up to the standard deduction amount).

Your standard deduction is increased by the following amount if, at the end of 2004, you are:

- An unmarried individual (single or head of household) and are:

65 or older or blind	$1,200
65 or older and blind	$2,400

- A married individual (filing jointly or separately) or a qualifying widow(er) and are:

65 or older or blind	$950
65 or older and blind	$1,900
Both spouses 65 or older	$1,900 *
Both spouses 65 or older and blind	$3,800 *

* If married filing separately, these amounts apply only if you can claim an exemption for your spouse.

To Figure Your Estimated Tax, Use:

- The **2004 Estimated Tax Worksheet** on page 4.
- The **Instructions for the 2004 Estimated Tax Worksheet** that begin on page 4.
- The **2004 Tax Rate Schedules** below.
- Your 2003 tax return and instructions, as a guide to figuring your income, deductions, and credits (but be sure to consider the **Changes Effective for 2004** that begin on page 1).

If you receive your income unevenly throughout the year (for example, because you operate your business on a seasonal basis), you may be able to lower or eliminate the amount of your required estimated tax payment for one or more periods by using the annualized income installment method. See Pub. 505 for details.

To amend or correct your estimated tax, see **Amending Estimated Tax Payments** on page 3.

Payment Due Dates

You may pay all of your estimated tax by April 15, 2004, or in four equal amounts by the dates shown below.

1st payment	April 15, 2004
2nd payment	June 15, 2004
3rd payment	Sept. 15, 2004
4th payment	Jan. 18, 2005*

*You do not have to make the payment due January 18, 2005, if you file your 2004 tax return by January 31, 2005, **and** pay the entire balance due with your return.

Note: *Payments are due by the dates indicated whether or not you are outside the United States and Puerto Rico.*

If, after March 31, 2004, you have a large change in income, deductions, additional taxes, or credits that requires you to start making estimated tax payments, you should figure the amount of your estimated tax payments by using the annualized income installment method, explained in Pub. 505. Although your payment due dates will be the same as shown above, the payment amounts will vary based on your income, deductions, additional taxes, and credits for the months ending before each payment due date. As a result, this method may allow you to skip or lower the amount due for one or more payments. If you use the annualized income installment method, be sure to file **Form 2210,** Underpayment of Estimated Tax by Individuals, Estates, and Trusts, with your 2004 tax return, even if no penalty is owed.

Farmers and fishermen. If at least two-thirds of your gross income for 2003 or 2004 is from farming or fishing, you may do one of the following.

- Pay all of your estimated tax by January 18, 2005.
- File your 2004 Form 1040 by March 1, 2005, and pay the total tax due. In this case, 2004 estimated payments are not required to avoid a penalty.

Fiscal year taxpayers. You are on a fiscal year if your 12-month tax period ends on any day except December 31. Due dates for fiscal year taxpayers are the 15th day of the 4th, 6th, and 9th months of your current fiscal year and the 1st month of the following fiscal year. If any payment date falls on a Saturday, Sunday, or legal holiday, use the next business day.

2004 Tax Rate Schedules

Caution. Do not use these Tax Rate Schedules to figure your 2003 taxes. Use only to figure your 2004 estimated taxes.

Single- Schedule X

If line 5 is: Over—	But not over—	The tax is:	of the amount over—
$0	$7,150	10%	$0
7,150	29,050	$715.00 + 15%	7,150
29,050	70,350	4,000.00 + 25%	29,050
70,350	146,750	14,325.00 + 28%	70,350
146,750	319,100	35,717.00 + 33%	146,750
319,100		92,592.50 + 35%	319,100

Head of household- Schedule Z

If line 5 is: Over—	But not over—	The tax is:	of the amount over—
$0	$10,200	10%	$0
10,200	38,900	$1,020.00 + 15%	10,200
38,900	100,500	5,325.00 + 25%	38,900
100,500	162,700	20,725.00 + 28%	100,500
162,700	319,100	38,141.00 + 33%	162,700
319,100		89,753.00 + 35%	319,100

Married filing jointly or Qualifying widow(er)- Schedule Y-1

If line 5 is: Over—	But not over—	The tax is:	of the amount over—
$0	$14,300	10%	$0
14,300	58,100	$1,430.00 + 15%	14,300
58,100	117,250	8,000.00 + 25%	58,100
117,250	178,650	22,787.50 + 28%	117,250
178,650	319,100	39,979.50 + 33%	178,650
319,100		86,328.00 + 35%	319,100

Married filing separately- Schedule Y-2

If line 5 is: Over—	But not over—	The tax is:	of the amount over—
$0	$7,150	10%	$0
7,150	29,050	$715.00 + 15%	7,150
29,050	58,625	4,000.00 + 25%	29,050
58,625	89,325	11,393.75 + 28%	58,625
89,325	159,550	19,989.75 + 33%	89,325
159,550		43,164.00 + 35%	159,550

Name Change

If you changed your name because of marriage, divorce, etc., and you made estimated tax payments using your former name, attach a statement to the front of your 2004 tax return. On the statement, explain all of the estimated tax payments you and your spouse made for 2004 and the name(s) and SSN(s) under which you made the payments.

Be sure to report the change to your local Social Security Administration office **before** filing your 2004 tax return. This prevents delays in processing your return and issuing refunds. It also safeguards your future social security benefits. For more details, call the Social Security Administration at 1-800-772-1213.

Amending Estimated Tax Payments

To change or amend your estimated tax payments, refigure your total estimated tax payments due (line 16 of the worksheet on page 4). Then, use the worksheet for amended estimated tax under **Regular Installment Method** in Chapter 2 of Pub. 505 to figure the payment due for each remaining payment period. If an estimated tax payment for a previous period is less than ¼ of your amended estimated tax, you may owe a penalty when you file your return.

When a Penalty Is Applied

In some cases, you may owe a penalty when you file your return. The penalty is imposed on each underpayment for the number of days it remains unpaid. A penalty may be applied if you did not pay enough estimated tax for the year or you did not make the payments on time or in the required amount. A penalty may apply even if you have an overpayment on your tax return.

The penalty may be waived under certain conditions. See Pub. 505 for details.

Paying by Check or Money Order Using the Payment Voucher

There is a separate payment voucher for each due date. The due date is shown in the upper right corner. Please be sure you use the voucher with the correct due date for each payment you make. Complete and send in the voucher **only** if you are making a payment by check or money order. To complete the voucher, do the following.

● Type or print your name, address, and SSN in the space provided on the voucher. If filing a joint voucher, also enter your spouse's name and SSN. List the names and SSNs in the same order on the joint voucher as you will list them on your joint return. If you and your spouse plan to file separate returns, file separate vouchers instead of a joint voucher.

● Enter in the box provided on the payment voucher only the amount you are sending in by check or money order. When making payments of estimated tax, be sure to take into account any 2003 overpayment that you choose to credit against your 2004 tax, but **do not** include the overpayment amount in this box.

● Make your check or money order payable to the "**United States Treasury.**" **Do not** send cash. To help process your payment, enter the amount on the right side of the check like this: $ XXX.XX. **Do not** use dashes or lines (for example, do not enter "$ XXX-- " or "$ XXX $\frac{XX}{100}$ ").

● Write "2004 Form 1040-ES" and your SSN on your check or money order. If you are filing a joint voucher, enter the SSN that you will show first on your joint return.

● Enclose, but do not staple or attach, your payment with the voucher.

● Mail your payment voucher and check or money order to the address shown on page 6 for the place where you live.

● Fill in the **Record of Estimated Tax Payments** on page 6 for your files.

Paying by Electronic Federal Tax Payment System (EFTPS)

You can use EFTPS to submit your estimated payment electronically using the Internet, computer software, or phone. You can schedule payments for withdrawal up to 365 days in advance. You can make payments weekly, monthly, or quarterly. For more information, call 1-800-555-4477 or 1-800-945-8400, or visit the EFTPS website at **www.eftps.gov.**

Paying by Electronic Funds Withdrawal

You may make one 2004 estimated tax payment when you electronically file your 2003 tax return by authorizing an electronic funds withdrawal from your checking or savings account. You will need to know your account number and your financial institution's routing number. You can check with your financial institution to make sure that an electronic withdrawal is allowed and to get the correct routing and account numbers. Whether or not you have a balance due on your electronically filed tax return, you can schedule one estimated tax payment with an effective date of April 15, 2004, June 15, 2004, or September 15, 2004. Check with your tax return preparer or tax preparation software for details. **Do not** send in a Form 1040-ES payment voucher when you schedule an estimated tax payment by electronic funds withdrawal.

Paying by Credit Card

You may use your American Express® Card, Discover® Card, MasterCard® card, or Visa® card to make estimated tax payments. Call toll free or visit the website of either service provider listed below and follow the instructions. A convenience fee will be charged by the service provider based on the amount you are paying. Fees may vary between the providers. You will be told what the fee is during the transaction and you will have the option to either continue or cancel the transaction. You can also find out what the fee will be by calling the provider's toll-free automated customer service number or visiting the provider's website shown below.

Link2Gov Corporation
1-888-PAY-1040ˢᴹ (1-888-729-1040)
1-888-658-5465 (Customer Service)
www.PAY1040.com

Official Payments Corporation
1-800-2PAY-TAXˢᴹ (1-800-272-9829)
1-877-754-4413 (Customer Service)
www.officialpayments.com

If you pay by credit card, you will be given a confirmation number at the end of the call. Fill in the **Record of Estimated Tax Payments** on page 6. Enter the confirmation number in column **(b)**, but **do not** include the amount of the convenience fee in column **(c)**. There is nothing to send in when you pay by credit card.

Instructions for the 2004 Estimated Tax Worksheet

Line 1. Adjusted gross income. Use your 2003 tax return and instructions as a guide to figuring the adjusted gross income you expect in 2004 (but be sure to consider the **Changes Effective for 2004** that begin on page 1). For more details on figuring your adjusted gross income, see **Expected Adjusted Gross Income** in Pub. 505. If you are self-employed, be sure to take into account the deduction for one-half of your self-employment tax.

Line 8. Include on this line the additional taxes from **Form 4972,** Tax on Lump-Sum Distributions, or **Form 8814,** Parents' Election To Report Child's Interest and Dividends. Also include any recapture of education credits.

Line 9. Credits. See the instructions for the 2003 Form 1040, lines 44 through 52, or Form 1040A, lines 29 through 34. However, be sure to see **Certain credits no longer allowed against alternative minimum tax (AMT)** on page 1.

Line 11. Self-employment tax. If you and your spouse make joint estimated tax payments and you both have self-employment income, figure the self-employment tax for each

2004 Estimated Tax Worksheet (keep for your records)

1	Adjusted gross income you expect in 2004 (see instructions above)	**1**		
2	• If you plan to itemize deductions, enter the estimated total of your itemized deductions. **Caution:** *If line 1 above is over $142,700 ($71,350 if married filing separately), your deduction may be reduced. See Pub. 505 for details.* • If you do not plan to itemize deductions, enter your standard deduction from page 2.	**2**		
3	Subtract line 2 from line 1	**3**		
4	Exemptions. Multiply $3,100 by the number of personal exemptions. If you can be claimed as a dependent on another person's 2004 return, your personal exemption is not allowed. **Caution:** *See Pub. 505 to figure the amount to enter if line 1 above is over: $214,050 if married filing jointly or qualifying widow(er); $178,350 if head of household; $142,700 if single; or $107,025 if married filing separately*	**4**		
5	Subtract line 4 from line 3	**5**		
6	**Tax.** Figure your tax on the amount on line 5 by using the **2004 Tax Rate Schedules** on page 2. **Caution:** *If you have qualified dividends or a net capital gain, see Pub. 505 to figure the tax.*	**6**		
7	Alternative minimum tax from Form 6251	**7**		
8	Add lines 6 and 7. Also include any tax from Forms 4972 and 8814 and any recapture of education credits (see instructions above)	**8**		
9	Credits (see instructions above). **Do not** include any income tax withholding on this line . . .	**9**		
10	Subtract line 9 from line 8. If zero or less, enter -0-	**10**		
11	Self-employment tax (see instructions above). Estimate of 2004 net earnings from self-employment $.................. ; if **$87,900 or less,** multiply the amount by 15.3%; if **more than $87,900,** multiply the amount by 2.9%, add $10,899.60 to the result, and enter the total. **Caution:** *If you also have wages subject to social security tax, see Pub. 505 to figure the amount to enter*	**11**		
12	Other taxes (see instructions on page 5)	**12**		
13a	Add lines 10 through 12	**13a**		
b	Earned income credit, additional child tax credit, and credits from **Form 4136** and **Form 8885**	**13b**		
c	**Total 2004 estimated tax.** Subtract line 13b from line 13a. If zero or less, enter -0- . . . ▶	**13c**		
14a	Multiply line 13c by 90% (66⅔% for farmers and fishermen) **14a**			
b	Enter the tax shown on your 2003 tax return (110% of that amount if you are not a farmer or fisherman and the adjusted gross income shown on line 35 of that return is more than $150,000 or, if married filing separately for 2004, more than $75,000) **14b**			
c	**Required annual payment to avoid a penalty.** Enter the **smaller** of line 14a or 14b . . ▶	**14c**		
	Caution: *Generally, if you do not prepay (through income tax withholding and estimated tax payments) at least the amount on line 14c, you may owe a penalty for not paying enough estimated tax. To avoid a penalty, make sure your estimate on line 13c is as accurate as possible. Even if you pay the required annual payment, you may still owe tax when you file your return. If you prefer, you may pay the amount shown on line 13c. For details, see Pub. 505.*			
15	Income tax withheld and estimated to be withheld during 2004 (including income tax withholding on pensions, annuities, certain deferred income, etc.)	**15**		
16	Subtract line 15 from line 14c. (**Note:** *If zero or less or line 13c minus line 15 is less than $1,000, stop here. You are not required to make estimated tax payments.*)	**16**		
17	If the first payment you are required to make is due April 15, 2004, enter ¼ of line 16 (minus any 2003 overpayment that you are applying to this installment) here, and on your payment voucher(s) if you are paying by check or money order. (**Note:** *Household employers, see instructions on page 5.*)	**17**		

of you separately. Enter the total on line 11. When figuring your estimate of 2004 net earnings from self-employment, be sure to use only 92.35% of your total net profit from self-employment.

Line 12. Other taxes. Except as noted below, enter any other taxes, such as the taxes on distributions from a Coverdell education savings account or a qualified tuition program, and early distributions from **(a)** an IRA or other qualified retirement plan, **(b)** an annuity, or **(c)** a modified endowment contract entered into after June 20, 1988.

Include household employment taxes (before subtracting advance EIC payments made to your employee(s)) on line 12 if:

● You will have Federal income tax withheld from wages, pensions, annuities, gambling winnings, or other income or

● You would be required to make estimated tax payments (to avoid a penalty) even if you did not include household employment taxes when figuring your estimated tax.

Do not include tax on recapture of a Federal mortgage subsidy, social security and Medicare tax on unreported tip income, or uncollected employee social security and Medicare or RRTA tax on tips or group-term life insurance. These taxes are not required to be paid until the due date of your income tax return (not including extensions).

Line 17. If you are a household employer and you make advance EIC payments to your employee(s), reduce your required payment for each period by the amount of advance EIC payments paid during the period.

Record of Estimated Tax Payments (Farmers, fishermen, and fiscal year taxpayers, see page 2 for payment due dates.)

Payment number	Payment due date	(a) Date paid	(b) Check or money order number or credit card confirmation number	(c) Amount paid (do not include any credit card convenience fee)	(d) 2003 overpayment credit applied	(e) Total amount paid and credited (add (c) and (d))
1	4/15/2004					
2	6/15/2004					
3	9/15/2004					
4	1/18/2005*					
Total	. . . . ▶					

*You do not have to make this payment if you file your 2004 tax return by January 31, 2005, **and** pay the entire balance due with your return.

Where To File Your Payment Voucher if Paying by Check or Money Order

Mail your payment voucher and check or money order to the Internal Revenue Service at the address shown below for the place where you live. **Do not** mail your tax return to this address **or** send an estimated tax payment without a payment voucher. Also, do not mail your estimated tax payments to the address shown in the Form 1040 or 1040A instructions. If you need more payment vouchers, use another Form 1040-ES package.

Note: *For proper delivery of your estimated tax payment to a P.O. box, you must include the box number in the address. Also, note that only the U.S. Postal Service can deliver to P.O. boxes.*

IF you live in . . . ▼	THEN use . . . ▼
Maine, Massachusetts, New Hampshire, New York, Vermont	P.O. Box 37001 Hartford, CT 06176-0001
Connecticut, District of Columbia, Maryland, New Jersey, Pennsylvania	P.O. Box 80102 Cincinnati, OH 45280-0002

Alabama, Florida, Georgia, Mississippi, North Carolina, Rhode Island, South Carolina, West Virginia	P.O. Box 105900 Atlanta, GA 30348-5900
Ohio, Virginia	P.O. Box 105225 Atlanta, GA 30348-5225
Delaware, Illinois, Indiana, Iowa, Kansas, Michigan, Minnesota, Missouri, Nebraska, North Dakota, South Dakota, Wisconsin	P.O. Box 970006 St. Louis, MO 63197-0006
Arizona, Utah	P.O. Box 1219 Charlotte, NC 28201-1219
Alaska, California, Hawaii, Idaho, Montana, Nevada, Oregon, Washington, Wyoming	P.O. Box 510000 San Francisco, CA 94151-5100
Arkansas, Colorado, Kentucky, Louisiana, New Mexico, Oklahoma, Tennessee, Texas	P.O. Box 660406 Dallas, TX 75266-0406

All APO and FPO addresses, American Samoa, the Commonwealth of the Northern Mariana Islands, nonpermanent residents of Guam or the Virgin Islands, Puerto Rico *(or if excluding income under Internal Revenue Code section 933)*, dual-status aliens, a foreign country: U.S. citizens and those filing Form 2555, 2555-EZ, or 4563	P.O. Box 80102 Cincinnati, OH 45280-0002
Permanent residents of Guam*	Department of Revenue and Taxation Government of Guam P.O. Box 23607 GMF, GU 96921
Permanent residents of the Virgin Islands*	V.I. Bureau of Internal Revenue 9601 Estate Thomas Charlotte Amalie St. Thomas, VI 00802

* Permanent residents must prepare separate vouchers for estimated income tax and self-employment tax payments. Send the income tax vouchers to the address for permanent residents and the self-employment tax vouchers to the address for nonpermanent residents.

Tear off here

Form **1040-ES**
Department of the Treasury
Internal Revenue Service

2004 Payment Voucher **4**

OMB No. 1545-0087

File only if you are making a payment of estimated tax by check or money order. Mail this voucher with your check or money order payable to the **"United States Treasury."** Write your social security number and "2004 Form 1040-ES" on your check or money order. Do not send cash. Enclose, but do not staple or attach, your payment with this voucher.

Calendar year- Due Jan. 18, 2005

Amount of estimated tax you are paying by check or money order.

Dollars	Cents

Type or print			
	Your first name and initial	Your last name	Your social security number
	If joint payment, complete for spouse		
	Spouse's first name and initial	Spouse's last name	Spouse's social security number
	Address (number, street, and apt. no.)		
	City, state, and ZIP code. (If a foreign address, enter city, province or state, postal code, and country.)		

For Privacy Act and Paperwork Reduction Act Notice, see instructions on page 5.

Page 6

Form 1040-ES
Department of the Treasury
Internal Revenue Service

2004 Payment Voucher 3

OMB No. 1545-0087

File only if you are making a payment of estimated tax by check or money order. Mail this voucher with your check or money order payable to the **"United States Treasury."** Write your social security number and "2004 Form 1040-ES" on your check or money order. Do not send cash. Enclose, but do not staple or attach, your payment with this voucher.

Calendar year- Due Sept. 15, 2004

Amount of estimated tax you are paying by check or money order.

Dollars	Cents

Your first name and initial	Your last name	Your social security number
If joint payment, complete for spouse		
Spouse's first name and initial	Spouse's last name	Spouse's social security number
Address (number, street, and apt. no.)		
City, state, and ZIP code. (If a foreign address, enter city, province or state, postal code, and country.)		

Type or print

For Privacy Act and Paperwork Reduction Act Notice, see instructions on page 5.

Tear off here

Form 1040-ES
Department of the Treasury
Internal Revenue Service

2004 Payment Voucher 2

OMB No. 1545-0087

File only if you are making a payment of estimated tax by check or money order. Mail this voucher with your check or money order payable to the **"United States Treasury."** Write your social security number and "2004 Form 1040-ES" on your check or money order. Do not send cash. Enclose, but do not staple or attach, your payment with this voucher.

Calendar year- Due June 15, 2004

Amount of estimated tax you are paying by check or money order.

Dollars	Cents

Your first name and initial	Your last name	Your social security number
If joint payment, complete for spouse		
Spouse's first name and initial	Spouse's last name	Spouse's social security number
Address (number, street, and apt. no.)		
City, state, and ZIP code. (If a foreign address, enter city, province or state, postal code, and country.)		

Type or print

For Privacy Act and Paperwork Reduction Act Notice, see instructions on page 5.

Tear off here

Form 1040-ES
Department of the Treasury
Internal Revenue Service

2004 Payment Voucher 1

OMB No. 1545-0087

File only if you are making a payment of estimated tax by check or money order. Mail this voucher with your check or money order payable to the **"United States Treasury."** Write your social security number and "2004 Form 1040-ES" on your check or money order. Do not send cash. Enclose, but do not staple or attach, your payment with this voucher.

Calendar year- Due April 15, 2004

Amount of estimated tax you are paying by check or money order.

Dollars	Cents

Your first name and initial	Your last name	Your social security number
If joint payment, complete for spouse		
Spouse's first name and initial	Spouse's last name	Spouse's social security number
Address (number, street, and apt. no.)		
City, state, and ZIP code. (If a foreign address, enter city, province or state, postal code, and country.)		

Type or print

For Privacy Act and Paperwork Reduction Act Notice, see instructions on page 5.

540-ES Voucher 1 at bottom of page

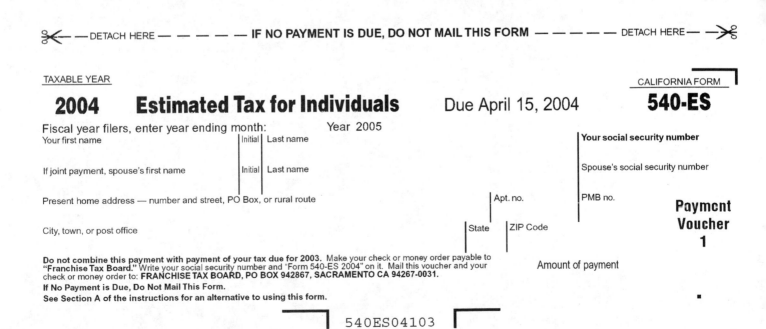

TAXABLE YEAR

2004   **Estimated Tax for Individuals**   Due April 15, 2004

CALIFORNIA FORM

540-ES

Fiscal year filers, enter year ending month: Year 2005

Your first name	Initial	Last name		**Your social security number**
If joint payment, spouse's first name	Initial	Last name		Spouse's social security number
Present home address — number and street, PO Box, or rural route			Apt. no.	PMB no.
City, town, or post office			State	ZIP Code

Payment Voucher 1

Do not combine this payment with payment of your tax due for 2003. Make your check or money order payable to "**Franchise Tax Board.**" Write your social security number and "Form 540-ES 2004" on it. Mail this voucher and your check or money order to: **FRANCHISE TAX BOARD, PO BOX 942867, SACRAMENTO CA 94267-0031.**
If No Payment is Due, Do Not Mail This Form.
See Section A of the instructions for an alternative to using this form.

Amount of payment

540ES04103

Blank

TAXABLE YEAR

2004 Estimated Tax for Individuals

Due June 15, 2004

CALIFORNIA FORM

540-ES

Fiscal year filers, enter year ending month: Year 2005

Your first name | Initial | Last name

Your social security number

If joint payment, spouse's first name | Initial | Last name

Spouse's social security number

Present home address — number and street, PO Box, or rural route | Apt. no. | PMB no.

Payment Voucher 2

City, town, or post office | State | ZIP Code

Do not combine this payment with payment of your tax due for 2003. Make your check or money order payable to "Franchise Tax Board." Write your social security number and "Form 540-ES 2004" on it. Mail this voucher and your check or money order to: **FRANCHISE TAX BOARD, PO BOX 942867, SACRAMENTO CA 94267-0031.**
If No Payment is Due, Do Not Mail This Form.
See Section A of the instructions for an alternative to using this form.

Amount of payment

540ES04103

✂ ← —DETACH HERE — — — — — **IF NO PAYMENT IS DUE, DO NOT MAIL THIS FORM** — — — — — DETACH HERE— → ✂

TAXABLE YEAR

2004 Estimated Tax for Individuals

Due Sept. 15, 2004

CALIFORNIA FORM

540-ES

Fiscal year filers, enter year ending month: Year 2005

Your first name | Initial | Last name

Your social security number

If joint payment, spouse's first name | Initial | Last name

Spouse's social security number

Present home address — number and street, PO Box, or rural route | Apt. no. | PMB no.

Payment Voucher 3

City, town, or post office | State | ZIP Code

Do not combine this payment with payment of your tax due for 2003. Make your check or money order payable to "Franchise Tax Board." Write your social security number and "Form 540-ES 2004" on it. Mail this voucher and your check or money order to: **FRANCHISE TAX BOARD, PO BOX 942867, SACRAMENTO CA 94267-0031.**
If No Payment is Due, Do Not Mail This Form.
See Section A of the instructions for an alternative to using this form.

Amount of payment

540ES04103

✂ ← —DETACH HERE — — — — — **IF NO PAYMENT IS DUE, DO NOT MAIL THIS FORM** — — — — — DETACH HERE— → ✂

TAXABLE YEAR

2004 Estimated Tax for Individuals

Due Jan. 18, 2005

CALIFORNIA FORM

540-ES

Fiscal year filers, enter year ending month: Year 2005

Your first name | Initial | Last name

Your social security number

If joint payment, spouse's first name | Initial | Last name

Spouse's social security number

Present home address — number and street, PO Box, or rural route | Apt. no. | PMB no.

Payment Voucher 4

City, town, or post office | State | ZIP Code

Do not combine this payment with payment of your tax due for 2003. Make your check or money order payable to "Franchise Tax Board." Write your social security number and "Form 540-ES 2004" on it. Mail this voucher and your check or money order to: **FRANCHISE TAX BOARD, PO BOX 942867, SACRAMENTO CA 94267-0031.**
If No Payment is Due, Do Not Mail This Form.
See Section A of the instructions for an alternative to using this form.

Amount of payment

540ES04103

2004 Instructions for Form 540-ES
Estimated Tax For Individuals

A   Purpose

Use this form to figure and pay your estimated tax. **Estimated tax is the tax you expect to owe for 2004 after subtracting the tax you expect to have withheld and any credits you plan to take.** These estimated tax payments do not apply to your 2003 tax liability. Use these instructions and the 2004 Estimated Tax Worksheet to determine if you owe estimated tax for 2004 and to figure the required amount. If you need to make a payment for your 2003 tax liability, make a separate payment for any balance due shown on your 2003 tax return. Use form FTB 3519, Payment Voucher for Automatic Extension for Individuals, or form FTB 3567, Installment Agreement Request, or call (800) 338-0505.

Generally, the required estimated tax amount is based on the lesser of 90% of the current year's tax or 100% of the prior year's tax. **Note:** Certain taxpayers are limited in their use of the prior year's tax as a basis for figuring their estimated tax. See paragraph C for more information. You can check the estimated payments we've received by going to our Website at **www.ftb.ca.gov** and clicking "Check Account Balance."

If you increase your withholding, more of your 2004 state tax liability will be withheld throughout the year. Doing so could eliminate the need to make a large payment with your tax return. Or, it could eliminate the need to make quarterly estimate payments. To increase your withholding, complete Employment Development Department (EDD) Form DE-4, Employee's Withholding Allowance Certificate, and give it to your employer's appropriate payroll staff. You can obtain this form by calling EDD at (888) 745-3886 or through the Internet at **www.edd.ca.gov/taxrep/de4.pdf**, or you can get this form from your employer.

Note: Form DE 4 specifically adjusts your California state withholding and is not the same as the Federal Form W-4, Employee's Withholding Allowance Certificate.

B   Who Must Make Estimated Tax Payments

Generally, you must make estimated tax payments if you expect to owe at least $200 ($100 if married filing separately) in tax for 2004 (after subtracting withholding and credits) and you expect your withholding and credits to be less than the **smaller** of:

1. 90% of the tax shown on your 2004 tax return; or
2. The tax shown on your 2003 tax return.

Note: You do not have to make estimated tax payments if you are a nonresident or new resident of California in 2004 and did not have a California tax liability in 2003.

If you and your spouse paid joint estimated tax payments, but are now filing separate returns, either of you may claim all of the amount paid, or you may each claim part of the joint estimated payments. If you want the estimated tax payments to be divided, notify the FTB before the end of the tax year in which you wish to file separate returns so that the payments can be applied to the proper account. The FTB will accept in writing, any divorce agreement (or court ordered settlement) or a statement showing the allocation of the payments along with a notarized signature of both taxpayers. The statements should be sent to:

JOINT ESTIMATE CREDIT ALLOCATION M/S F-225
TAXPAYER SERVICES CENTER
FRANCHISE TAX BOARD
PO BOX 942840
SACRAMENTO CA   94240-0040

C   Limit on the Use of Prior Year's Tax

Individuals who are required to make estimated payments, and whose 2003 adjusted gross income is more than $150,000 (or $75,000 if married filing separately), must figure estimated tax based on the lesser of 90% of their tax for 2004 or 110% of their tax for 2003. This rule does not apply to farmers or fishermen.

D   When to Make Your Estimated Tax Payments

For estimated tax purposes, the year is divided into four payment periods. Each period has a specific payment due date. If you do not pay enough tax by the due date of each of the payment periods, you may be charged a penalty even if you are due a refund when you file your income tax return. The payment periods and due dates are:

For the payment period:	Due date:
January 1 through March 31, 2004	April 15, 2004
April 1 through May 31, 2004	June 15, 2004
June 1 through August 31, 2004	September 15, 2004
Sept. 1 through Dec. 31, 2004	January 18, 2005

Filing an Early Return In Place of the 4th Installment. If you file your 2004 tax return by January 31, 2005, and pay the entire balance due, you do not have to make your last estimated tax payment.

Annualization Option. If you do not receive your taxable income evenly during the year, it may be to your advantage to annualize your income. This method allows you to match your estimated tax payments to the actual period when you earned the income. You may use the annualization schedule included with the 2003 form FTB 5805, Underpayment of Estimated Tax by Individuals and Fiduciaries.

Farmers and Fishermen. If you are a farmer or fisherman, and at least two-thirds of your 2003 and 2004 gross income is from farming or fishing, you may:

* Pay all of your estimated tax for 2004 by January 18, 2005; or
* File your tax return for 2004 on or before March 1, 2005, and pay the total tax due. In this case, you need not make estimated tax payments for 2004. Use form FTB 5805F, Underpayment of Estimated Tax by Farmers and Fishermen, to determine if you paid the required estimated tax. If the estimated tax is underpaid, attach the completed form FTB 5805F to the back of your return.

Fiscal Year. If you file your return on a fiscal year basis, your due dates will be the 15th day of the 4th, 6th, and 9th months of your fiscal year and the 1st month of the following fiscal year. If a due date falls on a Saturday, Sunday, or legal holiday, use the next business day.

E   How to Use Form 540-ES Payment Voucher

Use the Estimated Tax Worksheet and your 2003 California income tax return as a guide for figuring your 2004 estimated tax. **Caution:** If you filed Form 540 2EZ for 2003, do not use the Form 540 2EZ instructions for figuring amounts on this worksheet. Instead, get the 2003 California Resident Income Tax Booklet.

Note: This form is not an application for an installment agreement. If you are not able to pay your income tax, get FTB 3567, Installment Agreement Request Booklet or complete the form on line. Visit our Website at **www.ftb.ca.gov**.

There is a separate payment voucher for each due date. Please be sure you use the voucher with the correct due date shown in the top margin of the voucher. Complete Form 540-ES using black or blue ink:

1. Print your name, address, and social security number in the space provided on Form 540-ES.
2. Complete the payment box of the voucher by entering the amount of the payment that you are sending. Your entry must match the amount you are sending. Be sure that the amount shown on line 20 of the Estimated Tax Worksheet has been reduced by any overpaid tax on your 2003 return that you chose to apply toward your 2004 estimated tax payment.
3. Paying your tax:
   Check or money order – make your check or money order payable to **"Franchise Tax Board."** Write your social security number and "Form 540-ES 2004" on it and mail to the address on the voucher.
   Web Payment – To make a payment on line or to schedule a future payment (up to one year in advance), visit our Website at **www.ftb.ca.gov** and select "Payment Options." **Do not mail** the voucher to us.
   Credit card – Call (800) 272-9829 or visit the Website **www.officialpayments.com**. You will be charged a fee for this service. **Do not mail** the voucher if you pay by credit card.
4. Complete the Record of Estimated Tax Payments on page 2 for your files.
5. **Fiscal year filers:** Enter the month of your fiscal year end (located directly below the form's title).

F   Failure to Make Estimated Tax Payments

If you are required to make estimated tax payments and do not or if you underpay any installment, a penalty may be assessed on the portion of estimated tax that was underpaid from the due date of the installment to the date of payment or the due date of your tax return, whichever is earlier. Refer to the 2003 form FTB 5805 for more information.

2004 Estimated Tax Worksheet   Keep this worksheet for your records.

1   **Residents:** Enter your estimated 2004 California AGI. **Nonresidents and part-year residents:** Enter your estimated
    2004 total AGI from all sources .... **1** _____

2 **a** If you plan to itemize deductions, enter the estimated total of your itemized deductions .... **2a** _____
   b If you do not plan to itemize deductions, enter the standard deduction for your filing status:
       $3,070 if you are single or married filing a separate return
       $6,140 if you are married filing a joint return, head of household, or a qualifying widow(er) ..... **2b** _____
   c Enter the amount from line 2a or line 2b, whichever applies .... **2c** _____

3   Subtract line 2c from line 1 .... **3** _____

4   Tax. Figure your tax on the amount on line 3 using the 2003 tax table or tax rate schedules in the instructions
    for Form 540, Form 540A, or Long Form 540NR. Also include any tax from form FTB 3800, Tax Computation for Children with
    Investment Income; or form FTB 3803, Parents' Election to Report Child's Interest and Dividends .... **4** _____

5   **Residents:** Skip to line 6a. **Nonresidents and part-year residents:**
   a Enter your estimated California taxable income from Schedule CA (540NR), Part IV, line 46 .... **5a** _____
   b Compute the CA Tax Rate: <u>Tax on total taxable income from line 4</u> .... **5b** _.___ ___ ___ ___
                                  Total taxable income from line 3
   c Multiply the amount on line 5a by the CA Tax Rate on line 5b .... **5c** _____

6 **a** **Residents:** Enter the exemption credit amount from the 2003 instructions for Form 540 or Form 540A .... **6a** _____
   b **Nonresidents or part-year residents:** Enter the CA credit proration percentage. Divide line 5a by line 3. If more than 1 enter 1.0000 .. **6b** _.___ ___ ___ ___

7   **Nonresidents:** CA prorated Exemption credits. Multiply the total exemption credit amount by line 6b .... **7** _____

8   **Residents:** Subtract line 6a from line 4. Nonresidents or part-year residents subtract line 7 from line 5c................ **8** _____

9   Tax on accumulation distribution of trusts. See instructions for form FTB 5870A .... **9** _____

10 Add line 8 and line 9... **10** _____

11 Credits for joint custody head of household, dependent parent, senior head of household, child and dependent care expenses,
    and long-term care... **11** _____

    Nonresidents and part-year residents: For the child and dependent care expenses credit, use the amount from your 2003
    Long Form 540NR, line 54. For the other credits listed on line 11, multiply the total 2003 credit amount by the ratio on line 6b.

12 Subtract line 11 from line 10 .... **12** _____

13 Other credits (such as other state tax credit). See the 2003 instructions for Form 540, Form 540A, or Long Form 540NR ...... **13** _____

14 Subtract line 13 from line 12 .... **14** _____

15 Interest on deferred tax from installment obligations under IRC Sections 453 or 453A .... **15** _____

16 2004 Estimated Tax. Add line 14 and line 15. Enter the result, but not less than zero .... **16** _____

17 **a** Multiply line 16 by 90% (.90). Farmers and fishermen multiply line 16 by 66 2/3% (.6667) ..... **17a** _____
   b Enter 100% of the tax shown on your 2003 Form 540, line 34; Form 540A, line 23;
       or Long Form 540NR, line 43 .... **17b** _____
   c Enter the amount from your 2003 Form 540, line 17; Form 540A, line 14; or Long Form 540NR, line 21 .... **17c** _____
   d Is the amount on line 17c more than $150,000 ($75,000 if married filing a separate return)?
       Yes. Go to line 17e.   **No.** Enter the lesser of line 17a or line 17b. Skip line 17e and 17f and go to line 18 .... **17d** _____
   e Multiply 110% (1.10) by the tax shown on your 2003 Form 540, line 34; Form 540A, line 23; or Long Form 540NR, line 43.
       Go to line 17f .... **17e** _____
   f Enter the lesser of line 17a or line 17e and go to line 18 .... **17f** _____

    Caution: Generally, if you do not prepay at least the amount on line 17d (or 17f if no amount on line 17d), you may owe a
    penalty for not paying enough estimated tax. To avoid a penalty, make sure your estimated tax on line 16 is as accurate as
    possible. If you prefer, you may pay 100% of your 2004 estimated tax (line 16).

18 California income tax withheld and estimated to be withheld during 2004 (include withholding on pensions, annuities, etc)..... **18** _____

19 **Balance.** Subtract line 18 from line 17d (or line 17f if no amount on line 17d). If less than $200 (or less than $100,
    if married filing separately), you do not have to make a payment at this time .... **19** _____

20 **Installment** amount. Divide the amount on line 19 by 4. Enter the result here and on each of your Forms 540-ES. If you
    will earn your income at an uneven rate during the year, see Annualization Option in the instructions under paragraph D .... **20** _____

Record of Estimated Tax Payments

Payment voucher number	(a) Date	(b) Amount paid	(c) 2003 overpayment applied	(d) Total amount paid and credited add (b) and (c)
1		$	$	$
2				
3				
4				
Total .... ▶		$	$	$

Instructions for Form FTB 3522
Limited Liability Company Tax Voucher

General Information

Form FTB 3522 is used to pay the annual limited liability company (LLC) tax of $800 for taxable year 2004. An LLC should use this form if it:

- Has articles of organization accepted by the California Secretary of State (SOS);
- Has a certificate of registration issued by the SOS; or
- Is doing business in California.

You can download, view, and print California tax forms and publications from our Website at **www.ftb.ca.gov**

Access other state agencies' websites through the State Agency Index on California's Website at **www.ca.gov**

Who Must Pay the Annual LLC Tax

Every LLC that is doing business in California or that has articles of organization accepted or a certificate of registration issued by the SOS **is subject to the annual LLC tax of $800.** The tax must be paid for each taxable year until a certificate of cancellation of registration or of articles of organization is filed with the SOS.

How to Complete Form FTB 3522

Enter all the information requested on this form. To ensure the timely and proper application of the payment to the LLC's account, enter the SOS file number (assigned upon registration with the SOS), and the federal employer identification number (FEIN).

Note: If the LLC leases a private mailbox (PMB) from a private business rather than a PO box from the United States Postal Service, include the box number in the field labeled "PMB no." in the address area.

Where to Mail

Detach and mail the voucher portion with the payment to:

FRANCHISE TAX BOARD
PO BOX 942857
SACRAMENTO CA   94257-0631

When to Pay the Annual LLC Tax

The annual LLC tax is due and payable **on or before the 15th day of the 4th month** after the **beginning** of the LLC's taxable year (fiscal year) or April 15, 2004 (calendar year).

Note: The first taxable year of an LLC that was not previously in existence begins when the LLC is organized.

If the 15th day of the 4th month of an existing foreign LLC's taxable year has passed before the foreign LLC commences business in California or registers with the SOS, the annual LLC tax should be paid immediately after commencing business or registering with the SOS.

Example: LLC1, a newly-formed calendar year taxpayer, organizes as an LLC in Delaware on June 1, 2004. LLC1 registers with the SOS on August 16, 2004, and begins doing business in California on August 17, 2004. Because LLC1's initial taxable year began on June 1, 2004, the annual LLC tax is due September 15, 2004 (the 15th day of the 4th month of the short period taxable year). LLC1's short period (June 1, 2004-December 31, 2004) tax return is due April 15, 2005. The annual tax payment for tax year 2005, with form FTB 3522 also is due April 15, 2005.

Penalties and Interest

If the LLC fails to pay its annual tax by the 15th day of the 4th month after the beginning of the taxable year, a late payment penalty plus interest will be assessed for failure to pay the annual LLC tax by the return due date. The penalty and interest will be computed from the due date of the tax to the date of payment.

Late Payment of Prior Year Annual LLC Tax

If a prior year LLC tax of $800 was not paid on or before the 15th day of the 4th month after the beginning of the taxable year, the tax should be remitted as soon as possible, using the appropriate taxable year form FTB 3522. **Do not** use any other form for payment of the tax. This will assure proper application of the payment to the LLC's account.

✂— DETACH HERE — — — — — — **IF NO PAYMENT IS DUE, DO NOT MAIL THIS FORM** — — — — — — DETACH HERE —✂

DUE 15TH DAY OF 4TH MONTH OF TAXABLE YEAR (fiscal year) **OR APRIL 15, 2004** (calendar year).

TAXABLE YEAR **2004**	**Limited Liability Company Tax Voucher**	CALIFORNIA FORM **3522**

For calendar year 2004 or fiscal year beginning month_____ day_____ year 2004, and ending month_____ day_____ year_____ .

Limited liability company name

Secretary of State (SOS) file number

DBA

Federal employer identification number (FEIN)

Address

STE. no.   PMB no.

City

State   ZIP Code

Make your check or money order payable to "Franchise Tax Board." Write the SOS file number, FFIN and "FTB 3522 2004" on the check or money order. Mail this voucher and the check or money order to:
FRANCHISE TAX BOARD
PO BOX 942857
SACRAMENTO CA   94257-0631

If amount of payment is zero, do not mail form } ▶

Amount of payment

352204103

FTB 3522 2003

Form **8832**
(Rev. September 2002)
Department of the Treasury
Internal Revenue Service

Entity Classification Election

OMB No. 1545-1516

Type or Print

Name of entity	EIN ▶
Number, street, and room or suite no. If a P.O. box, see instructions.	
City or town, state, and ZIP code. If a foreign address, enter city, province or state, postal code and country.	

1 **Type of election** (see instructions):

a ☐ Initial classification by a newly-formed entity.

b ☐ Change in current classification.

2 **Form of entity** (see instructions):

a ☐ A domestic eligible entity electing to be classified as an association taxable as a corporation.

b ☐ A domestic eligible entity electing to be classified as a partnership.

c ☐ A domestic eligible entity with a single owner electing to be disregarded as a separate entity.

d ☐ A foreign eligible entity electing to be classified as an association taxable as a corporation.

e ☐ A foreign eligible entity electing to be classified as a partnership.

f ☐ A foreign eligible entity with a single owner electing to be disregarded as a separate entity.

3 **Disregarded entity information** (see instructions):
a Name of owner ▶ ....
b Identifying number of owner ▶ ....
c Country of organization of entity electing to be disregarded (if foreign) ▶ ....

4 Election is to be effective beginning (month, day, year) (see instructions) . . . . ▶ ___ / ___ / ___

5 Name and title of person whom the IRS may call for more information

6 That person's telephone number
( )

Consent Statement and Signature(s) (see instructions)

Under penalties of perjury, I (we) declare that I (we) consent to the election of the above-named entity to be classified as indicated above, and that I (we) have examined this consent statement, and to the best of my (our) knowledge and belief, it is true, correct, and complete. If I am an officer, manager, or member signing for all members of the entity, I further declare that I am authorized to execute this consent statement on their behalf.

Signature(s)	Date	Title

For Paperwork Reduction Act Notice, see page 4.

Cat. No. 22598R

Form **8832** (Rev. 9-2002)

General Instructions

Section references are to the Internal Revenue Code unless otherwise noted.

Purpose of Form

For Federal tax purposes, certain business entities automatically are classified as corporations. See items **1** and **3** through **8** under the definition of **corporation** on this page. Other business entities may choose how they are classified for Federal tax purposes. Except for a business entity automatically classified as a corporation, a business entity with at least two members can choose to be classified as either an association taxable as a corporation or a partnership, and a business entity with a single member can choose to be classified as either an association taxable as a corporation or disregarded as an entity separate from its owner.

Generally, an eligible entity that does not file this form will be classified under the default rules described below. An eligible entity that chooses not to be classified under the default rules or that wishes to change its current classification must file Form 8832 to elect a classification. The IRS will use the information entered on this form to establish the entity's filing and reporting requirements for Federal tax purposes.

60-month limitation rule. Once an eligible entity makes an election to change its classification, the entity generally cannot change its classification by election again during the 60 months after the effective date of the election. However, the IRS may (**by private letter ruling**) permit the entity to change its classification by election within the 60-month period if more than 50% of the ownership interests in the entity as of the effective date of the election are owned by persons that did not own any interests in the entity on the effective date of the entity's prior election. See Regulations section 301.7701-3(c)(1)(iv) for more details.

Note: *The 60-month limitation does not apply if the previous election was made by a newly formed eligible entity and was effective on the date of formation.*

Default Rules

Existing entity default rule. Certain domestic and foreign entities that were in existence before January 1, 1997, and have an established Federal tax classification generally do not need to make an election to continue that classification. If an existing entity decides to change its classification, it may do so subject to the 60-month limitation rule. See Regulations sections 301.7701-3(b)(3) and 301.7701-3(h)(2) for more details.

Domestic default rule. Unless an election is made on Form 8832, a domestic eligible entity is:

1. A partnership if it has two or more members.

2. Disregarded as an entity separate from its owner if it has a single owner.

A change in the number of members of an eligible entity classified as an association does not affect the entity's classification. However, an eligible entity classified as a partnership will become a disregarded entity when the entity's membership is reduced to one member and a disregarded entity will be classified as a partnership when the entity has more than one member.

Foreign default rule. Unless an election is made on Form 8832, a foreign eligible entity is:

1. A partnership if it has two or more members and **at least** one member does not have limited liability.

2. An association taxable as a corporation if all members have limited liability.

3. Disregarded as an entity separate from its owner if it has a single owner that does not have limited liability.

Definitions

Association. For purposes of this form, an association is an eligible entity that is taxable as a corporation by election or, for foreign eligible entities, under the default rules (see Regulations section 301.7701-3).

Business entity. A business entity is any entity recognized for Federal tax purposes that is not properly classified as a trust under Regulations section 301.7701-4 or otherwise subject to special

treatment under the Code. See Regulations section 301.7701-2(a).

Corporation. For Federal tax purposes, a corporation is any of the following:

1. A business entity organized under a Federal or state statute, or under a statute of a federally recognized Indian tribe, if the statute describes or refers to the entity as incorporated or as a corporation, body corporate, or body politic.

2. An association (as determined under Regulations section 301.7701-3).

3. A business entity organized under a state statute, if the statute describes or refers to the entity as a joint-stock company or joint-stock association.

4. An insurance company.

5. A state-chartered business entity conducting banking activities, if any of its deposits are insured under the Federal Deposit Insurance Act, as amended, 12 U.S.C. 1811 et seq., or a similar Federal statute.

6. A business entity wholly owned by a state or any political subdivision thereof, or a business entity wholly owned by a foreign government or any other entity described in Regulations section 1.892-2T.

7. A business entity that is taxable as a corporation under a provision of the Code other than section 7701(a)(3).

8. A foreign business entity listed on page 5. See Regulations section 301.7701-2(b)(8) for any exceptions and inclusions to items on this list and for any revisions made to this list since these instructions were printed.

Disregarded entity. A disregarded entity is an eligible entity that is treated as an entity that is not separate from its single owner. Its separate existence will be ignored for Federal tax purposes unless it elects corporate tax treatment.

Eligible entity. An eligible entity is a business entity that is not included in items **1** or **3** through **8** under the definition of corporation above.

Limited liability. A member of a foreign eligible entity has limited liability if the member has no personal liability for any debts of or claims against the entity by reason of being a member. This determination is based solely on the statute or law under which the entity is organized (and, if relevant, the entity's organizational documents). A member has personal liability if the creditors of the entity may seek satisfaction of all or any part of the debts or claims against the entity from the member as such. A member has personal liability even if the member makes an agreement under which another person (whether or not a member of the entity) assumes that liability or agrees to indemnify that member for that liability.

Partnership. A partnership is a business entity that has **at least** two members and is not a corporation as defined on page 2.

Who Must File

File this form for an **eligible entity** that is one of the following:

• A domestic entity electing to be classified as an association taxable as a corporation.

• A domestic entity electing to change its current classification (even if it is currently classified under the default rule).

• A foreign entity that has more than one owner, all owners having limited liability, electing to be classified as a partnership.

• A foreign entity that has at least one owner that does not have limited liability, electing to be classified as an association taxable as a corporation.

• A foreign entity with a single owner having limited liability, electing to be an entity disregarded as an entity separate from its owner.

• A foreign entity electing to change its current classification (even if it is currently classified under the default rule).

   Do not file this form for an eligible entity that is:

• Tax-exempt under section 501(a) or

• A real estate investment trust (REIT), as defined in section 856.

Effect of Election

The Federal tax treatment of elective changes in classification as described in Regulations section 301.7701-3(g)(1) is summarized as follows:

• If an eligible entity classified as a partnership elects to be classified as an association, it is deemed that the partnership contributes all of its assets and liabilities to the association in exchange for stock in the association, and immediately thereafter, the partnership liquidates by distributing the stock of the association to its partners.

• If an eligible entity classified as an association elects to be classified as a partnership, it is deemed that the association distributes all of its assets and liabilities to its shareholders in liquidation of the association, and immediately thereafter, the shareholders contribute all of the distributed assets and liabilities to a newly formed partnership.

• If an eligible entity classified as an association elects to be disregarded as an entity separate from its owner, it is deemed that the association distributes all of its assets and liabilities to its single owner in liquidation of the association.

• If an eligible entity that is disregarded as an entity separate from its owner elects to be classified as an association, the owner of the eligible entity is deemed to have contributed all of the assets and liabilities of the entity to the association in exchange for the stock of the association.

Note: *For information on the Federal tax treatment of elective changes in classification, see Regulations section 301.7701-3(g).*

When To File

See the instructions for line 4.

A newly formed entity may be eligible for late election relief under Rev. Proc. 2002-59, 2002-39 I.R.B. 615 if:

• The entity failed to obtain its desired classified election solely because Form 8832 was not timely filed,

• The due date for the entity's desired classification tax return (excluding extension) for the tax year beginning with the entity's formation date has not passed, and

• The entity has reasonable cause for its failure to make a timely election.

   To obtain relief, a newly formed entity must file Form 8832 on or before the due date of the first Federal tax return (excluding extensions) of the entity's desired classification. The entity must also write "FILED PURSUANT TO REV. PROC. 2002-59" at the top of the form. The entity must attach a statement to the form explaining why it failed to file a timely election. If Rev. Proc. 2002-59 does not apply, an entity may seek relief for a late entity election by requesting a private letter ruling and paying a user fee in accordance with Rev. Proc. 2002-1, 2002-1 I.R.B. 1 (or its successor).

Where To File

File Form 8832 with the Internal Revenue Service Center, Philadelphia, PA 19255. Also attach a copy of Form 8832 to the entity's Federal income tax or information return for the tax year of the election. If the entity is not required to file a return for that year, a copy of its Form 8832 **must** be attached to the Federal income tax or information returns of **all** direct or indirect owners of the entity for the tax year of the owner that includes the date on which the election took effect. Although failure to attach a copy will not invalidate an otherwise valid election, each member of the entity is required to file returns that are consistent with the entity's election. In addition, penalties may be assessed against persons who are required to, but who do not, attach Form 8832 to their returns. Other penalties may apply for filing Federal income tax or information returns inconsistent with the entity's election.

Specific Instructions

Name. Enter the name of the eligible entity electing to be classified using Form 8832.

Employer identification number (EIN). Show the correct EIN of the eligible entity electing to be classified. Any entity that has an EIN will retain that EIN even if its Federal tax classification changes under Regulations section 301.7701-3.

   If a disregarded entity's classification changes so that it is recognized as a partnership or association for Federal tax purposes, and that entity had an EIN, then the entity must use that EIN and not the identifying number of the single owner. If the entity did not already have its own EIN, then the entity must apply for an EIN and not use the identifying number of the single owner.

A foreign person that makes an election under Regulations section 301.7701-3(c) must also use its own taxpayer identifying number. See sections 6721 through 6724 for penalties that may apply for failure to supply taxpayer identifying numbers.

If the entity electing to be classified using Form 8832 does not have an EIN, it must apply for one on **Form SS-4,** Application for Employer Identification Number. If the filing of Form 8832 is the only reason the entity is applying for an EIN, check the "Other" box on line 9 of Form SS-4 and write "Form 8832" to the right of that box. If the entity has not received an EIN by the time Form 8832 is due, write "Applied for" in the space for the EIN. **Do not** apply for a new EIN for an existing entity that is changing its classification if the entity already has an EIN.

Address. Enter the address of the entity electing a classification. Include the suite, room, or other unit number after the street address. If the Post Office does not deliver mail to the street address and the entity has a P.O. box, show the box number instead of the street address.

Line 1. Check box 1a if the entity is choosing a classification for the first time **and** the entity does not want to be classified under the applicable default classification. **Do not** file this form if the entity wants to be classified under the default rules.

Check box 1b if the entity is changing its current classification.

Line 2. Check the appropriate box if you are changing a current classification (no matter how achieved), or are electing out of a default classification. **Do not** file this form if you fall within a default classification that is the desired classification for the new entity.

Line 3. If an eligible entity has checked box 2c or box 2f and is electing to be disregarded as an entity separate from its owner, it must enter the name of its owner on line 3a and the owner's identifying number (social security number, or individual taxpayer identification number, or EIN) on line 3b. If the owner is a foreign person or entity and does not have a U.S. identifying number, enter "none" on line 3b. If the entity making the election is foreign, enter the name of the country in which it was formed on line 3c.

Line 4. Generally, the election will take effect on the date you enter on line 4 of this form or on the date filed if no date is entered on line 4. However, an election specifying an entity's classification for Federal tax purposes can take effect no more than 75 days prior to the date the election is filed, nor can it take effect later than 12 months after the date on which the election is filed. If line 4 shows a date more than 75 days prior to the date on which the election is filed, the election will take effect 75 days before the date it is filed. If line 4 shows an effective date more than 12 months from the filing date, the election will take effect 12 months after the date the election was filed.

Consent statement and signatures. Form 8832 must be signed by:

1. Each member of the electing entity who is an owner at the time the election is filed; or

2. Any officer, manager, or member of the electing entity who is authorized (under local law or the organizational documents) to make the election and who represents to having such authorization under penalties of perjury.

If an election is to be effective for any period prior to the time it is filed, each person who was an owner between the date the election is to be effective and the date the election is filed, and who is not an owner at the time the election is filed, must also sign.

If you need a continuation sheet or use a separate consent statement, attach it to Form 8832. The separate consent statement must contain the same information as shown on Form 8832.

Paperwork Reduction Act Notice

We ask for the information on this form to carry out the Internal Revenue laws of the United States. You are required to give us the information. We need it to ensure that you are complying with these laws and to allow us to figure and collect the right amount of tax.

You are not required to provide the information requested on a form that is subject to the Paperwork Reduction Act unless the form displays a valid OMB control number. Books or records relating to a form or its instructions must be retained as long as their contents may become material in the administration of any Internal Revenue law. Generally, tax returns and return information are confidential, as required by section 6103.

The time needed to complete and file this form will vary depending on individual circumstances. The estimated average time is:

Recordkeeping . . . 1 hr., 49 min.
Learning about the law or the form . . . 2 hr., 7 min.
Preparing and sending the form to the IRS . . . . 23 min.

If you have comments concerning the accuracy of these time estimates or suggestions for making this form simpler, we would be happy to hear from you. You can write to the Tax Forms Committee, Western Area Distribution Center, Rancho Cordova, CA 95743-0001. **Do not** send the form to this address. Instead, see **Where To File** on page 3.

Form **8716**

(Rev. October 2000)

Department of the Treasury
Internal Revenue Service

Election To Have a Tax Year Other Than a Required Tax Year

OMB No. 1545-1036

Type or Print

Name	Employer identification number

Number, street, and room or suite no. (or P.O. box number if mail is not delivered to street address)

City or town, state, and ZIP code

1 Check applicable box to show type of entity:
- ☐ Partnership
- ☐ S corporation (or C corporation electing to be an S corporation)
- ☐ Personal service corporation (PSC)

2 Name and telephone number (including area code) of person who may be called for information:

3 Enter ending date of the tax year for the entity's last filed return. A new entity should enter the ending date of the tax year it is adopting. . . . .

Month	Day	Year

4 Enter ending date of required tax year determined under section 441(i), 706(b), or 1378 . . . .

Month	Day

5 Section 444(a) Election. Check the applicable box and enter the ending date of the first tax year for which the election will be effective that the entity is (see instructions):
- ☐ Adopting
- ☐ Retaining
- ☐ Changing to

Month	Day	Year

Under penalties of perjury, I declare that the entity named above has authorized me to make this election under section 444(a), and that the statements made are, to the best of my knowledge and belief, true, correct, and complete.

▶ _____
Signature and title (see instructions)

▶ _____
Date

General Instructions

Section references are to the Internal Revenue Code unless otherwise noted.

Purpose of Form

Form 8716 is filed by partnerships, S corporations, and personal service corporations (as defined in section 441(i)(2)) to elect under section 444 to have a tax year other than a required tax year.

Attach a copy of the Form 8716 you file to Form 1065 or a Form 1120 series form (1120, 1120-A, 1120S, etc.), whichever is applicable, for the first tax year for which the election is made.

When To File

Form 8716 must be filed by the earlier of:

1. The 15th day of the 5th month following the month that includes the 1st day of the tax year the election will be effective or

2. The due date (not including extensions) of the income tax return for the tax year resulting from the section 444 election.

Items **1** and **2** relate to the tax year, or the return for the tax year, for which the ending date is entered on line 5 above.

Under Regulations section 301.9100-2, the entity is automatically granted a 12-month extension to make an election on Form 8716. To obtain an

extension, type or legibly print "Filed Pursuant To Section 301.9100-2" at the top of a properly prepared Form 8716, and file the form within 12 months of the original due date.

Where To File

File the election with the Internal Revenue Service Center where the entity will file its return. See the instructions for Form 1065 or a Form 1120 series form for service center addresses. For a foreign entity, file Form 8716 with the Internal Revenue Service Center, Philadelphia, PA 19255.

Effect of Section 444 Election

Partnerships and S corporations. An electing partnership or S corporation must file **Form 8752**, Required Payment or Refund Under Section 7519, for each year the election is in effect. Form 8752 is used to figure and make the payment required under section 7519 or to obtain a refund of net prior year payments. Form 8752 must be filed by May 15 following the calendar year in which each applicable election year begins.

The section 444 election will end if the partnership or S corporation is penalized for willfully failing to make the required payments.

Personal service corporations. An electing personal service corporation (PSC) should not file Form 8752. Instead, it must comply with the

minimum distribution requirements of section 280H for each year the election is in effect. If the PSC does not meet these requirements, the applicable amounts it may deduct for payments made to its employee-owners may be limited.

Use **Schedule H (Form 1120)**, Section 280H Limitations for a Personal Service Corporation (PSC), to figure the required minimum distribution and the maximum deductible amount. Attach Schedule H to the income tax return of the PSC for each tax year the PSC does not meet the minimum distribution requirements.

The section 444 election will end if the PSC is penalized for willfully failing to comply with the requirements of section 280H.

Members of Certain Tiered Structures May Not Make Election

No election may be made under section 444(a) by an entity that is part of a tiered structure other than a tiered structure that consists entirely of partnerships and/or S corporations all of which have the same tax year. An election previously made will be terminated if an entity later becomes part of a tiered structure that is not allowed to make the election. See Temporary Regulations section 1.444-2T for other details.

Acceptance of Election

After your election is received and accepted by the service center, the center will stamp it "Accepted" and return a copy to you. Be sure to keep a copy of the form marked "Accepted" for your records.

End of Election

The election is made only once. It remains in effect until the entity changes its accounting period to its required tax year or some other permitted year or it is penalized for willfully failing to comply with the requirements of section 280H or 7519. If the election is terminated, the entity may not make another section 444 election.

Signature

Form 8716 is not a valid election unless it is signed. For partnerships, a general partner or limited liability company member must sign and date the election.

For corporations, the election must be signed and dated by the president, vice president, treasurer, assistant treasurer, chief accounting officer, or any other corporate officer (such as tax officer) authorized to sign its tax return.

If a receiver, trustee in bankruptcy, or assignee controls the entity's property or business, that person must sign the election.

Specific Instructions

Line 1

Check the applicable box to indicate whether the entity is classified for Federal income tax purposes as a partnership, an S corporation (or a C corporation electing to be an S corporation), or a PSC.

A corporation electing to be an S corporation that wants to make a section 444 election is not required to attach a copy of Form 8716 to its **Form 2553,** Election by a Small Business Corporation. However, the corporation is required to state on Form 2553 its intention to make a section 444 election (or a backup section 444 election). If a corporation is making a backup section 444 election (provided for in item Q, Part II, of Form 2553), it must type or print the words "Backup Election" at the top of the Form 8716 it files. See Temporary Regulations section 1.444-3T for more details.

Line 2

Enter the name and telephone number (including the area code) of a person that the IRS may call for information needed to complete the processing of the election.

Line 4

For a definition of a required tax year and other details, see the instructions for Form 1065 or a Form 1120 series form, whichever is applicable, and section 441(i), 706(b), or 1378.

Line 5

The following limitations and special rules apply in determining the tax year an entity may elect.

New entity adopting a tax year. An entity adopting a tax year may elect a tax year under section 444 only if the deferral period of the tax year is not longer than 3 months. See below for the definition of deferral period.

Existing entity retaining a tax year. In certain cases, an entity may elect to retain its tax year if the deferral period is no longer than 3 months. If the entity does not want to elect to retain its tax year, it may elect to change its tax year as explained below.

Existing entity changing a tax year. An existing entity may elect to change its tax year if the deferral period of the elected tax year is no longer than the shorter of 3 months or the deferral period of the tax year being changed.

Example. ABC, a C corporation that historically used a tax year ending October 31, elects S status and wants to make a section 444 election for its tax year beginning November 1, 2000. ABC's required tax year under section 1378 is a calendar tax year. In this case, the deferral period of the tax year being changed is 2 months. Thus, ABC may elect to retain its tax year beginning November 1, 2000, and ending October 31, 2001, or change it to a short tax year beginning November 1, 2000, and ending November 30, 2000. However, it may not elect a short tax year beginning November 1, 2000, and ending September 30, 2001, because the deferral period for that elected tax year is 3 months (September 30 to December 31), which is longer than the 2-month deferral period of the tax year being changed. After filing the short year return (November 1, 2000, to November 30, 2000), and as long as the section 444 election remains in effect, the corporation's tax year will begin December 1 and end November 30.

Deferral period. The term "deferral period" means the number of months that occur between the last day of the elected tax year and the last day of the required tax year. For example, if you elected a tax year that ends on September 30 and your required tax year is the calendar year, the deferral period would be 3 months (the number of months between September 30 and December 31).

Paperwork Reduction Act Notice. We ask for the information on this form to carry out the Internal Revenue laws of the United States. You are required to give us the information. We need it to ensure that you are complying with these laws and to allow us to figure and collect the right amount of tax.

You are not required to provide the information requested on a form that is subject to the Paperwork Reduction Act unless the form displays a valid OMB control number. Books or records relating to a form or its instructions must be retained as long as their contents may become material in the administration of any Internal Revenue law. Generally, tax returns and return information are confidential, as required by section 6103.

The time needed to complete and file this form will vary depending on individual circumstances. The estimated average time is:

Recordkeeping . . . . 2 hr., 38 min.

Learning about the law or the form . . . .1 hr., 12 min.

Preparing and sending the form to the IRS. . . 1 hr., 17 min.

If you have comments concerning the accuracy of these time estimates or suggestions for making this form simpler, we would be happy to hear from you. You can write to the Tax Forms Committee, Western Area Distribution Center, Rancho Cordova, CA 95743-0001. **Do not** send the form to this address. Instead, see **Where To File** on page 1.

Form **SS-8**
(Rev. June 2003)
Department of the Treasury
Internal Revenue Service

Determination of Worker Status
for Purposes of Federal Employment Taxes
and Income Tax Withholding

OMB No. 1545-0004

Name of firm (or person) for whom the worker performed services	Worker's name

Firm's address (include street address, apt. or suite no., city, state, and ZIP code)	Worker's address (include street address, apt. or suite no., city, state, and ZIP code)

Trade name	Telephone number (include area code) ( )	Worker's social security number

Telephone number (include area code) ( )	Firm's employer identification number	Worker's employer identification number (if any)

If the worker is paid by a firm other than the one listed on this form for these services, enter the name, address, and employer identification number of the payer.

Important Information Needed To Process Your Request

We must have your permission to disclose your name and the information on this form and any attachments to other parties involved with this request. **Do we have your permission to disclose this information?** . . . . ☐ Yes ☐ No
If you answered "No" or did not mark a box, we will not process your request and will not issue a determination.

You must answer ALL items OR mark them "Unknown" or "Does not apply." If you need more space, attach another sheet.

A This form is being completed by: ☐ Firm ☐ Worker; for services performed _____ to _____ .
(beginning date)   (ending date)

B Explain your reason(s) for filing this form (e.g., you received a bill from the IRS, you believe you received a Form 1099 or Form W-2 erroneously, you are unable to get worker's compensation benefits, you were audited or are being audited by the IRS). ----------------------------------
----

C Total number of workers who performed or are performing the same or similar services _____ .
D How did the worker obtain the job? ☐ Application ☐ Bid ☐ Employment Agency ☐ Other (specify) _____ .

E Attach copies of all supporting documentation (contracts, invoices, memos, Forms W-2, Forms 1099, IRS closing agreements, IRS rulings, etc.). In addition, please inform us of any current or past litigation concerning the worker's status. If no income reporting forms (Form 1099-MISC or W-2) were furnished to the worker, enter the amount of income earned for the year(s) at issue $ _____ .

F Describe the firm's business. --

G Describe the work done by the worker and provide the worker's job title. --------------------------------
----

H Explain why you believe the worker is an employee or an independent contractor. ---------------------------
----

I Did the worker perform services for the firm before getting this position? . . . . ☐ Yes ☐ No ☐ N/A
If "Yes," what were the dates of the prior service? --
If "Yes," explain the differences, if any, between the current and prior service. -----------------------------
----

J If the work is done under a written agreement between the firm and the worker, attach a copy (preferably signed by both parties). Describe the terms and conditions of the work arrangement. ------------------------------------
----

Part I   Behavioral Control

1 What specific training and/or instruction is the worker given by the firm? ....

2 How does the worker receive work assignments? ....

3 Who determines the methods by which the assignments are performed? ....

4 Who is the worker required to contact if problems or complaints arise and who is responsible for their resolution? ....

5 What types of reports are required from the worker? Attach examples. ....

6 Describe the worker's daily routine (i.e., schedule, hours, etc.). ....

7 At what location(s) does the worker perform services (e.g., firm's premises, own shop or office, home, customer's location, etc.)? ....

8 Describe any meetings the worker is required to attend and any penalties for not attending (e.g., sales meetings, monthly meetings, staff meetings, etc.). ....

9 Is the worker required to provide the services personally? . . . . ☐ Yes   ☐ No

10 If substitutes or helpers are needed, who hires them? ....

11 If the worker hires the substitutes or helpers, is approval required? . . . . ☐ Yes   ☐ No
    If "Yes," by whom? ....

12 Who pays the substitutes or helpers? ....

13 Is the worker reimbursed if the worker pays the substitutes or helpers? . . . . ☐ Yes   ☐ No
    If "Yes," by whom? ....

Part II   Financial Control

1 List the supplies, equipment, materials, and property provided by each party:
    The firm ....
    The worker ....
    Other party ....

2 Does the worker lease equipment? . . . . ☐ Yes   ☐ No
    If "Yes," what are the terms of the lease? (Attach a copy or explanatory statement.) ....
    ....

3 What expenses are incurred by the worker in the performance of services for the firm? ....
    ....

4 Specify which, if any, expenses are reimbursed by:
    The firm ....
    Other party ....

5 Type of pay the worker receives: ☐ Salary   ☐ Commission   ☐ Hourly Wage   ☐ Piece Work
    ☐ Lump Sum   ☐ Other (specify) ....
    If type of pay is commission, and the firm guarantees a minimum amount of pay, specify amount $ _____ .

6 Is the worker allowed a drawing account for advances? . . . . ☐ Yes   ☐ No
    If "Yes," how often? ....
    Specify any restrictions. ....
    ....

7 Whom does the customer pay? . . . . ☐ Firm   ☐ Worker
    If worker, does the worker pay the total amount to the firm?   ☐ Yes   ☐ No   If "No," explain. ....
    ....

8 Does the firm carry worker's compensation insurance on the worker? . . . . ☐ Yes   ☐ No

9 What economic loss or financial risk, if any, can the worker incur beyond the normal loss of salary (e.g., loss or damage of equipment, material, etc.)? ....
    ....

Form **SS-8** (Rev. 6-2003)

Part III   **Relationship of the Worker and Firm**

1   List the benefits available to the worker (e.g., paid vacations, sick pay, pensions, bonuses). ....
....

2   Can the relationship be terminated by either party without incurring liability or penalty? . . . . ☐ **Yes** ☐ **No**
If "No," explain your answer. ....

3   Does the worker perform similar services for others? . . . . ☐ **Yes** ☐ **No**
If "Yes," is the worker required to get approval from the firm? . . . . ☐ **Yes** ☐ **No**

4   Describe any agreements prohibiting competition between the worker and the firm while the worker is performing services or during any later
period. Attach any available documentation. ....

5   Is the worker a member of a union? . . . . ☐ **Yes** ☐ **No**

6   What type of advertising, if any, does the worker do (e.g., a business listing in a directory, business cards, etc.)? Provide copies, if applicable.
....

7   If the worker assembles or processes a product at home, who provides the materials and instructions or pattern? ....
....

8   What does the worker do with the finished product (e.g., return it to the firm, provide it to another party, or sell it)? ....
....

9   How does the firm represent the worker to its customers (e.g., employee, partner, representative, or contractor)? ....

10   If the worker no longer performs services for the firm, how did the relationship end? ....
....

Part IV   **For Service Providers or Salespersons-** Complete this part if the worker provided a service directly to
customers or is a salesperson.

1   What are the worker's responsibilities in soliciting new customers? ....
....

2   Who provides the worker with leads to prospective customers? ....

3   Describe any reporting requirements pertaining to the leads. ....

4   What terms and conditions of sale, if any, are required by the firm? ....

5   Are orders submitted to and subject to approval by the firm? . . . . ☐ **Yes** ☐ **No**

6   Who determines the worker's territory? ....

7   Did the worker pay for the privilege of serving customers on the route or in the territory? . . . . ☐ **Yes** ☐ **No**
If "Yes," whom did the worker pay? ....
If "Yes," how much did the worker pay? . . . . $ _____ .

8   Where does the worker sell the product (e.g., in a home, retail establishment, etc.)? ....
....

9   List the product and/or services distributed by the worker (e.g., meat, vegetables, fruit, bakery products, beverages, or laundry or dry cleaning
services). If more than one type of product and/or service is distributed, specify the principal one. ....

10   Does the worker sell life insurance full time? . . . . ☐ **Yes** ☐ **No**

11   Does the worker sell other types of insurance for the firm? . . . . ☐ **Yes** ☐ **No**
If "Yes," enter the percentage of the worker's total working time spent in selling other types of insurance. . . . . _____ %

12   If the worker solicits orders from wholesalers, retailers, contractors, or operators of hotels, restaurants, or other similar
establishments, enter the percentage of the worker's time spent in the solicitation. . . . . _____ %

13   Is the merchandise purchased by the customers for resale or use in their business operations? . . . . ☐ **Yes** ☐ **No**
Describe the merchandise and state whether it is equipment installed on the customers' premises. ....
....

Part V   **Signature** (see page 4)

Under penalties of perjury, I declare that I have examined this request, including accompanying documents, and to the best of my knowledge and belief, the facts
presented are true, correct, and complete.

Signature ▶ _____ Title ▶ _____ Date ▶ _____
                (Type or print name below)

General Instructions

Section references are to the Internal Revenue Code unless otherwise noted.

Purpose

Firms and workers file Form SS-8 to request a determination of the status of a worker for purposes of Federal employment taxes and income tax withholding.

A Form SS-8 determination may be requested only in order to resolve Federal tax matters. If Form SS-8 is submitted for a tax year for which the statute of limitations on the tax return has expired, a determination letter will not be issued. The statute of limitations expires 3 years from the due date of the tax return or the date filed, whichever is later.

The IRS does not issue a determination letter for proposed transactions or on hypothetical situations. We may, however, issue an information letter when it is considered appropriate.

Definition

Firm. For the purposes of this form, the term "firm" means any individual, business enterprise, organization, state, or other entity for which a worker has performed services. The firm may or may not have paid the worker directly for these services. **If the firm was not responsible for payment for services, be sure to enter the name, address, and employer identification number of the payer on the first page of Form SS-8 below the identifying information for the firm and the worker.**

The SS-8 Determination Process

The IRS will acknowledge the receipt of your Form SS-8. Because there are usually two (or more) parties who could be affected by a determination of employment status, the IRS attempts to get information from all parties involved by sending those parties blank Forms SS-8 for completion. The case will be assigned to a technician who will review the facts, apply the law, and render a decision. The technician may ask for additional information from the requestor, from other involved parties, or from third parties that could help clarify the work relationship before rendering a decision. The IRS will generally issue a formal determination to the firm or payer (if that is a different entity), and will send a copy to the worker. A determination letter applies only to a worker (or a class of workers) requesting it, and the decision is binding on the IRS. In certain cases, a formal determination will not be issued. Instead, an information letter may be issued. Although an information letter is advisory only and is not binding on the IRS, it may be used to assist the worker to fulfill his or her Federal tax obligations.

Neither the SS-8 determination process nor the review of any records in connection with the determination constitutes an examination (audit) of any Federal tax return. If the periods under consideration have previously been examined, the SS-8 determination process will not constitute a reexamination under IRS reopening procedures. Because this is not an examination of any Federal tax return, the appeal rights available in connection with an examination do not apply to an SS-8 determination. However, if you disagree with a determination and you have additional information concerning the work relationship that you believe was not previously considered, you may request that the determining office reconsider the determination.

Completing Form SS-8

Answer all questions as completely as possible. Attach additional sheets if you need more space. Provide information for all years the worker provided services for the firm. Determinations are based on the entire relationship between the firm and the worker.

Additional copies of this form may be obtained by calling 1-800-829-4933 or from the IRS website at **www.irs.gov.**

Fee

There is no fee for requesting an SS-8 determination letter.

Signature

Form SS-8 must be signed and dated by the taxpayer. A stamped signature will not be accepted.

The person who signs for a corporation must be an officer of the corporation who has personal knowledge of the facts. If the corporation is a member of an affiliated group filing a consolidated return, it must be signed by an officer of the common parent of the group.

The person signing for a trust, partnership, or limited liability company must be, respectively, a trustee, general partner, or member-manager who has personal knowledge of the facts.

Where To File

Send the completed Form SS-8 to the address listed below for the firm's location. However, for cases involving Federal agencies, send Form SS-8 to the Internal Revenue Service, Attn: CC:CORP:T:C, Ben Franklin Station, P.O. Box 7604, Washington, DC 20044.

Firm's location:	Send to:
Alaska, Arizona, Arkansas, California, Colorado, Hawaii, Idaho, Illinois, Iowa, Kansas, Minnesota, Missouri, Montana, Nebraska, Nevada, New Mexico, North Dakota, Oklahoma, Oregon, South Dakota, Texas, Utah, Washington, Wisconsin, Wyoming, American Samoa, Guam, Puerto Rico, U.S. Virgin Islands	Internal Revenue Service SS-8 Determinations P.O. Box 630 Stop 631 Holtsville, NY 11742-0630
Alabama, Connecticut, Delaware, District of Columbia, Florida, Georgia, Indiana, Kentucky, Louisiana, Maine, Maryland, Massachusetts, Michigan, Mississippi, New Hampshire, New Jersey, New York, North Carolina, Ohio, Pennsylvania, Rhode Island, South Carolina, Tennessee, Vermont, Virginia, West Virginia, all other locations not listed	Internal Revenue Service SS-8 Determinations 40 Lakemont Road Newport, VT 05855-1555

Instructions for Workers

If you are requesting a determination for more than one firm, complete a separate Form SS-8 for each firm.

 Form SS-8 is not a claim for refund of social security and Medicare taxes or Federal income tax withholding.

If the IRS determines that you are an employee, you are responsible for filing an amended return for any corrections related to this decision. A determination that a worker is an employee does not necessarily reduce any current or prior tax liability. For more information, call 1-800-829-1040.

Index

CATALOG

...more from Nolo

	PRICE	CODE

BUSINESS

	PRICE	CODE
Becoming a Mediator: Your Guide to Career Opportunites	$29.99	BECM
Business Buyout Agreements (Book w/CD-ROM)	$49.99	BSAG
The CA Nonprofit Corporation Kit (Binder w/CD-ROM)	$59.99	CNP
Consultant & Independent Contractor Agreements (Book w/CD-ROM)	$29.99	CICA
The Corporate Minutes Book (Book w/CD-ROM)	$69.99	CORMI
Create Your Own Employee Handbook (Book w/CD-ROM)	$49.99	EMHA
Dealing With Problem Employees	$44.99	PROBM
Deduct It! Lower Your Small Business Taxes	$34.99	DEDU
The Employer's Legal Handbook	$39.99	EMPL
Everyday Employment Law	$29.99	ELBA
Federal Employment Laws	$49.99	FELW
Form Your Own Limited Liability Company (Book w/CD-ROM)	$44.99	LIAB
Hiring Independent Contractors: The Employer's Legal Guide (Book w/CD-ROM)	$34.99	HICI
Home Business Tax Deductions: Keep What You Earn	$34.99	DEHB
How to Create a Noncompete Agreement (Book w/CD-ROM)	$44.95	NOCMP
How to Form a California Professional Corporation (Book w/CD-ROM)	$59.99	PROF
How to Form a Nonprofit Corporation (Book w/CD-ROM)—National Edition	$44.99	NNP
How to Form a Nonprofit Corporation in California (Book w/CD-ROM)	$44.99	NON
How to Form Your Own California Corporation (Binder w/CD-ROM)	$59.99	CACI
How to Form Your Own California Corporation (Book w/CD-ROM)	$34.99	CCOR
How to Get Your Business on the Web	$29.99	WEBS
How to Run a Thriving Business: Strategies for Sucess & Satisfaction	$19.99	THRV
How to Write a Business Plan	$34.99	SBS
Incorporate Your Business	$49.95	NIBS
The Independent Paralegal's Handbook	$34.99	PARA
Leasing Space for Your Small Business	$34.95	LESP
Legal Guide for Starting & Running a Small Business	$34.99	RUNS
Legal Forms for Starting & Running a Small Business (Book w/CD-ROM)	$29.99	RUNSF
Marketing Without Advertising	$24.00	MWAD
Mediate, Don't Litigate	$24.99	MEDL
Music Law (Book w/CD-ROM)	$39.99	ML
Nolo's Guide to Social Security Disability	$29.99	QSS

Prices subject to change.

	PRICE	CODE
Nolo's Quick LLC	$29.99	LLCQ
Nondisclosure Agreements (Book w/CD-ROM)	$39.95	NAG
The Small Business Start-up Kit (Book w/CD-ROM)	$24.99	SMBU
The Small Business Start-up Kit for California (Book w/CD-ROM)	$24.99	OPEN
The Partnership Book: How to Write a Partnership Agreement (Book w/CD-ROM)	$39.99	PART
Sell Your Business: A Step by Step Legal Guide (Book w/CD-ROM)	$49.99	SELBU
Sexual Harassment on the Job	$24.95	HARS
Starting & Running a Successful Newsletter or Magazine	$29.99	MAG
CA Workers' Comp: How to Take Charge When You're Injured on the Job	$34.99	WORK
Tax Savvy for Small Business	$36.99	SAVVY
Workplace Investigations: A Step by Step Guid	$39.99	CMPLN
Working for Yourself: Law & Taxes for the Self-Employed	$39.99	WAGE
Your Crafts Business: A Legal Guide (Book w/CD-ROM)	$26.99	VART
Your Limited Liability Company: An Operating Manual (Book w/CD-ROM)	$49.99	LOP
Your Rights in the Workplace	$29.99	YRW

CONSUMER

	PRICE	CODE
How to Win Your Personal Injury Claim	$29.99	PICL
Nolo's Encyclopedia of Everyday Law	$29.99	EVL
Nolo's Guide to California Law	$24.99	CLAW
Trouble-Free Travel...And What to Do When Things Go Wrong	$14.95	TRAV

ESTATE PLANNING & PROBATE

	PRICE	CODE
8 Ways to Avoid Probate	$19.99	PRAV
Estate Planning Basics	$21.99	ESPN
The Exexcutor's Guide: Settling a Loved One's Estate	$34.99	EXEC
How to Probate an Estate in California	$49.99	PAE
Make Your Own Living Trust (Book w/CD-ROM)	$39.99	LITR
Nolo's Simple Will Book (Book w/CD-ROM)	$36.99	SWIL
Plan Your Estate	$44.99	NEST
Quick & Legal Will Book	$16.99	QUIC
Quicken Willmaker: Estate Planning Essentials	$49.99	QWMB

FAMILY MATTERS

	PRICE	CODE
Child Custody: Building Parenting Agreements That Work	$29.99	CUST
The Complete IEP Guide	$29.99	IEP
Divorce & Money: How to Make the Best Financial Decisions During Divorce	$34.99	DIMO
Do Your Own California Adoption: Nolo's Guide for Stepparents and Domestic Partners (Book w/CD-ROM)	$34.99	ADOP
Get a Life: You Don't Need a Million to Retire Well	$24.99	LIFE

	PRICE	CODE
The Guardianship Book for California	$39.99	GB
A Legal Guide for Lesbian and Gay Couples	$29.99	LG
Living Together: A Legal Guide (Book w/CD-ROM)	$34.99	LTK
Medical Directives and Powers of Attorney in California (Book w/CD-ROM)	$21.99	CPOA
Prenuptial Agreements: How to Write a Fair & Lasting Contract (Book w/CD-ROM)v	$34.99	PNUP
Using Divorce Mediation: Save Your Money & Your Sanity	$29.99	UDMD

GOING TO COURT

	PRICE	CODE
Beat Your Ticket: Go To Court and Win! (National Edition)	$21.99	BEYT
The Criminal Law Handbook: Know Your Rights, Survive the System	$34.99	KYR
Everybody's Guide to Small Claims Court (National Edition)	$26.99	NSCC
Everybody's Guide to Small Claims Court in California	$29.99	CSCC
Fight Your Ticket ... and Win! (California Edition)	$29.99	FYT
How to Change Your Name in California	$34.99	NAME
How to Collect When You Win a Lawsuit (California Edition)	$29.99	JUDG
How to Seal Your Juvenile & Criminal Records (California Edition)	$34.95	CRIM
The Lawsuit Survival Guide	$29.99	UNCL
Nolo's Deposition Handbook	$29.99	DEP
Represent Yourself in Court: How to Prepare & Try a Winning Case	$34.99	RYC
Sue in California Without a Lawyer	$34.99	SLWY

HOMEOWNERS, LANDLORDS & TENANTS

	PRICE	CODE
California Tenants' Rights	$27.99	CTEN
Deeds for California Real Estate	$24.99	DEED
Dog Law	$21.95	DOG
Every Landlord's Legal Guide (National Edition, Book w/CD-ROM)	$44.99	ELLI
Every Tenant's Legal Guide	$29.99	EVTEN
For Sale by Owner in California	$29.99	FSBO
How to Buy a House in California	$34.99	BHCA
The California Landlord's Law Book: Rights & Responsibilities (Book w/CD-ROM)	$44.99	LBRT
The California Landlord's Law Book: Evictions (Book w/CD-ROM)	$44.99	LBEV
Leases & Rental Agreements	$29.99	LEAR
Neighbor Law: Fences, Trees, Boundaries & Noise	$26.99	NEI
The New York Landlord's Law Book (Book w/CD-ROM)	$39.99	NYLL
New York Tenants' Rights	$27.99	NYTEN
Renters' Rights (National Edition)	$24.99	RENT

HUMOR

	PRICE	CODE
Poetic Justice	$9.95	PJ

	PRICE	CODE

IMMIGRATION

Becoming A U.S. Citizen: A Guide to the Law, Exam and Interview	$24.99	USCIT
Fiancé & Marriage Visas (Book w/CD-ROM)	$44.99	IMAR
How to Get a Green Card	$29.99	GRN
Student & Tourist Visas	$29.99	ISTU
U.S. Immigration Made Easy	$44.99	IMEZ

MONEY MATTERS

101 Law Forms for Personal Use (Book w/CD-ROM)	$29.99	SPOT
Bankruptcy: Is It the Right Solution to Your Debt Problems?	$21.99	BRS
Chapter 13 Bankruptcy: Repay Your Debts	$36.99	CHB
Creating Your Own Retirement Plan	$29.99	YROP
Credit Repair (Quick & Legal Series, Book w/CD-ROM)	$24.99	CREP
Getting Paid: How to Collect form Bankrupt Debtors	$29.99	CRBNK
How to File for Chapter 7 Bankruptcy	$34.99	HFB
IRAs, 401(k)s & Other Retirement Plans: Taking Your Money Out	$34.99	RET
Money Troubles: Legal Strategies to Cope With Your Debts	$29.99	MT
Stand Up to the IRS	$24.99	SIRS
Surviving an IRS Tax Audit	$24.95	SAUD
Take Control of Your Student Loan Debt	$26.95	SLOAN

PATENTS AND COPYRIGHTS

The Copyright Handbook: How to Protect and Use Written Works (Book w/CD-ROM)	$39.99	COHA
Copyright Your Software	$34.95	CYS
Domain Names	$26.95	DOM
Getting Permission: How to License and Clear Copyrighted Materials Online and Off (Book w/CD-ROM)	$34.99	RIPER
How to Make Patent Drawings Yourself	$29.99	DRAW
Inventor's Guide to Law, Business and Taxes (Book w/CD-ROM)	$34.99	ILAX
The Inventor's Notebook	$24.99	INOT
Nolo's Patents for Beginners	$29.99	QPAT
License Your Invention (Book w/CD-ROM)	$39.99	LICE
Patent, Copyright & Trademark	$39.99	PCTM
Patent It Yourself	$49.99	PAT
Patent Pending in 24 Hours	$29.99	PEND
Patent Searching Made Easy	$29.95	PATSE
Patenting Art & Entertainment: New Stategies for Protecting Creative Ideas	$39.99	PATAE
The Public Domain	$34.99	PUBL
Trademark: Legal Care for Your Business and Product Name	$39.99	TRD
Web and Software Development: A Legal Guide (Book w/ CD-ROM)	$44.99	SFT

	PRICE	CODE

RESEARCH & REFERENCE

Legal Research: How to Find & Understand the Law	$39.99	LRES

SENIORS

Long-Term Care: How to Plan & Pay For It	$21.99	ELD
The Conservatorship Book for California	$44.99	CNSV
Social Security, Medicare & Goverment Pensions	$29.99	SOA

SOFTWARE

Call or check our website at www.nolo.com
for special discounts on Software!

LLC Maker—Windows	$89.95	LLP1
PatentEase—Windows	$349.00	PEAS
Personal RecordKeeper 5.0 CD—Windows	$59.95	RKD5
Quicken Legal Business Pro 2005—Windows	$109.99	SBQB5
Quicken WillMaker Plus 2005—Windows	$79.99	WQP5

Order Form

Name

Address

City

State, Zip

Daytime Phone

E-mail

Our "No-Hassle" Guarantee

Return anything you buy directly from Nolo for any reason and we'll cheerfully refund your purchase price. No ifs, ands or buts.

☐ Check here if you do not wish to receive mailings from other companies

Item Code	Quantity	Item	Unit Price	Total Price

Method of payment

☐ Check ☐ VISA ☐ MasterCard
☐ Discover Card ☐ American Express

Subtotal	
Add your local sales tax (California only)	
Shipping: RUSH $9, Basic $5 (See below)	
"I bought 3, ship it to me FREE!"(Ground shipping only)	
TOTAL	

Account Number

Expiration Date

Signature

Shipping and Handling

Rush Delivery—Only $9

We'll ship any order to any street address in the U.S. by UPS 2nd Day Air* for only $9!

* Order by noon Pacific Time and get your order in 2 business days. Orders placed after noon Pacific Time will arrive in 3 business days. P.O. boxes and S.F. Bay Area use basic shipping. Alaska and Hawaii use 2nd Day Air or Priority Mail.

Basic Shipping—$5

Use for P.O. Boxes, Northern California and Ground Service.

Allow 1-2 weeks for delivery. U.S. addresses only.

For faster service, use your credit card and our toll-free numbers

Call our customer service group Monday thru Friday 7am to 7pm PST

Phone	1-800-728-3555
Fax	1-800-645-0895
Mail	Nolo
950 Parker St.
Berkeley, CA 94710

Order 24 hours a day @
www.nolo.com

Remember:

Little publishers have big ears.
We really listen to you.

Take 2 Minutes
& Give Us
Your 2 cents

Your comments make a big difference in the development
and revision of Nolo books and software. Please take a few
minutes and register your Nolo product—and your comments—with us.
Not only will your input make a difference, you'll receive special offers available
only to registered owners of Nolo products on our newest books and software.
Register now by:

PHONE
1-800-728-3555

FAX
1-800-645-0895

EMAIL
cs@nolo.com

or **MAIL** us
this registration card

fold here

Registration Card

NAME _____ DATE _____

ADDRESS _____

_____

CITY _____ STATE _____ ZIP _____

PHONE _____ E-MAIL _____

WHERE DID YOU HEAR ABOUT THIS PRODUCT? _____

WHERE DID YOU PURCHASE THIS PRODUCT? _____

DID YOU CONSULT A LAWYER? (PLEASE CIRCLE ONE)   YES   NO   NOT APPLICABLE

DID YOU FIND THIS BOOK HELPFUL?   (VERY)   5   4   3   2   I   (NOT AT ALL)

COMMENTS _____

_____

_____

WAS IT EASY TO USE?   (VERY EASY)   5   4   3   2   I   (VERY DIFFICULT)

We occasionally make our mailing list available to carefully selected companies whose products may be of interest to you.

❑   If you do not wish to receive mailings from these companies, please check this box.

❑   You can quote me in future Nolo promotional materials.
Daytime phone number _____.

OPEN 5.0

Nolo *in the* NEWS

"Nolo helps lay people perform legal tasks without the aid—or fees—of lawyers."

—USA TODAY

Nolo books are ..."written in plain language, free of legal mumbo jumbo, and spiced with witty personal observations."

—ASSOCIATED PRESS

"...Nolo publications...guide people simply through the how, when, where and why of law."

—WASHINGTON POST

"Increasingly, people who are not lawyers are performing tasks usually regarded as legal work... And consumers, using books like Nolo's, do routine legal work themselves."

—NEW YORK TIMES

"...All of [Nolo's] books are easy-to-understand, are updated regularly, provide pull-out forms...and are often quite moving in their sense of compassion for the struggles of the lay reader."

—SAN FRANCISCO CHRONICLE

fold here

Place
stamp here

Nolo
950 Parker Street
Berkeley, CA 94710-9867

Attn: OPEN 5.0